DATE DUE

EMOTIONS I
ORGANIZATIOI
BEHAVIOR

EMOTIONS IN ORGANIZATIONAL BEHAVIOR

Edited by

Charmine E. J. Härtel
Wilfred J. Zerbe
Neal M. Ashkanasy

LEA LAWRENCE ERLBAUM ASSOCIATES, PUBLISHERS
2005   Mahwah, New Jersey   London

Lawrence Erlbaum Associates, Inc., Publishers
10 Industrial Avenue
Mahwah, New Jersey 07430

Cover design by Kathryn Houghtaling Lacey

Library of Congress Cataloging-in-Publication Data

Emotions in Organizational Behavior, edited by Charmine Härtel, Wilfred J. Zerbe,
and Neal Ashkanasy.

ISBN 0-8058-5098-8 (cloth : alk. paper).

Includes bibliographical references and index.

Copyright information for this volume can be obtained by contacting the Library of Congress.

Books published by Lawrence Erlbaum Associates are printed on acid-free paper,
and their bindings are chosen for strength and durability.

Printed in the United States of America
10 9 8 7 6 5 4 3 2 1

Getting to a point like this where one writes a book requires much dedication, effort, and driving force. I have thought a lot about what is behind my driving motivation. I must say that it is not the task itself but the relationships I have with the people involved and those in my life. So I dedicate this book to those people whose names don't appear in any of the bylines but whose love or devotion fuels my passions and work. And I thank my children and partner, who have understood this and loved me more for it.

C.H.

I would like to dedicate this book to my late parents, Maurice Ashkanasy and Heather Ashkanasy.

N.A.

With thanks to the many people who have supported this work in countless ways: colleagues, friends, and family.

W.Z.

Contents

Foreword: Workplace Emotion: Where We've Been, Where We're Going, and Where We Ought to Be

Professor Russell Cropanzano

Workplace emotion has finally arrived! And none too soon for many of us. In the span of about a decade, emotion scholars have gone from lamenting the dearth of relevant research (Ashford & Humphrey, 1995; Pekrun & Frese, 1992) to celebrating a new explosion of interest (Ashkanasy, Härtel, & Daus, 2002; Brief & Weiss, 2002). There is more than just volume in this current cascade. Emotion researchers have begun to incorporate innovative research strategies, such as qualitative inquiry (Ayoko & Härtel, 2002; Rafaeli & Sutton, 1990; Sutton, 1991; Sutton & Rafaeli, 1988), experience sampling (Weiss, Nicolas, & Daus, 1999; Williams, Suls, Alliger, Learner, & Wan, 1991), and multidimensional scaling (Russell, Lewicka, & Nitt, 1989). Moreover, scholars have begun to hammer out historically thorny theoretical distinctions. For example, considerable work has distinguished moods from emotions (Weiss & Brief, 2002) and mapped the structure of affect (Cropanzano, Weiss, Hale, & Reb, 2003). Perhaps most exciting of all, workplace emotion has taken an interdisciplinary turn, incorporating work from sociology (Ashford & Humphrey, 1993; Hochschild, 1983), social psychology (Isen & Baron, 1991; Kelly & Barsade, 2001), clinical and counseling psychology (Härtel, Kibby, & Pizer, 2003), and personality (George, 1992, 1996; Judge & Larsen, 2001). This combination of conceptual openness and theoretical flexibility has become a hallmark of emotion research. In one form or another, all of these influences are manifest in this current book. Those of us with long-standing interest in emotion have seen a lot of significant developments in the course of our careers.

If you've read this far you must have at least a passing interest in workplace emotion. As such, you've made my first task easy—I probably don't need to convince you that the topic is, at least potentially, important. But why should you read on? By "on" I don't mean in the mundane sense of finishing this little foreword or even reading through the entire book (although I certainly hope that you do both!). Rather, I mean "on" in a more substantive sense, to refer to the workplace emotion literature as a whole. Why should you stick with it? You probably know that emotion research offers or could offer something now. But should you have confidence in its future? In preparing this foreword, I have thought long and hard about that future. My evaluation is optimistic, of course, but that optimism needs to be based on the potential for future accomplishment and not the dusty glory of past—even recently passed—achievements. It's no longer enough to shout that "Emotion matters!" because we've already convinced everyone (assuming that there was ever a large cadre of doubters). The task before us is to provide the shape and substance that will allow our literature to continue to grow.

Fortunately, we've reached an at least serviceable understanding of the major constructs—affect, mood, emotion, and well-being. With that small, but not insignificant, measure of theoretical cohesion, emotion research has elbowed its way to the table of organizational behavior. We are ready to begin our careers. That future will see chapters in undergraduate textbooks, doctoral seminars, quotes in major newspapers, and popular books on how feelings shape our experience at work (this last prediction has already come true). In broad outline, we know what our future looks like, but what will be the content of those books, quotations, seminars, and chapters? No doubt we will all have much to say, but right now I can't tell you what they will be.

Herein lies a special opportunity for you: In the years to come, you can be part of the intellectual adventure that will provide solutions for those questions. At this particular juncture of our history, the thrill does not come from what we know, but from what remains for us to learn. That's why I encourage you to read on—because the biggest questions have yet to be answered and because fascinating challenges await you and us. The remaining enigmas promise to keep emotion research vital and dynamic for many years to come.

I next argue that at least three challenges wait at the horizon of our understanding. I treat each of these as a tension or dialectic within our discipline. For me, the push-and-pull between superficially opposite-sounding ideas can lead to new insights. This is my personal special list of challenges, and I hope you enjoy it. Of course, it is only my own appraisal. You probably have your own favorite problems and your own ideas for solving them. This is as it should be. So we should take my small questions at face value—they're only questions—and not as anything else. Maybe someday I'll have an opportunity to hear your ideas!

My first challenge pertains to the relationship between power and subtlety. Emotion can be experienced in a holistic and all-encompassing fashion. We speak of being "carried away," "torn apart," "overwhelmed," or "giddy" with our feelings. These words carry communicative meaning only because they designate powerful shared human experiences. Yet despite this not infrequent sense of power and completeness, an emotion is a multifaceted—almost fragile—construct. Each emotion has different parts. Like children's Tinker Toys, at least some of these parts can be disassociated and rebuilt to form slight but important shades of meaning (Mascolo & Griffin, 1998; Mascolo & Harkins, 1998). Seemingly modest changes in how we interpret or analyze an event can alter the course of a torrent of feeling.

To illustrate this point, consider three closely related emotions: embarrassment, shame, and guilt. Each is similar, in that the terms refer to self-conscious evaluations of our own behavior. Additionally, each occurs when we do something that others (and probably we ourselves) perceive as wrong. Despite these basic similarities, there are subtle but important differences in the phenomenology of each. Shame is the most general. We experience the feeling of shame when we behave in such a way as to question our identity as a certain type of person. Guilt is like shame, only more narrowly defined. We experience guilt when we misbehave in a specific instance that does not directly confront our sense of self. That is, we are guilt-ridden when we fail to live up to our own moral standards. Unlike shame and guilt, embarrassment does not carry these moral connotations. We feel embarrassed when we do something silly or dumb, but not when we experience an ethical failure (for details and evidence, see Keltner & Anderson, 2000; Keltner & Buswell, 1997; Tangney, 1995; Tangney & Fischer, 1995).

Notice, of course, that the exact same event can provide any one of these three emotions, depending on how it is understood. Does it pertain to morality? Does it pose a challenge to one's identity? Different answers to these questions alter substantially our affective experience. What are we to make of this? Are emotions affective bulldozers that push aside all else? Or are they delicate will-o'-the-wisps that change their meaning—in some ill-defined psychological version of the Heisenberg Principle—upon close scrutiny of our experience? In some sense, emotions must be both subtle and powerful. Or, perhaps more precisely stated, from the arrangement of subtle events, powerful affective forces can be unleashed (Mascolo & Griffin, 1988; Mascolo & Harkins, 1998).

The second challenge pertains to the relative attention provided to negative and positive feelings. In an insightful paper, Ashford and Humphrey (1995) reminded us that people do more than think. They also feel. While none would gainsay this observation, we should add that people don't only feel bad (Seligman & Csikzentmihalyi, 2000). In fact, in one survey of psychological research, Myers and Diener (1995) determined that there were 17 publications on negative emotion for every one on positive well-being. To be sure, a complete understanding of the human experience requires an attention to the despair, loneliness, and anxiety that are sometimes a part of our lives. However, our theories of work behavior must make room for joy and love as well. Recognition of this possibility is likely to yield practical gains. For instance, several studies have found that psychological well-being is related positively to job performance (Cropanzano & Wright, 2001). Likewise, research by Moliner, Martínez-Tur, Peiró, Ramos, and Cropanzano (2003) found that positive feelings (operationalized as psychological engagement) and negative feelings (operationalized as burnout) contribute independently to the prediction of work outcomes.

The third challenge has to do with relationship between feeling and thinking. Emotion is not the antithesis of cognition. When workplace emotion was still struggling for acceptance, it might have made sense to draw sharp demarcations. Perhaps some felt that conceding an inch might open the door for a sort of intellectual imperialism. I can't speak with certainty about the past, but I do believe that we can be more open to integration in the future. Although emotions cannot be reduced to cognitions, research tells us that thinking is certainly involved. These influences are bidirectional, with affect influencing our thinking (e.g., Forgas & George, 2001; Isen & Baron, 1991) and our thoughts impacting how we feel (e.g., Reisenzein & Schoenpflug, 1992). The processes of cognition and emotion are heavily intertwined (Judge & Larsen, 2001)—so much so that it is difficult to clearly locate the boundary where one leaves off and the other begins. For instance, emotion involves affect, but it also requires that we label and interpret events (Mascolo & Griffin, 1988; Mascolo & Harkins, 1998; Pirola-Merlo, Härtel, Mann, & Hirst, 2002). Likewise, healthy human functioning depends on the close interplay of our thoughts and feelings (Goleman, 1998; Härtel et al., 2003). Judge and Larsen (2001) illustrated this point nicely by examining the case of Elliot. Elliot was a patient described by Damasio (1994). Brain damage caused Elliot to lose his capacity for affect, while retaining his cognitive capacity. This loss of feeling made Elliot less rational in his dealings with others. Among other things, he had trouble making evaluations and ranking priorities. Making a distinction between cognition and emotion is practically useful. These are big topics and taking them apart allows us to more closely scrutinize each. However, we should not lose sight of the underlying unity between these two sets of processes.

We emotion researchers have a lot to think about. However, as I have already argued the case for optimism is predicated on this road of unsolved mysteries. In the final analysis, I believe these challenges are part of an adventure. We have much to look forward to.

Read on and enjoy yourself . . .

Preface

This edition was conceived and compiled to meet the need for a comprehensive book for practitioners, academics and students on the research on emotions in organizational behavior. The book is the first of its kind to incorporate organizational behavior and bounded emotionality and is the third in a series of books on emotions.

The editors' primary aim is to communicate the research presented at the biannual *Emotions in Organizational Life* conference to a wider audience. With the exception of the six chapters coauthored by the editors and two invited chapters, each chapter in this book embodies papers from the 2002 conference. As such, we would like to express our deep gratitude to John Basch and Cynthia Fisher of Bond University who contributed to the organization of the conference. We would also like to express our appreciation to the 29 conference paper reviewers who provided us with constructive reviews of the papers submitted to the conference. Based on these reviews, quality research from around the world was carefully selected for inclusion in this volume. Of the 40 papers received from scholars for the conference, 26 were accepted. In particular, we would like to thank the following for their time and diligence in providing quality reviews:

Eliza Ahmed

Yvonne A. Athanasaw

Julie Baker

Sigal Barsade
Dr. Maree Boyle
Jamie Callahan
Sandra Christensen
Karen J. Crooker
Marie Dasborough
Scott Davies
James M. Diefendorff
Hillary A. Elfenbein
Cynthia D. Fisher
Yuka Fujimoto
Don Gibson
Michelle Greenwood
Alice C. F. Hsu
David Martínez Íñigo
Peter Jordan
Helen Lawson-Williams
Yongmei Liu
Shannon Lloyd
Sugumar Mariappanadar
Janet McColl-Kennedy
Lyn McDonald
Anthony T. Pescosolido
Michelle K. Pizer
Roni Reiter-Palmon
Lisa Scherer
David Schmidt
Lyndall M. Strazdins
Irv Summers
Jacintha Tan
Mary Tucker
Fairly Vanover
Terry Waters-Marsh
Mona White
Ursula Wright
Nancy Yanchus

The first book in this series, *Emotions in the Workplace: Research, Theory, and Practice*, provided a range of research regarding emotions within the work environment. The second book, *Managing Emotions in the Workplace*, provided research on the *management* of emotions. This edition, in contrast, looks at the range of research on emotions within an organizational behavior framework, organized in terms of the individual, interpersonal, and organizational levels. Particular emphasis has been placed on obtaining the leading research in the international sphere, and this book is intended to be as useful to the student of organizational behavior as to the managers of organizations.

Our choice of organizational behavior as the theme for this book reflects the growing acceptance of emotions in the mainstream of organizational studies. We believe it is the right time to update courses in the area of organizational behavior to include emotions and to bring together, for researchers and practitioners alike, the contributions emotions researchers are bringing to the understanding and management of organizational behavior.

Before taking you on this journey, we wish to thank those persons who have been especially important to bringing this compilation to you. Indeed, without their help, this edition would not have been possible. In particular, we are indebted to Debra Panipucci for her outstanding assistance in managing the administration of such an undertaking, and her invaluable contributions to the review and editing process. We are also deeply appreciative of the exceptional efforts of Victoria Strybosch throughout the review and editing process. Last but not least, we would like to thank editor Anne Duffy for believing in the value of such an endeavor. We are deeply grateful to her and the staff at Lawrence Erlbaum Associates for publishing and enabling this volume to reach people around the world.

About the Editors and Contributors

Neal Ashkanasy is professor of management in the UQ Business School at the University of Queensland. He has a PhD (1989) in social and organizational psychology from the University of Queensland. His research in recent years has focused on the role of emotions in organizational life. He has published in journals such as the *Academy of Management Review*, *Academy of Management Executive*, *Journal of Management*, and *Journal of Organizational Behavior*, and has edited the two earlier books on emotion. He is a past chair of the Managerial and Organizational Cognition Division of the Academy of Management.

Joyce E. Bono is an assistant professor in the Psychology Department at the University of Minnesota. She received her PhD in organizational behavior from the University of Iowa. The underlying motivation for Dr. Bono's research is discovering how individual differences and work relationships contribute to worker motivation and quality of work life, with a current focus on emotional experiences. Specifically, her recent projects examine the role of both employee personality and manager behaviors as antecedents of emotional labor. In addition to her interest in emotions as work, Dr. Bono conducts research on leadership, teaches organizational psychology, and works with both public and private organizations to improve leadership and management effectiveness.

Catherine Daus is an associate professor of psychology at Southern Illinois University Edwardsville. She obtained her PhD in 1994 from Purdue University in industrial/organizational psychology. Dr. Daus's current research focus is in the area of emotions in organizations, with particular emphasis on emotional labor, emotional intelligence, and customer service behaviors. She is also interested in diversity issues, stress and coping, and work attitudes—job satisfaction, in particular. Along with edited books, Dr. Daus has recently published in the *Academy of Management Executive*, *Journal of Management*, *Journal of Quality Management*, *Organizational and Human Behavior Processes*, and *Journal of Occupational and Health Psychology*.

Dorthe Eide is working as an assistant professor at the Bodø Graduate School of Business in Norway. Currently she is finishing her doctoral dissertation on the role of emotions and social interactions in knowing and learning in organizations, proposing a broad situated-relational approach instead of seeing, knowing, and learning in practice as a cognitive process of individuals or taking place as social cognition. She has mainly been teaching and doing research within organizational studies at the college level, as well as doing some minor work within industries. Besides literature within organizational studies, she draws on philosophy, sociology, anthropology, and psychology when exploring and elaborating emotions in organizations.

Professor Charmine Härtel is Chair of Strategic Business in the Deakin Business School, Melbourne, Victoria, Australia. She received her BA in psychology with distinction from the University of Colorado and completed her master's degree and PhD in industrial and organizational psychology at Colorado State University. Her current research and consulting activities focus on emotions and patterns of relating at work; development of emotional intelligence, diversity, leadership, and team effectiveness. She is the recipient of several awards, including recognition in Who's Who, the Richard M. Suinn Commendation Award for Excellence in Research and the Advancement of Psychology, the Martin E. P. Seligman Applied Research Award, the Distinguished Leadership Award from the International Directory of Distinguished Leadership, and the Jacob E. Hautaluoma Distinguished Alumni Award. She is author of three books and over 40 refereed journal articles, which have appeared in journals such as the *Journal of Management*, *Academy of Management Review*, *Applied Psychology: An International Review*, *Leadership Quarterly*, and *Journal of Applied Psychology*.

Dr. Yuka Fujimoto is currently researching diversity management issues with particular interest in the diversity effects on emotions. Her teaching focus is in the advanced human resource management (HRM). The key emerging concepts of strategic HRM are taught in this subject, and the concept of emotions is incorporated as the HR challenge in achieving business success. She has a wide range of industry experience in conducting research on emotional experience of workers. To date she has studied diversity effects on emotions across five industries in Australia, namely, banking and finance, construction, manufacturing, textile and clothing, and services, which add up to 15 multicultural organizations.

Cristina Galli is a PhD student in Cognitive Science at the University of Padova, Faculty of Psychology. She was awarded a 2-year research grant (2001–2002) from the University of Padova for the service jobs and emotional labor project. Her major research interest lies in the area of psychology of emotions, on topics such as emotions in the workplace, emotion regulation and its correlates in different work settings, concepts of emotion, and structure of the emotion lexicon in children, adolescents, and adults.

Matthew J. Grawitch is a graduate student at St. Louis University, where he is completing his PhD in organizational psychology. He received a BA and an MS in psychology from St. Louis University. His research interests focus on workplace affect at all levels within organizations, conducting applied research in both field and laboratory settings. He has published several articles examining the effect of mood on temporary workgroups, most notably with regard to group effectiveness and creativity. He also consults for public and private organizations in the areas of strategic planning and organizational assessment.

Dr. Kenneth S. Law is a professor at the Department of Management of Organizations, Hong Kong University of Science and Technology. His research interests include emotional intelligence, localization of human resources, meta-analysis, extrarole performance, and the application of structural equation modeling in behavioral research. In the past few years, he has worked on projects demonstrating the construct validity of emotional intelligence and its influences on life satisfaction and job outcomes.

Yongmei Liu is a doctoral student in the College of Business at Florida State University. Her current research interests include the social functions of emotion, and the role of emotion in team process and organizational change.

David C. Munz is professor of psychology at St. Louis University, where he is director of the psychology department's doctoral program in organizational psychology. He received a BS in psychology from the University of Cincinnati and a PhD in industrial and organizational psychology from the University of Oklahoma. His research interests include workplace affect at the individual, group, and organizational levels and the design and evaluation of workplace interventions at each of these levels. He has published or presented over 100 scientific articles and chapters on topics such as occupational stress, mood in workgroups, and affectivity's role in organizational assessment. He is a fellow of the American Psychological Association (APA) and a charter member of the American Psychological Society.

Debra Panipucci is a doctoral student in the Centre for Business Research, Deakin Business School. Her research interests include social influences and diversity in teams, with particular emphasis on the effects of perceived dissimilarity on intrateam behavior and the individual team member outcomes and feelings that result.

Pamela L. Perrewé is the Jim Moran Professor of Management in the College of Business at Florida State University. She received her bachelor's degree in psychology from Purdue University and her master's and PhD degrees in management from the University of Nebraska. Dr. Perrewé teaches a doctoral seminar in organizational behavior with an emphasis on emotions. She has focused her research interest in the areas of emotions, job stress, and personality. Dr. Perrewé has published over 70 book chapters and journal articles in outlets such as the *Academy of Management Journal*, *Journal of Management*, *Journal of Applied Psychology*, and *Journal of Occupational Health Psychology*.

Anthony T. Pescosolido is an assistant professor in the Department of Management within the Whittemore School of Business and Economics at the University of New Hampshire. His research interests include emergent leadership, the impact of emotions and emotional expression on group processes and productivity, and the group processes that lead to long-term group effectiveness. He has taught courses on organizational behavior, teamwork, and career development, and has facilitated workshops on emotional intelligence, teamwork, and leadership within a variety of manufacturing and service firms. His research has appeared in *Human Relations*, *Leadership Quarterly*, and *Small Group Research*.

Michelle K. Pizer is a graduate student in the Centre for Business Research, Deakin Business School, where she is completing her PhD in management. Her research focus combines an interest in the emotional experience of individuals with the world of work, directly reflecting her current work as a registered psychologist in private practice providing psychotherapy with a psychodynamic orientation and her previous management experience. She received a MBus from Swinburne University, where she conducted a case study investigating the differential experience of an organization's culture based on career success within the firm. Currently she is exploring, more specifically, the relationship between organizational culture and workplace emotions.

Robert S. Rubin is an assistant professor of management at DePaul University. He received his PhD in organizational psychology from St. Louis University and holds an MA in industrial/organizational psychology from Southern Illinois University Edwardsville. His research and teaching interests span human resources management and organizational behavior, including transformational leadership, managerial development, academic assessment centers, and emotions at work. His published work appears in outlets such as *Human Resource Man-*

agement Journal and *Leadership Quarterly*. In addition, Dr. Rubin has been a Human Resource/Organizational Development (HR/OD) consultant to a variety of industries including biotechnology, healthcare, and transportation.

Vicki M. Staebler Tardino, MA, is an organization development practitioner and, more recently, a doctoral candidate in organizational psychology at St. Louis University. For over 10 years she has consulted in internal and external capacities in business, academia, and government. In her work with organizations, emotion plays a role in many leadership and team development interventions. Her master's thesis examined perceptions of personal, social, and work-related consequences of emotional expression at work. Her more recent research interest is emotional labor. She has served on the Executive Committee of Gateway Industrial/Organizational Psychologists and is on the Board of the St. Louis Organization Development Network.

Meredith A. Vey earned her PhD in industrial and organizational psychology from the University of Minnesota. In addition to exploring the structure of work performance, Dr. Vey's research has focused on the motivational and affective determinants of performance, particularly in the areas of citizenship behavior and emotional labor. Her research interests also include human capital development and employee engagement as determinants of organizational performance. Dr. Vey is a research fellow at the Accenture Institute for High Performance Business in Cambridge, MA.

Mona White is a doctoral student in the Centre for Business Research, Deakin Business School. Her current research interests include the areas of business communication and negotiations, in particular, the differences and similarities in mass and personal communication within culture and cross-cultural negotiants between Australian and Chinese nationals in a business context. Having lived and worked in both China and Australia, her understanding and insight into each country's culture and people are invaluable to clients operating in these countries. She understands the types of problems and issues confronted by Australian companies entering the Chinese markets and the problems and issues confronted by Chinese companies entering the Australian market.

Dr. Chi-Sum Wong is a professor at the Department of Management, Chinese University of Hong Kong. His research interests include emotional intelligence, localization of human resources, career interests, job design, and application of structural equation modeling in behavioral research. In the past few years, he has worked on projects demonstrating the construct validity of emotional intelligence and its influences on life satisfaction and job outcomes.

Dr. Ping-Man Wong is the senior lecturer and head (2000–2003) of the Department of Educational Policy and Administration of the Hong Kong Institute of Education. As a school manager and former secondary school principal, Dr.

Wong is program leader of various leadership training programs for local principals, teachers, and students. He also has experiences in coordinating and training Sri Lanka principals and school inspectors of Cambodia in programs sponsored by the World Bank and the CAMSET. His other recent outputs related to emotion studies include a leadership training program for primary school teachers and pupils—an EQ perspective (2001), and emotional intelligence attitudes toward lives and attainment of educational goals (2001).

Xin Yao is a PhD candidate in organizational behavior/human resource management at the University of Washington Business School. Her research interests include emotional labor, impression management, humor, self theories, and social dilemmas. Her dissertation examines the psychological process of performing emotional labor in a customer service context. A lab study is adopted to investigate how external humorous stimuli and the way in which one carries out emotional labor may affect the extent to which one becomes psychologically exhausted. In addition, her curiosity about humor leads to a theoretical probing of its genesis and development during emotion sharing at the workplace.

Vanda L. Zammuner is a professor at the Psychology Faculty of the University of Padova (Italy) (Dipartimento di Psicologia dello Sviluppo e della Socializzazione). From 1978, she has given seminars, lecture cycles, and courses on topics related to social psychology. Currently she is giving courses on techniques of questionnaires and interviewing, and on psychology of emotions. She is a member of the Cognitive Science Doctoral Program at the University of Padova and of various national and international research societies, such as the European Association of Experimental Social Psychology (EAESP), the Psychonomic Society, International Society for Research on Emotions (ISRE; in the directive board 1994–1998). She has taught at and conducted research seminars at several European universities, including Bern, Amsterdam, Bielefeld, and Umea. She is the author of about 100 publications and presentations at both national and international meetings. Her research, often interdisciplinary in nature, is related to several sectors, including emotions, studied from different perspectives, and methodological issues, with special reference to cognitive processes implied in data collection methods. She regularly acts as referee for various international journals, such as *Cognition and Emotion* and *European Journal of Experimental Psychology*. Finally, she has organized international and national symposia, meetings, and conferences.

Wilfred J. Zerbe is associate dean (MBA Program) and professor of human resources and organizational dynamics in the Haskayne School of Business at the University of Calgary. His research interests focus on emotions in organizations, organizational research methods, service-sector management, and leadership. His publications have appeared in books and journals including the *Academy of Management Review, Industrial and Labour Relations Review, Canadian Journal of Administrative Sciences, Journal of Business Research, Journal of Psychology, Journal of Services Marketing*, and *Journal of Research in Higher Education*. He is also an active consultant and executive educator.

IN MEMORY OF JAN PATERSON

The winner of the inaugural Best Paper award at the first Emotions in Organizational Life Conference (EMONET) and valued colleague.

Dr. Jan Paterson, friend, colleague, mother, and partner, died 31 December 2002. She is survived by her husband of 35 years, Errol Paterson, one son, and numerous friends and admirers.

Jan's research passion was furthering the understanding and practice of change management processes and the tragic effects of such processes when the teachings of our field are ignored.

Jan's career in organizational psychology crossed over from a practitioner role in New Zealand to an academic in the psychology department at the University of Queensland before returning to New Zealand.

In amazing testimony of her commitment to the field, Jan produced three journal publications and one book chapter in the 7 months between the date she was diagnosed with cancer and her death. Jan continued to work as a re-engineering officer with Health Waikato right up to the date of her admittance to the hospital with a brain hemorrhage. During that time she worked closely with the director of nursing in an effort to assist the Waikato Nursing Staff with many major work changes. Although she deteriorated too much to complete the process, her input was accepted and put into practice with excellent results.

Jan was an individual of the highest integrity, a person who not only passionately valued social justice but also actively worked to create it. The quality of her character is captured well by one of the events held in celebration of her life. Jan was one of three trustees of the Noa Foundation, which provides the Maori people with business assistance. To acknowledge her assistance to the New Zealand Maori's, the Tainui Tribe sent a Whaka—a large war canoe containing about 50 warriors—20 km from Ngaruawahia to a point 500 meters upstream of the family house, where they turned and paddled down the Waikato River. As they approached her house on the down-river run, they raised their paddles in salute to her memory, keeping them raised until they passed the property. This was done with full ceremony, including a female elder standing on the bank chanting in Maori calling for Jan's spirit to witness the event. The scene was very moving, with a large crowd of neighbors, friends, and associates from the Maori community sharing in the event. The honor given was great, a recognition of nobility of character, as such salutes normally are reserved only for tribal chiefs.

Jan—We, your friends and colleagues, also raise our paddles to you, in memory of a person whose life is a legacy to what it means to live and work with integrity, generosity, and concern for a positive society.

—*Charmine E. J. Härtel*

1

Organizational Behavior: An Emotions Perspective

Charmine E. J. Härtel
Wilfred J. Zerbe
Neal M. Ashkanasy

All organizations make at least some decisions that hurt their employees and cause some level of distress or disruption. For instance, jobs may need to be cut or high performance levels may be demanded. Without recognition of emotions, however, organizations cannot deal effectively and humanely with the pain caused (Frost, 2003). Organizations that understand this and attend to keeping their environments emotionally healthy will create less emotional pain and reap more productive work behavior. Moreover, organizations that have this understanding, and also value having a culture that is emotionally constructive, can create organizational behavior that contributes to employees' emotional health.

This opening chapter provides an overview of organizational behavior theory and research and the paradigms that have dominated the field to date. Running through a discussion of rational notions of organizational behavior, to concepts of bounded rationality and most recently the call for bounded emotionality perspectives, we identify for the reader what a bounded emotionality perspective adds to the understanding of organizations. We then provide an overview of the remaining chapters in the book and how they contribute to the book's objectives.

ORGANIZATIONAL BEHAVIOR: AN OVERVIEW

Organizational behavior is an ever-expanding, dynamic field with a variety of theories and models used to describe how and why people interact differently within the workplace. The aim of this book is to provide the reader with a real-time approach to understanding organizational behavior with a particular focus on emotions, to increase understanding and awareness of the role of emotions within the workplace.

For the most part, organizational research tends to rest on the assumptions that human beings are rational creatures and that emotions are irrational and unproductive (Styhre, Ingelgard, Beausang, Castenfors, Mulec, & Roth, 2002). Therefore, to act in emotional or unpredictable ways is "unacceptable" (Antonacopoulou & Gabriel, 2001). Subsequently, emotion is excluded from the majority of research. Prior to 1992, the study of emotions was, with a few notable exceptions, essentially next to nonexistent in the management literature. Textbooks in the field, for example, provided no coverage of the role of emotions in work settings, except with respect to job satisfaction—factors that have since been shown to be largely cognitive (e.g., see Meyer & Allen, 1991; Wright & Staw, 1999). This began to change with the publication of Pekrun and Frese's (1992) chapter titled "Emotions in Work and Achievement," followed in 1993 by publication of Fineman's edited book *Emotion in Organizations* (1993a).

The momentum rapidly accelerated in the years following 1993, with particular intensity following Ashforth and Humphrey's (1995) call to action. By 2000, this culminated in a veritable explosion of literature. Edited books by Ashkanasy, Härtel, and Zerbe (2000), Ashkanasy, Zerbe, and Härtel (2002), Fineman (2000), Lord, Klimoski, and Kanfer (2002), and Payne and Cooper (2001) emerged, and special issues of journals guest edited by Fisher and Ashkanasy (2000b), Fox (2000), Humphrey (2002), and Weiss (2001, 2002) were requisitioned. This proliferation of literature was recognized in 2002 by the editors of the *Annual Review of Psychology*, who invited their first review of this literature (Brief & Weiss, 2002). The present volume is the latest addition to this upsurge of interest.

FROM THE COGNITIVE REVOLUTION
TO THE EMOTIONAL REVOLUTION

In 1976, Simon founded the concept of bounded rationality, arguing that rational economic theory was flawed because it failed to take proper account of the limitations of human rational thought. A core part of this paradigm was the definition of "irrational" and "arational" decisions, with emotion in the former category. Essentially, Simon's work marked the beginning of the cognitive revolution in economics and management theory. As such, emotional responses were treated as weaker than those based on reason.

In direct opposition, Mumby and Putnam (1993) introduced the term *bounded emotionality*, intended to be a foil to Simon's (1976) concept of "bounded rationality." Specifically, Mumby and Putnam reexamined bounded rationality and concluded that it failed to take sufficient account of the power of emotion. They suggested that "emotions constitute a way of knowing that differs from but complements traditional rationality" (p. 480). Thus, in effect, cognitive theory is flawed because it dismisses emotion as "irrational" and therefore beyond the pale of systematic analysis. As such, bounded emotionality formed "an alternative mode of organizing in which nurturance, caring, community, supportiveness, and interrelatedness are fused with individual responsibility to shape organizational experiences" (Mumby & Putnam, 1993, p. 474). It extends the idea of bounded rationality (and cognitive theory) to take in the idea that emotions can be analyzed systematically and should be included in models of organizational behavior and decision making.

Thus, just as bounded rationality signaled the beginning of the cognitive revolution (Ilgen, Major, & Tower, 1994), bounded emotionality marked the launch of the emotional revolution (Barsade, Brief, & Spataro, 2003).

Although emotion has always been a critical factor in organizational management (Mastenbroek, 2000), it was not until the emergence in the 1980s of critical management theory that the topic finally bubbled to the surface of management scholarship. Indeed, the idea of bounded emotionality emerged from the critical feminist perspective that, in turn, was presaged by Van Maanen and Kunda's (1989) seminal description of the organizational process of emotion management as well as Fineman's (1993a) seminal book in the area.

The emotional revolution was also reflected in the increasing interest in the study of emotions in the wider psychological and popular literature. The American Psychological Association launched a new journal, *Emotion*, in 2001, and books on emotions by Damasio (2003) and Goleman (1995) reached the best-seller lists. Ten years after Fineman's book, Barsade and her colleagues (2003) announced that the revolution was, indeed, a "paradigm shift."

AN EMOTIONS PERSPECTIVE OF ORGANIZATIONAL BEHAVIOR

Emotions are linked to organizational behavior in a number of ways. Generally speaking, when employees are unhappy, it shows in organizational behavior, because unhappy people are disconnected from their work (Frost, 2003, p. 33). Failure to understand the emotional aspects of organizational behavior means that an organization is unlikely to realize its toxic actions such as unreasonable company policies, disruptive coworkers or clients, abusive managers, and poorly managed change (Frost, 2003, p. 14). Further, they are unlikely to recognize and support the efforts of those trying to change and deal with the consequences of the toxic behavior, and thus are unlikely to retain those who can support a healthy organizational culture. Taking an emotions perspective of organizational behavior, on the other hand, can help leaders increase the happiness of their workers and assist employees to achieve positive outcomes for themselves even when painful events are encountered. Not only does implementing an emotions perspective of organizational behavior provide bottom-line benefits to the organization, it holds the promise of making it more ethical and socially responsible, as heartfelt caring for the needs of others has been linked to moral acts (Josselson, 1992).

Specifically, organizational behavior is a study of individuals and groups in organizations, and the ways in which they display attitude, actions, and behaviors (Weiss, 1996). In order to understand these attitudes, actions, and behaviors, emotion-based theories emerged, such as *emotional intelligence, affective events theory*, and *emotional labor*, as discussed in various chapters within this book. Such integration of emotions and organizational behavior assists the development of understanding, implications, and solutions of managing emotions within the workplace.

As can be seen, organizations are complex entities. Many revolutions, theories, and models have eventuated in an attempt to better describe organizational behavior. For the most part, research has tended to be based on assumptions of rationality, excluding notions of emotionality. However, a reliance on one dimension of work experience, such as rationality, overlooks alternative forms of organizational experience. "By shifting rationality to include intersubjective understanding, community, and shared interests, insights into alternative forms of organizing are created" (Mumby & Putnam, 1993, p. 480).

In this volume, we present a broad range of the latest research in emotions in organizational behavior. In particular, the latest research is gathered from Australia, France, China, Sweden, the United States, and Italy. Further, the book introduces new theories, models, and recent advances in emotions, such as Fujimoto and Härtel's model of the types of emotions arising in interactions among culturally diverse workteams and how these are shaped by organizational policies and practices.

FRAMEWORK OF THE BOOK

The book is segmented into five parts and comprises a total of 20 chapters. Part I of *Emotions in Organizational Behavior* introduces the reader to the concept of emotions. Parts II to IV discuss the concept of emotions on three levels of analysis: individual, interpersonal, and organizational. Finally, as organizational behavior is dynamic and ever-changing, part V discusses the role of emotions in organizational change.

Part I: Organizational Behavior and Emotions

Part I is a theoretical piece that illustrates the important role emotions play for individuals and groups and suggests that organizational behavior is enhanced through the careful management of emotions, knowledge, and learning. This chapter looks at why we are emotional through a discussion of the psychological development of emotions and an integration of this into the role of emotions in the workplace. The discussion is particularly useful for students and practitioners as it provides a sound basis for their knowledge in this field and leads into the subsequent chapters, which build on this knowledge basis.

Part II: The Individual Within the Organization

We then turn to the individual within the organization and how they manage their emotions within the workplace. Chapters 3 to 5 comprise empirical studies and build on part I by incorporating situational factors and the potential conflict arising from work roles. Together, these chapters demonstrate the importance of emotions to individual behavior and work experiences, providing insight on the organizational behavior strategies that can enhance behavior and experience.

In particular, chapter 3 discusses the emotional conflict that service providers experience when performing emotional process work. It details the link between coping with these emotions and the conflicting gender roles that societal rules impose upon us. Chapter 4 addresses the implications of emotion in employee counterproductive work behavior. Specifically, it discusses the effects of situational factors in the role of managing behavior within the workplace. It demonstrates that, if managed inappropriately, counterproductive work behavior results, which can have a detrimental effect on both the employee and the organizational setting.

Chapter 5 demonstrates that perceptual and attitudinal processes occur when diverse individuals interact, based on observable attributes. The individuals within the interaction have attitudes about these perceptions and respond in an affective way. The chapter provides important new insights on interactions between dissimilar persons and forwards a model of the affective response individuals have toward dissimilar team members that will be useful to both practitioners and researchers alike.

The final chapter in this section, written by the editors, integrates the contributions of each chapter with other state-of-the-art research to provide a bounded emotionality perspective on the individual in the organization.

Part III: The Interpersonal Within the Organization

Part III presents a combination of empirical and theoretical research on work-group dynamics, communication and emotions. This section is particularly pertinent for practitioners who seek further understanding and new strategies for dealing with organizational change.

Chapter 7 presents a theoretical model incorporating group affect into problem-solving activities. Specifically, it reviews the literature surrounding individual and group level affect in workgroups and provides a detailed explanation of each stage within the model: problem identification; brainstorming; solution development; and implementation. It suggests that the feelings of individuals within the group and the collective feelings of the group are influenced by the problem-solving process. Further, as groups mature, their level of affect is shown to become more influential over individual affect. As such, group level affect is influenced by, and will in turn, influence individual members' affect.

In order for organizational behavior to be effective, students, practitioners, and scholars must be aware of the importance of different identities and negotiation skills. Chapter 8 addresses this need, presenting a picture of intergroup dynamics and the barriers to effective negotiation. Drawing on affective events theory (AET) and communication accommodation theory (CAT), the chapter elucidates cross-cultural communication and negotiation and demonstrates application of the model using a Chinese–Australian negotiation scenario.

Chapter 9 discusses the impact of communication on emotion by addressing the role of humor in emotional workplace events. Specifically, it discusses the social sharing of emotion (SSE) process and the impact that humor has on the workplace at both the primary and secondary stages of this process. The chapter suggests that humor can be used in the "storytelling" of emotional events to allow individuals to cope with the initial negative aspect of the event, in both a social and a psychological manner.

The final chapter in this section, written by the editors, integrates the contributions of the other chapters in the section with other state-of-the-art research to provide a bounded emotionality perspective on interpersonal behavior in organizations.

Part IV: Organizational Processes, Structure, and Design

Part IV focuses on organizational processes, structure, and design, and on how the organization impacts individual and group emotions. The chapters included in this section integrate job design with individual differences, such as personality and motivation. In particular, chapters 11 and 12 are theoretical pieces aimed to develop an understanding of the emotional dimension of job design and the impact it has on employees. These are followed by chapters 13 and 14, which empirically test the cause and effects of emotional demands on employees. Each of these chapters argues that individual differences such as emotional intelligence and personality and job characteristics such as level of autonomy, complexity, and responsibility impact on the emotional demands of employees and their responses. In addition, they suggest that a variety of outcomes of emotional labor are possible, in particular, emotional exhaustion, depersonalization, personal accomplishment, physical complaints, role internalization, self-esteem, and job satisfaction.

Written by the editors, the final chapter in this section integrates the contributions of chapters 11 to 14 with other research to provide a bounded emotionality perspective on work characteristics.

Together, the chapters in this section introduce the reader to the demanding aspects of "emotional" jobs, that is, jobs that are designed to regulate emotional displays, the demands associated with emotional regulation itself, and behavioral responses to emotional regulation. The section also highlights how behavior in organizations is influenced to a large extent by organizational rules and norms, which both work through emotional responses and dictate the emotional characteristics of jobs.

Part V: Organizational Change and Changing Organizations

Part V concludes the book. It begins with a theoretical chapter on the notion of emotions and organizational change, which illustrates that in order to achieve effective continuous change, organizations need to develop emotional capabilities. They must understand the emotional consequences of their change actions and use these emotions to advance the change. Chapter 17 follows and proposes a new role for group leaders, the role of managing group emotion. The chapter shows that individual group members are perceived as leaders by others when they provide direction and guidance during times of ambiguity, particularly when this guidance involves the display of appropriate emotional responses to unsettling events. Such leadership resolves ambiguity, provides the group with the direction needed for action, and can increase group solidarity by creating both shared emotion and shared action within the group. The chapter provides important new insights on leadership, showing that the leadership in the management of group emotion is a leadership action that can be performed by different group members at different times.

Chapter 18 takes an emotions perspective of organizational culture, illustrating how it must be managed to gain employee commitment while avoiding a destructive, cultlike following. It introduces the concept of a healthy organizational culture, in terms of organizational environment that induces positive emotions and reduces negative emotions. It stresses the importance of organizational culture on employees' work experiences and how it can influence them for better or for worse. Further, it suggests that the elements of culture can be shaped by the organization to enable social control. As such, organizations must be careful to construct a culture avoiding the destructive and cultlike nature of commitment while enhancing the positive nature of commitment to the organization.

Chapter 19 provides a bounded emotionality perspective on organizational change and culture, and chapter 20 provides a conclusion to the book, drawing on the contributions of the book itself to present a comprehensive analysis of what an emotions perspective of organizational behavior offers.

Each chapter in this volume is designed to enhance practitioner knowledge and student interest in and understanding of how organizational behavior concepts translate into workplaces. The principles underlying the compilation of research in this book are both empirically and theoretically based to cover the scope of first-class research that has been performed by specialist scholars from across the world. Consequently, *Emotions in Organizational Behavior* is designed as a valuable learning facilitator for students and as a means for scholars and practitioners to incorporate the latest research into their knowledge of organizational behavior.

I

ORGANIZATIONAL BEHAVIOR AND EMOTIONS

2

Emotions: From "Ugly Duckling" Via "Invisible Asset" Toward an Ontological Reframing

Dorthe Eide

The ability to cope and act in capable ways with and through emotions has become vital as more people and organizations become involved in work intensive on social interactions, emotional labor, and/or changes. However, linking emotions to capable activity challenges traditional views on organizations and knowledge. This chapter argues that the shift from seeing emotions as an "ugly duckling" to an "invisible asset" is not sufficient in order to understand emotions in organizations; a more radical rethinking is needed. A situated-relational ontology is suggested where emotions are seen as one of the fundamental and inseparable parts of being human, and consequently also of human knowledge and action in organizations.

EMOTIONS AND KNOWLEDGE—INCOMPATIBLE PHENOMENA?

Knowledge and learning processes have gained increased legitimacy in society and organizations. They are claimed to be critical "invisible assets" and core processes in order to survive, innovate, and increase competitiveness (Drucker, 1993, 2001; Nonaka & Takeuchi, 1995; Quinn, 1992). As this claim becomes stronger, it becomes important—both for functional and for symbolic reasons—to explore critically what it means to know and work in organizations. If not, there is a high risk that we will only appreciate the kind of work and knowledge already understood, and thereby silence other voices of experience, knowledge, and opinions in organizational life and studies.

During the last decade the calls for rethinking emotions and knowledge increased, and at least two main alternative research schools have been identified. One view centers on knowledge processes in organizations where it is argued that knowledge is a critical resource, but where the idealized theoretical view of knowledge is argued to be out of touch with the meaning of knowledge in practice. The other school of thought within research, emotions in organizations, describes how emotions are present and constitute a vital resource in work. It also criticizes the traditional "rational" view for taking an overly dualistic view of cognition and emotions, as well as assuming that cognition tends to be rational whereas emotions tend not to be (e.g., Domagalski, 1999; Fineman, 1993a). There are examples where these two schools of thought overlap—for instance, both tacit knowledge and emotions are argued as invisible assets and/or human ways of knowing and being.

Rethinking Knowledge in Organizational Studies

The traditional view of emotions and knowledge has a common "root" in a positivistic/realism (i.e., functionalistic, to use the term of Burrell & Morgan, 1979) paradigm that depicts emotions as the "sand in the machinery" or, in other words, that emotions prohibit workplace effectiveness. Therefore emotions and knowledge came to be seen as two dualistic and incompatible phenomena. Scholars working within an interpretive-constructionist paradigm have claimed that traditional perspectives on human knowledge are insufficient (i.e., where knowledge is seen as only or mainly something explicit, "objective," general, theoretical, and often technical). Instead, versatile concepts of knowledge have been suggested (Bruner, 1990; Gherardi, 1999; Lave & Wenger, 1991; Polanyi, 1958; Schön, 1983) that involve dimensions such as the personal, relational, and social dimensions; the tacit, narrative, and explicit dimensions; and the local embedded and more general aspects. During the last decade, organizational studies have recognized and

> The life—
> and the love of everything—
> you must feel your way toward
> —with the rough skin of your
> hands—like a blind person learns
> the face of her lover
> through her fingertips.
> (Hans Børli, 1972, my translation)

focused on knowledge in practice, particularly through the subphenomena of *tacit knowledge* and *narrative knowledge*. Tacit knowledge means knowledge that is difficult to articulate fully in words; that is, most of what we know is tacit, and even the more explicit knowledge dwells in the tacit (see, e.g., Polanyi, 1966/1983). Narrative knowledge is largely discursive and expressive in words; it is a story-based way of understanding and makes meaning out of ongoing experiences in order to know oneself and the world (Bruner, 1990; Czarniawska, 1997; Polkinghorne, 1988). Both the tacit and the narrative/discursive are core processes in how people understand in everyday life, and are therefore central to organizational behavior and the concept of knowledge.

Even though our understanding of knowledge has developed and enlarged, science still seems to have problems with bringing emotions "back in" to organizational studies, particularly with regard to knowledge and processes related to intelligent/capable activity. This is a field that appears to be among the most dominated by cognition and/or traditional instrumental rationality. Is this the last "bastion" where emotions are the "ugly duckling"? When it comes to learning in organizations, emotions have recently been claimed to be the most promising and unexplored dimension (Höpfl & Linstead, 1997). Is this the case for knowledge in organizations as well? Yes, I will argue; the next vital step is to include emotions in studies of learning and knowledge in organizations.

Toward Integrating and Rethinking Emotions

Ashkanasy (1995, p. 2) argued that it is time to place "Cinderella" in the limelight and to include emotions in order to make organizational studies "more complete." In present working life it has become more apparent that human actions are often emotional because a growing number of occupations and trades are characterized by emotionally intensive work, especially due to increasing focus on service quality, customer orientation and rapid changes (Fineman, 1993a, 2000; Van Maanen & Kunda, 1989). Coping with one's own and others' emotions seems vital, but can also be difficult. The emotional dimension can be a smaller part of the service "product" or it can be a critical part of the core process of customer service (Forseth, 2001). However, indicating that emotions can be related positively to knowledge does not resonate well with the traditional and "rational" views on knowledge and organizations.

The main purpose of this chapter is to contribute in the rethinking discourse of emotions and knowledge. My argument is twofold: First, in order to grasp human emotions and knowing in practice, we need to engage in a more radical rethinking that includes an ontological choice. Here a broad situated-relational approach (within the interpretive-constructionist paradigm) is suggested. Second, stemming from this ontology is the basic assumption that being human involves emotions; therefore, human knowledge can involve emotions as well. By arguing that emotions have a fundamental role, I do not mean that other human aspects (e.g., cognition) should be omitted. My point is not to throw out one for the other but rather to aim for a broader and more integrated view on human being and human activity.

This chapter is divided into four sections: First, I briefly review traditional views of emotions in society and organizations. Second, more recent views on emotions in organizations and work are addressed, particularly the view of emotions as an invisible asset in emotionally intensive work. Third, an ontological reframing of emotions and knowledge is suggested and elaborated. Finally, implications are summarized.

EMOTIONS AS THE "UGLY DUCKLING"[1]

Emotions have been viewed as the "ugly duckling" within the triangular of
three distinct faculties of affect/emotion, cognition (how people think, know,
reason), and will (conation, motivation) (Forgas, 2000). During the Victorian
period (about 1820–1920) the prevailing view developing was that emotions
needed to be structured and controlled (May, 1983), whereas reason and science became the new promising force for industry and governmental activity.
Since this first phase of industrialization, Western cultures and especially science have mainly celebrated so-called instrumental, rational, and/or cognitive
views on humans and organizations, such as the machine view of organizations
(see Morgan, 1986). Instead of the religious dogma in the Middle Ages, with
one almighty God and truth, science became the new "hero" in the search for
the truth. Personal aspects such as feelings and intuition, as well as other types
of values and rationality (e.g., care and substantial rationality,[2] practical sense/
judging), were ignored, suppressed, or in other ways treated as "sand in the
machinery." Emotions were seen as something that characterized primitive
creatures and cultures, including children, women, or artists, and therefore
became as the antithesis of both scientific work and of knowledge (Bendelow
& Williams, 1998; Carnall, 1995; Morgan, 1986).

Existential phenomenology replied by asking, "But what sort of world do
we dwell in?" (Luijpen, 1962, p. 88). Human philosophers (e.g., Heidegger,
1927/1996; James, as cited in Forgas, 2000) recognized a close relationship in
thinking, feeling, and behavior, and started to question and protest against
the rationalism of their time (late part of the 1800s and beginning of 1900s).
Something vital was missing and had gone wrong when natural science ruled
the "playground" alone. Not even psychology assigned much importance to
emotions in the two most dominant paradigms of behaviorism and cognitivism (Forgas, 2000).

Within organizational studies, Weick (1979) and Fineman (1993a) among
others argued against the "machine" perspective of organizations and human
beings. Bruner (1990) claimed that cognitivism still suffers from insufficiency
due to the machine metaphor assumed when discussing learning and knowledge. Nonaka (1994) argued that the rational and hierarchical view of organizations and knowledge hinders the understanding and facilitation of knowledge creation and innovation. However, this "rational" view is not purely
historical. Ashkanasy (1995, pp. 1–2) argued that research still seems to be
"influenced by the Weberian belief that emotions and feelings are not proper

---

[1]The term *the ugly duckling* is inspired by the fairy tale with the same name by the Danish poet
H. C. Andersen.

[2]For example, care rationality has often been seen as female and emotional, opposed to the instrumental technical/economical rationality, which was seen as a male rationality and where emotions were excluded (Martinsen, 1989).

subjects for serious study." Today an increasing number of researchers have become aware of the importance of including emotions and more implicit aspects when studying organizational life and capable action/knowledge. One may argue that it is high time that management and organizational scholars start including the everyday emotional life in their studies and theories (Ashforth & Humphrey, 1995), and then studying the many sides of emotions and not only seeing them as irrational.

> We are left with an image of an actor who thinks a lot, plans, plots and struggles to look the right part at the right time. But we do not hear this actor's anger, pain, embarrassment, disaffection or passion and how such feeling relates to actions — except when it forms part of the organizational script.
> (Fineman, 1993a, p. 14)

In summary, I argue that the view of cognition as something more important than, and as something separable from, other human aspects and meanings is definitely being challenged. The question is, however, are we moving toward more fruitful alternatives?

EMOTIONS IN ORGANIZATIONS— AN INVISIBLE ASSET?

In more recent writings on emotions in organizations, different perspectives of emotions are taken. The two most common and complementary conceptual views are the *psychoanalytic* and the *social constructional* perspectives (Fineman, 1997). The former sees emotions as mainly an inner individual and private process (see Calori, 1998), whereas the latter argues that emotions are mainly something relational, social, cultural, and thereby also public (e.g., Gergen, 1994; Sandelands & Boudens, 2000; Strati, 1998). Both views can study what, why, and how feelings are expressed and repressed. For example, this can be carried out in a study of the differences and similarities between groups (e.g., the front line vs. the back line). In addition to, or partly overlapping with, the two views, there is a rapidly growing school of thought—emotional intelligence—that addresses the role of emotions in capable action and in learning (see Goleman, 1998; Mayer & Salovey, 1997).

This section does not address the main recent views in depth; instead, I focus on emotionally intensive work and studies thereof, which tend to draw on one or more of the three lines. My purpose is to show problems with addressing emotions mainly as an invisible asset to be utilized and managed in organizations in instrumental ways. In this way, the examples can be seen as arguments against stopping the rethinking of emotions, with the idea that emotions are an invisible asset. In the third section I suggest and elaborate a third and more radical rethinking. However, first, what is emotionally intensive work and how can it be problematic?

Emotionally Intensive Work

Emotions have received increasing attention and importance in organizations because a large, if not the largest, part of the
workforce in Western countries work
within service industries or service work.
The number of employees who are paid
to express positive emotions and attitudes such as commitment, sensitivity,
care, and hospitality (e.g., through smil-

> People working in customer service
> roles find their employers specifying
> how they act and dress, what they
> say and even what they should
> think and feel . . .
> Service staffs are paid as much for
> their "emotional labor" as for their
> technical skills.
> (Guerrier, 1999, pp. 212 and 234)

ing, greetings such as "welcome" and "have a nice day"), while not expressing
negative emotions or other feelings and identities, are increasing. Such work is
also termed *emotional labor* and involves emotional management, as one is
supposed to control and manage one's feelings so they are appropriate when
"on stage" with customers. Hospitality and frontline work in particular are often described as intensive regarding emotions; "the word 'hospitality' con-
jures up images of warm, smiling welcomes" (Guerrier, 1999, p. 211). In this
type of work, emotions are argued an "invisible asset," that is, an unrecog-
nized, intangible and/or central resource in the organizations:

> We can think of emotion as a covert resource, like money, or knowledge, or physi-
> cal labor, which companies need to get the job done. Real-time emotions are a
> large part of what managers manage and emotional labor is no small part of what
> trainers' train and supervisors supervise. It is a big part of white-collar "work."
> (Hochschild, 1993, p. xii)

Rather than biasing and neglecting emotions, I argue that emotions are
more often seen as an invisible asset for the individual and particularly the organization both in practice and in the more recent theoretical schools of
thought briefly introduced earlier. One main reason for this change in the view
on emotions (from "ugly duckling" to "invisible asset") seems to be the global
ideas of service management, quality, and customer orientation, and the necessity of these in successful business transactions. Such ideas are not only
cognitive (i.e., mental models and structures, thinking, and information processing), they are also embedded with emotions, meanings, and values that direct and shape the internal and external activities of the involved organizational members. The service itself is highly intangible, displayed by and
creating feelings and symbols. Learning and maintaining appropriate emotions through contextual situated "feeling rules" have therefore been argued
to be a central component in service work, both in so-called low-skilled work
(e.g., fast-food restaurants) and in occupations acquired through university
degrees (e.g., doctors, teachers, and consultants).

Van Maanen and Kunda (1989) claimed that emotions, such as moods, are a matter of contextual appropriateness put into use. Emotions are therefore viewed as manageable by oneself and others, and are largely about being able to act in an appropriate manner; that is, emotions can be managed and utilized in an instrumental way, as is exhibited by knowing how to dress. Furthermore, such competent emotional labor and management does not depend on *deep acting* (i.e., the actual feelings behind the *occupational mask*) (Hochschild, 1983). One general assumption in recent studies on emotions in organizations is, according to Sturdy and Fleming (2001), that *surface acting* (i.e., expressing feelings that are not felt, e.g., putting on a smiling mask when one does not feel like smiling) for a period does not matter because one assumes that surface practicing results in internalization. Goffmann (1959) described such an internalization process, where explicit knowledge and emotions become part of the person and thereby become implicit and deep knowledge and emotions. It seems reasonable that newcomers or persons who have recently experienced new ideas (e.g., in training) often, but not always, experience such an internalization process.

When persons "fake it in good faith," as Hochschild (1983) termed it, they manage the feelings so that they adhere to some standardized "rule" or ideal (e.g., smile or look sad at the appropriate places), and they have internalized this formal or informal "rule"—that is, it has become part of the persons and they understand, identify with, share and follow it. "Faking it in bad faith" is, on the other hand, when persons put on the same mask, but do so only because someone else (e.g., their superior) expects them to; they do not understand the purpose of doing so, or do not share the purpose—rather, they tend to distance themselves from it (e.g., as a nonbeliever or in a cynical way). "Faking it in good faith" can be stressful, but some might even see it as fun.

I do not dispute that emotions have many qualities: positive, negative, and the unknown. I argue, however, against making emotions a new kind of asset to be exploited in a highly instrumental way. Such *emotional engineering* (management, control, utilization for economical purposes) is not a new approach; Descartes (see Taylor, 1995, p. 281) did so when arguing for the rational control over passion by proposing a functionalistic theory of emotions. Some of the approaches to emotions in organizations are oriented toward too much emotional manipulating and dehumanizing of emotions and work. Fineman (2000) warned about the increasing tendency of so-called "emotional management" or "emotional intelligence" when popularized as a managerial "quick fix." The increase in emotionally intensive work has reintroduced the problem of authenticity versus inauthenticity that was first introduced by Heidegger (1927/1996). For example, Fineman (2000, p. 6) questioned, "What happens to self when self and emotions are to be compromised and consumed as a commodity?"

This is a significant question, which is addressed and discussed in this chapter, and which is a main reason for continuing the rethinking of emotions. The movement in organizational theory and practice from viewing emotion as "ugly duckling" toward emotions as "invisible assets" involves significant ethical dilemma and work environment problems, which indicates that this approach to emotions has problematic limitations. I next show empirical examples of problematic aspects when emotions mainly are approached as an invisible asset to manage and utilize in the workplace.

Consequences of Emotionally Intensive Work

There are many consequences of emotionally intensive work. Based on recent empirical studies of service work, I show and discuss four arguments against viewing emotions mainly as something easily manageable or purely concerned with surface acting.

First, in-depth studies within the hospitality industry (Eide & Lindberg, 1997) show that customers can see through surface acting and subsequently experience the customer interaction as *false and untrustworthy*. Hotel customers, for example, describe such interactions as negative, especially if the conference host or receptionist continues to smile, instead of really being able and willing to help:

> "I, and four other guys were just about to check into the hotel. Two girls were in the reception. One of these girls put on a false 'pro' attitude which was perceived by all of us as a very arrogant attitude, and it was very irritating."
>
> "When I was about to arrange the course, the receptionist showed little accommodating attitude. I just got a feeling of insecurity towards the accomplishment of the whole course. I simply had to talk to the manager, and he provided me with a person with a more accommodating attitude." (Eide & Lindberg, 1997, p. 4)

Managers and various occupational groups of employees in hotels also point out the importance of being natural during interactions. For example, an illustration of such an argument told to us by a receptionist was, "To be service minded is exaggerated. One has to be natural. If you like to work with people, it will come naturally" (Eide & Lindberg, 1997, p. 5). We found in our study (Eide & Lindberg, 1997) that being able to help and interact with customers face to face is often complex and involves doing far more than just smiling or repeating simple phrases like "have a nice day" at the right time, as has also been found in Australian hotels (Faulkner & Patiar, 1997). Service or other relational work, therefore, is neither completely manageable by oneself or others, nor is it primarily a theatric surface performance as indicated by Goffmann (1959) and Pine and Gilmore (1998). Customers may distrust surface acting as they are able to "read between the lines," and customer interactions are basically relational, that is, reciprocal and dialogical, not mainly monological and in the control of only one part. For this reason the work, including the emotions and knowledge, cannot and should not be standardized a priori. The dynamic, reciprocal, and complex customer interactions depend on the service worker's *ability and willingness* to see, judge, relate, and cope with different customers and situations (Eide & Lindberg, 1997). In short, being highly capable is far more than just wearing prescribed masks with a false or felt smile, repeating simple expressions, and using other prescribed simple "scripts" in static ways. The relational and complex nature of the interactions depends rather on another emotional side of the work, that is, the emotional attunement, sensitivity, and intuitions that guide the practical judgments and practical knowing (I return to this point later in the chapter).

Second, studies (Forseth, 2001; Hochschild, 1983) also showed that prescribed emotional rules (e.g., smiling) can make the work more *alienating* and blur personal and work life in a way that commercializes not only the feelings of customers, but also those of employees. Being service-minded can increase the pressure, cause stress, and develop into serious *personal and work environment problems* such as burnout. These problems are increasing because emotions are not only a large part of work life, they are more often argued as a critical "tool" for an increasing number of occupations. Forseth (in Myhr, 2001, p. 18, my translation[3]) comments that "it is not only that you have to use emotions. You also have to be clever when doing it."

When emotions are assumed to be "the key tool" that makes a difference in customer service, this "little extra" often means that one is able to get into the spirit of the work (i.e., to be committed and to identify with and live for the work and customers). Service workers with emotional burnout problems tend to cope by being more impersonal and cynical in interactions with customers, which reduces the quality of service created (Forseth, 2001). Furthermore, Forseth (2001) found that traditional care workers (i.e., in health and education sectors) tend to be more prepared for work where the care about others is central than the new groups within private and public sectors. The study included a group of approximately 1,000 employees from three industries: banking, nursery, and retail. Forseth (2001) found that 50% of the bank employees are more or less emotionally exhausted, as are 40% and 34% in the two latter industries. Also, the high number and level of radical changes in the industries increased the tensions, anxiety, and emotionality. In my view, Forseth's (2001) study indicates that the ability to cope with emotions is critical in at least three ways:

1. In the core production (i.e., interactions with the customers or other actors), emotions are a central part of how and what is being "produced." There-

---

[3]"My translation" means that I have translated the quote from a Scandinavian language into English.

fore, emotions are also something an employee must be able to know, draw on, and cope with in a capable way.

2. Emotions become more complex and tense due to a perceived increase due to continual changes in organizations. This tends to influence most trades and organizations in society and across cultures. Blackler, Reed, and Whitaker (1993, p. 857) asserted that the postindustrial society stretches the collective and individual cognition toward their capable limits. But is the consequence only cognitive? I argue that what is "stretched," involved, and critical in order to act, interact, and cope in capable ways is also highly *emotional*. How one feels and is able to live and work with one's own and others' emotions has become a more pressing issue in recent society; however, it is not only about being flexible and adaptive.

3. If one is not able to cope with emotional pressure following from one or both of the two aforementioned situations (see 1 and 2), one may experience negative stress, burnout or develop other problems.

The third reason for not addressing emotions as an invisible asset that is easily managed and utilized is the observed *temporality and vulnerable side of interacting in capable ways*. My ethnographically inspired, hermeneutical study of receptionists in four hotels (Eide, 2000, in press) shows that the assumed cycling from more explicit (e.g., prescribed rules) to internalized knowledge, feeling, and acting is not the only critical change that can take place. Highly capable receptionists who are dedicated to a service-care ideology can begin questioning their own practice and their continued desire to do it. They balance belief and practice on one side, and struggle with doubt and a possible change in dedication on the other. The mode(s) of practicing (i.e., identity, knowing, and doing) what they believe in, find meaningful, and experience daily in interactions with customers may gradually shift toward less capable practice.

The three reasons addressed thus far can be seen as a critical lens toward work being intensive on emotions since they mainly address problems. However, Hardy, Lawrence, and Phillips (1998, p. 81) asserted that the critical lens is too narrow and needs to be balanced with other views that do not "lead to a similar conclusion as that of the rational view of organizations: both conclude that emotions are (or should be) the private domain of individuals and should not be considered as organizational phenomena." Further, if only using a critical lens one runs the risk of overlooking the many positive aspects of such work and of emotions in organizations. A fourth reason for not addressing emotions as an invisible asset to be managed and utilized is that such an approach can ruin the meaning and positive sides of emotions in organizations. The limitations of only seeing the problems in service work were illustrated when reinterpreting the results of a Norwegian national work environment study conducted by Grimsmo (1996a, 1996b) in which he concluded that the hotel and restaurant industries have the worst work environment. However, the negative conclusion was mainly due to an assumption built into the survey (i.e., that a high number of customer interactions always caused stress and other negative problems). This assumption is, however, highly questionable because more in-depth studies of the hospitality industry have shown that receptionists and other front-line workers often argue the opposite, as illustrated in, "customers are different. It is through relations with customers that they [receptionists] are challenged, i.e. that they learn, develop, encounter variation, participation and social contact, and experience meaning" (Eide, Jensen, & Lilleby, 1996, p. 7, my translation). First, this shows that general models and assumptions may lead to incorrect conclusions because they do not grasp the fact that there can be considerable *differences* among individuals, occupations, and sociocultural contexts. Second, it shows that work involving a high degree of emotions and social interactions can be experienced as *highly meaningful, learning, and fun*, if the work is varied and accommodates autonomy, initiative, and personal style (i.e., being natural caring and relating rather than mainly prescribed, false, and controlled). These experiences also covary with a strong interest and dedication in meeting new people and caring for people. If such interest and dedication are not present, then the assumption that a high level of customer interaction is stressful and negative for the work environment is more accurate. Such lack of interest and dedication can be due to that the organization has hired the "wrong" person(s) for frontline work, or the person has become sour.

Emotions in Work—A First Conclusion

In summary, emotions are not only present, but are often *central* to being able and willing to do the work in capable ways, especially in work with a high degree of customer interactions. A fundamental question for managers within hospitality and service organizations more generally is how to facilitate and organize so that the customers feel welcome and cared for. Bureaucratic control and heavy standardization tend to be alienating, inflexible, and risky in regard to the interhuman tasks and competence, as the many subordinate ways of interacting cannot be dictated a priori by a manager or trainer in the same way as is possible with more technical tasks. Surface acting and emotional management are a part of everyday life, but this does not mean that emotions in work are purely a phenomenon to manipulate. On the contrary, studies show that emotionally intensive work is far more complex, paradoxical, and dependent on knowing, relating, and dedicating as a whole person. What modes of emotions and knowledge are we dealing with, and how can we understand the complex, dynamic, and subtle layers of emotions and knowledge? These questions are the focus of the remainder of this chapter.

EMOTIONS AS PART OF A LARGER WHOLE:
AN ONTOLOGICAL REFRAMING

Rather than assuming the traditional dualisms of "cognitive" versus "emotions," or addressing emotions mainly in functionalistic ways, I propose to undertake a more radical rethinking, that is, an *ontological* reframing. By *ontology* I mean the more fundamental assumptions about the world and about human nature. Furthermore, I suggest that a *situated-relational ontology be assumed*. This ontological view represents a shift that tries to overcome and rethink some of the main dualisms in science, such as individual versus environment, mind versus body, thinking versus action, and cognition as rationality versus emotions as irrationality. This ontology includes a mixture of writers within the interpretive-constructionist paradigm. As I show, Aristotle inspires some of the vital writers contributing to this ontology. Aristotle argued in Greek antiquity that pathos, ethos, and logos were not distinctly separate (dual), as was assumed during the Enlightment, nor did he see emotions only as something private but rather as largely public and social. The main thesis argued by this ontological view is that human beings and their more fundamental conditions for actions are situated in within four main situators: as "a whole person" (i.e., with body, emotions, and cognition, not either–or), "in-relations" (i.e., relations with things, others, and self), "in-worlds" (i.e., in different physical, social, and cultural contexts), and "in-history" (i.e., a time involving the past, present, and future). This section begins by introducing key terms and assumptions in this ontology and gradually moves more specifically to the consequences of how to understand emotions and knowledge/knowing. In addition to seeing emotions as intertwined with cognition, and as having both personal and collective sides, I further argue that emotions are *relational* and *part of a larger whole*.

Emotions in Organizations as Relational and Part of a Larger Whole—An Introduction

The organizational psychologist Weick (1995, p. 39) suggested a relational view, claiming that emotions "do not grow within us but between us." The Norwegian psychiatrist Finn Skårderud (2002) was critical of the traditional dualism of body versus soul or body versus mind, and suggested that a broader integrated understanding is needed:

> We feel. We think. We have a body. And we relate to other human beings. These four phenomena together constitute our mental life . . . How our feelings and our thoughts develop has to do first of all *with our meetings*. It is about individuals we meet. And how we meet. And where and when we meet. Culture means that within us there are depositions of all the meetings that we have ever participated in. (Skårderud, 2002, p. 228, my translation)

Skårderud elaborated emotions, cognition, and body as vital and not excludable sides of being human and relating in the world; feelings were also argued as having a particular role in becoming a more whole integrated person:

> Our feelings make us whole human beings . . . help us move forward in life. The will (lust) drives us toward other humans . . . The healthy shame makes sure that the excitement does not become too intense and that we get a grip on ourselves. The fear holds back the foolhardiness . . . There is one factor that protects against many things: good self-esteem. (Skårderud, 2002, pp. 228 and 235, my translation)

Emotions were, here, seen as both positive and negative, not either–or; his view seems similar to my own in this regard. The Norwegian philosopher Arne Næss (1998) also assumed a relational approach when arguing for an integrated view of human beings by claiming that emotions should not be seen as something one "has." Rather, these emotions are part of being human and originate from the situated, relational being/becoming in the world:

> *Emotions are not things, that we own.* They are some(-"thing") that originates in the meeting with ourselves-and-the-world. . . . And it is not so that we only have feelings, just as seldom as we have relations, but in inner circumstances *we are emotions and relations.* We cannot make ourselves external to ourselves. The thoughts, feelings and relations that we identify with are a part of us in a wider sense. The emotions that we have for a bus driver, for example, depend upon whether or not we perceive him or her as a subject—a co-human, or as an object—a part of the bus that gets us where we want. The goal must be to meet other co-creatures with almost our whole self. (Næss, 1998, p. 24, my translation)

Viewing emotions as relational in this way fits well with what I see as a broad situated-relational approach, because it does not exclude or largely downgrade the personal and deeper sides like some social constructionist writers (e.g., Gergen, 1994) seem to do. Emotions, I argue, should be situated not only within the specific relation and/or the sociocultural world, but also within at least the two further ontological situators—that is, within time, as well as within the whole bodily person.

A Broad Situated-Relational Ontology

Here, I concentrate on the core ideas suggested by Heidegger (1927/1996). For a broader and more in-depth elaboration of a situated-relational ontology, and the consequences for emotions, knowledge, and learning, see Eide (in press).

The following idea indicates the essence of the situated-relational ontology: "This with-like (mithaften) being-in-the-world, the world is always the one that I share with others . . . Being-in is Being-with others" (Heidegger, 1927/ 1996, p. 118). This primordial view, also known as an ontological structure, highlights concepts such as *situatedness*, *attunement*, and *fore-understanding*. Heidegger also elaborated other fruitful concepts that are relevant both for understanding emotions and knowing, such as the terms *care for self* and *authenticity*. Meaning and interpretations are vital in an ontological sense, and this view is also shared by other approaches, such as constructivism within the interpretive paradigm. Constructivism depicts human nature as an individual and cognitive phenomenon. Heidegger (1927/1996) did not interpret human beings, meaning, and interpretation as purely cognitive.

The individual and cognitive sides are important in the ontological approach, but they are also part of a larger complexity because human nature and meaning are multidimensional and have their origins in the broader situatedness (Heidegger, 1927/1996). People develop and act by means of the situatedness (in body, in relations, in worlds, and in history/time), not as an autonomy-cognitive individual or a completely cultural determined "actor." Rather than viewing the individual as neutral or distanced, being situated means always being attuned one way or another and with a fore-understanding. It reaches beyond traditional dualism between rationality as thinking and irrationality as emotions (Guneriussen, 1996). Therefore, this approach is particularly fruitful for rethinking emotions and humanistic ways of knowing (including knowledge).

Before elaborating further on conceptualizations of human nature, I find it useful to emphasize the following: I share the notion that there are problematic sides with elaborating views of human beings in general terms, because every human is unique. Consequently, it is necessary to separate between analyses on an ontological level (i.e., discussion about humankind and worldview) and an ontic or existential level that involves discussion about the unique phenomenon or person in question. For instance, the situated-relational ontology proclaims attunement as an ontological notion (i.e., that involves every human). How attunement emerges ontically is never obvious a priori because it depends on the context, relations, and people involved. Simply stated, we can say generally that human beings are emotional beings, just they are thinking beings at an *ontological level*, but what a person feels or thinks in a specific situated time and place or how a person expresses the feelings or thoughts must be studied empirically as it varies at an *ontic level* (Heidegger, 1927/1996).

Attunement and Understanding—Emotions and Knowledge as Blurred

Because human beings are situated, they find themselves *attuned*. But what does attunement mean? We know that it involves deeper emotions, and Fløistad (1993) argued that it is a kind of state of being tuned/attuned. Lindberg

(2001) asserted that, due to the situatedness of human beings, attunement is neither something inward, nor something determined from the outward, but something that

> ontically depends on the *in-world-existence*, while finding oneself is primordially ontological. . . . Dasein is indicated by situatedness, which again is indicated by attunements (and feelings). But every human is born with, and [has] developed, different possibilities for attunement and different ability to sense it. . . . *To be "at-tuned" means to be tuned within the world a certain way.* (Lindberg, 2001, pp. 96 and 99–100)

The attunement, as a deep emotion, depends on the individual's belonging to the world and interacting in the world; it is relational and does not only involve the inner individual. Attunement, according to Heidegger (1927/1996), is the primary way of discovering and understanding "the world, other individuals, and ourselves" (Lindberg, 2001, p. 97). Attunement, therefore, provides insight and a sense of a " 'being-there-feeling' which is necessary for our ability to grasp reality, act and think" (Lindberg, 2001, p. 101). Angst is a kind of attunement that can provide the break leading to movement and change. In short, Heidegger (1927/1996) elaborated attunement as a precondition that occurs before thinking, insight, and acting; I therefore elaborate further by focusing on attunement and its role for understanding and knowledge. Central in his elaboration is also the hermeneutical process and the situatedness in history, which means that any understanding follows from a fore-understanding (see Gadamer, as cited in Linge, 1976), and the shift between parts and the whole (e.g., that the explicit knowledge or that which we have in focus always dwells in the larger whole of the tacit understanding and knowledge; see Polanyi, 1958, 1966/1983, and Polanyi & Prosch, 1975; more discussion follows).

Both situatedness and attunement show the dynamic and infinite nature of being and understanding, because "the attunements can be destroyed and can change, show that a human is always already attuned" (Heidegger, as cited in Fløistad, 1993, p. 196, my translation). Fløistad (1993) questioned where attunements and feelings end, and where the cognitive sides of understanding begin. His answer is clarified next:

> It is through the attunement that we primarily recognize and understand ourselves, the world and other humans . . . *the attunements and feelings are the primary source of our consciousness* of things, ourselves, and our fellow beings. (Fløistad, 1993, p. 196, my translation)

This notion can be exemplified by how one answers the question "How are you?" A reply can be based on the situated feeling of the situation as a human being within time and place. Every relation with, and understanding of, others, things, or self therefore is based on attunement and situatedness; attunement has a kind of cognitive function for summing up the situation. Fløistad (1993) believed that it could be thus in many situations, but was critical of this concept as a general claim about understanding. Dreyfus (1991, p. 185), however, argued that Heidegger's (1927/1996) notion of understanding is not a cognitively distanced phenomenon. Alvesson and Sköldberg (1994) argued, when discussing Heidegger, that all "understanding right from the beginning ('always already') is colored by emotional attunements; therefore there is no purely cognitive or rational understanding" (Alvesson & Sköldberg, 1994, p. 136, my translation).

My own view is that the situatedness of the whole person means that our understanding always (and not only sometimes) is partly based on attunement and perhaps other kinds of emotions. Human knowledge is primarily about understanding[4] where tacit knowledge and emotions are involved in the horizon of understanding. Active knowledge (i.e., knowing) is already incorporated with emotions; that is, it is not a purely cognitive knowledge or a purely passive, rational, or theoretical one, particularly not when it is included as a part of one's practice. Such understanding of the world, oneself, and others is a vital part of being, becoming and knowing.

In summary, the attunement based on the broad (the four types of) situatedness means that emotions are included at different levels and are intertwined with understanding and knowledge. Emotions are not only a matter of the surface level, the present, the isolated individual, or something irrational. For pedagogical purposes, I have made a simplified sketch—at an analytical level—that includes the key concepts and their relations in a situated-relational approach that focuses on emotional and cognitive aspects (Fig. 2.1).

The situatedness in body, time, relations, and world(s) involves three key ontological structures of being and becoming that have to do with our deep existence: "understanding" (i.e., a vague or clear understanding of our basic existential conditions, such as where we are), "thrown" (i.e., the person finds her/himself thrown into a situation that the person partly may have chosen, and that partly is determined), and "falling" (toward the world and future). These three states depend on the situatedness, and they interact continually and contribute to three states of being: a colored "horizon" (a historical, cultural-based fore-understanding), "attunements," and "approach" (with attention). These three states of being do not exist in isolation, and all three can bring insight that contributes to tacit feelings and knowing (knowledge) and also contributes to "external relational activities" in the world. Such external activity includes feelings being directly and indirectly expressed in interactions. Due to the relational nature of "being" in the world, situatedness can continually be altered, which can in turn alter the three key structures and consequently the three states of being, and so on.

---

[4]Polanyi (1958) argued strongly for the importance of understanding in knowing and knowledge.

This can be exemplified by classical situations where persons move rapidly between contexts and situations. I use here an event experienced personally of two people who attended a classical concert (it could just as well have been a fine restaurant, party, or work meeting) dressed in informal clothes shortly after returning from an exciting trip to the Postojna caves in Ljubljana (in Slovenia). They were in a good mood after the trip, but short of time because the arranged trip was delayed. Therefore they had no time to change clothes; in fact, they nearly missed the concert. They were sitting and smiling, expressing how happy they were that they made also

this experience-based event in time. However, they gradually became aware of a new situatedness as they also began to feel uncomfortable, because other people were dressed very formally. The change of context had been too fast; they became aware that they were not appropriately dressed so the situation became unpleasant. The attention that should have been directed to the music was not; they were too focused on others in the audience and on self; it there-

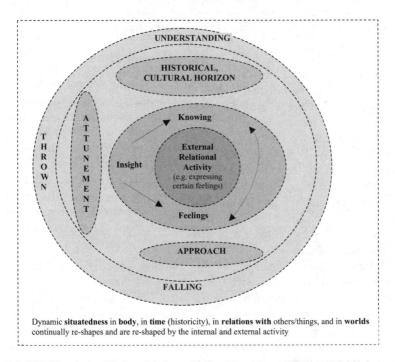

FIG. 2.1. A simplified model of emotions and cognition at different individual levels.

fore ruined their music experience. This shows that the experience at the concert that normally should have resulted in great enthusiasm also depended on the broader situatedness and not only the isolated listener or the musicians playing.

Further Discussion of Heidegger's Ideas

Like Heidegger (1927/1996), Charles Taylor (1995) also argued that emotions delve deeply into who we are, what we experience, and what is significant to us. Therefore, emotions elevate our attention and contribute to a certain understanding and "movement." As emotions are one of the ontological characteristics of being human, emotions are not something we can "step in and out of"— or neglect (Taylor, 1995). Understanding emotion and cognition as ontological characteristics of human nature means that they are intertwined and interdependent. Present-day society is criticized for idealizing consciousness and action as something driven by the explicit, objective, and general; in doing this, he reclaimed the key points of interpretive writers:

> The more well-known argument—forwarded by Wittgenstein, Heidegger, Michael Polanyi and others . . . Rules do not adapt themselves—no matter how extensive and detailed they are. Norms and ideals always demand new interpretations in new situations. (Taylor, 1995, p. 294, my translation)

Here the vital role of meaning, interpretation, and tacit knowledge in action is addressed. Furthermore, Taylor (1995) situated emotions in a larger whole, that is, as part of the self that is seen as relational in a dialogic way. Self-consciousness does not develop as distanced inner thinking. It develops when living in the world, as "we become self-conscious through thinking, feeling and interacting" (Nyeng, 2000, p. 168, my translation). Self-understanding, identification, and development cannot develop without first participating in a culture, and articulation is a vital part of it.

> What we need to explain is people living their lives; the terms in which they cannot avoid living them cannot be removed . . .
> We cannot just leap outside of these terms altogether, on grounds that their logic doesn't fit some model of "science."
> (Taylor, quoted in Nyeng, 2000, p. 119)

Humans experience genuine kinds of emotions that are characterized as "strong evaluations" and subject-related emotions that are fundamental when trying to understand human beings (Grimen, 1995). Animals also experience desires of the first order, whereas only humans can experience those of the second order, that is, judging whether our desires are desirable. It is the latter that characterizes strong evaluations/judgments (Grimen, 1995). Examples of genuine human emotions include pride, shame, love, sense of worth, morality, dignity, and evil (see Taylor, 1985, p. 102). For example, other animals do not feel shame, machines of course do not feel at all; even so, machine metaphors have been so popular. These unique emotions are possibly due to the vital role of language in our lives and our situatedness in social practices. For this reason, even prearticulated emotions are dependent on language and are often interpreted emotions (Taylor, 1985). Human beings are described as a continually self-interpreting and narrating animal where meaning and emotions are fundamentally dynamic and intertwined:

> This is an animal whose *emotional life incorporates a sense of what is really important* to him, of the shape of his aspirations, which *asks to be understood, and which is never adequately understood*. His understanding is explicated at any time in the language he uses to speak about himself, his goals, what he feels, and so on; and in shaping his sense of what is important, it also shapes what he feels. (Taylor, 1985, p. 74)

Emotions can *express meanings and understanding* because strong judgments and values are anchored in emotions and struggling. This anchoring is why emotions motivate us and make us attentive[5] (Grimen, 1995, p. 28). Kirkeby (2001, pp. 88–89) claimed that certain emotions, such as conscience, justice, and honesty, can express deep and strong judgments. Such judgments and emotions are seen as originating from active participation in social practices and from the integration of the three basic aspects of humanity, that is, of emotions, thought (reason), and will. The idea that emotions can carry and be a mode of expressing values and knowledge dates back to Aristotle (1998). Drawing on both Aristotle and Heidegger, Taylor (1995, p. 158) argued that *practical judging and orientation* take place in the gestalt of the unique human emotions. Meaning, emotion, and action originate in the relational sphere and not just in the inner and private spheres, as in the constructivist approach. This does not mean that human action is solely determined and "written" by outside sources, as that would be an externally orchestrated monologue and not be dialogical.

Taylor's (cited in Nyeng, 2000, p. 83, my translation) *concept of emotions* includes at least four subterms: *affections, feelings, attunements*, and *sensations*. The last concept—sensations—is a joint term for bodily expressions of all kinds of emotions, particularly those that follow strong affections. To only address this side of emotions is, however, a limited view of emotions, as that would merely measure physical changes during anger or reduce emotions to bodily conditions alone. According to a situated-relational approach, emotions are interpreted emotions with meanings. A feeling cannot be understood as an isolated phenomenon because it is embedded within a larger whole, as a "system" of feelings and other aspects contributing to a web of significance. What

---

[5]It is a well-known argument that attention is central to knowledge and learning. In my view, emotions can contribute both to increase and to decrease the attention.

are important when a person is angry are the circumstances—for example, did the person experience an injustice? Thereby, sensations and bodily expressions are not seen as the core of emotions. However, I argue that the body "can tell" by means of intuition and deeper emotions what is "right" for the person. Drawing on the notion of attunement, Taylor (cited in Nyeng, 2000) also argued that human beings are always attuned one way or another, but often are not conscious of it. This attunement means that a human is not neutral when confronting things and others. Anxiety is one example of attunement; it is a deep and fundamental emotion that threatens the existence and ontological security of the person, whereas fear is seen as a feeling directed toward something more specific (Giddens, 1991; Nyeng, 2000). The different terms can be described as follows—I quote at length:

> In a way we can say that attunements and affections make up the two endpoints. Everything "in between" is feelings. Both endpoints are characterized by very limited distance and reflection. However, while *the attunements are the emotional fundaments that life exists upon, the affections represent the immediate manifestations of emotional "shaking,"* that which is strong, that puts us out of play, but which is usually over just as fast as it comes into being . . . I live in an immediate and all-absorbing here and now . . . *Feelings are processed experiences that are emotionally loaded—a processing that integrates emotional involvement and reason-based reflection and argumentation in a more distanced attitude* to the object and power of emotions. (Nyeng, 2000, p. 85, my translation)

All these terms are seen as partly different but related sides of emotions. I share this view; it should be noted that, for example, Salovey and Mayer (1990, p. 186) defined emotions far more narrowly and saw emotion as something shorter and more intense than mood. Mood, in my opinion, approaches attunement and is part of the larger concept of emotion.

The process of reflecting and articulating feelings makes it possible to grasp what it means to be human, and to "create an individualized and authentic self in the first person" (Nyeng, 2000, p. 90, my translation). When Taylor (1995) claimed that emotions are fundamental, it was because emotions are integrated into the existence as ontological phenomenon and the deeper, more implicit, and unarticulated are present and significant parts of being. When emotions are articulated, the implicit background for actions becomes more conscious: "To articulate a framework is to explicate what makes sense of our moral responses" (Taylor, cited in Gergen, 1994, p. 104). Life can become more human through reflexive awareness since we can reach more of the deeper values of life. Articulating brings emotions into language, and thereby more into focus and into a public space, although what is articulated is always only the tip of the iceberg (Grimen, 1995). Articulations can make us more aware of who we are, what are important to us, and it can also change how we understand and feel about a situation and ourselves (Taylor, 1985). Thus articulation is not only a representation or translation into an articulated form. It can also have an intervening function:

> Formulating how we feel, or coming to adopt a new formulation, can frequently change how we feel. *When I come to see* that my feeling of guilt was false, or my feeling of love self-deluded, the emotions themselves are different. (Taylor, 1985, p. 100)

By claiming that exerting falseness tends to change the emotion, Taylor (1985) also asserted that emotions can be constituted and shaped by our understanding and interpretations, and not just the other way around as Heidegger (1927/1996) seemed to suggest. Furthermore, articulations can also increase the emotions: "I can describe my emotions by describing my situation, and very often I must do so really to give the flavour of what I feel" (Taylor, 1985, p. 101). Articulation therefore influences how we interact with the world, how and who we are.

Does this mean that experiencing a beautiful rainbow or an exciting football match is not meaningful enough unless it is articulated? I do not interpret this claim on articulation as such; however, the point is that we need to be more aware of what is important to us. Taylor (1985) seemed to assign greater significance to the more explicit and verbally articulated aspects and to self-consciousness than Heidegger (1927/1996) did, and more than other proponents of his ideas such as Bourdieu (1990) and Dreyfus (1991, p. 4), who argued that "what is most important and meaningful in our lives is not, and should not be, accessible to critical reflection." However, critical reflection and articulation are not the same as we might narrate on what we feel without reflecting on it. As I understand it, there are also many situations where we can both know and feel with sufficient meaning without having to articulate it explicitly in words; sometimes articulating might even ruin the meaning.

Compared to Heidegger (1927/1996), Taylor (1995) also elaborated more about the social and public side of life, which I see as a vital contribution to the understanding of human beings and of emotions. There is blurred distinction between the experiences of (lived) emotions versus emotional cultures; I argue that both should be included when trying to study and understand emotions. A vital strength in Taylor's elaboration of emotions is that he does not erode the separation between the surface and the depths or between the private and the public. The differences are needed in development and communication, and not only in deep genuine relations (Nyeng, 2000). Differences shown in contrasting dialogues can contribute to deeper value experiences. It can separate the more instrumental values or superficial expressive values and emotions from deeper significant life values. This is a vital difference between Taylor's discussion (1995; cf. Nyeng, 2000) compared to social constructionist writers that tend to focus too much on the expectations and surface acting. At the same time, Taylor criticized the consumer society as an instrumental, sur-face community that lacks focus on real meanings. He argued that today's frag-mented and individualized selves only seek to satisfy instant pleasure and that this hampers meanings and relations. Strong values that are expressed as gen-uine emotions point toward goals to strive for and orient us so that the result is something that is right/good or better/worse.

A Knowledge Concept Where Emotions Are a Part

The situated-relational approach results in a different understanding of hu-man emotions compared to the "ugly duckling" or "invisible asset" views, that the ontological change also has conse-quences for the meaning of understand-ing, knowledge, and the grounds for ac-tion have also been briefly indicated. How to conceptualize human knowledge is further explored next. Aristotle (1998) elaborated on a versatile (although hier-archical) concept of knowledge and hu-man beings as early as the Greek period of antiquity; he was a great inspiration for the two main writers (Heidegger and Taylor) already discussed. Versatile views

> The Aristotelian description makes us think of real practical insight and understanding as an integrated activity that calls upon the whole soul . . .
> Often relying on the intellectual ability can actually be a hindrance for true ethical sensing by putting itself in the way of, or undermining, the emotions and sensitivity. (Nussbaum, 1995, p. 85, my trans-lation)

of knowledge relate knowing to emotions and intuition. In other approaches, intuition has often been seen as a primitive knowledge (see Simon, quoted in Sinclair & Ashkanasy, 2001; cf. Cooper, 2001), or as no knowledge at all, whereas others see intuition and even emotions as part of highly capable action and knowledge (Schön, 1983; Sjöstrand, 1997; Strati, 2000, 2001). Two exam-ples of the latter are illustrated:

> That *intuition* has an unsolvable connection with *emotions* seems *undeniable* to me, this has nothing to do with an obscurity of intuitive representations, but has to do with its *richness and unity*. (Larsson, 1892/1920, p. 5, my translation)

> Into *every act of knowing* there enters a *tacit and passionate contribution* of the person knowing what is being known, and that this coefficient is not mere imper-fection, but a *vital component* of all knowledge. (Polanyi, 1958, p. 312)

Larsson and Polanyi share Aristotle's (1998) view that intuition and emo-tions can increase the ability to see, understand, and act in a powerful way due to its ability to connect a range of parts into a unit. Polanyi (1958, freely quoted) claimed that all knowledge, more or less, includes and depends on personal and tacit knowledge, as "we know more than we can tell." Polanyi

(1958) and Polanyi and Prosch (1975) elaborated how all knowing and knowledge include *dwelling-in* tacit elements and *tacit integration*. The tacit integration takes place as a "from-to-attention," constituted by the content in focus (i.e., the focal attention) and the tacit content (background, i.e., the subsidiary attention), "showing that all thought contains components of which we are subsidiary aware of in the focal content of our think-

> **We know** a person's face, and can recognize it among a thousand, indeed among a million. Yet we usually **cannot tell how** we recognize a face we know. So most of this knowledge cannot be put into words ... We recognize the moods of the human face, without being able to tell, except quite vaguely, by what signs we know it.
> (Polanyi, 1969, pp. 4 and 5)

ing, and that all thought *dwells in its subsidiaries*, as if they were parts of our body" (Polanyi, 1966/1983, p. x).

Trying to articulate the tacit into explicit more or less fails because much of our knowledge (e.g., as shown in the quotation about recognizing faces) is expressed as, and relates to, feelings and activities in action. These two kinds of attentions are vital parts, I argue, in any approach in practice. This contention occurs not only in the private life or in craftwork, but also in the practical research work:

> Even when attempts are made to state them explicitly, what these explicit statements mean can be known only by the scientists in the particular field involved. There is much that cannot be made explicit because it lies at *the level of feelings* about fitness and in working attitudes that betray an essentially imaginative grasp of how things in that field may be expected to work or to be. (Polanyi & Prosch, 1975, p. 186)

Later Wittgenstein (1953/1992) also elaborated on understanding and knowledge by pointing to the limitations of explicit rules and the vital role of personal and social practice for knowledge. Learning to "see" and understand human affairs, and the use of language, is not a rule-based technique to apply in a fixed system such as mathematics. Only experienced individuals can draw upon the rules in highly capable actions, and then feelings inform and guide this use:

> What one learns is not technique; one learns to *judge* correctly. There are also rules, but they build no system, and only experienced individuals can apply them properly ... The genuineness of the expression cannot be proved; one must *feel* it. (Wittgenstein, 1953/1992, pp. 261–262, my translation)

It is thus when distinguishing faces, when reading a poem, or when knowing what word to use when talking, or how to move the body and the ski when skiing. Certain rules become a part of us, incorporated into the self-identity and what we know, in a bodily, emotional, and anonymous way. The "rules" lo-

cate us in a culture. We do not know them
as explicit rules and cannot give full accounts of them because such "rules" are
tacit, dynamic, and social, and differ from
the logic of formal rules that are general,
static, and explicit (Wittgenstein, 1953/
1992). Polanyi (1958, 1966/1983) and
Wittgenstein (1953/1992) are now vital
sources for organizational scholars in rethinking the discourse of knowledge in
organizations.

> *When I read a poem, a story with
> emotions, then something takes
> place within me that does not take
> place when I only scan the rows to
> be informed . . .*
> *The composition sounds different.
> I carefully attend the tone. Some-
> times a word has a false tone, is
> too strong or too weak.*
> (Wittgenstein, 1953/1992, p. 247,
> my translation)

Sketches Toward a Model

Based on the theoretical elaboration and empirical studies discussed so far, I
suggest that interactional emotional work, which constitutes a large part of hospitality and service industry, cannot be fully managed by the manager or the employee, as social interactions often are reciprocal, complex, dynamic, and unfore-
seen—that is, they are basically *relational and dialogic* in nature and not
monologic and static. Also, the other (the customer or colleague) and the particular relationship that originates between the involved parts have and should have
a real influence on the process; therefore, the core production cannot be fully
managed by the manager or the employee alone. How then does one understand
and approach knowledge and learning? One main implication is that the experience-based practical judgment and understanding become more critical as the
employee must be able and willing to act in capable ways on the spot. These
ways of knowing draw on and dwell in the more emotional and intuitive ways of
being and acting. How knowledge in practice is relational and emotional, and
how emotions are relational, are illustrated in Fig. 2.2. My intention in using this
model is not to propose an overall and universal theory of emotions in knowledge
and work, but to propose an alternative understanding of emotions and knowledge according to the situated-relational approach. The sketch is based on the
theoretical discussions and empirical interpretations of my hotel receptionist
study (Eide, 2000; Eide & Lindberg, 1997), which can also be seen as a more
practical illustration and elaboration of Fig. 2.1.

Person B is the individual focused on and followed in the figure. Like person B, persons A and C also participate in both situations characterized as "in-
action" and "processing about-action." The four levels of being, knowledge,
and emotions described in the left box exist both when the person is in situations characterized as "in-actions" and as "processing about-actions," because the latter situation is at the same time also a kind of "in-action" here and
now. The approach, attention, talk, and other activities tend, however, to differ
depending on what kind of main situation one participates in. Knowledge and

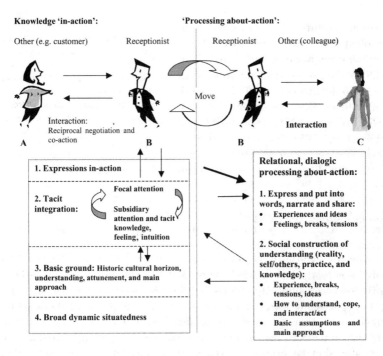

FIG. 2.2.   Knowledge in practice as relational and emotional.

emotions are described as intertwined, leveled, process/activity and relational in the figure.

On the *levels*, knowledge and emotions can be expressed in action, in the tacit integration, and in the basic ground according to the situatedness; the two latter are the resonators for the two former levels. In this way I claim that knowledge (knowing) in practice is always (a) more or less emotional and not only cognitive, and (b) not only present at a surface level and explicit. What characterizes the levels below the explicit (i.e., the less visible parts of the "iceberg") can be difficult, if not impossible, to manage and hide behind the occupational mask, as deeper feelings can show in one's eyes, body language, and other aspects of the approach in the interactions. Emotions are present in the tacit integration of understanding and knowledge at least as an attunement due to the situatedness.

All levels are somehow situated—for example, they are relational and contextually dependent in that they are shaped (colored) by, and may be more or less shared by, the community and life world in which the person work. A metaphor that partly symbolizes this is the difference in the development of a flower in sour versus healthy soil. A caring and positive person and/or subcommunity of front-line staff, or even a whole organization, can become "sour" (frustrated, careless, insecure or arrogant) if the interactions and experiences become largely negative. In some organizations you may sense the atmosphere upon entering the room, or you may gradually notice it during interactions with the employees, for example, through lack of hospitality, respect, or ability to solve problems. When the "soil is good," however, the interactions may proceed like "a smooth dance" even when they are complex.

Knowledge and emotions are described as *multirelational* in the figure, as they are seen as developing not only within one particular dyad but also through participation in various interactions among different subjects and across both interactions characterized as "in-action" and those characterized as "processing about-action." For receptionists, both "in-action" and "processing about-action" often took place as social interactions, but the "other" participating in the interaction varied. Experiencing breaks and dilemmas may challenge reality, self, what you/we do, and the knowledge and meaning; such challenging experiences primarily originate in interactions with others who are not receptionists, that is, most often employees from other sections and especially managers, and less often with customers or fellow receptionists. Even though the receptionists normally worked alone in the reception (because the organizations were small) and mainly met during work shifts and formal meetings, the "processing about-action" mainly took place in informal interactions with fellow receptionists. Such processing of experiences, tensions, and ideas often meant renegotiating and reconstructing personal, and perhaps also collective, practices—including knowledge and emotions. Past, present, and/or future experiences that received attention, often due to some kind of break and tension (e.g., how to cope with the angry boss, discussed later), were expressed in conversations, narratives, and other less oral ways. Together they produced outcomes (e.g., coping strategies, how to understand self/work) that later became part of the horizon of understanding, as well as of knowledge and emotions. Social processing about action therefore can be more vital than just being a social gathering or personal/social therapy. It can be a vital way to learn and develop the ability and will to know and feel within the community of practice and organization.

I next illustrate a slightly different side of how emotions and knowledge are relational and intertwined by pointing to the role of insecurity followed by inattention to the customer, versus security and attention at the customer. Attention to the customer and the ongoing situation has been shown to be vital for performing the work in a capable way (Eide & Lindberg, 1997). A further elaboration of knowledge and emotions, as well as empirical examples interpreted within a situated-relational approach, can be found in Eide (in press).

The Angry, Scolding Boss
(An Example From Front Office Work)

To obtain a concrete illustration of how emotions and knowing can be intertwined in service work (from my hotel study), I have chosen a vignette, "The

Angry-Scolding Boss." Among other things, the vignette is related to the phenomenon where the characteristics and expectations of manager–employee interactions (MI) intersect and spill over into the characteristics and expectations of employee–customer interactions (CI).

One of the receptionists—we will call Kristin—describes how she finds it difficult to cope with and act in her work in a competent way due to the temper of the boss: "He gets angry so easily." One thing is the anger, she argues, but what is worse is the unpredictability and that others, even customers, may overhear:

> "One never knows when it will come. I feel insecure. For example, sometimes I can lower the price and it is OK. Other times when we do the same thing, we are scolded. Yelling and verbal snapping makes you nervous and it is strenuous. What makes it worse is that we are scolded when everybody can hear. Even worse, we are scolded when the customers are listening."

Being scolded, particularly when customers are listening, symbolizes a meaning, in her view, that deviates from how she and the colleagues understand and practice customer orientation. Kristin continues:

> "I have experienced how difficult it is to suggest improvements or to talk about problems with the boss due to his unpredictability. One day I went in to his office and asked a question. When I went back to the reception he yelled at me, 'Are you stupid?' Guests were in the reception and heard. What sort of customer orientation is that? It makes me insecure about myself."

Being insecure is not a good condition when one needs to interact capably in customer interactions. Rather, it hampers one's ability to act in capable ways, partly because it takes the attention away from the customer, and thereby reduces the ability to sense, understand, and relate. In addition, it does not look good when customers overhear such reprimands either. This example shows how the receptionist's participation in customer interactions (CI) and interactions with the manager (MI) are intertwined; the latter creates breaks and tension not only for the receptionist but probably for the customer as well. A similar situation happened when the hotel became the local supplier for a national airline company. The boss argued that the contract was important to the hotel, routines had to be altered, and the involved customers were followed up very closely to prevent failure and to learn. Several small "crises" had already taken place and this had increased the insecurity and the frequency of the reprimands. One receptionist describes one of the "crises":

> "One morning the crew guests were not awakened. That is critical. When the boss heard it, the receptionist ['Marit'] on duty was heavily scolded at the recep-

tion desk. The scolding took place even before finding out what caused the mistake. It turned out to be a technical mistake in the call terminal. The next day Marit was crying when she came to work."

When Marit came to work the next day, Kristin was on duty, and they interacted (RI, receptionist interaction) during the work shift. Marit expressed through verbal and nonverbal ways what had happened and how she felt. She was particularly afraid that the boss might start scolding her or others when customers were listening. Together, while expressing, articulating, and processing the experiences and how they felt, the receptionists coconstructed how to make sense of and cope with the situation in order to go on with their work and life. The social construction that developed during the interaction was something like this: "Do not worry, it's the boss's problem. We just have to make the best of it and do all that we can for the guests." Indirectly they took responsibility and reconstructed themselves as heroes, and the boss as the stupid and irresponsible one. The social support and social relational constructions created by their camaraderie made the reconstruction possible. The example also shows how participation across interactions with three different kinds of others, that is, in the three different kinds of interactions (CI, MI and RI), can become a web and interplay of subprocesses in an integrated learning process where emotions are part of the learning process and result.

In the instance just mentioned, the event was at least temporarily solved in a positive way. It even seemed to strengthen the identity of the receptionists. However, Marit could have become so self-centered and uncertain that she could have become unable or unwilling to interact with the customers in a knowledgeable and learning manner. This could have occurred if all the vital attention that should be on the customer and their mutual interaction process was turned toward herself and/or the manager. She might have stopped really seeing and relating dialogically with the customer. The anxiety can also grow and spread to most or all the receptionists, and thereby start a more radical change in the personal and social practice in a broader sense (i.e., including how they feel, think, act, talk, identify, know, and learn). As part of this, the individual or the whole community of receptionists may start to question their roles and work. This doubt was not only expressed in the hotel with the "angry boss," but also less tension-filled examples were observed. For example, one argued, "Since the boss does not seem to care and regard me as an important and knowledgeable person, why should I care and regard my work and role as important?" Highly capable and dedicated receptionists expressed the tension and doubt about how long they were going to be willing to continue the employment, or be able and willing to work so hard and carry out their duties in a caring and competent way.

Being able and willing to care for others (e.g., guests, customers, users, and colleagues, and thereby the work) is relational. One basic question shows this relational nature: Is an organization with managers that really care for their employees more likely to get employees that really care for their customers and the organization as a larger whole? There are several indications of this type of connection in my study. In the case just described, it was the fellow colleagues that really cared and contributed to the social negotiation concerning the care ideology and identity. In this way, individuals other than the manager can maintain this vital role as participators in the relational reconstruction of practice, emotions, and knowledge. The case, however, also shows that the manager is nevertheless significant to the practice of caring—in this case as a threat—both on a short- and a long-term basis: A doubt had been planted, and it gnawed and could enlarge if replanted.

CONCLUSION

My first line of argument in this discussion of emotions was to show the importance of discussing ontological assumptions (i.e., to rethink the view of human nature and the world) for understanding more about emotions and knowledge. Assuming that human beings are whole persons situated in time, body, and in relation, when being in the world, means that we are multidimensional and thereby emotional beings. This fundamental condition is, therefore, also present in human knowledge in practice. We cannot "step in and out" of ontological conditions, nor fully distance ourselves from, or manipulate, how we feel. I have also argued that the move from viewing emotions as an "ugly duckling" to mainly seeing them as an "invisible asset" to be managed and utilized instrumentally is still a cynical and limited view. It does not grasp properly the nature and role of emotions in human life. Emotions can be "good" and "bad," and they occur at both deeper and surface levels; however, they are a fundamental part of being human. I have suggested that a broad situated-relational approach can contribute to a more versatile, holistic, and relational understanding of emotions. Figure 2.3 summarizes the core points of the three main views of emotions explored in this chapter.

I hope I have demonstrated that the common dichotomy of rational versus emotional, knowledge versus feeling, somehow collapses within a situated-relational approach. This has conceptual implications; there is no pure rationality or cognition without emotions, and vice versa, in human organizational practice. This view on rationality has similarities with Domagalski's (1999, p. 838) description of rationality in organizational practice, "organizational actors quite rationally draw upon their emotions to evaluate their circumstances." Also, it comes close to Fineman's (1993a) description of good communication as dependent on the ability and will to read the situation of, and interact with, a constant mix of messages that are embedded with feelings. Practice, like leadership, is more about acting than planning; it is more about practicing skills

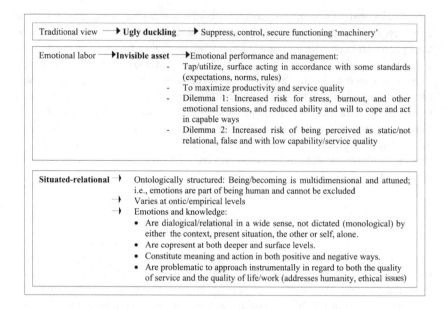

FIG. 2.3.   Three main ways of approaching emotions.

than about following scientific or other explicit methods and rules (Bryman, 1996; Mintzberg, 1990; Sjöstrand, 1997). Rules cannot formulate practice because practice is more contextual, more relational, and messier (Bourdieu, 1990; Bruner, 1990; Wittgenstein, 1953/1992). Further, rules have no use without people using them; they are always depending on actors that know and act. Stretching emotions too far can decrease the ability and will to interact in capable ways. From this follows a first practical implication: Capable interaction cannot mainly be organized a priori through explicit knowledge (e.g., standardized rules, emotional or voice scripts), as capable action and knowledge depend on living human beings that are situated and that know and act. This involves tacit knowledge where understanding, attention, judging, emotions, and intuition are involved parts in a larger process. Thus, even highly capable employees can become less capable if becoming insecure and moving the attention to self or other persons, things, or routines that takes the attention away from what is the core process (e.g., the customer interaction).

A second practical implication of the earlier theoretical discussion on emotions, which also resonates well with my empirical findings in the hospitality study, is that the employees' desire to care and act in capable ways in customer interactions is "created," "reconstructed," or "reduced" during participation in and across interactions, including the interactions with managers. Questions such as "Why should I care when the manager does not seem to care for the guests and for me?" seem fundamental to receptionists and should be no less vital for managers. Such questioning and doubt have consequences for the quality of service and for the work environment. But why is it so? My suggestion and conclusion is that care is relational, infinite, and vulnerable, not inborn or only about the individual sphere, for example, as fixed personality characters (e.g., as a fixed EQ rate). It involves, and is constituted by, emotions, identity, action, respect, and knowledge, which all are situated, relational and reciprocal subphenomena—not monologues. Care is not something one develops and then has and owns forever; rather, it is modes of being and doing overlapping with ability and will; all are dynamic and relational, and they are continually tested and reconstructed in relations in worlds. Being met with respect, appreciation, and care by important others seems to increase the likelihood that the person also respects, appreciates, and cares for others and the self. Being yelled at or in other ways not being interacted with in a way where one is respected, appreciated, and cared for creates doubts and questions the practice of the persons. This can then reduce the ability and will to know and care. Such a change in the dominating attunement of the person also alters the approach, attention, and carefulness, which also results in a change in knowledge in practice (e.g., carelessness).

Emotions have been irrationalized or neglected for too long; now emotions also are seen as something positive. This chapter shares this goal, but it also exposes an alternative to the more recent cynical view wherein emotions are seen as a new "gold mine" that mainly should be exploited and managed. Human beings as well as the quality will suffer under such instrumental control.

ACKNOWLEDGMENTS

An earlier version of this text was part of a paper presented at EGOS 17th Colloquium, Sub Theme Group 27: Knowing as Desire, Lyon, 5–7 July 2001; I would like to acknowledge the comments from participants in this group. My colleagues Elisabet Ljunggren and Jean Jaminon contributed with inspiring ideas in the first phase of this text. Frank Lindberg, as well as the three blind reviewers and the editorial team, proposed significant comments on later versions. None of them, however, bears any responsibility for its contents. Finally, I acknowledge the financial support of Bodø Graduate School of Business, Economic Research Fund, and Nordland College.

II

THE INDIVIDUAL
WITHIN THE
ORGANIZATION

3

"You Wait Until You Get Home": Emotional Regions, Emotional Process Work, and the Role of Onstage and Offstage Support

Maree V. Boyle

This chapter explores the connections between emotionalized regions within organizations and the kinds of emotional process work that occur within these regions. A study of an emergency service organization over an 18-month period found that the performance of emotional process work is a vital stage in the overall performance of emotional labor within this industry. Interviews with emergency service workers also indicated that a substantial amount of emotional process work occurs within one of three emotional regions within the organization—the "offstage" (or nonwork) region. The organization in question, known here as the Department of Paramedical Services (DPS), relies heavily on informal "off stage" emotional support. Thoits's (1985) work on emotional process work and Goffman's (1959) work on regions are used to demonstrate how the individual management of emotion and the organizational ordering of emotional regions are intertwined closely. Organizational implications for the overreliance on offstage forms of support are also discussed briefly.

Although we don't get enough training in how to cope, the expectation is that you have to cope. . . . So you can do your job, you can let the tears flow but you still have to be efficient at what you are doing. At least until you get back to the station. But that doesn't usually happen. You wait until you get home . . .

The principal aim of this chapter is to explore how the existence of emotional regions within organizations and the individual practice of emotional process work as part of emotional labor are intertwined. This discussion is based on qualitative field data collected over an 18-month period within an emergency services organization specializing in prehospital emergency care. The organization in question, the Department of Paramedical Services (known hereafter as the DPS), could best be described as an emotion-laden organization, where emotionality is central to the raison d'être of the organization.

The linkage between emotional regions within organizations and emotional process work is illustrated through a closer examination of the offstage (or nonwork) region within the DPS. Thoits's (1984, 1985, 1991) work on emotional process work and Goffman's (1959) work on regions will also help illustrate how, in this instance, emotional process work can be "privatized" and thus removed from the realm of organizational responsibility.

This chapter is divided into the following sections. First, I provide an overview of the research site and design. Second, I discuss the concepts of emotional regions, emotional labor, and emotional process work, and how these relate to the study discussed here. Third, I provide a detailed and richly narrative style account of the nature of emotional labor and how it is performed within the DPS. Within this section I also highlight the different approaches to the performance of emotional labor in front-stage regions, which includes illustrations of surface and deep acting, and the process of emotional "switching." Fourth, I illustrate the nature of offstage support within the DPS, and discuss how the overreliance on this kind of support may leave an organization such as the DPS vulnerable to the negative financial consequences of occupational stress.

EMOTIONAL CULTURES, REGIONS, AND DRAMATURGY

Emotional culture within organizations consists of three components: emotional vocabularies (Gerth & Mills, 1953; Gordon, 1981), emotional norms (Gordon, 1989; Hochschild, 1979, 1983; Scheff, 1979, 1990), and meanings of power and status (Kemper, 1978). Gordon (1990) also differentiated between institutional and impulsive orientations within emotional cultures. Institutional meanings of emotions are those given by organizational members when they are in full control of their emotions. Members effect achievement and maintenance of institutional norms, and in doing so continue to uphold and reproduce emotional culture (Gordon, 1989).

In formal organizations such as the DPS, the application of impulsive modes of emotional expression is considered either deviance or indicative of faulty socialization (Gordon, 1981; Thoits, 1989). However, permission to express impulsive emotion is granted to those with power and status, typically middle- and upper-class men of Anglo–Celtic origin (Hochschild, 1983; Pierce, 1999). These "status shields" also apply to relationships between clients and organizational members. Those with greater professional status are less likely to witness impulsive orientations to emotion than those with lower status (Hochschild, 1983). For example, patients are less likely to exhibit displays of extreme emotion in the presence of medical consultants than they are in front of clinical staff that are considered of lower status.

The concept of emotional region is derived from Goffman's (1959) dramaturgical perspective. Performance, which is a central component of an organization, is defined as "all the activity of a participant on a given occasion that serves to influence any of the other participants" (Goffman, 1959, p. 26). Performances are only successful when individuals can show that their actions are genuine, while sustaining simultaneously a "front" that is considered authentic (Goffman, 1959, p. 28).

Successful performance is also staged by teams "who share both the risk and discreditable information in a manner comparable to a secret society" (Goffman, 1959, p. 108, as cited in Manning, 1992). Teams are organized by "directors" who manage disputes and delegate responsibility. Teams also act in "front regions," which are defined as spaces within which they perform for their public (Goffman, 1959, pp. 102–114). Teams "rehearse, relax, and retreat" to "back regions," spaces hidden from publics' view when front region performances are "knowingly contradicted as a matter of course" (Goffman, 1959, pp. 110–114). Goffman's (1959) conceptualization of front and back regions is used here heuristically to develop further Fineman's (1993b) notion of the "emotional architecture" of organizational culture, in which he suggests within organizations physical spaces exist in which different feeling rules apply.

The concept of emotional culture builds on Gordon's (1981) original conceptualization, joining both Goffman's (1959) description of regional behavior and audience segregation and the differentiation perspective of organizational culture (Martin, 1992), which recognizes the importance of subcultures. Therefore, emotional culture can be observed within three "regions"—front- or onstage, backstage, and offstage. The front-stage sector is where emotional labor is performed, whereas the backstage sector is where interaction with organizational members happens and where emotional process work is likely to occur. In comparison, offstage regions are located outside the physical realm of the organization itself. As Hosking and Fineman (1990) asserted, differentiation between front-stage and backstage organizational emotionality helps us understand the nature and consequence of emotional labor, particularly within the context of emotional culture.

EMOTIONAL LABOR AND EMOTIONAL PROCESS WORK

Recent research on the links between the performance of emotional labor and emotional dissonance indicates that a complex array of factors has both positive and negative effects on the individual's emotional well-being in the workplace (Hartel, Hsu, & Boyle, 2002). These factors include the quality of the immediate workplace emotional climate in which the service encounter occurs (Ashforth & Humphrey, 1995), the influence of gendered cultural norms (Wharton, 1993), the degree of job control and routinization (Leidner, 1993; Van Maanen, 1991), and the quality of organizational responses to stress induced by emotional labor (Kunda & Van Maanen, 1999).

Early work on the conceptualization and operationalization of emotional labor created a clear distinction between emotion work and emotional labor (Hochschild, 1979, 1983). Expanding on Hochschild's (1983) definition of emotional labor previously discussed, Hochschild (1983) also argued that emotive dissonance was an inevitable consequence of emotional labor because it resulted in a transmutation of the private emotional region into the public commercial region. However, emotion as a process involves the appraisal of a series of affect-related events, which may involve the experience of discrete or private emotions such as sadness or envy. Although the context in which the appraisal and subsequent emotional regulation take place may change from a public to private one, the process of appraisal, attribution, and regulation of emotion is essentially the same (Weiss & Cropanzano, 1996).

Therefore, I propose that emotional process work is an integral part of emotional labor, and is an extension of the service provider–client interaction. In addition, I also propose that organizational response to this aspect of an employee's work influences significantly both the quality of the service outcome and the levels of individual employee stress fitness and emotional health.

Emotional Process Work

Emotional process work occurs before, during, and after a service encounter, and involves a number of strategies that enable the employee to maintain a normative emotional state. Thoits (1984, 1985) explained that when emotional management techniques fail and individuals are unable to deal satisfactorily with "deviant" or "outlaw" emotions such as disgust, extreme anger, or hatred, they then have to process this failure as a violation of feeling or expression norms. Thoits (1985) cited two conditions that she viewed as central to the prediction of emotion work failure: the persistence of deviant or outlaw emotions, and the absence of social support. Thoits (1985) explained that when individuals are committed to competent identity enhancement and are aware of a discrepancy between situational feelings and emotional norms, attempts at emotional process work follow, and self-attributions of deviance occur as a result of persistent failure to create an individual normative state. For example, if a paramedic felt extreme anger after attending a case such as child abuse, this would be considered the emotional norm for this particular situation. However, if the same officer felt nonchalant or disinterested about the same case, he might attempt to move his feelings closer to the emotional norm for this situation. If he were unable to do this, then he would be more likely to label his own emotions as deviant.

Therefore, Thoits's (1984, 1985, 1991) work has implications for how emergency service organizations confront the reality of work stress and the maintenance of appropriate emotional climates within the organization. Within an emergency service context, emotional process work occurs after a case has been completed and involves a variety of strategies that are designed to assist the officer to return to a normative emotional state. The parameters of a normative state are determined by both societal and organizational cultural norms, and are influenced by gender, national culture, and generational emotional norms. Emotional process work may be as simple as one officer acknowledging to another officer that the previous patient was rude or obnoxious, or it may involve many weeks of coping with a major traumatic event such as a plane crash. All officers "do" emotional process work, and the degree to which they accomplish successfully emotional normality varies according to level of experience, degree of social support, and ability to cope with the demands of emotional norms and feeling rules that the organization places on them.

RESEARCH SITE AND DESIGN

The DPS provides prehospital emergency care to subscribers to its service. It is a public-sector organization that has developed a culture emergent from a combination of both militaristic and not-for-profit influences. The DPS is a male-dominated organization, with over 90% of the on-road staff being men. As part of their duties as "caring" paramedics, the DPS on-road staff are expected to perform as emotionally complex individuals while simultaneously adhering to a strict hegemonically masculinist code of conduct. Officers are expected to display the "softer" emotions of compassion, empathy, and cheerfulness in public, while refraining from the expression of grief, remorse, or sadness in the company other officers. Although this expectation is not harsh in itself, it becomes untenable when the DPS relies heavily on the "privatizing" of emotional process work.

Using Thoits's (1991) work on social support as a basis, emotional process work is defined as the emotion work in which officers engage after emotional labor has been performed. Although this practice incorporates what Hochschild (1983) referred to as emotional management, in this particular context it is used to differentiate between the processes used while emotional labor is being performed, and those utilized to make sense of the interaction to which emotional labor is central.

In keeping with Hochschild's (1983) original definition, emotional labor is defined here as the appropriate level of display, feeling, and exchange that occurs between the service provider and the service recipient. Therefore, the practice of emotional labor includes both individual emotion work and emotion management of others' feelings. In the DPS context, emotional labor is specifically defined as the management of the emotional interface between paramedic and patient, and/or persons located within the vicinity of the interaction with whom the officer needs to communicate with in order to successfully accomplish the task at hand.

This ethnographic style qualitative study of the emotional labor practices within ambulance work utilizes a triangulated approach that involves extensive observation of work routines and practices. Given that self-reports of intangible and unobservable feelings and inner emotion work may be difficult to validate through formal interviews only, I chose this observational methodological approach because I considered it the most appropriate way of accessing this kind of data (James, 1993). Document analysis of training and human resource materials, recruitment practices, and organizational mission statements was also performed.

My approach to ethnographic research is influenced by the classic anthropological approach, which requires the researcher to adopt the role of "professional stranger" (Agar, 1996). According to Van Maanen (1988), this kind of ethnographic study can be categorized as more of a "critical" than "realist" account of the culture of the DPS. Therefore, it does not focus exclusively on my personal experience as a fully immersed participant, but rather is a critical account of organizational emotionality within the workplace. Although I was physically and emotionally involved in particular cases, I did not wear a uniform, was not permitted to comfort or reassure patients, and was not fully accountable to the DPS as an employee or volunteer. My own experiences in the field did not involve "doing emotion" in the same way that ambulance officers did. This psychic distance from the actual work in which officers engaged is indicative of the well-documented dilemma field-workers face when they are restricted in their ability to gain unlimited and pure access to informants in the field (Hubbard, Backett-Milburn, & Kemmer, 2001).

Fieldwork was conducted within the DPS over an 18-month period. During that time I conducted 500 hours of observation, and attended and partially observed 110 cases. I observed cases with 50 on-road officers, 9 of whom were women. In addition to these observations, I conducted 30 in-depth interviews with officers across the 7 DPS geographical regions. I also attended training sessions, spent time within communication call centers, and held informal discussions with senior managers and counselors about DPS policies regarding posttraumatic stress disorder and stress debriefing.

An ethnography is a written representation of either a whole or parts of a culture, and carries serious intellectual and ethical responsibilities (Van Maanen, 1988). Therefore, every effort has been made to protect the identities of the paramedics who agreed to be interviewed for this study. The names of these interviewees have been changed to maintain anonymity. Care has been taken to choose names that do not correspond with those officers who were observed or interviewed. At no time during fieldwork were patients' names recorded.

ON-STAGE AND BACKSTAGE REGIONS: THE DPS AND THE PERFORMANCE OF EMOTIONAL LABOR

Emotional labor is an integral part of a paramedical officer's work day. Several aspects of paramedic work impinge on how and why emotional labor is performed. They include the management of patients' emotions through surface and deep acting; the management of one's own emotions through emotional switching; generational and geographical differences between officers; and training to perform emotional labor. Hochschild (1983) differentiated between surface and deep acting, in that surface acting involves a superficial expression of the appropriate emotion. Deep acting involves the combination of the actual exhortation along with the expression of the emotion. Emotional switching is an emergent category from the data, and it involves the ability to change one's emotional demeanor quickly. In paramedic work this occurs frequently, particularly in the move from a highly emotionally charged job to one that is less taxing and emotionally demanding.

There are four emotional labor practices that are specific to paramedical work: the ability to manage the patients' and one's own anxiety; managing people who are out of their usual environment; being able to cope with a constant state of uncertainty; and the ability to simultaneously "care for" and "care about" others (James, 1993). This section focuses on emotions through surface and deep acting, as they are a critical component of a paramedical officer's position.

Surface Acting

Most paramedical officers admit that they do a significant amount of surface acting. This involves smiling, teasing, and light humor, all of which should be taken at face value only. During the study's observations, there were several occasions when officers were friendly toward the patient but then complained bitterly about the patient's attitude or expectations after the patient had been transported. In these cases, patients complained about the length of time spent for the ambulance to arrive, which irritated the officers, because lengthy delays were often out of their control.

Although officers generally displayed a friendly demeanor in front of most older patients, several officers either ignored dementia patients, or treated quiet or depressed patients in a condescending manner. A more somber demeanor was observed on several night shifts, when officers treated many intoxicated, indigenous, or adolescent patients.

During observations, officers reported that they used surface acting techniques with almost every patient. Whether it be sharing a joke with a shy or fearful patient, smiling in the face of a belligerent one, or developing a "neutral" expression when having to coax an intoxicated person into the back of the ambulance, officers view acting as part of their work. However, they also distinguish between surface acting, that is, expressing positive or negative emotions even if they are not authentic, and deep acting, when officers are required to actually feel the emotion they are projecting. Officers define surface acting either as the act of expressing positive feelings, especially in circumstances where the situation does not lend itself to positive emotionality, or as the suppression of negative emotions, such as sadness or disgust. In both circumstances, the performance requires officers to give something that is either themselves, or denies parts of themselves.

There are many techniques officers use to perform surface acting successfully. Humor was cited as the major strategy used, and during observations it was the most common way of engaging with patient: As one senior officer stated:

> If you can make someone laugh or smile you've got the battle half won. Treat them like an equal. Get their mind off their worries. Have a joke with them or whatever. If you get their mind off what's hurting them you're well on your way.

According to Francis (1994), humor as emotion management involves a sophisticated cultural performance, which strengthens and often restores normal feelings. Francis (1994) also stated that humor is used as an integrative device that effectively reduces (or redefines) an external threat. This bonding process often occurs at the expense of the excluded person or persons.

A good example of how humor is used to alleviate patients' and relatives' anxiety was when a man in his eighties was transported home from a hospital after a hip replacement operation. Officers needed to be able to gauge how much humor they can perform, and in this case, they used the opportunity to make light of a delicate situation. When the patient arrived home, the officers sensed that the relatives needed much reassurance, as they seemed particularly anxious about the difficulty the patient would experience walking up the front stairs. The officers were extremely jovial, and joked with both the patient and his relatives. One of the younger officers even took the crutches and ran up and down the sidewalk outside the house with them. The relatives were not offended by this, and even seemed to appreciate the mild joke at the patient's expense. This is an example where the officers judged correctly how much humor was acceptable, and even used the permission given by the relatives to engage in "horseplay."

However, there are occasions when humor either fails or is unappreciated. When a form of surface acting has failed, officers have the option of reverting to silence or changing the topic of conversation to strictly medical issues (Palmer, 1983). In the case of long trips from rural areas to metropolitan hospitals and vice versa, humor is one of many strategies officers used to quell irritable patients. As this officer of 6 years indicated, there is often a difference between the type of surface acting performed on a longer and shorter trips:

> I think a lot of DPS officers joke a lot of things off and they've got standard lines that they can use to laugh it away and maybe try to get this person around through humor. But there's a bit of a difference there between city and country too because where I am I'll probably have a patient on board a maximum of twenty minutes. So for me, it's quite easy. I can put up with them and be nice to them for that period of time and then I can just refer them on. But with a country person having to put up with a whinger from the back of the bush to the city on a long trip would be extremely difficult. There are two in the car, and if by the end of the day you're starting to become weary you can swap over. . . . All you can do is what is within your power at the time. All you can do is try to be friendly, try to understand where they're coming from.

During the course of an average day shift, officers transport many nonurgent cases. These cases usually involve a low level of technical skill, although they often involve a considerable amount of surface acting. Many nonurgent patients are older frail women, sometimes suffering from dementia, and some officers expressed a significant amount of ambivalence toward these patients. Although all officers I observed transporting these patients expressed either positive emotions or affective neutrality, in many cases officers expressed dislike or discomfort about these cases to other officers after these patients had been transported. For example, one younger officer referred to nonurgent cases as "granny-busting." Others referred to these cases as "humpers" or "geries," which refer to older patients who have difficulty walking or communicating. As one officer of 20 years explains, this kind of emotional distancing is a vital part of the job for officers who are barely out of adolescence:

> DPS officers dissociate very well. I mean, how can you not? The DPS is now made up of officers in their late teens to early thirties who have all got families and they pull kids out of pools and go to motor accidents. In a lot of cases they're treating elderly people around the same age as their parents with the same sort of complaints. If they don't dissociate themselves with that patient emotionally they get caught up in the web of themselves. And occasionally you do.

As one officer explained, emergency service workers are exposed to more emotionally distressing situations in the course of one shift than many people would experience in a year. This unsanitized experience of the social world is one that most officers come to accept as "part of the job." Officers also justify their tendency to distance themselves emotionally as part of the process of developing a veneer. The following quote is from an officer with 8 years of experience who explained that developing such a shield is important part of acting out the professional role of the paramedical officer:

> A lot of people may be upset but you just harden because you do see so much of death and dying . . . it's just a part of life. We're not isolated from it the way the general public is. Years ago everyone saw death and dying. There was a lot more blood around, we killed our own animals. It's not that we're necessarily special, it's just that we keep seeing what most people saw forty or fifty years ago. We also get to see a lot more inappropriate behavior and people trying to cope with things. If you don't have that veneer, if you don't have some hardness, you're not going to survive.

Therefore, surface acting is not only a strategy for managing patients' emotions; it is also considered an important method in managing one's own emotions and emotional conflicts. Many officers admit that developing an extreme focus at the scene of major trauma, what they describe as tunnel vision, is the most common method of suppressing or denying individual emotional responses. This form of affective neutrality is also considered necessary for both managing the anxiety of the patient, and appearing professional:

> You become more job orientated. You see the patient as a job. You don't see them as a person. Once you get them settled down you might give them some reassurance. It's a professional thing. You have to close it out. It's very hard to explain.

Thus, officers' perception of professionalism involves successful accomplishment of an affectively neutral performance. In this respect, ambulance officers are not unique. What distinguishes DPS officers is the degree to which they find themselves in situations that call on them to engage in deep acting.

Deep Acting

In the context of the DPS, deep acting involves the management of all aspects of an affective state, including the ability to change how one is feeling about an event or person. The most common deep acting technique officers referred to was when a patient was objectified. This was achieved through officers developing the image of the patient as a thing or object, and in doing so, temporarily suspending any emotional attachment they may have to the patient as a human being. Although most officers admit that this strategy should not be used frequently, many explained that high levels of stress and emotional exhaustion encourage the overuse of this strategy. One officer justified the use of this technique by highlighting that deep acting strategies are no different from those used by other health professionals:

The analogy of a piece of meat was given to me early on in my DPS career and it's right. I mean, it's a terrible term. But the analogy I was given was that a surgeon treats a patient as a piece of meat and does his best possible job on it. Carves it like Michelangelo carved David and then puts it back. And that's the way DPS paramedics do their job. If they get emotionally tied to it then they can't effectively do the job.

Smith and Kleinman (1989) explained this tendency toward objectification by drawing comparisons between the socialization processes of military recruits and medical students. Both undergo a process of desensitization where emotions are blunted by sleep deprivation and changes in the way students perceive human bodies.

Although some officers overuse surface and deep acting strategies needed to achieve emotional distancing, others are prone to emotional attachment with patients, particularly those who remind an officer of a relative, child, or loved one. Many officers I spoke to explained that all officers are prone, at some time during their careers, to communicate inappropriate emotional messages to the relatives of the dying patient, because officers find it difficult to reconcile their lifesaving role with the very real possibility of losing the patient.

Most of the officers who had worked in the DPS for many years described circumstances where they had given false hope to a patient or relative because they were unsure or unable to perform the kind of emotional labor specific to that context. A common example was giving false hope to the relatives of burn victims based on the percentage and degree of burns to the body. Officers stated that they were most likely to fail in their efforts to engage in deep acting at the end of a series of night shifts, after a series of urgent cases in one shift, or when they failed to dissociate successfully.

Cases involving critically ill children were cited as the most risky in this instance. This is similar for the majority of emergency service personnel, most of whom cited cases involving the death of, or serious injury to, children as the most emotionally challenging (Palmer, 1983). The cases I observed involving children always evoked a different response from officers in that they appeared to work at a faster pace. One officer explained that apart from the fact that many officers had young children themselves, they also felt added pressure to always save the child, regardless of the severity of the case. This demands of officers a dramaturgical performance that is quite distinct from adult cases. The following quote from an officer with 8 years of experience illustrates the extreme emotional and physical pressure officers finds themselves under during the course of attempting to save a child's life:

> When you walk into a scene where there's a child who is ill, if it's a SIDS or something, there are so many expectations. The parents, especially with SIDS, know the child's dead. You know the child's dead. But if the child's still warm you have

to give them every opportunity. . . . You see, there's so much expectation on us
when we go into a situation we can't turn around and go to pieces because then
we're not doing our job.

The death of a child is probably one of the few instances where a strong
emotional reaction to a case is legitimized. Although several younger officers
expressed angst about this, most officers believed that that an increase in the
acceptance of public displays of grief, if only for children, is a positive change
within the emotional culture of the DPS.

In summary, the majority of officers interviewed and observed cited emotional labor as an important "tool" in the DPS officers' repertoire of skills.
During the course of observation, the officers described a number of surface
and deep acting techniques utilized in the performance of emotional labor.
These included managing the emotions of patients through extortion and suppression of emotion. The specific techniques also included use of humor to
manage anxiety, the avoidance of false hope, emotional distancing through developing tunnel vision, disparaging stereotypes, and the categorization of patients into deserving and undeserving cases. Officers also spoke of the process
of hardening through developing an emotional veneer of affective neutrality
and professionalism.

One of the most enjoyable and frustrating aspects of paramedical work is
the unpredictability of each shift. An officer may be kept busy with many
nonurgent cases in the morning, only to find that the afternoon is quiet. Then,
just before the end of the shift, the officer may be called to several urgent
cases. As such, the paramedic cannot predict exactly what he or she will be doing on any one shift.

Nonurgent cases make up the bulk of an ambulance officer's work, particularly on day shifts and during the early part of night shifts. Although an urgent
case involves less technically skilled work than nonurgent cases, it does involve
a considerable amount of emotional labor. However, there is no compulsion to
perform emotional labor during nonurgent cases, and many officers express
ambivalence regarding how much "skill" is involved in these cases. For example, some officers are very frank about their assessment of nonurgent cases as
boring, dead end, and no better than "driving a taxi." Although it is highly
likely that officers would attend an urgent case during every shift in urban regions, in provincial and rural areas officers may have to settle for weeks of
nonurgent cases.

However, although some officers may complain about too little stress, others experience shifts that are almost dangerously frantic. The effects of too
much or too little stress in emergency services have been documented by
Mitchell (1984). A busy night shift may consist of up to 10 urgent cases, and
each of these may be legitimate. The constant pressure to be emotionally "up"
for the duration of a shift often takes its toll, and many officers argue that it

takes up to 3 days to recover both physically and emotionally from this. One officer who has a military background described how being "up" for extended periods of time can extract an emotional price off-stage:

> We did about six urgent cases in an eight-hour shift recently and each one needed to be urgent. I was up here all the time and I never actually got down. If you do a nine- or ten-hour shift, you just go all the time. You start to get up and up and up and you end up staying there. After fourteen hours, it's a long time to maintain that. When I get home, I just want to veg out. . . . But everyone else wants company [at home] and I find that hard to cope with at times. It's hard for them to understand, and it's not their fault.

The extraordinary amount of organizational change that has occurred within the DPS in recent years has meant significant changes in the volume of work that an officer is expected to handle. An emphasis on structural efficiency has led the DPS to undertake an efficiency drive, thus resulting in officers having to do more work but with less resources. These changes include a reduction in the number of officers rostered to cover weekend shifts and sick leave, and fewer breaks between cases.

The level of work intensification or "speed-ups" as described by Hochschild (1983) that DPS officers have experienced in recent years are similar to what Hochschild's flight attendants experienced during the 1980s. The DPS officers are now expected to attend more cases during a shift while still providing the same quality of service. This means that there is less time between cases in which to emotionally process the previous job. This workload increase is particularly problematic in urban regions. Officers spoke angrily about the lack of time available to "come down" between jobs, especially from a previously stressful urgent case. Many expressed regret at initially supporting organizational change because they felt it had failed to meet the practical needs of customer service.

Increased expectations to perform more efficiently with less organizational support have ramifications for how officers switch emotionally from one type of case to another. Although most officers make the switch successfully from a nonurgent to an urgent case, the reverse switch is often problematic. Problems arise when officers are sent back out on the road immediately following a difficult emergency code. Officers complained that this was a frequent occurrence, even when the officers involved need to change their clothing. This following quote illustrates how officers negotiate time for themselves in the face of ever-increasing demands to "always be ready":

> Like you've done CPR and your car is a mess and they'll be saying on the way back, do you mind doing this job for us and you've got to get on the radio and tell these people, no. I'm not doing it. I'm coming back, and having a shower and I'm going to get changed. So, the way I work it out now is I go and do a case, I do the

paper work and I don't call free until I've done that, and if we're run all day long, I
will stop and I will have my break. . . . Whether they know it or not, they'll lose me
for 30 minutes. I don't like doing that because there might be an emergency that
might be pending, they might be looking for you. But that's the only way I can
pace my day.

One officer expressed the view that management often placed unreasonable
expectations on officers regarding emotional switching from one type of code
to another, particularly in cases where the patient died:

It used to affect me and I used to wonder why I couldn't be demobilized for a
time, because it felt quite cold. . . . It felt quite cold with regards to administration and management, that they could be so callous as to give me another three
geriatrics after I've finished a cot death case or something like that. I started to
do things to protect myself, to overcome the emotional states, so it doesn't worry
me anymore.

What this officer referred to when discussing "overcoming emotional
states" is the emotional process work that occurs between codes either by oneself or with a partner.

Coping and Emotional Labor

Despite the fact that officers now are required to have more academic creden-
tials to gain permanent employment, formal training for emotional labor is still
a rare occurrence. At the shop floor level, emotional labor may be considered
"the best tool to have." However, in terms of resource allocation for training,
technical skills are still given primacy. This has implications for how the DPS
approaches the whole issue of emotionality. Younger officers who are being
trained as technological experts may be better equipped to cope with the intensity of trauma work because they have developed the technical competence
needed to accomplish successfully their work. However, the reality is that a
vast majority of the workday is comprised of mundane, nonurgent work. It is
during these cases that the bulk of the emotional labor is performed. Conversely, it is after major trauma cases that the bulk of emotional process work
is conducted. Even after 100 years, the DPS has yet to successfully prepare officers for this.

This narrative of emotional labor within the DPS also illustrates the degree
to which the DPS officers switch constantly from frontstage to backstage regions. If emotion were the *only* major component of the switch between front-
and backstage, officers would find this process straightforward and unprob-
lematic (Lois, 2001; Spitzer & Neely, 1992). However, a major part of the
switch from one region to the other is the ability to change from what is essentially a "feminine" demeanor in the front-stage region to one that is conven-

tionally masculine in the backstage region. Generally speaking, backstage regions include base stations, truck stops, gas stations, and any place where the officer is not "onstage" and performing emotionally for a public.

In the case of the DPS, backstage emotional process work involves a range of practices, including rapid speech patterns, the telling of "war" stories, and the use of black humor. In extreme cases, backstage processing may involve formal critical incident debriefing, which involves a counselor alerting officers to signs and symptoms of posttraumatic stress. However, many officers find this level of support inadequate for processing much of what an officer experiences throughout a working shift because of the gendered constraints of male-dominated team dynamics, which influence what is acceptable in backstage areas. Explanations for this phenomena are varied and complex and beyond the scope of this chapter (for a full review, see Boyle, 2002). However, officers do receive considerable emotional support from offstage regions, as discussed in detail next.

THE ROLE OF OFFSTAGE SUPPORT IN THE DPS

To state that spouses provide a significant amount of emotional support to DPS officers is something of an understatement. The expectation that the family, particularly the spouse, will provide offstage emotional support is based on the assumption that a certain kind of emotional gender asymmetry exists within heterosexual relationships. As Duncombe and Marsden (1993, 1995) explained, this gender asymmetry is an indicator of a form of emotional power, which is situated within the wider context of continuing gender inequalities of societal resources and power. Although the central feature of men's lives may be the rational, affectively neutral workplace, "women carry the emotional responsibility for the private sphere" (Duncombe & Marsden, 1995, p. 150). This includes the performance of emotion work that sustains the relationship itself.

During earlier DPS administrations, spouses not only provided emotional support, but were also intensely involved in providing ancillary labor to help run the organization. Spouses assisted in raising funds, provided secretarial assistance, and sometimes acted as surrogate counselors, especially in rural and remote areas. Thus, there was an expectation that wives would be as "wedded" to the organization as their husbands (Finch, 1983).

Although this reliance on women's ancillary labor may have been exploitative in principle and often in practice, the benefit of co-opting women into the service meant that the whole family enjoyed considerable status within the community. Conversely, the local DPS officer was "owned" by the community, which meant that officers and their families were expected to adhere to strict moral and behavioral codes. This applied particularly to senior DPS officers, whose role was to care for the ambulance "family," as well as the whole community.

As community role models and representatives, officers stationed in rural and remote areas often found themselves with no emotional support outside their family. Several rural officers interviewed believed that community members viewed them as "above" feelings or emotion. This hero status meant that officers were expected to perform in a superhuman fashion. It was expected that emotional support either was received from their immediate families, or was something that male DPS officers did not need. Thus, officers were only ever the givers of public emotional support, never the receivers. This situation was even more difficult for young officers who had no significant other or spouse living in the community.

Although most officers who work in urban and provincial centers do not experience this constant blurring of the boundaries between work and home, there is still an implicit assumption by the DPS that officers will receive most of their emotional support offstage. In this study the majority of officers interviewed and/or observed were male and married with children. With the exception of one officer, all officers admitted that they would find it difficult to do their job without the support of their spouse. They also admitted that the emotional stress of ambulance work often placed significant pressure on their relationships. In some cases, they cited this as the main reason for marital breakdown and subsequent divorce.

Officers also believe difficulties arise when there is a tension between balancing how much they disclose to family members about work, and the amount of process work an officer chooses to engage in individually. As one officer illustrated, "protecting" family members from the unpleasant and gruesome parts of the job is in itself an extension of the workday. Therefore, emotional labor continues after hours in the form of shielding the family from the extreme aspects of ambulance work. A station manager explained that "shielding" his wife and children from the more unpleasant aspects of his job was important:

> I think my wife has to be fairly unique to be able to put up with some of the stuff I bring home. But I don't bring everything home to her. There are certain things that I won't discuss with her. I told her not to look at my textbooks. The pictures that are in them are just too graphic. I find it distressful to look at them myself, particularly if you've got kids the same age as the kids in the pictures in these books.

Officers also reported that spouses become frustrated when an officer chooses to be selective about how much disclosure occurs at home after a shift. As an officer of over 20 years' standing explained, there is a thin line between deciding what the officer thinks is distressing for the spouse, and guessing what the spouse will want to hear:

She can say, I can understand the nature of your job but she can't identify with the job. If I go home and tell her what I've seen, she's got to now deal with that problem. And there are very few women in that context who can deal with that situation. No matter how much they say, I want you to tell me. You've got to deal with a lot yourself and talk to people you can trust but still not totally keep your family out of it. That's a mistake. You're going to fall down in a big way if you do that. You've got to do a balancing act, you have to say, I can tell you this much. I can tell you this happened, but I can't tell you that happened.

Several officers reported that they negotiated "routines" with their spouses for dealing with difficult shifts. It is not surprising then, that the longest serving officers were the ones who were willing to discuss these routines and their relative successes or failures. The success of these routines in defusing anger or frustration depended on the spouse being committed to doing this kind of emotional process work. For example, an ambulance "couple" that has been married for over 20 years has developed a routine whereby the officer "signals" to his spouse if he needs emotional space when he comes home:

Over time my wife had learned that if I walk in and my mannerisms are such, then she'll just walk out the other door. She'll just go away and leave me alone for an hour or two. Until I've processed it and dealt with it and put it where it's supposed to go. Then I'll walk out and we'll start from there.

Learning when to "go away" is an expectation with which many spouses have extreme difficulty coping, particularly younger couples with children. One young officer stated that his spouse "hounded" him at the end of every shift to tell her everything that had happened during the day. When he refused to comply, she became frustrated and this often led to marital conflict. The officer's main problem with this situation was that he had little private space in which he could process the day's events and emotions.

By their own admission, many officers became intolerant and irritable at what they perceived as the triviality of life outside the DPS. Requests from spouses to behave like "average" men outside of work and within the family environment, together with shift work and the ensuing irregular sleeping and eating patterns, led to conflict about issues of support. One officer who had recently divorced after 15 years of marriage admitted that his inability to cope with the emotional switch from work to home was one of the major contributing factors to the breakdown of his marriage:

Why am I the Mr. Fixit for everyone? . . . I've fixed up fifteen patients' problems today, and then I come home and she's got a migraine and she wants me to cook dinner, and I think, no! I've clocked off. You cook dinner. You get very intolerant.

In addition to providing direct emotional support, spouses often have to deal with the officer frequently being absent from social gatherings. This can lead to tension within the extended family, as the spouse has to do the emotion work of allaying fears as to why the officer is not in attendance. Although the absent father is not all that unusual at school functions, for an officer involved in a traditional heterosexual relationship, continual absences from family events may cause problems as the family may view the marital relationship as dysfunctional or abnormal.

Although there is no evidence to suggest that DPS officers have a higher than average divorce rate, there is some validity in suggesting that officers who have young children are under considerable offstage pressure compared with officers who have served for longer periods and whose families are older and more established. It is argued here that younger, married, and rural officers have the greatest need to develop sound emotional process skills, for it is these groups that may be at greatest risk of emotional exhaustion if their offstage support is inadequate or deficient. Offstage emotional process work may involve something as simple as a short amount of time and space away from family and friends, or it may be as complex as a close relationship with a religious minister or health professional such as a psychologist to help them deal with their emotional conflict (Boyle & Healy, 2003).

CONCLUSION

This chapter attempted to discuss the emotional conflict experienced during emotional process work, and the role of offstage support. Specifically, it examined a study involving the DPS, an emergency service organization where emotions are a central part of the job.

There are a number of reasons why the DPS has not fully recognized and compensated the emotional component of a paramedic's work. The DPS was, and still is, a "harsh" cultural entity, consisting of a paradoxical mix of cultural values and practices, such as display of "softer" emotions to the public (i.e., compassion, empathy, and cheerfulness) and an expectation that officers will not display emotional expressions of grief, remorse, or sadness. In other words, officers were expected to keep up a constant "masculine" demeanor of self-control and stoicism, while simultaneously presenting a "caring" and "feminine" demeanor to patients.

In terms of emotional expression, this expectation is not harsh. This expectation becomes problematic when the organization deems that only a narrow range of feelings can be expressed publicly. Officers who express emotions outside the acceptable range risk harassment and ostracism.

Despite this, officers were generally positive about performing emotional labor. This is in contrast to Hochschild's (1983) findings, where the flight attendants spoke of emotional labor as a burden that often led to a lack of connection with others. Of course, there are specific reasons why there is this difference between the two groups, and some of them have little to do with emotional labor itself. For example, flight attendants are prone to suffer dislocation because of the travel involved. Spending many nights away from home, constant disruption of personal routines, and the stress of flying all combine to create a sense of alienation. In contrast, ambulance officers do not experience the same level of disruption or dislocation, despite the similarities of performing emotional labor.

DPS advertising campaigns explicitly promote men as carers. Many of the posters and television advertisements show male officers in caring poses such as holding the hand of a child or an older person. Indeed, the fact that the DPS has a baby carseat rental service attests to their commitment to be seen as a caring organization. However, men are not usually associated with the act of caring in public. Therefore, officers have to reconcile this traditionally feminine act with the fact that they are still men. Men benefit emotionally from the traditionally patriarchal arrangements that separate home and work. In an orthodox Marxist sense, this means that men are able to sell their labor power because they are able to reproduce emotionally within the private sphere (Milkie & Peltola, 1999). However, this arrangement is contingent on women being available to engage in emotion work at home. The DPS is heavily dependent on this public/private arrangement as a means of providing informal and offstage emotional support to male officers.

As the DPS culture is strongly adherent to hegemonically masculine practices and ideologies (see Connell, 1995), it would be fair to assume that the majority of male DPS officers are heterosexual and practice a conventionally heterosexual lifestyle. Apart from student officers, all officers interviewed or observed were married with children. In most cases. the male officers were the principal earners in the family. Many officers commented on the level of emotional support they received from their spouses, and most believed they could not do their work efficiently if this support was unavailable.

According to some officers, when they are experiencing marital problems, their work performance diminishes. If they are unable to secure emotional support from elsewhere, they are likely to be more vulnerable to emotional stress at work. The DPS then is almost totally dependent on officers receiving emotional support from outside of the organization. The distinction between work and home then becomes blurred as spouses, partners, and occasionally good friends and relatives assume the role of employee assistance counselor. They are, by default, "hidden" employees of the DPS.

Therefore, the DPS is ill-equipped to cope with a rise in the number of men and women who lack offstage emotional support. The individualistic and masculinist cultural framework within which the DPS operates is unable to provide the kind of emotional support needed by most officers, because as a masculinist culture, it does not recognize that men need public as well as private forms of emotional support. The culture is not tolerant of the existence of an emotionally complex paramedic, because to do so would require the acknowledgment of multiple masculinities (see Connell, 1995).

DPS officers are allowed to "step out of" the traditional hegemonic frame within the confines of performing emotional labor. However, emotional labor does not terminate when patients leave the hospital. It has process characteristics and extends beyond the boundaries of the narrowly defined service provider–client relationship (Dodier & Camus, 1998, as an example). Failure by the DPS to acknowledge the need for officers to have the time, space, and permission to engage in emotional process work as a valid part of ambulance work and often results in increased levels of emotive dissonance and emotional exhaustion (Thoits, 1991). This does not always occur as a result of the interaction with the patient, but can occur when the officer realizes that the organization objectifies his or her emotional self. This happens when the DPS fails to acknowledge that part of its responsibility to its organizational members is to take into consideration the time needed to replenish the mind, body, and spirit when developing operational procedures and policies (Boyle & Healy, 2003).

Thus, the DPS has privatized this part of its responsibility to officers by asserting that emotional process work is something that should occur primarily in the private sphere of the home and family. Given the state of flux that familial arrangements are in, this strategy holds considerable risk for the organization in question. The DPS has based its strategy on the assumption that most officers are involved in orthodox hegemonic heterosexual relationships where the female spouse sees it as her role to manage the emotions of her male partner.

If support cannot be found within the private sphere, and if traditional male friendships prove to be inadequate in terms of providing emotional support, then this can lead to officers neglecting to engage in emotional process work.

The quote at the beginning of this chapter illustrates nicely the connections between front-stage expectations, and back- and offstage realities. The front-stage emotional culture deems that officers "cope" under all circumstances, regardless of the amount of emotional pressure placed on officers. As representatives of the DPS, the community expects officers to perform at their emotional peak with patients—yet from an organizational perspective, maintaining emotional health is an individual responsibility. Officers have to usually wait until they get home to deal with emotion and receive support, which indicates the lack of recognition classifying emotional process work as actual "work."

Although the DPS is an organization literally saturated with emotion, emotional support for DPS officers is mainly viewed by the organization as something that needs to primarily occur off-site and not the responsibility of the organization. Although emotional process work occurs during organizational time, particularly in backstage regions, a closer inspection of the structure and culture of the organization indicate a serious level of emotional denial. Anecdotal evidence suggests that employees appear more likely to engage in acts of resistance if an organization fails to either recognize or legitimate the consequences of emotional labor for front-line employees. In turn, this has implications for the overall level of individual as well organizational well-being.

4

The Role of Emotion in Employee Counterproductive Work Behavior: Integrating the Psychoevolutionary and Constructivist Perspective

Yongmei Liu
Pamela L. Perrewé

We argue that many forms of counterproductive work behavior (CWB) can be understood better through an examination of individuals' emotional adaptive efforts trying to survive in the organizational setting. An emotion-based, process model of CWB is developed based on two emotion theories: the psychoevolutionary theory and the constructivist view of emotion. We view emotion as a chain of cognitive, emotional, and behavioral reactions to stimuli events, and discuss several "problem points" in the emotion process that may lead ultimately to CWB. The chapter concludes with a discussion of organizational implications and suggestions for future research and practice.

Workplace aggression and violation, employee theft, sabotage, and many other forms of employee counterproductive work behaviors (CWB) have drawn increasing theoretical attention among management researchers in recent years (Spector & Fox, 2002). In the literature, CWB has been given different names and definitions, including deviant workplace behavior (e.g., Hollinger, 1986), antisocial behavior (e.g., Robinson & O'Leary-Kelly, 1998), and dysfunctional behavior (e.g., Collins & Griffin, 1998). Although some have examined CWB in general, others have focused on specific types of behaviors such as aggression and violence (e.g., Fox & Spector, 1999; Greenberg & Barling, 1999), employee theft (e.g., Greenberg, 1990), and sabotage (e.g., Giacalone & Knouse, 1990). There are also differences in researchers' emphases on either individual differences or situational factors as primary antecedents of CWB (for a more complete and detailed review, see Spector & Fox, 2002). Some theoretical perspectives that have been used include social learning theory (Bandura, 1977), justice theory (Greenberg, 1990), and attribution theory (Martinko, Gundlach, & Douglas, 2001; Martinko & Zellars, 1998).

It is worth noting that, despite the increasing volume of research on this topic, there has been relatively little effort exploring the role of emotion in employees' conducting CWB. Imagine an extreme situation in which a person has no feelings of anger. Facing a colleague's insulting language or action, he or she might simply inquire why the colleague would have done so, and then rationally find out where the problem lies and try to solve it. Chances are that the insulting behavior will be stopped and the problem solved without any major influences on the subsequent interaction between the two (although in some instances the apparent calmness of the target may even further irritate the perpetrator, such as when he or she interprets the calmness as arrogant or pretending). Unfortunately, in daily organizational life, insulting behavior often leads to strong feelings within the target, such as guilt, shame, and anger (Gabriel, 1998). Negative emotions such as anger often motivate retaliations such as attacking back in the same manner, which is often how CWB is induced in organizations (cf. Folger & Skarlicki, 1998). It is not hard to imagine that employees who conduct such violent behaviors as shooting a supervisor or physically attacking a coworker must have undergone some strong inner emotional experiences. Of course, it is fair to say that not all CWBs have to do with emotions. For example, checking personal e-mails during working hours or work avoidance often have more to do with poor work ethics than emotions. However, it is still quite possible for emotions to play a significant role. For example, intentionally slowing the pace of work may well involve strong emotions such as anger toward the supervisor.

Our review of the literature revealed some research addressing the role of emotion in CWB. Spector and Fox (2002) argued that emotions play a central role in CWB. Specifically, they proposed that negative emotions are likely to lead to CWB, especially when employees are exposed continuously to emotion-arousing events. Martinko and colleagues (2001) argued that feelings of guilt, shame, anger, and frustration mediate the relationship between individual attribution of perceived disequilibrium in the workplace and subsequent CWB. In their empirical studies, Fox and colleagues (Fox & Spector, 1999; Fox, Spector, & Miles, 2001) found that negative emotions serve as a mediator through which employee's experience of situational constraints induces CWB. This line of research, however, left unexplored exactly *how* the emotional mechanism functions as is involved in CWB. In addressing the gap in the current literature, we draw on two influential theories of emotion and propose a process model of CWB. We believe to identify the emotional antecedents of CWB will help not only to understand it better, but also to control it effectively, and, further, to enhance individual and organizational well-being.

THEORETICAL BACKGROUND

CWB has been defined as behaviors that have a direct and visible negative effect on either organizations or their members (e.g., Spector & Fox, 2002). With a few exceptions (e.g., Martinko et al., 2001), passive forms of CWB (those directed to self such as drug use and depression) have been ignored largely. However, it seems appropriate to include such behaviors in the CWB category because they tend to influence negatively productivity and will, over time, have a corruptive influence on organizational climate (Robinson & O'Leary-Kelly, 1998). It is reasonable to expect that such less overt forms of CWB could at times become equally harmful to both the organization and the individual. Therefore, for the purpose of this chapter, we adopt a broad definition of CWB to include all employee behaviors, intended or unintended, that are directed at the organization, other organization members, clients and customers, or self, and have the potential to hurt organizational productivity and well-being. Thus, according to our definition, behaviors such as expressing fake emotions all the time, or consistently working overtime without attending to health problem, may also belong within the CWB category.

The rest of the chapter is organized as the following: First, we introduce the psychoevolutionary theory (Plutchik, 1980) and the constructivist view of emotion (Averill, 1980). We then discuss how these two theories can be integrated meaningfully and applied in an organizational setting. Next, we present a process model, drawn from the psychoevolutionary theory, which explains CWB from an emotion-based perspective. The purpose of this chapter is to provide a theoretical framework within which CWB is understood better.

Although research on emotions in organizations has been a newly immerged area of interests to most organization researchers (Ashforth & Humphrey, 1995; Fineman, 2000), systematic research on human emotions can be traced back to at least a century ago when William James (1884) asked, "What is an emotion?" Since then, numerous emotion theories have developed in the literature. Ashforth and Humphrey (1995) identified two streams of research in the field of emotions that take very different approaches, the *naturalist* perspective and the *social constructivist* perspective. According to them, the naturalist perspective takes a biological perspective, examining emotion based on the physical reactions and individual genetic attributes; the social constructionist perspective posits that emotions are learned, and they take on socially defined meanings and rules in the process of learning. Both approaches have developed a useful framework in explaining emotions, but do so with very different foci. Many researchers (e.g., Fineman, 2000; Lazarus, 1991; Porter & Samovar, 1998), however, believe that a sound theory of emotions should look to the interplay of the two because neither of the two provides a complete understanding of human emotions. Following this school of thought, we built our theory based on the belief that the two poles of theorizing on emotion are not necessarily contradictory rather they compliment each other.

Psychoevolutionary Theory of Emotion

Psychoevolutionary theory of emotion, developed by Plutchik (1980), is one of the biological oriented theories of emotions. Building on Darwin's early work on the expression of emotions of human beings and animals, Plutchik (1980) posits that emotions serve as a basic function of survival by helping to organize animal and human behavior in a way that is appropriate to the immediate environment. Emotions are described as having a purpose, either unconscious or deliberate. Plutchik (1980) proposed that the purpose of emotion is adaptation, and that emotions are activated in an individual when issues of survival are raised in fact or by implication. He argued that the effect of the emotional state is to create an interaction between the individual and the event that precipitates the emotion, which usually serves to reduce the disequilibrium and reestablish a sense of equilibrium (Plutchik, 1980, 1989).

From an evolution point of view, Plutchik (1980) argued that emotion should not be treated as simply a feeling state. Rather, it is understood best when viewed as a chain of complex and loosely connected cognitive, emotional, and behavioral responses (i.e., *emotional chain*) to a *stimulus event*. As a major part of his theoretical development, Plutchik (1980) proposed that the occurrence of certain stimuli events is followed by cognition, which in turn will be followed by introspective feelings; the feeling state is only one step in the emotional chain and will serve to motivate certain goal-directed behaviors; when successfully conducted, such behaviors will lead to desired consequences (Plutchik, 1980). For example, when a man encounters a dangerous animal, the cognition of danger will motivate the inner feeling of fear, which prompts him to run and, consequently, protects the person from being attacked.

Plutchik (1980) argued further that there are a number of *problem points* in the emotional chain which disrupt the smooth flow of the emotional chain. First, the initial cognition may be in error so that the threat is misperceived or misinterpreted. Second, the feeling generated by the cognition can be blocked, modified, or distorted. Third, appropriate reactions to feelings may (or may not) occur due to either environmental or internal restraints, or both. Finally, depending on whether appropriate and effective behavior occurs, the goal or purpose of the emotional chain may (or may not) be served. If the desired purpose or goal of the behaviors is not fulfilled, the unaccomplished goal will serve as new stimulus to motivate further actions to reduce the imbalance (Plutchik, 1980). For example, we discussed previously the man encountering the dangerous animals; if he runs away but cannot find any protection, he may begin to cry. Here, crying is an emotional expressive behavior, motivated by the felt emotion of fear, probably with the purpose of release the inner tension.

Plutchik's (1980) approach to studying emotions provides a useful way from which CWB can be examined. Later, we discuss this framework and note that many forms of CWB have an emotion element and are people's conscious or unconscious efforts to adapt to the environmental stimuli. These efforts turn out to be counterproductive only when either the organization's or the individual's well-being is (or will be) harmed. However, before this is discussed, we modify the framework to ensure that it is suitable for our discussion and application in the organizational setting.

One element to be added to the framework before the psychoevolutionary perspective can be applied readily to the organizational setting is the influence of the social context. Focusing on the biological side of emotion and trying to explain human and animal behaviors within a general framework, Plutchik (1980) deliberately limited his discussion regarding the influence of social environment on human behavior only. Although he did mention briefly the mechanisms of emotional regulation in his theory, he did not go so far as to incorporate them into the general framework. For example, he gave a description of how a little boy who gets angry with his mother may seek other ways (such as kicking his dog) to release the anger instead of expressing his feelings to the mother. Plutchik (1989) also talked about the role of social institutions in controlling the expression of emotions—for example, how anger and aggression are channeled into socially acceptable pathways through the social institutions of sports and war.

In summary, from the psychoevolutionary theory perspective, emotions are survival mechanisms based on evolutionary adaptations. Emotions are best described as a complex chain of events with stabilizing feedback loops that produce some kind of behavioral homeostasis (Plutchik, 2001).

The Constructivist View of Emotion

Human behaviors can become much more complex when it comes to the social setting. That is predominantly why researchers from social psychology and sociology have critiqued the biology-oriented examination of human emotions. Thoits (1989) argued that the strict biological explanation of emotions would lose its meaning and significance when one looks at the complex social context within which emotions take place. This is consistent with several other perspectives for theorizing in emotions (e.g., Hochschild, 1983; Kemper, 1984; Shott, 1979; Zurcher, 1982), one of which is the constructivist view of emotion (Averill, 1980) is one of the examples.

From a sociological viewpoint, Averill (1980) argued that human emotions are socially constructed and inherit important social meanings. He viewed emotions as transient roles that individuals take in the drama depicted by the society within which individuals are involved. Thus, the social norms provide shared expectations about appropriate behaviors and exert powerful influences on individuals' actual behaviors. From this perspective, emotions are best described as roles, which are both socially constructed and individually enacted. Individuals interpret actively their own emotions based on the explicit or implicit rules and norms provided by societies. Further, individuals act based on these interpretations, and expect others to interpret the emotions using similar rules accordingly. Thus, emotions also serve as signals of appropriate actions under certain social contexts (Averill, 1980; Zurcher, 1982).

Averill (1980) emphasizes the passion characteristic of emotion, in contrast to emotion as an action. In other words, emotions are not actions that people take. Rather, people don't usually have control over their emotions, and indeed, sometimes they are overcome by them.

In his research, Averill (1980) also discussed the possible influence of conflict between personal norms (i.e., individual expectancies about one's own behavior) and social norms (i.e., shared expectancies about appropriate behavior) in shaping individual emotional responses and experiences. He argued that behaviors that are consistent with personal norms but not social norms are liable to be deemed inappropriate, and that well-socialized individual norms reflect social norms. Thus, it is reasonable to expect that individuals will seek actively emotional cues that are appropriate in certain social contexts in an effort to match their personal norms with social norms.

In summary, it is evident that from the social psychological perspective, emotions are built on one or more biological systems of behaviors, and the meaning of emotion, or its functional significance, is embedded primarily in the sociocultural system (Parkinson, 1996; Thoits, 1989). Thus, it is necessary to consider the broader social context within which the emotions take place to fully understand individuals' emotional behaviors.

APPLYING A SOCIAL PSYCHOEVOLUTIONARY PERSPECTIVE TO THE ORGANIZATIONAL SETTING

Upon closer examination, it is evident that, despite the different emphasis of the two approaches discussed previously, they have interesting similarities. First, both the psychoevolutionary theory of emotion and the constructivist view argue that emotion is not a simple feeling state. Specifically, both theories agree that cognitive and behavioral elements in emotions. In the psychoevolutionary theory of emotion, this is evident from the argument of emotions as a chain of cognition, feelings, and behaviors. From the constructivist view of emotion, this is evident in Averill's (1980) argument that emotions are interpretations and roles. This is a critical understanding. On one hand, this underscores the importance of understanding emotions within the context rather than isolated feeling states. On the other hand, it also implies that emotions are important in the understanding of cognitions and behaviors (Fisher & Ashkanasy, 2000a; Fineman, 2000; Weiss & Cropanzano, 1996).

Second, both theories agree that emotion has a survival value, although they may differ on the meaning of *survival*. It is evident that the psychoevolutionary theory of emotion emphasizes the individual's physical and psychological experiences, whereas the constructivist view of emotion emphasizes the social facet of human emotions and describes the individual as an active role taker in the social context. At the same time, the psychoevolutionary theory of emotion looks at survival at its basic biological level, whereas the constructivist view of emotion adds to survival a social meaning, namely, the survival of self or the self identity. When examining individual behaviors in contemporary organizations, however, the second meaning of survival becomes more salient. For example, dying from hunger may not be as significant a concern for an employee as losing a job from which he obtains a sense of belonging and meaning. The latter case and other concerns, such as belonging to certain social groups (e.g., middle-class, professionals), having certain reputations, and being loved and well accepted, are usually the meanings of *survival* in the modern social setting. In fact, Plutchik (1980) acknowledged identity as a fundamental existential crisis for all organisms and acknowledged it as a more complex issue when applied to human behaviors.

Therefore, it appears that two of the most diverse theories of emotions within the literature share common ground and tend to differ primarily in focus and emphasis. Thus, we propose that by integrating the psychoevolutionary theory and the constructivist view of emotion, a social psychoevolutionary perspective can be applied readily to the organizational setting.

Conceptual Model

We put the psychoevolutionary theory in the psychodynamic context that the constructivist perspective implies, and developed a model of CWB from the emotion perspective (see Fig. 4.1). In daily organizational life, individuals are exposed to work events or other stimuli events occurring outside the workplace (i.e., life events). Upon encountering the stimuli events, individuals perceive information selectively in ways prescribed by situational factors and individual characteristics; in this process some information may be lost during the perception and interpretation process, and some other information may be misinterpreted (Motowidlo, 1986; Weick, 1995). These perceptions influence further the feelings of individuals, and a disequilibrium feeling may result, which often leads to emotional tension.

The direct link between stimulus events and feelings indicates that it is also possible for stimuli to lead directly to inner feelings (Zajonc, 1984). It is important to note that there is still an unresolved debate as to whether cognitive appraisal is a necessary precondition for elicitation of emotion (Lazarus,

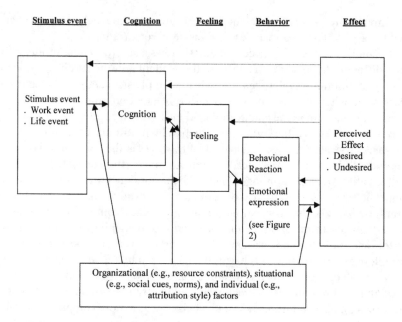

FIG. 4.1. An emotion-based process model of counterproductive work behavior.

1984), or whether there are circumstances under which affect may precede cognition (Zajonc, 1984). Although many argue that cognition is a necessary precondition (Lazarus, 1991), or an intertwining part (Solomon, 2000), of emotion, some have shown that emotions could be induced without the involvement of cognition (Zajonc, 1980). It has also been found that emotion can influence cognition and behaviors (Staw & Barsade, 1993). For example, research has found that emotional states may affect an individual's cognition ability (Isen & Means, 1983) and social orientation (Staw & Barsade, 1993; Staw, Sutton, & Pelled, 1994). Taking all this literature into consideration, we depict the relationship as non-recursive to show that cognition and feelings may influence each other in a cycling manner.

To rebuild the emotional balance result from stimuli events or cognitive appraisal, individuals actively involve themselves in behaviors (including emotional expression) that are intended for certain desired effects. In certain situations, discussed later in this chapter, the behaviors can be counterproductive in nature. The behavioral reactions to inner feelings can then lead to consequences, which may (or may not) be the desired effects or goals. Depending on whether the purpose is satisfied, another episode of emotional experiences may (or may not) follow.

The arrows (pointing left) from "perceived effect" back to the stimulus event, cognition, feelings, and behavior represent situations in which the desired effects are not fulfilled. These unfulfilled goals may serve as new stimuli events that invoke a entire new chain of emotional reactions, or induce new perceptions, feelings, or behavior reactions that may lead to CWB. Theoretically, these feedback loops in the emotional chain only end when the desired goals (either the original or the adjusted ones) are achieved. To better illustrate the point, an example is in order. Imagine an employee who failed to get an expected promotion (stimulus event). Imagine further that she interpreted it as unfair (cognition) and felt angry (feeling). In a department meeting, therefore, she "caused a scene" by publicly offending her supervisor (behavioral reaction) to try to release her emotional tension (desired effect). Rather than regaining her emotional balance, however, she may instead be punished by the organization (undesired effect). The punishment then may serve as a new stimulus event that intensifies the worker's perception of unfairness (new cognition), which induces her subsequent feelings of frustration (new feeling) and sabotage (new behavioral reaction).

It is important to note that the entire process of the emotional chain is influenced by organizational, situational, and individual factors (cf. Averill, 1980; Parkinson, 1996; Thoits, 1989; Hochschild, 1983). For example, organizations often have explicit requirements or implicit expectations for employees' emotions in the forms of feeling rules, defined by Hochschild (1983) as the social guidelines for individuals as to what emotions to have in certain situations. Situational factors, such as being in a football game or a department meeting, also provide cues to individuals' emotional expressions and behaviors, where individuals consciously get themselves "psyched up" or "calmed down" (Zurcher, 1982). Overall, the social influences both enrich and constrain individuals' emotional experience. They enrich emotional experiences by providing the tacit knowledge on how things should be perceived, giving cues that indicate which emotion and behavior are socially appropriate. At the same time, they constrain emotional expression by imposing social rules that individuals must follow in order to survive. In addition, individual differences in such factors as attribution style and emotional stability (Martinko & Zellars, 1998) also influence how stimuli events are interpreted and reacted to. In all, the conceptual model posited that the emotional chains that are invoked by stimuli events and shaped by the organizational, situational, and individual factors serve as critical antecedent of CWB.

Emotional Adaptation

According to the psychoevolutionary theory of emotion, the adaptive function of emotion depends on the smooth flow of the entire emotional chain. In situations where links between two constructs are distorted, the entire process from stimulus to behavior and subsequent effect becomes problematic. Unfortunately, in modern organizational settings, there are many factors such as intense competition and large-scale environmental change (Cascio, 1995) that may hinder or block the adaptation process, as is discussed in detail in later sections.

At each of the linking point in the proposed model two possibilities coexist, both of which may lead to CWB. The first occurs where the link is hindered, blocked, or distorted. For example, when a feeling of anger toward a customer cannot be expressed due to organizational policies, it is then redirected toward organizational property or coworkers. The second is when the chain functions smoothly but in a way that harms the organization. For example, an outburst of extreme anger in the case just mentioned may be due to the accurate appraisal of the situation (e.g., abuse by the customer) and be effective in helping the person regain emotional balance (i.e., fulfill the goal of emotions). However, such expression of anger clearly has negative implications for organizational outcomes (e.g., customer satisfaction and retention). Thus, even adaptive emotions may lead to CWB.

A Taxonomy of CWB Based on Emotion

To understand better how emotional adaptation and maladaptation affect CWB, we have developed a taxonomy of CWB. It should be noted that the emotional chain might be adaptive and functional from the perspective of individual, but not necessarily be so from the social perspective of the society, which is, in our case, the organization.

As indicated in Fig. 4.2, based on the notion of emotional adaptation, CWB can be classified into four different categories according to its individual and social implications. We propose that the conventionally defined CWBs, such as abuse of others, threats, work avoidance, and sabotage (Fox et al., 2001), are behaviors that are adaptive from the individual's perspective but maladaptive from the social perspective. However, there are three other forms of CWB that are understudied. First are those CWBs that are maladaptive to both individual and society, including self-destruction, drug use, and depression (as shown in the bottom left quadrant in Fig. 4.2). Second are those that are maladaptive individually but seem to be adaptive socially at the surface level (see the bottom right quadrant in Fig. 4.2). Such behaviors include passive emotional regulation behaviors such as suppression of negative emotional expressions (Gross, 1999) and surface acting when performing emotional labor (Grandey, 2000; Hochschild, 1983). This type of behavior is maladaptive in the sense that it may be harmful for the physical and psychological well-being (Grandey, 2000; Gross, 1998b; Hochschild, 1983), as well as the cognitive ability, of individuals (Gross & Levenson, 1997; Richards & Gross, 2000). Finally, CWBs that are adaptive both to the individual and the immediate social groups (see upper left quadrant in Fig. 4.2). This includes deviant behaviors (e.g., stealing) attempting to adhere to certain organizational cultures or group norms. Viewing CWB

Emotional adaptation from the social

perspective

		Adaptive	Maladaptive
Emotional adaptation from the individual perspective	Adaptive	Unethical behaviors attempt to adhere to organizational culture (Hidden form of CWB)	Abuse of others, threats, work avoidance, work sabotage, overt acts (Mostly studied forms of CWB)
	Maladaptive	Suppression of negative emotions, high level of emotional labor (Understudied forms of CWB)	Self-destruction, drug use, depression (Understudied forms of CWB)

FIG. 4.2.   A taxonomy of CWB as employee emotional adaptation behaviors.

from the emotional adaptation perspective highlights that these three forms of CWB should be emphasized in organizational research since they could be harmful equally to the individual and the organizational well-being.

In the preceding subsection, we discuss situations where a linking point in the emotional chain becomes problematic, which, we propose, is how CWB is induced. It is important to understand that although CWB can be induced when only one of the linking points become problematic (i.e., each problem point can lead directly to CWB), it is through the mechanism of the entire emotional chain that the antecedents of CWB function. Thus, we cannot understand fully the process of the influence without examining the complex chain of emotional adaptation. In other words, viewing CWB from this perspective helps to better understand CWB.

Stimuli and Cognition

The organizational context has a strong influence over individual behaviors. Events occurring daily in the workplace can serve as important antecedents of strong emotional and behavioral reactions (Weiss & Cropanzano, 1996). Injustice events are likely to induce CWB (Greenberg & Barling, 1999). For example, supervisor's emotional abuse of subordinates has been found to be associated with pervasiveness of fear and breakdown of employees (Harlos & Pinder, 2000). Many extreme cases of workplace aggression and violence also seem to be direct responses to workplace injustice (Cropanzano & Greenberg, 1997). We argue that organizational injustice should be related positively to CWB through cognition and/or feelings.

However, it is usually not the objective event itself that serves as the immediate cause of CWB. In the organizational setting, people actively construct their own realities based on the limited information readily available, and through the socialization and collective sense-making with other organizational members (Weick, 1979). Thus, it is important to examine individuals' cognitive appraisal of a stimulus event beyond its objective attributes. Both individual differences (e.g., attribution style) and contextual factors (e.g., environmental uncertainty) influence individuals' cognitions. We discuss both factors in detail next.

Attribution Style. Attribution style is a traitlike individual characteristic that directs the individual's attention when one makes causal reasoning. Attribution styles influence individuals' appraisals as to their relationship to the situation. For example, individuals who have an external attribution style tend to attribute success or failure to the environment; in contrast, those with an internal attribution style tend to attribute success or failure to themselves. There is evidence that attribution style influences the relationship between organizational frustration and CWB, such that, in reaction to frustration, individuals who tend to make external attribution are more likely to sabotage than their internal counterpart (Storms & Spector, 1987). It has also been proposed that individuals who have an external attribution style are more likely to exhibit aggressive and violent behaviors as a result of aversive outcomes than employees who tend to make internal attributions (Martinko & Zellars, 1998). Thus, it is reasonable to expect that individuals' attribution style will influence their cognitive appraisal of events.

Environmental Uncertainty. The modern work environment is characterized by constant changes, which has resulted in additional pressures both on organizations and individuals (Cascio, 1995; Greenberg & Barling, 1999). On the one hand, changes bring about a high level of uncertainty, and therefore the need to process more information within a constrained time limit. On the other hand, information gathering and processing become problematic due to the limited cognitive capability of individuals (Simon, 1997). For example, research indicates that during threatening situations, individuals, groups, and organizations tend to become more rigid and rely on less information for decision making (Staw, Sandelands, & Dutton, 1981). In addition, there are situations where management feels it is necessary to withhold information from the employees for a certain period of time, which makes it more difficult for employees to fully comprehend the actual situation at the time the stimulus event occurs. Situations simultaneously involving information overload and a lack of information may increase the possibility of misinterpreting certain events, which can generate further frustration and stress among employees (Spector, 1997). Increasing stress within the workplace is associated with CWBs, such as theft (Greenberg, 1990), interpersonal aggression, and sabotage (Chen & Spector, 1992). However, misinterpretation or distorted perception is also possible in less stressful situations. For example, role overload and role ambiguity may influence individuals' feelings of control over situations and affect further how they perceive situations (Perrewé & Ganster, 1989). Thus, we expect that individual differences (e.g., attribution style) and situational factors (e.g., uncertainty) affect the relationship between the stimulus event and the cognition such that the misinterpretation or distorted perception of work or life events can occur and lead to CWB. As an example, individuals with an external, pessimistic attribution style are more likely to interpret stimuli events negatively. Further, situations that are characterized with uncertainty and stress are likely to be related positively to employees' misinterpretation of stimuli events.

Cognition and Feeling

Even with the stimuli being perceived as fully and as functionally as possible, the cognition may not lead to appropriate feelings that are both adaptive to individuals and beneficial to organizations. The reasons are twofold. First, the adaptive feelings may not be elicited from the perception. Second, when the adaptive feeling is elicited within an employee, it may not be beneficial to the organization. We discuss each scenario next.

There are a number of factors that will influence people's elicitation of emotions. In the extreme case, individuals may lack certain kinds of emotions, such as love or fear. For example, Damasio (1994) reported a subject who lost his ability to get in touch with his own emotions. More commonly, being in certain moods may also predispose individuals to feel certain emotions and not others. For example, an individual in a bad mood may be irritated more easily than one who is in a good mood. From a social norm perspective, strong display and feeling rules may influence and, over time, guide individuals to learn not only what emotions to express but what emotions to experience (Hochschild, 1983; Scherer, 1986; Zurcher, 1982). For example, people may initially find it appropriate socially to express sadness when attending a funeral, and over time the perception of a funeral setting will actually generate feelings of sadness inside the person. In a work setting, when a supervisor reprimands publicly an employee for a misdeed, even if he or she believes that the comments are justified, the simple fact of being criticized in public may generate a feeling of shame or humiliation. Feelings of shame may motivate further retaliation behaviors toward the supervisor. Thus, we expect that individual factors (e.g., disability) and social and organizational norms affect the relationship between cognition and feelings such that an accurate perception may still lead to an inability or unwillingness to elicit or express appropriate feelings, which may further result in CWB.

A more typical case in organizations is when individually and psychologically adaptive emotions are expressed with a potentially negative implication for organization, which is especially true when the emotions are ones commonly viewed as negative (e.g., anger). There are several situational and individual psychological factors that may induce employee negative feelings.

Injustice. Perceived unfairness is an important situational factor that induces negative emotions (Spector & Fox, 2002). Two types of justice have been frequently discussed, procedural and distributive justice. Procedural justice refers to the degree to which procedures are perceived as fair in decision making and resource allocation. Distributive justice reflects the perceived fairness of the rewards employees receive for their performance inputs. Perceptions of injustice are associated with counterproductive behaviors such as employee theft, withdrawal, aggression, and other forms of CWB (Fox et al., 2001; Greenberg, 1990; Greenberg & Barling, 1999). Research illustrates that distributive justice also induces employee theft in striving to restore a balance between their rewards and contributions to a job (Greenberg, 1990, 1993). As suggested by O'Leary-Kelly, Griffin, and Glew (1996), workplace violence may ensue when employees perceive valued outcomes (e.g., promotions, compensation) as having been distributed unfairly. In contrast, research also illustrates that fair procedures can minimize the dissatisfaction resulting from poor outcomes (Greenberg, 1990) and can promote employee citizenship behavior (Organ & Ryan, 1995).

Violation of Psychological Contract. Psychological contracts refer to employees' beliefs about the reciprocal obligations between themselves and their organization (Rousseau, 1989). It is argued that that the content of psychological contracts is not always clear and may become difficult for organization to fulfill, as when organizations undergo dramatic changes such as corporate restructuring, large scale downsizing, and increased reliance on temporary workers (McLean Parks & Kidder, 1994; Morrison & Robinson, 1997). Although such changes are becoming increasingly necessary for organizations (Cascio, 1995), it may result in various levels of employees' perceptions of violation of psychological contracts by the organization (McLean Parks & Schmedemann, 1994; Robinson, Kraatz, & Rousseau, 1994). Similar to distributive injustice, violation of psychological contracts may also lead to the employee engaging in behaviors such as theft or sabotage in order to "get even" (Morrison & Robinson, 1997).

Loss of Control. Perceived control is a critical concept in coping with stress. Research has found consistently that high level of perceived control leads to better task performance and a lower level of felt stress appraised (Averill, 1973; Langer, 1975; Thompson, 1981; Thompson, Armstrong, & Thomas, 1998). Unfortunately, within organizations, changes such as technology modernization and large-scale downsizing often introduce considerably high levels of job insecurity, therefore resulting in feeling of loss of control for employees (Greenberg & Barling, 1999). Possible consequences of a loss of control include feelings of powerlessness, loss of identity, anxiety, and stress, which may result in aggression or other forms of CWB in an effort to regain feelings of control. Thus, we argue that perceptions of injustice, violation of psychological contract, and loss of control will affect the relationship between cognition and feelings. Specifically, when feelings of injustice, a violation of a psychological contract, and loss of control are high, perceptions of an event may lead to more negative feelings, which will induce CWB.

Feeling and Behavior

Felt emotions bear strong influence on subsequent behaviors (Weiss & Cropanzano, 1996). Although positive feelings may bind people together (Kemper, 1984) and facilitate interpersonal relationship (Fredrickson, 1998), negative feelings such as anger and sadness tend to pull people apart (Kemper, 1984). Research indicates that negative emotions are related to both organization- and person-targeted CWB (Fox et al., 2001). It is worthwhile noting that the negative emotions may be adaptive reactions to negative stimulus event in the strict physiological and psychoevolutionary sense (e.g., anger may serve as warnings that intend to avoid harmful behaviors of others from happening next time); however, such individually functional behaviors may become socially harmful and dysfunctional in a social setting, as demonstrated by anger-induced aggression (Folger & Skarlicki, 1998). Thus, we argue that the hedonic tone of felt emotion affects the feeling–behavior relationship such that negative emotions are positively related to conduction of CWB.

Interestingly, individuals' good intentions to behave in a socially desirable way can prove equally to be harmful strategically for organizations. For example, suppression of negative emotions has been found to cause stress among flight attendants because of the discrepancies between felt emotion and expressed emotions (Hochschild, 1983). (Boyle discusses this study in detail in a chapter in this book.) We examine next the influences of social and organizational norms, as well as feeling rules, on the linkage between feeling and behavior.

Social and Organizational Norms. An individual's behavior is a function of social influences (Bandura, 1977). Certain organizational culture factors such as organizational values and integrity influence the extent to which employees engage in CWB (Boye & Jones, 1997). Workgroup context also has a significant influence on antisocial behaviors of individual employees (O'Leary-Kelly et al., 1996; Robinson & O'Leary-Kelly, 1998). Further, individuals' antisocial behaviors become stronger as their group experiences enrich and they begin to become socialized with the deviant norms (Robinson & O'Leary-Kelly, 1998). In fact, in some organizations employee theft was so institutionalized that it served as a symbol indicating the employee was well socialized within the organization (Altheide, Adler, Adler, & Altheide, 1978).

Social norms also influence an individual's selection of targets to whom they express particular emotions. For example, anger toward a supervisor tends to be viewed as highly inappropriate behavior at work. Thus, people who feel angry with their supervisors may resort to targeting their anger toward coworkers or subordinates, or even organizational property, which are all potentially counterproductive.

Feeling Rules.   In certain organizations or occupations, there are strong feeling rules, and emotional labor is deemed part of the work role. Often negative emotions are not deemed appropriate to be expressed at work (cf. Schaubroeck & Jones, 2000). For example, Mundy (1998) found that crying remains as a more serious violation of office etiquette than stereotypical manly reactions such as displayed anger and shouting. Often, employees are trained and required to suppress their negative feelings, which can lead to emotional dissonance (Hochschild, 1983; Morris & Feldman, 1997). The negative emotional energy also accumulates inside the individual and could lead one to resort to CWB to regain emotional balance. Thus, we argue that social and organizational norms and feeling rules will affect the relationship between feelings and behavior such that employees may not behaviorally express their felt emotions, which induces CWB.

Behavior and Effect

Even if adaptive behavior is conducted properly, the desired effect or purpose may not be fulfilled. For example, an employee's complaint regarding his unfair wage may not be responded to immediately, or an expression of anger toward a coworker may not stop the coworker's insulting behavior. Therefore, the fulfillment of the desired effects of employees depends significantly on organizational and situational factors, such as resources availability and task structures. First, organizations (or the behavior target) may lack the resources to which they can draw on to react to the emotional adaptation requirement. For example, facing increasing employee dissatisfaction because of a noisy working environment, an organization may not be able to provide a better one simply due to financial constraints. When a lack of resources interferes with employees' hygiene and/or career development needs, it may lead to frustration among employees (Spector,

1978, 1996), which gives rise to CWB such as aggression, hostility, sabotage, and theft (Chen & Spector, 1992). Second, task structures such as level of task interdependency also affect the degree to which a desired effect is obtainable. Organizations as cooperative systems are characterized by interdependency (Thompson, 1967) and interlocking behavior (Weick, 1979). Thompson (1967) suggested that there are three types of interdependency (pooled, serial, and reciprocal), which range from connected loosely to closely tied relationships among individual behaviors. In the case of serial and reciprocal interdependency, one person's goals (desirable effects) depend heavily on the way others behave. When one person conducts a behavior that influences negatively the interdependent relationship, a negative pattern of interlocking behaviors may be formed and influence further subsequent interpersonal exchange. Thus, when task interdependency is high, interpersonal conflicts become more likely (Earley & Northcraft, 1989). Based on this research, we argue that resource constraints and task structures affect the relationship between behavior and outcomes such that even appropriate behaviors may fail to induce the desired effect.

As long as the gap between the desired and actual effect exist, the tension will act as new stimulus event, which induces another round of cognitive, emotional, and behavioral reactions. In this case, an escalation of CWB may occur. Thus, an unfulfilled desired effect will serve as a new stimulus event, or lead directly to negative cognition and/or negative emotions, which will induce another round of emotional reactions leading to same or other forms of CWB.

Complex Combinations of the Problem Points

It is important to understand that situations in which only one link becomes problematic will be the simplest scenario. In reality, multiple links in the process may be hindered, blocked, or distorted, which will make the situation more complex. Thus, the already mentioned problem points are only the simplest illustration of the mechanism through which the emotional chain leads to CWB. It is also possible for two or more linkages to become problem points and function together. For example, a stimulus event can be misinterpreted and, simultaneously, an inappropriate negative feeling is generated. When these complex combinations of the problem points occur, which is probably closer to the real situations occurring daily in the organizational life, the whole emotional adaptation mechanism and the consequences of the emotional chain become less predictable and CWBs become more likely.

CONCLUSION

In this chapter, we proposed an emotion-based process model of CWB. The central message is that many forms of CWB can be understood better by examining the emotional adaptation efforts made by employees. Integrating the social constructivist view of emotion with the framework provided by the psychoevolutionary of emotion, we proposed that CWB occurs when one or multiple linking points in the emotional chain become problematic. Organizational, situational, and individual factors play significant roles in CWB because they influence each of the linking point in the emotional chain.

The organizational implications for conceptualizing CWB as being emotion based are numerous. First, the emotional chain perspective indicates that many factors leading to CWB are actually under the control of employers. Second, control at an early stage of the emotional chain may be more effective and fruitful than at a later stage. Third, this approach also suggests that a healthy work environment that allows for a wider range of emotional expression is very important both for the employee and the organization. Research has suggested that employees appreciate being allowed to talk through their emotional experiences. In an interesting piece of research, Vince and Broussine (1996) used illustrations to access the complex emotions that managers experience during an organizational change process. They found that being able to express and discuss personal feelings about change helped middle managers both to release their emotional tension and to promote a better understanding between top management and middle managers. It is possible that a caring, emotionally honest work environment may help to reduce CWB. Finally, organizations may consider offering employee training on emotion, such as emotional control and regulation, in order to help employees gain a better understanding of their own emotions and enhance their emotional health (Jordan, Ashkanasy, Härtel, & Hooper, 2002).

The model has a few limitations. First, it is possible that the proposed model may not be able to explain all occurrences of CWB. For example, in the case of theft, it may be simply an ethical problem rather than an emotional issue. However, the model is useful for understanding a major portion of CWB. Besides, based on previous conceptual and empirical research (e.g., Spector & Fox, 2002), it is expected that the model will explain a significant portion of variance for various forms of CWB.

Second, we have focused primarily on the effects of situational factors rather than individual differences. We acknowledge that individual differences play important roles in CWB. For example, factors such as locus of control and emotional stability are likely to influence the way people respond to their work and life events, and therefore the possibility for individuals to involve in CWB (Martinko & Zellars, 1998; Martinko et al., 2001). Despite this, O'Leary-Kelley and colleagues (1996) suggested that too much of an emphasis on individual differences as antecedent factors could be misguiding for organizational practices. Consistent with their thoughts, we have focused mainly on situational factors and discussed individual difference factors only where it is necessary.

Despite the limitations, we believe the model nonetheless contributes to the literature with a better understanding of CWB, and highlights many opportunities for future research. First, empirical investigations are needed to explore whether individual difference factors play a more prominent role within the model. For example, it will be interesting to see whether factors such as emotional self-monitoring or deep acting (i.e., to align inner feeling with the social requirement) will help in an individual's emotional adaptation process in a way that is beneficial both to self and to the organization. Research indicates that when employees successfully changed their mood states to align with the organizational context, they may actually experience more positive emotions at work (Grandey, 2000), which is beneficial for both individuals and the organization.

It is also interesting to determine whether the current model explains both CWB and OCB. Spector and Fox (2002) showed that emotion can serve as a link in explaining both CWB and employees' voluntary contributions that go beyond specified task performance or the psychological contract with the employer (i.e., organizational citizenship behavior, OCB). It is reasonable to expect that emotional chains characterized by favorable cognitive appraisal of stimuli events and positive feelings are likely to induce employee extrarole behaviors, such as helping, with the desired effect of maintaining positive emotions and/or positive social interactions with coworkers (cf. Staw et al., 1994).

Finally, the model is yet to be empirically tested. As mentioned earlier, emotion may not explain all forms of CWB. Through empirical studies, specific forms of CWB that have an underlying emotional mechanism may be identified. Due to the process-focused nature of the model, a qualitative research design, such as critical event technique (Flanagan, 1954) and experience sampling methodology (cf. Fisher, 2000).

To sum up, this chapter contributes to the literature with an emotion-based process model of CWB based on psychoevolutionary theory and a constructivist view of emotion. It was argued that CWB is understood better by highlighting the emotional antecedents in the emotional chain. Contextual factors (organizational and family/social factors) can generate events in the form of uncertainty and stress. Individuals differ as to their cognitive ability and awareness of their own emotional states, which, under stressful situations, leads to distorted cognition and feelings of self-identity being threatened, and, in turn, leads to self-protection. Such intention of self-protection under stressful situations may lead to maladaptive behaviors in the forms of CWB. It is worth noting that emotions involved in one emotional chain could be very complex, such as feelings of anger and joy, or shame and pride, or fear and excitement, all at the same time. Further, positive feelings may also lead to CWB, as people attempt to maintain a good mood. Organizational structure or culture may not be supportive enough for positive emotional expression, which gives rise to emotional tension. Emotional chains that fail to generate the desired consequences may lead to further increased tension/emotional energy and, possibly, maladaptive behavior.

ACKNOWLEDGMENTS

We thank Mark Martinko, Robert Plutchik, Paul Spector, and three anonymous reviewers for their insightful comments in developing this chapter.

5

Emotional Experience of Individualist-Collectivist Workgroups: Findings From a Study of 14 Multinationals Located in Australia

Yuka Fujimoto
Charmine E. J. Härtel
Debra Panipucci

Globally, the increasing diversity in the workforce means that the effectiveness of contemporary organizations rests largely on their ability to be open to the differences associated with different cultures. Prejudice, or the negative affective response to perceived dissimilar others, is a significant barrier that organizations must deal with to realize this goal. This chapter makes a unique contribution to the area of diversity and emotions management by considering how cognitive and affective reactions to dissimilar others impacts on individual, group, and organizational outcomes such as hope, intergroup anxiety, trust, perceived fairness, deviant behavior, and task performance. More importantly, this chapter outlines how organizational human resource management practices can alter the consequences of dissimilarity in the workforce and manage more effectively the impact that this has on organizational behavior.

Due to an increase in workforce diversity in recent years, prejudice, or the negative affective response to others perceived as dissimilar, has become an important strategic issue in organizations (Cressey, 2001; Dass & Parker, 1996; Dibben, 2001). Indeed, a number of organizational scholars have foreshadowed that the extent of the effectiveness of contemporary organizations will be determined largely by their ability to be open to dissimilar races, ethnic groups, and the values associated with different cultures (e.g., Dass & Parker, 1996).

Although scholars recognize the need to understand better the effects of diversity on organizational culture and productivity (Eagly & Wood, 1999), discourse in workforce diversity research has evaded largely the issues of stereotyping, prejudice, and discrimination (Linnehan & Konrad, 1999). Further, affect-based theories are adopted rarely in empirical studies of diversity within organizations, despite the well-established affective basis for prejudice (cf. Ashkanasy, Härtel, & Daus, 2002).

In this chapter, we underscore the importance of taking an emotions perspective on the study and management of diversity. In particular, we show how cognitive and affective reactions to dissimilar others impact on individual, group and organizational outcomes such as hope, intergroup anxiety, trust, perceived fairness, deviant behavior and task performance. We also demonstrate how the characteristics of an organization's climate and human resource (HR) policies and practices influence the likelihood of individuals having negative affective reactions (prejudice) to dissimilar others, and the negative emotional consequences of poor relationships.

THE VALUE OF DIVERSITY MANAGEMENT

Studies of both organizational and national diversity have demonstrated that a major deterrent to realizing the positive potential cultural diversity has to offer is prejudice between people whose race or ethnicity is dissimilar to that of dominating employee groups in positions of power and influence (e.g., Bochner & Hesketh, 1994; Fullerton, 1987). Through the perception of similarity/dissimilarity, observable differences (such as age, gender, and race) are subject to categorization processes (Brickson, 2000; Graves & Powell, 1995; Härtel & Fujimoto, 1999; Linnehan & Konrad, 1999). These processes activate stereotypes and beliefs about certain people. Prejudice is a "social emotion triggered by beliefs about a group's characteristics and relationship to one's own group . . . negative beliefs lead to negative emotions" (Linnehan & Konrad, 1999, p. 403). The costs of this prejudice include psychological pain, physical suffering, economic costs, lost opportunities, and denial of the rights to life, liberty, and hope (Snyder & Miene, 1994). Creating openness to perceived differences through managing diversity is proposed to combat these negative experiences. Thus, managing cultural diversity not only improves the operational aspect of the organization, it improves the emotional experience of employees' work life, which is reflected in such things as hope, confidence, satisfaction, and reduced levels of stress, anxiety, and tensions in the workplace (Fujimoto & Härtel, 2002).

In the past, governments have fostered organizations' acceptance of diversity through equity policies such as Equal Employment Opportunity (EEO) and Affirmative Action (AA). However, such legal and regulatory interventions have been viewed as ambiguous and ineffective in improving the quality of work life of employees (Gilbert & Ivancevich, 2000). It is, therefore, important for organizations to go beyond simply satisfying legal mandates, to formulate and implement diversity-open policies and practices that best suit their organization's demographic composition. In recognition of this need, there is an expanding literature base on managing diversity with particular reference to the development of management policies and practices that recognize and value diversity in the workplace (Roosevelt, 1996). In this chapter, we are concerned with identifying diversity management policies and practices that thwart employees' tendency to feel dislike for others perceived as dissimilar and improve the work life of those typically discriminated against—the minority-group members in the organization. We tackle this issue by focusing on the triggers of prejudice in diverse workgroups.

Full utilization of diversity can only be achieved when prejudices are overcome. As a result, those who overcome prejudices will contribute their strengths as well as accepting the dissimilar talents brought by perceived dissimilar others. The present research aims to incorporate the concept of self with the cultural orientation of collectivism and individualism to identify the key outcomes of differences in cultural orientation for the individual, the group, and the organization. In particular, we look at the group dynamics, individuals' positive and negative emotional experience of work, affectively driven attitudes, and affectively and attitudinally driven negative and positive employee behaviors. An overview of the model developed herein is provided in Fig. 5.1.

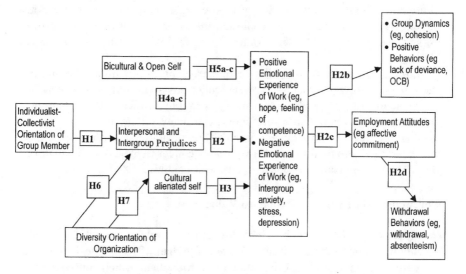

FIG. 5.1. Moderators and consequences of affective response (prejudice) toward dissimilar others in workgroups comprised of individualists and collectivists.

THE PERCEPTION OF DISSIMILARITY
AND ITS EFFECT

Across the cultures of the world, the most important dimension of cultural difference is the relative emphasis on individualism versus collectivism (Triandis, 1990). This dissimilarity reflects individual differences in racioethnicity, values, and views of the self (Hofstede, 1980; Probst, Carnevale, & Triandis, 1999; Triandis, 1980). An important clue to identifying effective ways in managing diversity for positive outcomes should be provided by ascertaining the key triggers of negative emotional responses to the perception of cultural dissimilarity, such as the expression of prejudice.

For the purpose of our research, we define prejudice based on that by Stephan and Stephan (1993) as the low affection associated with perceived dissimilar others. It comprises of emotional reaction like hatred or affection as well as evaluative reactions such as dislike or approval (Stephan, 1999). This definition of prejudice highlights that diversity is an important potential trigger of affective events, which, more often than not, are negative.

Perceived Dissimilarity Based on Race

Race, which individuals often use to infer one's values and self-orientation, is among the most significant stereotype-evoking characteristics (Greenhaus, Parasuraman, & Wormley, 1990; Milliken & Martins, 1996). The term *race* is defined as a definite combination of physical characteristics associated with national origin or as a group of people sharing the same culture (e.g., Western vs. Eastern nations) (Cox & Nkomo, 1993; *Oxford Dictionary Thesaurus*, 2001).

Although race is a powerful factor in stereotype formation and prejudice, there is hope for relationships between collectivists and individualists as research shows stereotypes based on such observable characteristics usually operate only when relationships are superficial. However, even if race doesn't provoke the negative stereotype expected, the inevitable difference in values, which are a distinguishing feature of both collectivism and individualism, threatens the realization of harmonious relationships.

Perceived Dissimilarity Based on Values

Values are defined as a nonobservable higher order concept thought to provide a structure for organizing attitudes (Hogg & Vaughan, 1998). Value differences arise from the independent orientation of individualists, which contrasts with the interpersonal orientation of collectivists. Individualists emphasize an "I" consciousness through independent values such as primary concern for personal goals and immediate family (Hofstede, 2001). Collectivists, on the other hand, express a "WE" consciousness through interdependent values such as cohesive in-groups, mutual obligations, and concern for one's groups with unquestioning loyalty (Hofstede, 2001).

Values influence the individualist–collectivist interaction (ICI) after social categorization based on observable differences because as members interact with one another, stereotypes are replaced subsequently by a deeper level knowledge of the psychological features of one another (Harrison, Price, & Bell, 1998). In other words, as relationships deepen, people are less affected by stereotypes associated with observable characteristics such as race, and more affected by unobservable characteristics such as values. Consequently, this impacts the way in which we interact with others and, thus, our organizational behavior.

Although values refer to implicit differences and are not easily detected, Harrison et al. (1998) argue that actual dissimilarity in values has great potential for influencing organizational outcomes. For example, individualists may define a good employee as one who states explicitly individual goals and stands up for his or her rights, whereas collectivists may define a good employee as one who follows collective norms and maintains social harmony in the group (Chen & DiTomaso, 1996). Therefore, in individualist cultures, dissimilarity in values may result in unfair performance appraisals based on evaluating collectivist employees as too submissive, lacking confidence, and lacking initiative (Chen & DiTomaso, 1996). As a consequence, these values represent a major obstacle to effective ICI interactions.

In summary, values shape attitudes and behaviors through shaping an individual's self-concept (Marsella, Devos, & Hsu, 1985; Wagner & Moch, 1986). This self-concept refers to the processes of individuals' thoughts, perspectives, feelings, and desires, which, in turn, affect their interaction, and emotion, with others (Deschamps & Devos, 1998). Thus, we argue that actual dissimilarity in values will tend to be a negative affective event, eliciting negative affect, negative group dynamics, and negative work-related behaviors. The overarching proposition we discuss in this chapter is, therefore:

Differences in values associated with the independent orientation of individualists and the interpersonal orientation of collectivists will be correlated positively with negative group dynamics, and negative work-related behaviors such as prejudice.

THE CATEGORIZATION PROCESS

Categorization processes are evoked during ICIs based on the perception of differences. Self-categorization theory states that people tend to classify themselves and others into various social categories (Turner & Oakes, 1989). In-group and out-group distinctions are formed on the basis of categorizations, dictating the extent to which another person is included in an interaction (Brewer, 1979; Dunbar, Saiz, Stela, & Saez, 2000; Miller, 1998; Mor Barak, 2000; Moreland, 1985).

The attraction to those perceived as similar, and the subsequent in-group/ out-group distinctions, activate negative stereotypes and prejudices that cause group members to make biased attributions (Allport, 1954; Hewstone & Ward, 1985; Jackson, Stone, & Alvarez, 1993; Taylor & Jaggi, 1974). Therefore, based on social identity theory, which states that prejudice results from the need for a positive social identity with an in-group (Tajfel, 1981), both individualists and collectivists may possess prejudices against each other due to the definition of their own in-group.

The negative affective and behavioral effects of ICI can be explained by a human's inclination to be attracted to those who hold similar attitudes and opinions (Byrne, 1971) and, thus, form part of their in-group. Individualists tend to define their in-group as individuals or groups who are in agreement with them on personally important issues and values (Rokeach, 1960). Conversely, collectivists tend to define the in-group based on social memberships related to them or who are concerned for their welfare such as family, friends, or people from similar racial backgrounds (Gudykunst, Yoon, & Nishida, 1987; Triandis, 1972, 1990).

INDIVIDUALIST–COLLECTIVIST
IN-GROUP/OUT-GROUP PREJUDICE

The cause and type of prejudice depend on a person's values. Individualists may possess prejudices against collectivists based on both racioethnicity and values as they place greater emphasis on defining the in-group according to similar values and beliefs than do collectivists (Triandis, 1990). As such, individualists' negative affect or prejudices toward collectivists' dissimilar values may present the greatest challenge to obtaining positive employee behaviors. For example, research indicates that individualists feel smaller social distance from collectivists whose values are similar to their own than from European Americans whose values are dissimilar to their own (Rokeach & Mezei, 1966).

Collectivists, in contrast, may hold prejudice against individualists as a result of intergroup anxiety. Intergroup anxiety refers to concerns for negative outcomes, such as rejection and disapproval, arising from in-group members' perceived dissimilarity toward out-group members (Stephan, Ybarra, Martinez, Schwarzwald, & Tur-Kaspa, 1998). Collectivists experience intergroup anxiety as they place greater emphasis on interdependence such that the self is almost defined entirely in the context of significant others (Stipek, 1998). As such, research reveals that collectivists tend to place a stronger emphasis on in-group/out-group membership than do individualists (Gudykunst et al., 1987), thus eliciting their in-group favoritism within the ICI setting.

The numerical status of group members may also impact on in-group/out-group distinctions and behavior toward those perceived as dissimilar. Although cultural minority group members tend to discriminate less than majority group members, indicating their recognition of the superiority of members of the majority group (Moscovici & Paicheler, 1978), research indicates that minority-group membership, and a socially disadvantaged status, activate intergroup comparison and increase competitive behavior toward the majority-group members of individualists (Espinoza & Garza, 1985). In addition, studies have shown that minority members display higher levels of intergroup differentiation and in-group favoritism than do majority members (Gerard & Hoyt, 1974).

Key Outcomes for the Individual, the Group, and the Organization

Although the major difference between individualists and collectivists is in value orientations, we must not forget that the members of each group also tend to be dissimilar in racioethnicity. Research states that such observable differences often lead to prejudices and negative short-term effects because of the stereotypes evoked (Harrison et al., 1998; Pelled, 1996). For example, supervisors tend to categorize subordinates as either in- or out-group members early in their relationship when little information exchange has occurred between the two (Tsui, Egan, & Porter, 1994). This out-group status impacts heavily on the work experience of these employees. Minority-group members tend to perceive less support and feel less attraction and commitment, which, in turn, result in higher rates of absenteeism and turnover (Cummings, Zhou, & Oldham, 1993; Greenhaus, Prasuraman, & Wormley, 1990; Pelled, 1996; Tsui, Egan, & O'Reilly, 1992; Tsui & O'Reilly, 1989). These negative findings underscore the costs involved with ineffective diversity management.

Prejudice has a further detrimental effect on minority members' emotional experience of work and attitudes. It tends to increase their propensity to engage in negative group dynamics such as self-segregation from individualists, and in negative employee behaviors such as turnover and absenteeism (e.g., Kanter, 1977).

The Mediational Role of Self-Representation on ICIs

The previous discussion on prejudice and social identity suggests that the effectiveness of ICI is influenced highly by how individuals within ICI contexts represent themselves in relation to others (Brewer & Gardner, 1996; Brickson, 2000; Markus & Kitayama, 1991). In particular, individualists tend to define the "self" using an independent perspective, whereas collectivists take an interdependent view (Markus & Kitayama, 1991). The independent self refers to a self-concept that is differentiated from all others, whereas the interdependent self refers to a self-concept that reflects assimilation to others or significant social groups. The independent self of individualists and the interdependent self of collectivists explain the tendency for individualists to use the individual as the unit of analysis for social behavior, and for collectivists to use the group (Triandis, 1998). Thus, collectivists view more from an intergroup perspective than do individualists, whereas individualists view more from an interpersonal perspective than do collectivists, as demonstrated in the previous discussion of the "I" and "WE" perspective.

The implication of the different perspectives of collectivists and individualists for ICIs is that collectivists tend to create close groups that possess a stable relationship derived from long-term group membership, whereas individualists tend to create open groups that are flexible in changing their memberships (Triandis, Dunnette, & Hough, 1994; Ziller, 1965). Therefore, we propose that the different self-representations adopted by individualists and collectivists (ICs) play a mediational role in the emotional quality of ICI. Further, the limited understanding of the effect of self-representation on ICIs pose a serious hindrance to this area of research (Brewer & Gardner, 1996; Brickson, 2000). This chapter attempts to address this research gap with the effect of self-representations on ICIs explained in detail next.

Dissimilar Self-Representation Explains Negative ICI Effects

Following from the previous discussion, a number of differences exist between individualist and collectivist group members, which may result in negative ICI effects. For instance, when an individualist is in a group where the majority of members are collectivists, he or she may perceive negative stereotypes deriving from the dissimilar collectivist value of high group identity and in-group favoritism. Further, collectivists expect to gain group benefits from the group, whereas individualists expect to gain personal benefits from the group. As such, the individualists' desire to transcend the group means they are no more likely to favor people within the group than from outside the group, as long as there is a personal benefit in the relationship. Therefore, the individualists may perceive that their personal benefit is thwarted by their need to be unconditionally loyal to the group, thus creating new emotion. The self-reliant orientation of the individualist may also be perceived as selfishness (Bellah, Madsen, Sulivan, Swindler, & Tipton, 1986) and thus pose another hindrance to effective ICI.

Similarly, collectivists are expected to find working with individualists difficult because their core principle is to work cooperatively with in-group members and to not seek personal benefits. As such, when a collectivist is in a group where the majority of members are individualists, the collectivist may feel that his or her group benefits are thwarted because of high independence within the in-group. Further, the collectivists within such a group are expected to perceive negative stereotypes deriving from the dissimilar individualist value of high personal identity and to possess intergroup anxiety and fear of abandonment from the in-group.

EFFECT OF THE INDEPENDENT
SELF-REPRESENTATION OF INDIVIDUALISTS

Although individualists may exhibit prejudice toward those with dissimilar values to themselves, they are also expected to have an open group boundary, exhibiting openness to those with similar values, regardless of group membership. Individualists exhibit more prejudice toward a person when the person has a negatively valued characteristic than do collectivists (Crandall et al., 2001). However, research indicates repeatedly that individualists demonstrate openness when collectivists share their values (Rokeach & Mezei, 1966). Therefore, when ICs meet for the first time, individualists are expected to be more open compared to collectivists as long as collectivists agree with individualists on issues that lead to their achievement.

The tendency for individualists to have an open group boundary appears to lead to a cooperative orientation toward groups; however, individualists' orientation to independence means they may also have a greater concern with attaining high status and distinctiveness (Triandis et al., 1994). Consequently, although collectivists emphasize unconditional relatedness to their in-group, individualists emphasize conditional relatedness that calculates carefully the costs and benefits of their relationships with others (Kim, Triandis, Kagitcibasi, Choi, & Yoon, 1994; Triandis, 1998). Research has found that Western participants tend to define themselves as a unique individual to a group when their group membership has a negative value for their self-image. However, when group memberships have a positive value for their self-image, they tend to emphasize their group membership more than individual attributes (Simon, Pantaleo, & Mummendey, 1995). Individualists, therefore, are expected to possess interpersonal prejudices against collectivists, negatively affecting relationships between individualists and collectivists when there is division in values. The emotional experience of individuals in workgroups comprised of people with different cultural orientations is likely to be characterized by the presence of more hassles than workgroups homogeneous in orientation unless care is taken in the formation and management of such groups.

EFFECT OF THE INTERDEPENDENT
SELF-REPRESENTATION OF COLLECTIVISTS

Like the individualist group within the ICI context, the strong intergroup perspectives of collectivists may lead to intergroup prejudices that affect negatively the IC relationship (Perdue, Dovidio, Gurtman, & Tyler, 1990). There is an ethnocentric quality to the collectivist cultures' intergroup orientation in that they expect their perception of the in-group to be valid universally, and everything is scaled and rated with reference to the in-group (Triandis, 1990). Moreover, the salience of the numeric minority membership and socially disadvantaged status of collectivists also accentuate their intergroup prejudices. Research shows that intergroup prejudices by collectivists affect negatively the behavioral integration of individualists with collectivists. When cross-cultural groups are formed for the first time, members from collectivist cultures behave less cooperatively than members of individualist cultures (Gabrenya & Barba, 1987). In other words, collectivists with intergroup perspectives see individualists as out-group members and act less cooperatively toward individualists.

Based on the foregoing review, it is hypothesized that:

H1.   The more individualist a person, the more the person leans toward *interpersonal* prejudice, and the more collectivist a person, the more the person leans toward *intergroup* prejudice.

H2.   The *interpersonal* prejudice of individualists and the *intergroup* prejudice of collectivists will be associated negatively with an individual's emotional experience.

Negative outcomes arise from in-group members' attraction to those perceived as similar, which, in turn, leads to the exclusion, or cultural alienation, of others who are perceived as dissimilar (Zenger & Lawrence, 1989). In particular, collectivists may perceive threats to their self-representation, which may lead to feelings of intergroup anxiety. The intergroup anxiety perceived by these group members, in turn, leads to prejudice toward the individualist members (Britt et al., 1996). As a consequence, prejudices held by individualists toward collectivists, and vice versa, facilitate collectivists' feelings of cultural alienation within individualist groups or organizations. Subsequently, cultural alienation caused by perceived discrimination may affect negatively the relationship between ICI and employees' emotional experience of work. Organizational policies and practices need, therefore, to foster emotionally constructive interactions between employees holding different cultural orientations.

H3.   Higher levels of cultural alienation in collectivists will be associated with lower levels of positive emotional experience of work and higher levels of negative emotional experience of work.

Fostering Emotionally Constructive Individualist–Collectivist Interactions

Although the literature is replete with cross-cultural studies of individualism and collectivism, little information is available on the factors that foster emotionally constructive ICI within organizations. In fact, although the differences in values associated with individualists and collectivists may provide an important source of negative affective events in diverse workgroups, there is research suggesting that these differences could also be a source of positive affective events. For example, research shows that members who are dissimilar in values and beliefs can develop more creative and better alternatives in problem solving than similar members (McLead & Lobel, 1992). The question that is raised, therefore, is, *"What determines whether culturally-based value differences result in negative versus positive affective events?"*

We suggest two reasons, which have diversity management implications. First, we contend that individuals' orientation to cross-cultural experience, defined by the variables of bicultural self, open-self, and intercultural experience, determines one's affective predisposition to cultural difference. Second, we contend that a diversity climate of openness is associated with cultural differences triggering positive, rather than negative, affective reactions. Each is discussed in detail next.

The Moderating Role of an Individual's Affective Predisposition to Cultural Difference on ICIs

Although cultural values are very influential in shaping the self-representation of individuals (Marsella et al., 1985; Triandis, 1989), there are other factors that contribute. This chapter describes the individual characteristics which moderate the process of perceived dissimilarity and ICI. In particular, we propose that individuals may possess both individualist and collectivist cultural orientations regardless of their cultural origins (Singelis, 1994; Yamada & Singelis, 1999) through their level of openness and experience, and that this impacts on their cognitive and affective reactions to dissimilar others.

Bicultural Self. Our discussion so far has been in reference to separate independent and interdependent orientations. However, Singelis (1994) and Yamada and Singelis (1999) found that the independent and interdependent self could coexist in individuals regardless of one's culture. In agreement, Triandis (1989) suggested that both allocentrics (interdependent self) and idiocentrics (independent self) exist within a culture. Similarly, in an empirical study of stress-coping behavior among American and East Asian students, Cross and Markus (1991) found that East Asian students developed an independent self-representation similar to their American counterparts. However,

98   FUJIMOTO, HÄRTEL, PANIPUCCI

their study also found that the East Asian students still had a more developed
interdependent self-representation than did American students, meaning that
one's self-concept can become bicultural. We propose that there are individuals who hold a balance of both individualist and collectivist values (i.e., have a
bicultural self-concept) and that these impact positively on their cognitive and
affective reactions to perceived dissimilarity.

The self-representation that demonstrates this phenomenon of both high
interdependence and independence has been termed the bicultural self
(Cross & Markus, 1991; Yamada & Singelis, 1999). Individuals with a
bicultural self are expected to demonstrate reduced prejudice associated with
collectivist and individualist cultures.

H4a.   The bicultural score will be correlated negatively with interpersonal
       prejudice in individualists. Similarly, the bicultural score will be
       correlated negatively with intergroup prejudice in collectivists.

H5a.   Consequently, bicultural self will be associated positively with em-
       ployees' positive emotional experience of work and related inversely
       to employees' negative emotional experience of work.

We propose two factors that lead to a bicultural self: individual's openness
(*open self*) and intercultural experience. These are discussed next.

Open Self

The interpersonal prejudice and intergroup prejudice sometimes observed in
ICIs indicate that ICs hold negative stereotypes toward each other's group
(Ashmore & del Boca, 1981). Negative cultural stereotypes are automatically
activated in the presence of the member of a stereotyped group regardless of
one's prejudice level (Devine, 1989). Research findings indicate that high- and
low-prejudice Whites categorized Blacks as poor and aggressive (Devine,
1989). The low-prejudice person, however, controlled their automatically activated stereotypes in considering Black–White interactions whereas high-prejudice persons did not (Devine, 1989). Research findings also indicate that low-
prejudice participants are more accurate than high-prejudice participants in
estimating their partner's attitudes (Scodel & Mussen, 1953).

The individual with low prejudice is termed here as "the open self." Those
with an open self are expected to accept and try to understand self-representations dissimilar to their own, which enables them to develop a bicultural
self. The open self may encompass a more positive meaning of self in dealing
with perceived dissimilar others. For example, those with an open self will not
only be open to those with dissimilar self-representations, but they will also be
open to others perceived as dissimilar (such as in gender or knowledge).
Therefore, it is hypothesized that:

H4b.   The openness score will be correlated negatively with interpersonal prejudice in individualists. Similarly, the openness score will be correlated negatively with intergroup prejudice in collectivists.

H5b.   Consequently, an open self will be associated positively with employees' positive emotional experience of work and related inversely to employees' negative emotional experience of work.

Intercultural Experience

An individual's intercultural experience may also shape their self-representation so that it comprises both an interdependent and an independent self-view (Singelis, 1994; Yamada & Singelis, 1999). Intercultural experience may arise from spending time abroad in another culture, from daily interaction within a culturally diverse community, or through having parents from different cultures (Singelis, 1994; Yamada & Singelis, 1999). Research shows that individuals with intercultural experience demonstrate cultural flexibility (Bhawuk & Brislin, 1992). That is:

H4c.   The intercultural experience score will be correlated negatively with interpersonal prejudice in individualists. Similarly, the intercultural score will be correlated negatively with intergroup prejudice in collectivists.

H5c.   Consequently, intercultural experience will be associated positively with employees' positive emotional experience of work and related inversely to employees' negative emotional experience of work.

In summary, positive key outcomes during ICIs are predicted to be impeded largely by members possessing prejudices against perceived dissimilar others. ICIs are therefore expected to achieve positive outcomes when prejudices among dissimilar members are overcome. Further, the paradoxical effect of ICIs also indicates the need for a proactive role by organizations. In light of this, organizations need to develop techniques and procedures to facilitate increasing openness for actual individual differences and the ability to perceive the world from the view of actual dissimilar others (Byrne, 1971). The main way organizations can achieve this is through their human resource policies and practices, which are discussed next.

The Moderating Role of Human Resource Management Policies and Practices in ICI

Although organizations recognize the importance of diversity management, there is still a gap between recognition and action (Noble, 1994). Research shows that although they are leading the way in diversity management, only one-third of U.S. employers had any sort of diversity policy (Carrell & Mann, 1993). Moreover, about half of them were related to EEO/AA requirements (Carrell & Mann, 1993), which are the predecessors to diversity and are not capable of reducing prejudice and obtaining the full utilization of ICs.

In addition to the lack of diversity management, the United States has focused previously on individualistic human resources management (HRM), deemphasizing collectivist HRM, which is insufficient for achieving positive emotional experiences and behaviors in a diverse workforce (Cascio, 1995). As we have shown, organizations will be competitively disadvantaged if they do not realize the importance of, and act to facilitate, the relationships among ICs.

Fostering Diversity Openness

The contextual features of an organization are crucial to the development of effective ICIs, as they influence the self-representation of individuals and determine the effectiveness of relationships that emerge between members (Brickson, 2000). HRM practices typified by individualistic values emphasize personal achievement through clearly defined task responsibilities and reward of individual performance rather than groups (Deutsch, Katz, & Jensen, 1968). The down side for organizations is that such HRM practices encourage employees to focus on a concern for one's own welfare over that of the group's (Brickson, 2000), demotivating them from pursuing other's welfare (Batson, 1998). Exclusive reliance on such individualistic HRM practices then may exacerbate the effect of interpersonal prejudices of individualists. In a similar vein, collectivistic HRM practices such as equality in reward allocation promote individuals' group achievement rather than personal achievement (Ramamoorthy & Carroll, 1998), which motivates individuals to enhance their group's welfare over the individual's welfare (Brickson, 2000; Sherif, 1966). Consequently, we propose that a combination of individualistic and collectivistic policies and practices within an organization, through the development of diversity openness, will have the most positive influence on key affective, attitudinal, and behavioral outcomes of IC workgroups than either could on their own.

HRM policies and practices that foster openness to both an individual's culture and dissimilarity will shape employee attitudes and behaviors and reinforce an organizational culture of diversity openness, thereby enhancing the organization's ability to facilitate effective utilization of ICI (Härtel & Fujimoto, 1999; Kossek & Lobel, 1996). Organizations are more likely to be viewed as valuing differences if: Top management are committed to diversity management; resources are provided (human, financial, technical) for diversity-oriented programs; ongoing cultural diversity training is provided; effective ICI performance is recognized; selection criterion such as "the ability to work with diverse members" is included; constructive conflict is fostered; and minority members are supported. These organizational policies and practices establish a culture of dissimilarity openness, which is expected to reduce the prejudice level of IC members. Specifically, it is proposed that HRM policies and practices are crucial contributors to ICs' emotional experiences, group dynamics, attitudes, and behaviors.

H6. In organizations with IC workgroups, higher levels of diversity-oriented human resource management policies and practices will be associated with lower levels of prejudice.

H7. In organizations with IC workgroups, higher levels of diversity-oriented human resource management policies and practices will be associated with lower levels of cultural alienation.

STUDY 1

To date, there is no published measure of assessing an organization's diversity openness available. Therefore, it was necessary to undertake a study to identify a scoring system, which would enable independent judges to rate the extent to which an organization's HR policies and practices are diversity oriented. Fifty structured interviews with persons representing different stakeholder perspectives (e.g., HR managers, union representatives, equity officers, diversity trainers and consultants, and members of ICI groups) were conducted over a 5-month period in Australia. Also, where feasible, the organization's documentation of their HR strategy and policies were analyzed with the aim of identifying differentiating features related to diversity.

The interviews were transcribed verbatim, and the resulting documents were sorted by abstracts into 347 cards. The cards were analyzed using two stages of an unforced Q-sort methodology. In the first stage, five diversity experts were asked to sort the cards into any category of their choosing without any foreknowledge of the research objectives. Their categories were then grouped into prime categories, represented by 99 cards. In the second stage, the 99 cards were converted into survey format and 32 participants were asked to rate each of the 99 items using a 7-point Likert-type scale ranging from *very diversity closed* to *very diversity open*. A principal components factor analysis with varimax rotation suggested a stable factor structure of four factors with 47 of the 99 items loading adequately and simply on to those four factors. Next, 19 participants with more than 1 year of work experience in an organization with more than 500 employees were asked to think about their organization and indicate the extent to which they agreed or disagreed with each of the statements. The principal components factor analysis with varimax rotation suggested a stable two-factor structure comprised of 21 items. Factor 1 reflected the level of diversity openness in the organization, and Factor 2 reflected an ongoing recognition and support for minority members. An additional 15 items were added from the organization's documentation of HRM policies and practices and a literature review of diversity management. The resultant set of 36 items formed the diversity orientation survey used in Study 2.

STUDY 2

Study 2 aimed to assess empirically the model of the moderators and consequences of affective response (prejudice) toward dissimilar others in workgroups comprised of individualists and collectivists (see Fig. 5.1). Employee surveys were administered electronically and in person to 359 employees across 14 organizations. The supervisor of the participant's workgroup completed Section 2 of the survey, which asked them to evaluate their workgroup's organizational citizenship behavior, task performance, and prevalence of deviant behaviors.

The final survey, the diversity orientation survey, was developed in Study 1 and was administered to at least two HR managers in organizations with more than 400 employees. Included in this survey were individualistic and collectivist HRM policies and practices questionnaires to assess the cultural orientation of the organization.

Individualistic organizations were sampled randomly by selecting organizations from the Business Who's Who database of Australia. Collectivistic organizations were selected randomly from Japanese firms listed by the Japanese Embassy of Australia and by contacting organizations that had participated in Study 1. Approximately 50 organizations with more than 100 employees were approached to participate. The final sample comprised of 14 organizations, of which 7 were Japanese, 3 were Australian, 2 were European, and 2 were American.

Measures

Value Orientations. Individualists and collectivists were identified using the 17-item, 6-point Likert-type questionnaire developed by Triandis (1986). The scale shows strong convergent validity ($r = .73$). For individualism, a composite score of both self-reliance with hedonism and separation from ingroup was computed by taking the mean of the items in the scale. Applying the formula reported in Triandis (1986), individualism = (0.07 × self-reliance with hedonism) + (0.11 × separation from in-group). For collectivism, a composite score of both family integrity and interdependence and sociability was computed by taking the mean of the items in the scale. Applying the formula reported in Triandis (1986), collectivists = (0.57 × family integrity) + (0.25 × interdependence and sociability).

Interpersonal and Intergroup Prejudices. Singelis's (1994) independent and interdependent self-construal scale was adapted to measure the prejudice dimension of interpersonal prejudice and intergroup prejudices. The reliability of the measure was reported as Cronbach alpha = .73 (Singelis, 1994). Participants were asked to indicate on a 7-point Likert scale the degree of like and dislike felt toward examples representing the collectivist interdependent self and the individualist independent self. Mean scores were used in all analyses involving these constructs.

Cultural Alienated Self. Cultural-alienated self was measured with the 7-item, 7-point Likert scale adapted from Jessor and Jessor (1977). The response scale ranged from *strongly agree* to *strongly disagree*. The cultural-alienated self score was created by computing the mean of the items in the scale.

Bicultural Self. Singelis's (1994) independent and interdependent self-construal 19-item, 7-point Likert scale ranging from *strongly disagree* to *strongly agree* was adapted to measure the bicultural self. As a bicultural person is expected to have a liking toward both an interdependent and an independent person, unlike the prejudice measure already described, the interdependent and independent scales were not reverse coded so that the maximum rating (7) would be *like*. The bicultural self score was measured as the average score of the interdependence score and interdependence score.

Open Self. Diversity openness was measured with the 4-item, 7-point Likert scale (ranging from *strongly disagree* to *strongly agree*) adapted from Fujimoto, Härtel, Härtel, and Baker (2000). The items were derived through a review of the diversity literature and represent the following aspects of openness to perceived dissimilarity: (a) expectations toward perceived dissimilarity; (b) in-group/out-group classification; (c) causal attribution toward failure or success; and (d) openness–closeness to perceived dissimilarity. The scale has a reported reliability of .78. A predictive validity of .21 was shown for the scale in a study of cross-cultural service performance.

Diversity Climate of Openness. Diversity climate of openness was measured with a 36-item, 7-point Likert scale (1 = *strongly agree* to 7 = *strongly disagree*). It comprised two scales, namely, diversity-open HRM policies and practices and combined individualist and collectivist HRM policies and practices. Items for the diversity-open HRM policies and practices scale were derived in Study 1.

Three of Ramamoorthy and Carroll's (1998) HRM practices preferences scales were modified to measure combined individualist and collectivist HR policies and practices. The progressive HRM scale and equity in reward allocation scale assessed individualist HRM practices, and the equality in reward allocation scale assessed collectivist practices. Participants were asked to indicate agreement with each statement with respect to HRM within their organization. Responses were given on a 7-point Likert-type scale ranging from *strongly agree* to *strongly disagree*. The average score on the progressive HRM scale, the equity in reward allocation scale, and the equality in reward allocation scale was used to represent the level of combined individualist and collectivist HRM policies and practices in the organization.

Emotional Experience of Work. Individual experiences at work were categorized into negative and positive emotions (Fujimoto & Härtel, 2002). The negative emotion category comprised situational anxiety, stress, depression, job-related tension, and lack of supervisory support. The positive emotion category comprised hope, confidence in skills and knowledge, and organizational-based self-esteem (Fujimoto & Härtel, 2002). The average score was created for each emotion category. Depression, situational anxiety, and stress were measured by the 7-item, 4-point Likert-type Depression Anxiety Stress Scales (DASS) (Lovibond & Lovibond, 1995), which has high reported internal consistency (Brown, Chorpita, Korotitsch, & Barlow, 1997). Job-related tension was measured with the 13-item, 5-point Likert-type scale developed by Kahn, Wolfe, Quinn, Snoek, and Rosenthal (1964). Reliability of the measure was reported as Cronbach alpha = .83. Lack of supervisory support was measured with the 4-item, 7-point Likert scale developed by Pearce, Sommer, Morris, and Frideger (1992). The reported internal consistency reliability of the scale ranged from .88 to .95. Feelings of lack of supervisory support were measured by computing the mean of the reverse-coded supervisory support items. Organization-based self-esteem was measured with the 10-item, 7-point Likert-type scale developed by Pierce, Gardner, Cumming, and Dunham (1989). The average reliability of the measure was reported as Cronbach's alpha of .91. Confidence in skills and knowledge was measured with the 3-item, 7-point Likert scale developed by Wagner and Morse (1975). The internal consistency reliability of the measure was reported as .96. Hope was measured by taking the mean of the 4-item, 4-point Likert-type scale developed by Snyder et al. (1991). Reliability of the measure was reported as Cronbach alpha ranging from .74 to .84.

RESULTS

Results are grouped together by hypothesis for ease of presentation. Regression analyses were conducted to test the seven hypotheses.

H1.   The more individualist a person, the more the person leans toward interpersonal prejudice, and the more collectivist a person, the more the person leans toward intergroup prejudice.

This hypothesis was supported ($F(1,342) = 17.33, p < .0001, R^2_{Adj} = .05, \beta = .22$). This indicates that the more individualist a person, the more the person leans toward interpersonal prejudice. Similarly, the more collectivist a person, the more the person leans toward intergroup prejudice.

H2.   The interpersonal prejudice of individualists and the intergroup prejudice of collectivists will be associated negatively with an individual's emotional experience.

Analyses showed some support for the second hypothesis. Specifically, support was found for a relationship between negative emotion and intergroup prejudice ($F(1,355) = 8.9053, p = .003, R^2 = .024, \beta = .21351$) and between positive emotion and interpersonal prejudice ($F(1,351) = 20.3075, p = .000, R^2 = .004, \beta = -.29094$). Although not significant, the directions of relationships were in the predicted direction for negative emotion and interpersonal prejudice ($F(1,354) = 1.0084, p = .316, R^2 = .003, \beta = .061389$) and for positive emotion and intergroup prejudice ($F(1,352) = 3.0328, p = .082, R^2 = .006, \beta = -.13656$).

H3.   Higher levels of cultural alienation in collectivists will be associated with lower levels of positive emotional experience of work and higher levels of negative emotional experience of work.

Hypothesis 3 was supported. Negative emotion was higher with higher cultural alienation for collectivists ($F(1,196) = 10,3,9, p = .0015, R^2_{Adj} = .05, \beta = .18$), and positive emotion was lower with higher cultural alienation ($F(1,196) = 10.4, p = .0015, R^2 = .05, \beta = -.18$). Unexpectedly, this was also true of individualists ($F(1,196) = 24.6, p < .0001, R^2_{Adj} = .11, \beta = .24$), and there was no difference in the slopes between the two groups.

H4a.   The bicultural score will be correlated negatively with interpersonal prejudice in individualists. Similarly, the bicultural score will be correlated negatively with intergroup prejudice in collectivists.

This hypothesis was not supported ($p > .1$) for either individualists ($F(1,144) = 2.89$, ns) or collectivists ($F(1,196) = 3.09$, ns).

H4b.   The openness score will be correlated negatively with interpersonal
       prejudice in individualists. Similarly, the openness score will be cor-
       related negatively with intergroup prejudice in collectivists.

Support was found for this hypothesis but for individualists only $(F(1,124)$
$= 7.51, p = .0071, R^2 = .057091, \beta = -.56)$. However, the relationship between
interdependent prejudice and openness for collectivists was in the predicted
direction $(F(1,175) = .0373, ns, \beta = -.03)$.

H4c.   The intercultural experience score will be correlated negatively with
       interpersonal prejudice in individualists. Similarly, the intercultural
       score will be correlated negatively with intergroup prejudice in
       collectivists.

This hypothesis was not supported for individualists $(F(1,134) = .0110, ns)$
or for collectivists $(F(1,180) = .0043, ns)$.

H5a.   Bicultural self will be associated positively with employees' positive
       emotional experience of work and related inversely to employees'
       negative emotional experience of work.

The relationship between negative emotion and bicultural self was significant but in the opposite direction to that predicted $(F(1,342) = 18.3752, p <$
$.0001, R^2 = .05, \beta = .18)$. Although not significant for the relationship between
positive emotion and bicultural self, the relationship was in the predicted direction $(F(1,342) = 3.2014, p = .0745, \beta = .09)$.

H5b.   Open self will be associated positively with employees' positive emo-
       tional experience of work and related inversely to employees' nega-
       tive emotional experience of work.

Although the predicted relationships were not significant, they were in the
predicted direction $(F(1,312) = .0012, ns, \beta = -.0008$ for negative emotion
and $F(1,311) = .1143, ns, \beta = .008)$.

H5c.   Consequently, intercultural experience will be associated positively
       with employees' positive emotional experience of work and related
       inversely to employees' negative emotional experience of work.

Although the predicted relationships were not significant, they were in the
predicted direction for negative emotion $(F(1,320) = 1.1161, ns, \beta = -.01064)$
and for positive emotion $(F(1,319) = 2.5776, p = .1094, \beta = .008)$.

H6. In organizations with IC workgroups, higher levels of diversity-oriented human resource management policies and practices will be associated with lower levels of prejudice.

Although this hypothesis was only supported for interpersonal prejudices, the relationship was in the predicted direction for intergroup prejudices. Breakdown of the significant relationships showed a negative correlation between interpersonal prejudice and collectivist HR practices ($F(1,337)$ = $10.1031, p = .0016, R^2 = .03, \beta = -.096$), between interpersonal prejudice and diversity climate ($F(1,337) = 4.27, p = .0396, R^2 = .013, \beta = -.10302$), between interpersonal prejudice and equity in reward systems ($F(1,337)$ = $8.9578, p = .003, R^2 = .0259, \beta = -.07647$), and between interpersonal prejudice and progressive HR practices ($F(1,337) = 3.9829, p = .011878, R^2 = .01168, \beta = -.11878$).

H7. In organizations with IC workgroups, higher levels of diversity-oriented human resource management policies and practices will be associated with lower levels of cultural alienation.

General support was found for this hypothesis, with three of the relationships being significant and the remaining relationship being in the predicted direction. Breakdown of the significant relationships showed a negative correlation between interpersonal prejudice and collectivist HR practices ($F(1,334)$ = $7.8509, p = .0054, R^2 = .023, \beta = -.11143$), between interpersonal prejudice and diversity climate ($F(1,334) = 13.9921, p = .0002, R^2 = .04, \beta = -.24145$), and between interpersonal prejudice and progressive HR practices ($F(1,334)$ = $15.8732, p < .0001, R^2 = .045368, \beta = -.30707$).

DISCUSSION

This chapter had two aims. The first was to show how cognitive and affective reactions to dissimilar others impact on individual, group, and organizational outcomes such as hope, intergroup anxiety, trust, perceived fairness, deviant behavior, and task performance. The second was to demonstrate how the characteristics of an organization's climate and human resource (HR) policies and practices influence the likelihood of individuals having negative affective reactions (prejudice) to dissimilar others and the negative emotional consequences of poor relationships.

The Cognitive and Affective Reactions to Dissimilar Others

A major deterrent to realizing the positive potential cultural diversity has to offer is the affective and cognitive responses between dissimilar people. These responses are shaped largely by the values the individual holds (Marsella et al.,

1985; Wagner & Moch, 1986). This chapter presented a model of individual-ist–collectivist interactions (ICIs), which incorporated an individual's values with the person's intercultural experience, linking them to key outcomes for the individual, the group and the organization.

Specifically, we found that individuals are more inclined to exhibit a certain type of prejudice based on their own cultural values. For instance, people who hold individualist values are more likely to lean toward forms of interpersonal prejudice, whereas people with more of a collectivist nature are more likely to hold intergroup prejudice. However, we did not find evidence in this study of a relationship between bicultural values and prejudice levels.

The direction of relationships conformed to the hypothesis that openness and intercultural experience are inversely related to a person's tendency to be prejudiced. However, the relationship was significant only for individualists on the openness construct.

Emotional Experience From Perceived Dissimilarity.   This chapter exam-ined the affective consequences of diversity, which has been identified as an important factor overlooked largely in diversity research (Ayoko & Härtel, 2000; Fujimoto et al., 2000; Linnehan & Konrad, 1999). We found a significant relationship between interpersonal prejudice and the positive emotional expe-riences of hope, confidence in skills and knowledge, and organizational based self-esteem, and between intergroup prejudice and the negative emotional ex-periences of situational anxiety, stress, depression, job-related tension, and lack of supervisory support.

Further, when individuals feel culturally alienated they are more likely to experience negative emotions, and less likely to experience organizational-based self-esteem, confidence in skills and knowledge, and hope. This occurs regardless of whether a person places greater emphasis on self or group achievement.

Although the prediction that an open self and intercultural experience would be associated with positive emotional experience and inversely associ-ated with negative emotional experience was not upheld, the predictions were in the hypothesized direction. The same was true for the hypothesized rela-tionship between bicultural values and positive emotions. An unexpected find-ing, however, was the significant positive relationship between negative emo-tional experience and bicultural self. This finding may reflect the presence of a third variable operating, such as the presence of a poor climate for diversity openness, which would lie in contradiction to the values of a bicultural person. Future studies should assess the effect of the diversity climate on the relation-ship between bicultural self and emotional experience.

This chapter makes a significant contribution to both diversity research and research into emotions. It has tackled the difficult issues of stereotyping, prejudice and discrimination, which are frequently ignored in the literature

(Linnehan & Konrad, 1999), yet have been shown to create psychological pain, physical suffering, economic costs, lost opportunities, and denial of the rights to life, liberty, and hope (Snyder & Miene, 1994). We, ourselves, have found that they have a powerful impact on the emotional experiences of individuals in the workplace. Through gaining understanding of how stereotypes and prejudice impact on emotions, we can better understand our own and other's emotions and increase the capabilities of individuals, groups, and organizations to manage constructively emotions (Shih et al., 1999).

The Influence of an Organization's Climate and Human Resource (HR) Policies

The second purpose of this chapter was to examine how the characteristics of an organization's climate and human resource (HR) policies and practices influence the likelihood of individuals having negative affective reactions (prejudice) to dissimilar others and experiencing the negative emotional consequences of poor relationships. One of the key ways in which organizations can influence employee openness to perceived differences and the ability to perceive the world from the view of actual dissimilar others is through their human resource management policies and practices. In fact, there is an expanding literature base on managing diversity with particular reference to the development of management policies and practices that recognize and value diversity in the workplace (Roosevelt, 1996). This research area posits that group boundaries can be manipulated to reduce intergroup bias and conflict through diversity practices and interventions (Dovidio et al., 1997). Yet little research exists on *how* these practices and interventions impact on the cognitions and affect of employees, particularly when one party is dominated by another. This chapter attempted to address this gap through looking at the orientation of HR policies and practices to individualist, collectivist and diversity values.

Specifically, we argued that HRM policies and practices themselves reflect cultural value orientations. Furthermore, we demonstrated that HRM policies and practices that motivate individuals to enhance their group's welfare over the individual's welfare (Brickson, 2000; Sherif, 1966) can exacerbate the tendency for individualists to feel interpersonal prejudices toward collectivists. Subsequently, we proposed that the HRM policies and practices with the most positive influence on key affective, attitudinal, and behavioral outcomes of IC workgroups would comprise both individualist and collectivist values.

We found that organizations with HR policies and practices that were diversity oriented, that is, comprised of both individualist and collectivist values, showed lower levels of interpersonal prejudice and cultural alienation. This has significant consequences for our earlier findings. It suggests that when workgroups are comprised of both individualists and collectivists, organizations need to integrate both individualist and collectivist policies and practices into their HRM in order to overcome the inclination of individualists working in an individualist country to feel interpersonal prejudice toward collectivist team members. Further, we found that individuals who feel culturally alienated, regardless of which value orientation they lean toward, are more likely to experience situational anxiety, stress, depression, job-related tension, and lack of supervisory support. However, organizations can combat this with diversity-oriented policies and practices and can increase the individual's feelings of organizational-based self-esteem, confidence in skills and knowledge, and hope.

In order for organizations to effectively manage ICIs, we must develop a better understanding of the ICI process and its relationship to individual, group and organizational outcomes. It is crucial that we gain a better understanding of the organizational capabilities and practices required to manage culturally diverse groups and minimize negative emotional experiences while improving positive emotional experiences at work. A number of scholars have identified the need for research to examine the effect of organizational culture and human resource management initiatives for diversity management (e.g., Linnehan & Konrad, 1999). It is only through increasing knowledge and awareness of how organizational policies and practices impact on the cognitive and affective reactions of their employees to dissimilar others, that effective management of diversity will be realized.

Taking a bounded-emotionality perspective of organizations, we demonstrated how diversity is an environmental variable that can be a source of negative or positive affective events, depending on the characteristics of the individuals and diversity management practices present in an organization. Using this vantage point, we also demonstrated how the culturally shaped individual difference of cultural orientation results in particular prejudice tendencies and influences the emotional experience of individuals at work. These outcomes, as such, may be moderated by an organization's HR policies and practices.

CONCLUSION

Prejudice refers to the negative affective response expressed toward a person who is perceived as dissimilar. This chapter determined that the different ways in which ICs perceive the self lead to a different basis for prejudice in ICs. Further, propositions were offered and supported with respect to how prejudice might impact on group dynamics and employees' attitudes, emotional experience, and behaviors at work. Together, the findings suggest that organizations comprised of ICs are best served by a diversity-open climate, progressive HR policies and practices, and both collectivistic and individualistic HR practices. The findings provide strong evidence that an organization's

HR policies and practices can moderate group dynamics, individuals' negative emotional and positive emotional experience of work, employment attitudes, positive employee behaviors, and withdrawal behavior. In the 21st century, understanding diverse individuals' perspectives, values, and affective events will help organizations move closer to achieving work environments that promote constructive and healthy emotional, cognitive and behavioral reactions at work. This chapter makes a step toward that understanding.

6

A Bounded Emotionality Perspective on the Individual in the Organization

Neal M. Ashkanasy
Wilfred J. Zerbe
Charmine E. J. Härtel

Traditionally, books on organizational behavior proceed in a linear fashion from the individual, to groups, and then to the organization as a whole. This volume is no exception. Organizations exist only because of the people within them. Consequently, understanding organizations first of all requires understanding the people who populate them, and especially their needs, drives, and capabilities. It is all the more surprising therefore to find that organizational behavior scholars, and behavioral science researchers in general, were so slow to appreciate the centrality of emotion in organizations (see Ashforth & Humphrey, 1995). Indeed, even today, many scholars are reluctant to accept an emotions-oriented explanation of motivation and behavior (e.g., Becker, 2003). Interestingly, and as Weiss and Brief (2002) pointed out, early organizational behavior scholars were deeply interested in the role of feelings and emotion, but this research seems to have withered with the rise of behaviorism in the 1940s and 1950s.

From the perspective of the present volume, the major breakthrough in bringing the study of emotions to the individual level of analysis was Weiss and Cropanzano's (1996) introduction of affective events theory (AET). This theory emphasized the dynamic and interactive association of emotion, behavior, and performance in organizations. More recently, Ashkanasy (2003a) proposed a "multi-level theory of emotions" (p. 3), which puts AET at the core of the model and extends its discussion to five levels: within-person, between-person, interpersonal dyads, groups, and organization. In a follow-up article, Ashkanasy (2003b) emphasized that the integrating factor across the five levels

of analysis is the neurobiological basis of emotion. In this respect, human beings are bound to behave in ways predetermined by their neurobiological architecture. In the introduction to our first book (Ashkanasy, Härtel, & Zerbe,
2000), we made a similar point—that understanding emotions in organizational settings requires first an understanding of the mechanisms underlying
the generation and control of emotion.

The chapters in this section do not deal specifically with the neurobiology
of emotion, but drive home a corollary—that emotions constitute the essence
of behavior in organizations: a message that lies at the core of the present volume. This point is especially salient in Maree Boyle's analysis of the performance of emotional work within an emergency services organization in chapter
3. In Boyle's rich account, which takes a dramaturgical perspective (Goffman,
1959), members of the Department of Paramedical Services (DPS) engage in
emotional work in three "emotional regions." But it is not only in the obviously
emotion-laden aspects of emergency service work that emotion work is required, but "offstage"—in the work areas behind the scenes, and especially after work—that Boyle found the most interesting manifestations of emotion
work. Here, workmates, family members, and the wider community provide
essential emotional support to stressed DPS officers, most of whom are men.
Yet, perhaps not surprisingly, the department seems to be unable or unwilling
to recognize the importance of support. Consistent with the rational organization model prevalent in the public service, there seems to be an expectation
that, somehow, departmental officers are heroes—that they are able to control
their emotions at work, and to deal with the emotional consequences afterward. Thus, the burden of this role is placed on the officers' informal networks. Amazingly, this seems by and large to have worked. But the point here
is not so much the issue of the organization's responsibility toward the welfare
of its employees, but the finding that emotion is so central to the performance
of work by the employees, both on and off duty. In this instance, even the department's indifference is subsumed in an organizational environment where
emotion and emotion management lie at the very core of organizational effectiveness.

In chapter 4, Yongmei Liu and Pamela Perrewé delve more deeply into the
murky underside of organizational behavior—which they refer to as "employee
counterproductive work behavior" (CWB). Taking an approach based on ideas
of emotional adaptation, Liu and Perrewé seek a less superficial understanding of CWB than is available through the traditional behavioral and cognitive
models of organizational behavior. But CWB, which often involves acts of anger driven by deep feelings of hurt, is inherently emotion charged. Liu and
Perrewé bring together two streams of thought—psychoevolutionary theory
(Plutchik, 1980) and the constructivist view of emotion (Averill, 1980)—and
integrate them in an intriguing and original model of the genesis of CWB. In
this model, CWB is not some form of irrational behavioral response to a per-

ceived stimulus, but is a natural response to environmental pressures, and is derived from a basic need for survival in the organizational context. As with Boyle's examples, emotion is not something that can be tacked on or managed in the conventional linear sense. Instead, emotion forms the basic kernel underlying particular behaviors—in this case, CWB.

Chapter 5 is the third chapter in this section. Here Yuka Fujimoto, Charmine Härtel, and Debra Panipucci delve into understanding the emotional dimensions of diversity and that most fundamental of human instincts: individualism versus collectivism. Their results demonstrate that individual attitudes in respect of collectivism-individualism and diversity are related to emotional experiences. This research raises some intriguing questions about the interactions of diversity and emotion (see also Ashkanasy, Härtel, & Daus, 2002b), and the way that organizational members' feelings about their work are conditioned by the way they feel about their fellow workers and the work environment. Viewed through the lens of Liu and Perrewé's model of CWB, it would seem that the same processes of psychoevolution and constructivism are operating here too, in that organizational members react instinctively to perceived threats in their working environment. Therefore, when a threat is seen to derive from the makeup of the work group, emotional responses related to basic survival are triggered.

In summary of the chapters in this section: All bring different perspectives to the topic of emotions at the individual level of organizational analysis, but at the same time all bring a consistent theme that emotion lies at the core of organizational behavior. This holds true irrespective of whether organizational behavior is altruistic (Boyle) or counterproductive (Liu and Perrewé). It also holds true with respect to attitudes toward diversity and working together. As Ashkanasy (2003b) stressed, the unifying thread is that all human beings are ultimately dependent on their neurobiology for the way they think, feel, and behave.

The implication of this conclusion is obvious in many ways, but apparently not so obvious for many years to scholars working in the field of organizational behavior research. Despite the early interest in emotions, as noted by Weiss and Brief (2001), scholars of organizational behavior in the following years concentrated their efforts on developing sophisticated models that were seriously flawed in their failure to account for the emotional underpinnings of individual behavior. The chapters in this section of the book help to make a start on redressing this shortcoming.

III

THE INTERPERSONAL
WITHIN THE
ORGANIZATION

7

Individual and Group Affect in Problem-Solving Workgroups

Matthew J. Grawitch
David C. Munz

A large volume of literature suggests that positive affect can facilitate individual problem solving. The effect of positive affect stems from its influence on processes related to perception, cognition, and motivation. More recent research has begun to examine the relationship between affect and different stages of group problem solving. In this chapter, we propose a theoretical framework to understand the relationship between affect and group performance at various stages of problem solving that synthesizes individual- and group-level research. This framework, the Group Affect Problem Solving (GAPS) model, shows relationships between individual affective processes and group affective norms at the problem identification, brainstorming, solution development, and implementation stages of the group problem-solving process. Additionally, we offer propositions underlying the GAPS model to be examined empirically in future research. Research issues and practical implications are also discussed.

Modern organizations seek continuously to maximize their human capital. Often, employees, working within problem-solving groups (e.g., cross-functional, quality improvement, or reengineering teams), generate ideas or solutions to the challenges faced by their organization and may manage the implementation of those solutions (Uhl-Bien & Graen, 1998). Therefore, it is important to understand individual- and group-level constructs that influence outcomes at various stages of the problem-solving process.

Affect at the individual and group levels contributes to our understanding of group problem-solving performance, because of its pervasive effect on motivation and information processing (Gendolla, 2001). Affect is defined as "mental states involving *evaluative feelings*, in other words psychological conditions when the person feels good or bad, and either likes or dislikes what is happening" (Parkinson, Totterdell, Briner, & Reynolds, 1996, p. 4). Affect has consequences for both the individual and the group, especially in the regulation of that affect (Carver, 2001; George, 1990).

Using previous research as a guiding framework, the current chapter delineates the Group Affect Problem Solving (GAPS) model that integrates both individual- and group-level affect research (Fig. 7.1). The GAPS model is a theoretical model that presents four key stages involved in effective group problem solving: problem identification, brainstorming, solution development, and implementation. The model illustrates a macro-level problem-

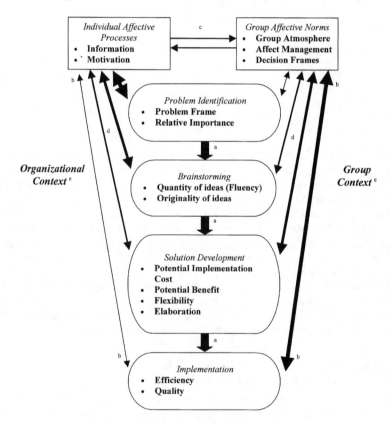

FIG. 7.1.   The Group Affective Problem Solving (GAPS) model. a, Indicates that outputs at one stage of problem solving serve as input into the next stage; b, represents transactions (all double arrows indicate transactional relationships); c, indicates mutual influence over time; d, indicates differential influence (increasing arrow density equals increasing influence over time, and decreasing arrow density equals decreasing influence over time); e, signifies the importance of context to problem-solving stages and affect constructs.

solving process typically used in organizations. The model also contains two key elements that influence group problem solving: individual affective processes and group affective norms. In order to explicate the model and the rationale supporting it, we explore both the individual and group affect constructs in detail. Then, we discuss each link in the GAPS model using current empirical research to support and hypothesize specific relationships. Additionally, we propose and discuss the implications of context, with an emphasis on organization and group factors that may influence model relationships. Finally, we present practical implications and research opportunities to bridge the gap between theory, research, and practice.

THE STRUCTURE OF INDIVIDUAL AFFECT

Affect at the individual level encompasses a wide variety of psychological phenomena, including emotions and moods. Affective experiences provide information about the state of the individual in transaction with the environment. These affective experiences motivate behavior in any given situation (Forgas, 2002; Forgas & Vargas, 2000; Fredrickson, 2001; Gendolla, 2001; Nemanick & Munz, 1997; Parkinson et al., 1996). For example, research suggests that individuals experiencing positive affect are motivated to engage in proactive or prosocial behaviors (e.g., helping behaviors), whereas individuals experiencing negative affect are motivated to engage in avoidance or withdrawal behaviors (e.g., distraction; Parkinson et al., 1996). Until recently, affect was discussed primarily in terms of a circumplex composed of two conceptually and statistically independent dimensions: activation and hedonic tone (Russell, 1980). All affective experiences could be mapped along these two dimensions. The *activation* dimension relates to the level of physiological arousal inherent in the experience, and the *hedonic tone* dimension refers to the pleasantness or unpleasantness of the experience. Thayer (1967, 1978) further defined dimensions related to energy and calmness, and Watson and colleagues (Watson & Clark, 1997; Watson, Clark, & Tellegen, 1988) defined dimensions of positive and negative affect. Additionally, recent efforts have integrated different conceptualizations of affect into a unified affect circumplex as depicted in Fig. 7.2 (Yik, Russell, & Feldman Barrett, 1999).

THE FUNCTION OF INDIVIDUAL AFFECT

The affective circumplex provides a theoretical conceptualization of affect from a structural perspective, but it does not provide a conceptualization of the functionality of affect (Carver, 2001). Carver argued that although affect may be understood in structural terms, those structural components do not explain

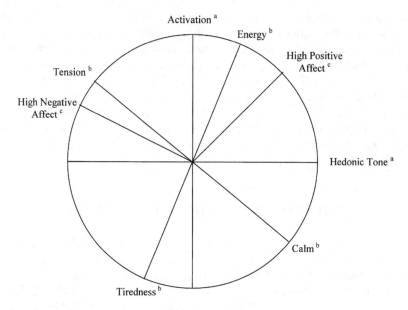

FIG. 7.2.   An integration of several common affect constructs: a, dimensions identified by Russell (1980); b, dimensions identified by Thayer (1967, 1978); c, dimensions identified by Watson, Clark, and Tellegen (1988). Adapted from Yik, Russell, and Feldman Barrett (1999).

the function of affect. Instead, Carver proposed that affect is best understood as two separate functional systems: an approach system and an avoidance system, both of which have received significant theoretical and physiological support (Carver, 2001; Carver & Scheier, 1999) and identify closely with social psychological theories of motivation and self-discrepancy (i.e., promotion/prevention focus; Higgins, 1998).

The Approach System

The *approach system* is activated when the goal is to obtain or achieve a positive outcome (Carver, 2001), motivating individuals to seek growth and accomplishment (Higgins, 1998). Therefore, approach processes motivate the individual toward positive outcomes, and the individual evaluates the progress made in achieving those outcomes or goals through continuously operating self-regulatory mechanisms (Carver & Scheier, 1999). That is, as approach processes inform the individual that exceptional progress is being made toward a positive outcome, high positive affect results, in the form of positive mood, elation, or eagerness (Carver, 2001). However, when the approach system informs the individual that inadequate progress is being made toward a positive outcome, then low positive affect results, in the form of sadness, depression, or tiredness (Carver, 2001). As Carver argued, the experience of positive affect also initiates the approach system, causing individuals to emphasize or focus on the obtainment or achievement of a positive outcome (Carver, 2001). Figure 7.3 provides a graphical presentation of the approach system.

The Avoidance System

The *avoidance system* is activated when the goal is to avoid or minimize a negative outcome (Carver, 2001), motivating individuals to seek safety and security (Higgins, 1998). Avoidance processes motivate the individual away from negative outcomes, and the individual evaluates the progress made in avoiding those outcomes through continuously operating self-regulatory mechanisms (Carver & Scheier, 1999). In other words, as avoidance processes inform the individual that exceptional progress is being made to move away from a negative outcome, low negative affect results, in the form of relief, calmness, or relaxation (Carver, 2001). However, when the avoidance system informs the individual that insufficient progress is being made to move away from a negative outcome, then high negative affect results, in the form of anxiety, negative mood, fear, or irritability (Carver, 2001). As Carver argued, the experience of negative affect also initiates the avoidance system, causing individuals to emphasize or focus on the avoidance of negative outcomes. Figure 7.3 provides a graphical presentation of the avoidance system.

IMPLICATIONS OF THE FUNCTIONAL PERSPECTIVE

Because of its emphasis on goals and goal achievement, the functional perspective offers implications for understanding the relationships indicated by the GAPS model. Approach and avoidance processes that result from and pro-

Approach Process		Avoidance Process	
Doing Well +	Elation, Eagerness	Doing Well +	Relief, Calmness
	Neutral		Neutral
Doing Poorly −	Sadness, Depression	Doing Poorly −	Fear, Anxiety

FIG. 7.3. Graphical representation of approach and avoidance mood outcomes. Adapted from Carver (2001).

duce affect influence how that affect is regulated and directed toward the development of effective group norms and performance. In essence, the functional perspective purports an ongoing gap analysis, in which an individual evaluates progress made toward positive goals and standards and away from undesired outcomes (also known as control theory; Carver & Scheier, 2002). High positive affect results from a *decrease* in the gap between positive goals and the individual's current state, whereas low positive affect results from an *increase* in the gap between positive goals and the individual's current state. Alternatively, high negative affect results from a *decrease* in the gap between negative outcomes and the individual's current state, whereas low positive affect results from an *increase* in the gap between negative outcomes and the individual's current state.

The functional theory's emphasis on goals and standards aligns suggests a *transactional approach* to affect (Carver, 2001). A transactional approach accounts for the importance of individual characteristics (e.g., personality), environmental conditions (i.e., events in the external world), and the mutual influence each exerts to create the momentary states that individuals experience (Carver & Scheier, 2002). Because the functional theory proposes that individuals set goals and standards to be achieved (approach standards) or avoided (avoidance standards), the progress that is continuously evaluated includes characteristics of the person (e.g., differences in approach/avoidance emphasis, different goals), environment conditions (e.g., aspects of the environment that facilitate or impede progress), and mutual influences between the person and the environment (e.g., the type of goals an individual sets causes him or her to seek out specific environmental events that influence the progress toward those goals). These self-evaluations then result in a particular affective state.

Within the functional paradigm affect serves two important roles: (a) an informational role and (b) a motivational role (Gendolla, 2001). The GAPS model indicates that both roles influence the outcomes of problem-solving workgroups. Affect influences how information is perceived, synthesized, and cultivated within the group (the informational role), and it influences the desire of workgroup members to engage in specific types of behavior (the motivational role).

The Informational Role

The informational role of affect occurs in the influence on perception and information processing. Positive and negative affect occur due to separate self-evaluative processes, and the influence on perception and information processing tends to be congruent with the type of affect. High positive affect resulting from the approach system signals that sufficient progress is being made toward positive outcomes. Therefore, less attention is required in critically evaluating environmental events and characteristics, allowing individuals to perceive and process information at a more global level (Gasper & Clore, 2002). Conversely, high negative affect resulting from the avoidance system signals that insufficient progress is being made away from negative outcomes. Consequently, more attention is required in critically evaluating environmental events and characteristics, causing individuals to perceive and process more localized information (Gasper & Clore, 2002). Essentially, positive affect allows individuals to focus on the forest, whereas negative affect causes individuals to focus only on the trees.

The difference in focus that results from the experience of positive and negative affect also influences cognitive flexibility. Individuals experiencing high positive affect exhibit greater cognitive flexibility than individuals experiencing other types of affect (e.g., low positive, high negative affect; Isen, 2000). Because high positive affect signals alignment with positive goals and outcomes, the individual redirects cognitive resources away from intense environmental scanning and toward other more relevant tasks, exploring a wider variety of behavioral options when making decisions and increasing the efficiency with which information is synthesized (Fredrickson, 2001; Isen, 2000), positive outcomes especially relevant to our later discussion of the GAPS model.

Because of the self-referent nature of affect (i.e., affect resulting from self-evaluations of one's own progress), information and appraisals congruent with the experienced affective state are often primed. For example, positive affect has been found to prime information (Doherty, 1998; see also Isen, 2000) and appraisals (Munz, Benaka, & Walters, 2000) with a positive valence, whereas negative affect has been found to prime information (Doherty, 1998) and appraisals (Munz et al., 2000) with a negative valence. This priming filters individual experiences through either a positive or negative lens, leading to perceptions and cognitions congruent with the current affective state.

The Motivational Role

The motivational role of affect was discussed to a degree earlier. What is of importance to the GAPS model is how affect manifests itself in an individual's motivation to engage is certain types of behaviors. The functional theory proposes that individuals strive to approach positive outcomes and avoid negative outcomes, but the affect that results from the continuous self-evaluations must be *managed* (i.e., affect regulation), which can occur consciously or unconsciously (Larsen, 2000; Mayer, 2000; Parkinson & Totterdell, 1999; Parkinson et al., 1996; Thayer, Newman, & McClain, 1994). Individuals may engage in a variety of affect management strategies, from active mood management (e.g., relaxation techniques) to withdrawal-avoidance techniques (e.g., avoiding other people; Thayer et al., 1994). The extent to which individuals actively manage affect depends on their ability to recognize and monitor their affective states (Swinkels & Giuliano, 1995) and use that information as input to select appropriate cognitive and behavioral mechanisms for affect regulation (Martin, Ward, Achee, & Wyer, 1993). Therefore, affect management is likely to result in different regulation strategies when the approach system has been initiated than when the avoidance system has been initiated (Carver, 2001).

Because positive affect generally results from approach processes, in which the goal is to obtain or achieve positive outcomes, previous research has suggested that positive affect is related positively to positive outcomes (e.g., satisfaction, commitment, prosocial behaviors; Brief & Weiss, 2002; Munz, Huelsman, Konold, & McKinney, 1996). Alternatively, because negative affect generally results from avoidance processes, in which the goal is to avoid or evade negative outcomes, this same research has suggested that negative affect is related positively to negative outcomes (e.g., turnover, turnover intentions, burnout; Brief & Weiss, 2002; Munz et al., 1996; Parkinson et al., 1996). In spite of this, negative affect provides information that the interface between the individual and the environment is suboptimal and in need of improvement. As a result, it can serve to motivate behavior toward improving transactions with the environment, resulting in positive outcomes (e.g., process improvements) if appropriate actions are taken to reframe, remove, or improve the conditions that reinforce negative affect (George & Zhou, 2002). The differential predictive validity of positive and negative affect provides more evidence that affect operates through separate underlying motivational processes reflecting an approach-avoidance paradigm (Carver, 2001).

Affect, through the approach and avoidance transactional systems, has a pervasive effect on an individual's functioning, influencing perceptions, information processing, motivation, and behavior. In workgroups, affect has important implications for both the individuals that operate within that group and the group itself. Consequently, before discussing the GAPS model in depth, we must first understand how affect manifests itself in a group, and how individual-level affect develops into group affect constructs, which then reinforce individual-level affect.

FROM INDIVIDUAL TO GROUP AFFECT

Individual affective processes have consequences for workgroups, due to their effects on the individual members of the group and the group's affective norms (George, 1990). *Group affective norms* refer to those norms that develop within groups and govern the experience, management, and use of affect within the group. The GAPS model highlights three important affective norms that can develop within workgroups: group atmosphere, affect management, and decision frames. In subsequent sections, we discuss how these group affective norms develop from individual affective processes and how they influence the GAPS model.

Group Atmosphere

Group atmosphere refers to the general atmosphere or climate of the group (Bierhoff & Müller, 1999). A positive group atmosphere is one that is open, honest, and constructive, resulting from the consistent experience of positive affect by group members. That is, a positive group atmosphere is one in which approach processes play a significant role in helping the group to develop positive interactions among members (e.g., conflict has positive consequences and should be managed effectively). A negative group atmosphere is one that is tense and often destructive, resulting from the consistent experience of negative affect by group members. In other words, a negative group atmosphere is one in which avoidance processes play a significant role in shaping how group members relate to each other (e.g., conflict has negative consequences and should be avoided). The group atmosphere results from processes of mutual influence at a conscious level, whereby group members influence each other through explicit means (George, 1990). For example, if group members convey positive attitudes toward the group, those attitudes are likely to result in increased positive affect within the group (Grawitch, Munz, Elliott, & Mathis, 2001).

Additionally, group members may influence the affect experienced by other group members unconsciously, a process known as *affect contagion* (Doherty, 1998; Hatfield, Cacioppo, & Rapson, 1994; Neumann & Strack, 2000). Affect contagion occurs through unconscious mimicry processes, in which group members begin to mimic the affective expressions of other group members (e.g., facial expressions, postures, voice tone; Hatfield et al., 1994; Laird et al., 1994). Due to cognitive and physiological feedback mechanisms, this mimicry leads to affective convergence within the group (Hatfield et al., 1994). Over time, these processes result in consistent levels of affect within the group setting (also known as *affective tone*; George, 1990), which influences the group atmosphere (Bierhoff & Müller, 1999). Groups that develop a negative atmosphere engage in fewer prosocial behaviors and are less satisfied with the group (Bierhoff & Müller, 1999; George, 1990). Workgroups that cultivate consistent positive affect among their members create an open, honest, and constructive group environment, a key element in group problem-solving success.

Affect Management Norms

Affect management norms develop as group members reinforce each other's affect regulation strategies and refer to those processes sanctioned by the group as acceptable means of affect regulation (Marks, Mathieu, & Zaccaro, 2001).

As members of the group begin to sanction implicitly and explicitly certain affect regulation behaviors, especially as those behaviors relate to successes and failures experienced by the group, affect management norms develop (Marks et al., 2001). These norms can have significant consequences on the ability of group members to manage both positive and negative affect effectively, most notably as that affect results from conflict, feedback, and evaluation. There is a direct relationship between affect management norms and affective outcomes, such as cohesion and satisfaction with the group (Marks et al., 2001), and work improvement processes (George & Zhou, 2002). Of importance to the GAPS model is that affect management norms instituted explicitly and implicitly by the group determine the type of affect that is accepted, promoted, and regulated actively by the group, creating an affective group norm. For example, if the group has few strategies for decreasing negative affect when it occurs (e.g., when conflict arises), then negative affect will have a stronger influence on the group. Although affect management norms do not influence performance outcomes directly, they serve to reinforce the experience and regulation of affect within the workgroup and may contribute to the group atmosphere (Bierhoff & Müller, 1999).

Decision Frames

Decision frames represent the way in which workgroups frame potential opportunities and actions. *Decision frames* refer to the extent to which the group seeks to approach potentially positive outcomes or avoid potentially negative outcomes (Higgins, 1998). Research has suggested that positive and negative affect influence the decision frames of individuals (Higgins, 1998; Isen, 2000). Additionally, it is evident that a decision frame produces a response bias congruent with that frame (Friedman & Förster, 2001). For instance, at the individual level, positive affect promotes approach processes, resulting in increased motivation to take calculated risks that may bring potentially greater benefits, thus maximizing desired outcomes (promotion-focused frame). Negative affect promotes avoidance processes, resulting in increased motivation to accept low-cost, low-risk decisions, thus maintaining security and avoiding negative outcomes (prevention-focused frame). At the group level the promotion-focused frame leads to more calculated risks with the expectation of greater benefits for the group, whereas the prevention-focused frame leads to decisions to engage in less risky, more conservative alternatives (Levine, Higgins, & Choi, 2000). Therefore, promotion-focused frames consider the problem and the solution in terms of maximizing positive outcomes, whereas prevention-focused frames consider the problem and the solution in terms of minimizing negative outcomes. Little research has examined the relationship between affect and decision frames at the group level directly. However, if members of a group experience positive or negative affect consistently, resulting in a positive or negative atmosphere, the group may be more likely to adopt decision frames consistent with that atmosphere. Groups that have developed a positive group atmosphere may be more likely to use promotion-focused decision frames, whereas groups that have developed a negative group atmosphere may be more likely to use prevention-focused decision frames. Consistent positive or negative affect within a group may result in a consistent group-level frame that can affect how problems are solved and the subsequent actions that result.

THE GAPS MODEL

The previous sections defined individual affective processes and group affective norms. In this section we focus on the problem-solving process in order to describe the GAPS model more fully. The GAPS model is a theoretical model that integrates affect and group problem-solving research at each stage of the problem-solving process. First, we describe the four broad problem-solving stages and present key indicators and outcome measures for each stage. Then, we propose relationships between the components of the model in an attempt to synthesize previous research at the individual and group levels and suggest effects of affect on group problem-solving outcomes. Throughout our discussion we present five important propositions or key assumptions underlying the GAPS model.

Problem-Solving Stages Defined

The GAPS model presents four general problem-solving stages used by groups in organizations. The first stage of the problem-solving process is the *problem identification stage*. This stage emphasizes the adequate description of the problem and its seriousness (Orlitzky & Hirokawa, 2001). Of additional consequence is the extent to which the problem is defined as an opportunity to grow and achieve (promotion-focused frame) or as an opportunity to seek safety and security (prevention-focused frame; Levine et al., 2000). In many instances, management engages in problem identification and then assigns the identified problem to a project, reengineering, or problem-solving group to solve (Uhl-Bien & Graen, 1998).

There are at least two criteria for evaluating problem identification effectiveness: the decision frame applied to the problem and the relative importance of the problem. Because of the difference in emphasis using a promotion-focused versus a prevention-focused frame, promotion-focused frames lead to an increase in the types and number of ideas that are considered in both the brainstorming and solution development stages (Levine et al., 2000). A second important criterion at this stage refers to the relative importance of the identified problem. Serious problems are more likely to energize the problem-solving group to devote the time and energy required to develop effective solutions than are less serious problems (Orlitzky & Hirokawa, 2001). When selecting from a variety of potential problems on which to direct the effort of a group, an emphasis should be placed on solving more serious problems. Table 7.1 presents ways to measure the problem frame and the relative importance of

TABLE 7.1
Proposed Indicators and Possible Measures
of Group Problem-Solving Criteria

Indicators	Possible Measures
Problem Identification Stage	
Problem frame	Ratings of promotion-focused and prevention-focused qualities of the problem statement
	Rankings of problem statements from most to least promotion focused and most to least prevention focused
Relative importance	Rankings of potential problems from most to least important by relevant stakeholders (e.g., employees, management, customers)
	Ratings of problem importance by relevant stakeholders
Brainstorming Stage	
Quantity of ideas (fluency)	Count of the number of ideas generated
Originality of ideas	Ratings of the uniqueness of each idea
Solution Development	
Potential implementation cost	Ratings of potential solution cost by management
	Rankings of solutions from least to most cost
Potential benefit	Ratings of potential solution benefit by management
	Rankings of solutions from least to most beneficial
Flexibility	Cross-functional management ratings to assess the degree to which solution appeals to multiple stakeholder groups
	Management ratings of the complexity and multifaceted nature of the solution
Elaboration	Ratings or rankings of the number of ideas generated during brainstorming integrated into the solution
	Ratings or rankings to evaluate the completeness of a given solution (e.g., clarity)
Implementation	
Efficiency	Estimates of time, budget
	Ratio of performance to time
Quality	Ratings of quality dimensions, either inductively or deductively derived

Note. The indicators and measures presented here represent some criteria for evaluating outcomes at the various stages of problem solving. They by no means provide an exhaustive list.

the problem in the problem identification stage through the use of ratings and rankings.

The second stage of group problem solving is the *brainstorming* stage. In this stage the group generates as many ideas as possible to be used in solving the problem, without evaluating the merit of those ideas (Kramer, Fleming, & Mannis, 2001; Offner, Kramer, & Winter, 1996). Therefore, the goal of brainstorming is to generate a list of possible ideas for solving the problem before proceeding onto the next stage.

Evaluating brainstorming effectiveness can include two important criteria: the quantity and the originality of ideas. The quantity of ideas generated by a brainstorming group is commonly referred to as *fluency* (Paulus, 2000). The larger the number of ideas, the more likely the group is to develop a multifaceted solution that accounts for multiple viewpoints (Paulus, 2000). Although generating a large number of ideas may be important at later stages of problem solving, generating *original* ideas is also important (Paulus, 2000). If a group generates novel or original ideas, then the group is more likely to develop a creative solution (Unsworth, 2001). Although some ideas may not seem feasible at the time, they provide creative input into the later stages of problem solving. Table 7.1 presents ways to measure fluency and originality in brainstorming through the use of frequencies and ratings.

The third stage of problem solving requires that the ideas generated during brainstorming be evaluated and synthesized into a *solution* or *recommendation*. This stage may result in the creation of multiple alternative solutions to be evaluated (Orlitzky & Hirokawa, 2001), or it may result in a single recommended solution. In some problem-solving groups, solution development may culminate only in recommendations to be evaluated by management. A group may also revisit various problem-solving stages as it receives feedback from various sources (e.g., management, the environment; Marks et al., 2001).

Solutions developed at this stage can be evaluated using at least four criteria: cost, potential benefit, flexibility, and elaboration. *Cost* refers to the estimated amount of resources required to effectively implement the solution, estimated as time, money, or manpower (Sundstrom, DeMeuse, & Futrell, 1990). *Potential benefits* may include increases in organizational goal attainment (e.g., increased return-on-investment), organizational capabilities (e.g., the establishment of in-house training facilities), or softer organizational measures (e.g., employee participation or commitment; Levine et al., 2000). *Flexibility* refers to the extent to which a solution considers multiple perspectives or contains a multifaceted approach (Paulus, 2000). A solution that addresses and integrates the views of multiple stakeholder groups has a high degree of flexibility. Thus, a new product solution that contains a customer-focused component (e.g., seek customer input), an employee-focused component (e.g., training in sales), and a marketing component (e.g., advertising) would be a more flexible solution than one containing only an employee-focused component. Finally, *elaboration* refers to the ability of the group to synthesize and integrate the ideas generated during brainstorming and its ability to articulate that solution (Paulus, 2000). The ability to integrate a variety of ideas generated during brainstorming into one solution and to articulate that solution becomes important if the solution is to be implemented effectively and have the desired outcomes. Table 7.1 presents ways to measure cost, potential benefit, flexibility, and elaboration through ranking and rating methods.

The final stage of problem solving involves the *implementation* of the solution. This stage is often the most complicated, time-consuming, and difficult (Floyd & Lane, 2000; Katzenbach & Smith, 1994). In some organizations, individuals outside the problem-solving group may be responsible for this final stage. Implementation requires knowledge of the system within which it is to occur, the ability to develop contingencies in the event of setbacks, the flexibility to experiment with alternate approaches, and the support (e.g., time, expertise, finances) required to institutionalize change (Uhl-Bien & Graen, 1998).

At this stage, at least two evaluation criteria are important. The first concerns the *efficiency* with which implementation occurred. Efficiency can refer to the amount of time required to implement the proposed solution, or it may refer to the degree to which the activities occurred under budget. The second evaluation criterion is *quality*. Quality implementation processes are those that allocate the appropriate resources to ensure that it occurs fully and effectively (Katzenbach & Smith, 1994; Sundstrom et al., 1990). For example, if an organization chooses to institute quality control processes, it must allocate the appropriate type and amount of resources (e.g., technology, training) to ensure that those quality control processes are implemented effectively. Table 7.1 presents ways of measuring implementation effectiveness.

As discussed, the various stages of problem solving follow a logical progression from problem identification to implementation. *Proposition 1* of the GAPS model suggests that outputs at one stage serve as inputs into subsequent stages of the group problem-solving process. That is, the results of problem identification influence the ideas generated during brainstorming, which serve as the input into the solution, which serves as the input into implementation. *Proposition 1* argues that when evaluating a solution, whether in research or applied settings, the number and originality of ideas generated during brainstorming will influence the quality of the solution generated by the group. Therefore, if groups do not generate enough creative ideas during brainstorming, the resulting solution will be negatively affected.

Although the group problem-solving stages are key elements in the GAPS model, the stages are influenced by and influence affect. The GAPS model proposes two specific bidirectional relationships between affect and group problem-solving performance. The bidirectional nature of these relationships reflects the transactional nature of the GAPS model. *Proposition 2* suggests that both individual affective processes and group affective norms influence and are influenced by the problem-solving process. *Proposition 2* suggests that not only do individual affective processes and group affective norms serve as input into the problem-solving process, but they can also be considered outcomes of the process. Outcomes at each stage of the problem-solving process serve as feedback to both the individual and the group about performance, the processes used to achieve performance, and the norms that have developed within the group. Therefore, positive performance at any one stage may result in increased positive affect that will influence the next stage in the process (George & Zhou, 2002). Negative performance, on the other hand, may result in negative affect, which may signal a need to adjust processes or norms within the group (George & Zhou, 2002). If the negative affect is not managed appropriately, it will become reinforced, creating a negative group atmosphere.

In the next subsection, we discuss in more detail the relationship between *individual affective processes* and performance at each stage of the problem-solving process. Then, we discuss the relationship between *group affective norms* and performance at each stage of the process. These proposed relationships were derived through the synthesis of both individual- and group-level research, as well as some hypothesized relationships.

Relationship Between Individual Affective Processes and Performance

Based on previous literature at both the individual and group levels, individual affective processes may influence performance at all four stages of the problem-solving process. With regard to problem identification, research has suggested that affect influences an individual's orientation toward approach or avoidance (Carver, 2001; Erez & Isen, 2002). Positive affect facilitates an orientation toward approach, and negative affect facilitates an orientation toward avoidance. Consequently, during problem identification, positive affect is likely to foster a motivation among individual group members to perceive the problem as an opportunity to approach potential positive outcomes, whereas negative affect is likely to foster a motivation among individual group members to perceive the problem as an opportunity to avoid potential negative outcomes. Similarly, positive affect promotes an orientation toward more serious or important problems and away from less important problems. Grawitch, Munz, Elliott, and Mathis (2003) induced positive and neutral affect within workgroup members and asked them to identify important problems within their organization. Grawitch et al. (2003) obtained peer rankings of the identified problems and determined that when group members were induced to experience positive affect, their groups identified more important problems than did groups whose members were induced to experience neutral affect. The results suggested that positive affect orients group members toward more important problem domains and away from less important domains.

With regard to brainstorming, positive affect increases both the overall number of ideas and the number of original ideas that are generated by individuals (Isen, 2000). Additionally, this research has suggested that negative affect has no effect on individual-level idea generation. Isen (2000) argued that increased cognitive flexibility results from the experience of positive affect, which leads to the generation of a greater number of ideas. Although there have been few studies conducted at the group level, our research suggests that when group members are induced to experience positive affect, there is little or no effect on fluency (i.e., the absolute number of ideas generated; Grawitch et al., 2003; Grawitch, Munz, & Kramer, 2003). Instead, when asked to brainstorm ideas to solve a particular problem, induced positive affect increases the originality of the ideas (Grawitch et al., 2003). In comparison, induced negative affect has no effect on group brainstorming outcomes as compared to neutral affect (Grawitch et al., 2003).

In terms of solution development, no research has examined the relationship between individual-level affective processes and performance at the group level. Instead, using individual-level research as a source of hypotheses, we propose four sets of relationships between affect and performance at this stage of problem solving. *First*, positive affect promotes expanded cognitive functioning within individuals, allowing them to synthesize information more effectively (Isen, 2000; Isen & Means, 1983) and to consider a wider variety of options before making a decision (Fredrickson, 2001). Therefore, we hypothesize that positive affect permits group members to more efficiently synthesize and integrate the ideas they generated during brainstorming, increasing solution elaboration. *Second*, because positive affect allows individuals to see the broader system and process information at a systems level (Gasper & Clore, 2002), we hypothesize that positive affect permits group members to consider a systems perspective and integrate the concerns of multiple stakeholders, increasing solution flexibility. *Third*, positive affect increases the motivation to approach positive outcomes, increasing the desire for growth and achievement (Carver, 2001; Higgins, 1998). Hence, we hypothesize that positive affect motivates group members to focus on maximizing positive outcomes, leading to solutions that possess a higher potential benefit, which may also increase the potential implementation cost. *Finally*, because negative affect motivates individuals away from potential threats and toward safety and security (Carver, 2001; Higgins, 1998), we hypothesize that negative affect leads to solutions that possess less potential risk (and benefit), but also less potential cost. These four hypotheses require focused empirical attention in future research.

The influence of individual affective processes on implementation may be somewhat more complex than the influence on problem identification, brainstorming, and solution development. In many organizations one group generates the solution, and a second group implements it (Katzenbach & Smith, 1994). The effectiveness of that implementation may be influenced by the quality of the solution that was developed. If the solution is complex and requires broad participation, implementation processes may require the addition of more group members or the development of subgroups (Katzenbach & Smith, 1994). Therefore, implementation may be viewed as a series of activities, resulting in assessments of each activity required for effective implementation.

Our research suggests that positive affect has an effect on a group's ability to implement its own solution. Grawitch et al. (2003) found that groups whose members were induced to experience positive affect received higher overall performance scores and were more efficient in their implementation processes than were control groups. Consequently, it may be that positive affect allows groups responsible for implementation to more effectively (a) determine how to implement a solution, and (b) anticipate system-wide effects and plan contingencies.

Relationship Between Group Affective Norms and Performance

Although the direct relationship between affect and group performance at the various stages of problem solving result from individual affective processes, group affective norms also play a role in problem-solving performance. *Proposition 2* of the GAPS model suggests that individual affective processes influence the development of group affective norms, which in turn influence the individual affective processes operating within the group setting. This proposition is based on the premise that group members influence each other's affective experiences, which in turn influence the affective norms of the workgroup (George, 1990). As group members begin to sanction others' affective reactions and affect management strategies, those affective reactions and strategies influence the group's affective norms. For example, if group members sanction venting as an affect management process either explicitly (e.g., members encourage others to blow off steam when upset) or implicitly (e.g., members listen attentively as another member vents), then venting becomes an accepted means of regulating negative affect. Additionally, if the group does not develop effective strategies for regulating negative affect when it occurs, the group is likely to develop a more negative group atmosphere. As affect regulation and group atmosphere norms develop, they begin to influence the affective experiences of members of the workgroup, creating a consistent level of affect within the group (George, 1990).

For group affective norms to influence the problem-solving process, they must have time to develop. *Proposition 3* of the GAPS model directly follows *Proposition 2* and states that as groups mature, group affective norms become more influential and individual affective processes become less influential. In the GAPS model, this is represented by the decreasing density (thickness) of the arrows stemming from individual affective processes and the increasing density (thickness) of the arrows corresponding to group affective norms. This is not to say that individual affective processes disappear as groups mature. Instead, group norms drive individual processes (Tuckman, 1965). That is, individual affective processes become more a product of group affective norms than individual-level factors. Furthermore, as stable, long-term groups revisit the problem-solving process (e.g., a long-term group focuses on solving a new problem), the influence of group affective norms may remain consistent.

There has been little published research examining the influence of group affective norms on problem-solving performance at the group level. When discussing the relationship between group atmosphere and decision frames to problem-solving performance, we are discussing hypothesized relationships based on our review and understanding of the literature.

The Importance of Group Atmosphere to Performance.   The group atmosphere has the ability to influence all four stages of the group problem-solving process. A positive group atmosphere leads to a more open and constructive environment, whereas a negative group atmosphere leads to a critical, harsh environment (Bierhoff & Müller, 1999). Based on the work of Bierhoff and Müller (1999), we hypothesize that during the problem identification, brainstorming, and solution development stages, the group atmosphere determines how forthcoming and open group members are in presenting their ideas. In the problem identification stage, a positive group atmosphere allows group members the opportunity to discuss organizational problems more openly, resulting in the identification of more serious problems that require immediate attention. Because of its destructive qualities, a negative group atmosphere does not permit group members to discuss potential problems openly, resulting in the identification of less difficult and more superficial problems.

In the brainstorming stage, we propose that a positive group atmosphere leads individuals to provide as many ideas as possible, without fearing criticism from other group members, but that a negative group atmosphere leads group members to censor their ideas for fear that other members will criticize those ideas. The fear of criticism in idea-generating groups is also known as evaluation apprehension and may cause groups to generate fewer ideas than they would without the presence of evaluation apprehension (Diehl & Stroebe, 1991; Kramer et al., 2001; Offner et al., 1996). Our position is that a positive group atmosphere results in more ideas overall and more original ideas than a negative group atmosphere.

In the solution development stage, we hypothesize that the group atmosphere has a similar influence. A positive atmosphere fosters a more open and constructive environment in which to evaluate ideas (Bierhoff & Müller, 1999) and reach the optimal solution. Because of the open and constructive nature of the positive group atmosphere, the resulting solution may possess high flexibility, elaboration, and an optimized cost-benefit ratio. Conversely, a negative group atmosphere leads to destructive criticism, causing group members to censor themselves to avoid confrontation. This may result in a solution that has low flexibility (limited in addressing the views of multiple stakeholder groups) and low elaboration (addressing only a subset of the organizational system rather than the total system).

Finally, in the implementation stage, a positive group atmosphere should foster teamwork and cooperation among group members because of the mutual respect that is created by that atmosphere (Katzenbach & Smith, 1994). Alternatively, a negative group atmosphere should undermine the cooperation and teamwork required for effective implementation. As a result, a positive group atmosphere may result in greater implementation efficiency and quality, whereas a negative atmosphere may inhibit both efficiency and quality.

The Importance of Decision Frames to Performance.   The group atmosphere influences group problem-solving effectiveness through the constructive or destructive nature of group interactions, but the decision frame may influence problem-solving effectiveness through more cognitive means. The decision frame refers to the extent to which the group seeks to approach (or avoid) potentially positive (or negative) outcomes and serves as a focal point for ideas and solutions (Levine et al., 2000). At the problem identification stage, the decision frame influences the ways in which the group identifies and defines the problem. A promotion-focused (or prevention-focused) frame motivates the group to attain positive (or avoid negative) outcomes. Therefore, the decision frame used by the group in the problem identification stage serves as a source of approach or avoidance motivation throughout the problem-solving process.

In the brainstorming stage, the way the problem is framed influences the types of ideas that are generated (Levine et al., 2000). For example, a group considering the issue of customer satisfaction might frame the problem as "How do we reduce customer complaints?" and consequently, conservative ideas to improve the status quo may result (e.g., lower defect rates, better sales training) that are directed at avoiding negative outcomes (i.e., customer complaints). If the group frames the problem as "How do we increase customer satisfaction?" many of the same ideas may result, but additional innovative ideas may also surface, especially ideas that may change the status quo (e.g., expand our product lines, offer additional services), directed at attaining positive outcomes (i.e., customer satisfaction). Therefore, we hypothesize that at the brainstorming stage, groups using a promotion-focused frame produce more ideas and more original ideas than groups using a prevention-focused frame.

The expanded problem conceptualization is also likely to influence the solution developed by the group. Groups using a promotion-focused frame adopt riskier solutions than those using a prevention-focused frame (Levine et al., 2000). These promotion-focused solutions may possess higher potential benefits for the organization (or a lower cost-benefit ratio) and greater flexibility. When implementing the solution, a promotion-focused frame, because it emphasizes the maximization of achievement and growth, is more likely to lead to experimentation than a prevention-focused frame, which emphasizes the maximization of safety and security (Floyd & Lane, 2000; Levine et al., 2000).

As discussed, both individual and group affect play a role in the various stages of group problem solving. Many of the relationships just discussed are hypothesized relationships, because of the lack of empirical research. When considering the application of the GAPS model to organizations, an additional issue that must be addressed is context.

The Importance of Context in Understanding GAPS Relationships

Problem-solving groups operate within a specific context that includes both organizational and group factors (Sundstrom et al., 1990). These factors may alter the influence of affect at various stages of the problem-solving process. As a result, contextual factors can have implications for the application of the GAPS model.

Organizational Context

Two organizational context factors that are especially relevant to the GAPS model are performance management systems and organizational culture. These two factors provide a strong normative influence on behavior. *Performance management systems* influence the extent to which groups are rewarded for group performance. The system used to reward performance can foster higher levels of interdependency among group members, making processes of mutual affective influence more possible. Further, the extent to which the organization rewards and reinforces group performance outcomes, especially solution quality and implementation effectiveness, can serve as a continuous source of feedback (George & Zhou, 2002), creating stronger relationships between individual affect and group performance.

Organizational culture is another contextual factor that can influence relationships in the GAPS model. First, cultural norms about the expression of affect in the workplace may influence the development of group processes to effectively manage that affect. Many organizations assume that affective expression is incongruent with the desired tone of the workplace. Consequently, employees are often discouraged from expressing their genuine affective states, when those affective states violate organizational norms. Instead, employees are often compelled to express only those affective states that are sanctioned by the organization (i.e., emotional labor; Fisher & Ashkanasy, 2000a; see also previous chapters of this book). If individuals within a workgroup are implicitly or explicitly discouraged from affective expression in the workplace, then the group will have difficulty developing effective affect management norms.

Additionally, culture can be a determinant of initial affective processes that individuals bring with them to a new group setting. For example, if an organization regularly uses workgroups to identify solutions but then never actually implements those solutions, the organization may establish norms that participation in such groups is a waste of time (Schein, 1990). In those cases negative affect may pervade problem-solving groups initially, and over time, this negative affect may create a negative group atmosphere and few positive outcomes.

Group Context

Group contextual factors can also influence the GAPS model. Although many group-level factors can influence the development of affect in workgroups, we discuss two important factors: (a) the duration of the group's existence, and (b) the functional nature of group composition.

The *duration of a group's existence* has been proposed to play an important role in the development of group affective norms. Grawitch et al. (2003) argued that there are differences in the expected duration of a group's existence from the moment the group is designed or conceived. That is, some groups are designed to be long-term workgroups, chartered to complete on-going or recurring tasks over a prolonged period of time or to complete large-scale projects within the organization. Many of these groups can be thought of as long-term workgroups. These groups accomplish the daily business of the organization, and they are generally responsible for maintaining or increasing some desired performance standard. Alternatively, other groups tend to be short-term in nature, or temporary workgroups. These workgroups are brought together for a finite period of time within which they are chartered to complete one or more given tasks (Uhl-Bien & Graen, 1998), such as launching a new product. Once the assigned task is completed, temporary workgroups disband, although some may develop into long-term groups. Often, short-term temporary workgroups do not have the time required to develop group processes, reducing or negating the relative influence of group affective norms on problem-solving performance.

The *functional nature of group composition* can also influence the GAPS model. Some groups are composed of members from the same functional unit (e.g., a group of marketing analysts). These workgroups are organized according to "similarity in the skills, expertise, and resource use of members" (Uhl-Bien & Graen, 1998, p. 341). They have open lines of communication and coordination, permitting members to better interact with each other because of their common background and training. Conversely, other groups are cross-functional. They are composed of a variety of individuals from different functional areas within the organization and often bring together individuals with dissimilar, but complementary, skills, educations, and backgrounds (Katzenbach & Smith, 1994).

Because they come from different functional units, members of cross-functional groups often represent different subcultures within the organization, bringing potentially conflicting normative influences to the group setting. This may increase the amount of time required for cross-functional groups to develop effective norms for regulating and using affect (Uhl-Bien & Graen, 1998). Because cross-functional groups often have difficulty communicating and resolving conflict (Uhl-Bien & Graen, 1998), they also may experience greater levels of negative affect in the early stages, which may lead to a negative group atmosphere or prevention-focused decision frame. Because of the difficulties that exist in cross-functional groups, we propose that functional groups develop more effective affect regulation norms in significantly less time than cross-functional groups.

The organizational and group context has implications for the relationships in the GAPS model. However, the model itself suggests several application and research directions. That is, although the GAPS model does require future research, some of the relationships discussed could be capitalized on by problem-solving groups in organizations. In the final subsections we focus on both practical and research implications.

Practical Implications of the GAPS Model

Although the GAPS model is a theoretical model and requires extensive future research, there are some practical implications that can be drawn from its foundational research. *First*, drawing on previous individual-level research, the GAPS model indicates that both positive and negative affect possess functional utility and therefore must be capitalized on in the problem-solving context (George & Zhou, 2003). Positive affect offers the benefits of expanded cognitive processing, which can lead to more creative solutions (e.g., Fredrickson, 2001; Isen, 2000). Consequently, groups should maximize, to the extent possible, a consistent level of positive affect within the group, including the establishment of a positive group atmosphere, effective means of regulating affect, and promotion-focused decision frames.

The experience of negative affect also provides functional utility within the problem-solving context, as long as negative affective experiences do not become a regular occurrence within the workgroup. Previous individual-level research suggests that negative affect can serve as information regarding the effectiveness of processes to achieve performance (George & Zhou, 2002).

Therefore, occasional negative affective experiences within the group setting may point to improvements required in some area of group functioning. Groups should attempt *actively* to manage negative affect when it surfaces to manage and improve the group proactively and effectively (Marks et al., 2001). If the informative value of negative affect is avoided or only managed *passively*, then negative affective experiences within the workgroup may become more consistent, resulting in a negative group atmosphere (Bierhoff & Müller, 1999). Interventions can be designed to: (a) educate workgroup members on the benefits of both positive and negative affect, (b) train groups in active affect management strategies, and (c) facilitate the development of positive individual processes and group norms.

Second, the GAPS model specifies that problem-solving groups function best in contexts that facilitate group effectiveness. Contextual factors (e.g., performance management systems, culture) that diminish the capacity of problem-solving groups to achieve optimal performance should be minimized. Alignment of organizational context factors facilitates optimal levels of performance in a variety of workgroups, especially problem-solving workgroups (Sundstrom et al., 1990). For example, if a problem-solving workgroup is expected to function as a cohesive unit, there should be some incentives for group performance, rather than an emphasis only on individual performance. Key organization members must examine the expectations they have about problem-solving groups (e.g., how information is shared, commitment to the group and group performance), and promote organizational context factors that enhance the desired results.

Opportunities for Future Research

There are four broad opportunities for future research implicated by the GAPS model. *First*, an opportunity exists to test the theoretical links in the model. For example, research has yet to examine fully how group affective norms influence the various stages of problem solving, and until recently, little research has focused on the relationship between the functional aspects of affect and problem solving at the group level (Grawitch et al., 2003). *Second*, future research should test the four propositions that we set forth based on the model. For example, future research may determine whether the quality of outcomes at one stage of group problem solving (e.g., brainstorming) influences the quality of outcomes at the next stage of problem solving (e.g., solution development). Or, future research may test directly the proposition that individual affective processes influence the development of group affective norms, which reinforce and maintain individual affect. *Third*, by testing the links in the model and the propositions of the model, future research will refine and explicate more fully the ways in which affect (both positive and negative) influences group problem solving. *Finally*, the specific mechanisms through which affect influences group problem solving need to be examined. Although we have suggested several potential explanations for the relationship between affect and group problem-solving performance (e.g., informational and motivational effects), future research should more closely examine the mechanisms through which affect influences group problem solving at each stage of the process. For example, future research may determine that positive affect increases brainstorming performance due to its effects on the cognitive flexibility of group members rather than through an increase in the approach motivation of group members.

CONCLUSION

The purpose of this chapter was to discuss the implications of affect on group problem-solving processes and performance using a transactional model. The GAPS model provided us a means of examining functional affective processes that occur at the individual level and the opportunity to explore and hypothesize additional relationships between group-level affective norms and group problem-solving performance. We discussed in some detail the relationship between individual affective processes and group affective norms, and we proposed a reinforcing system in which individual affective processes influence the development of group affective norms which reinforce individual affective processes. We offered a series of hypotheses and propositions related to the GAPS model. Finally, we explored both the practical and research implications of the model. Although it is a theoretical model that has received little directed empirical attention, we believe the GAPS model provides a starting point for examining the relationships of both individual and group affect with group problem-solving performance.

ACKNOWLEDGMENTS

The authors thank Tim Huelsman, Tom Kramer, and Bob Rubin for their helpful comments on previous drafts and presentations of this chapter.

8

Nonsense Makes Sense: Humor in Social Sharing of Emotion at the Workplace

Stefan Meisiek
Xin Yao

The purpose of this theoretical chapter is to suggest a model of humor in the social sharing of emotion at the workplace. With this in view we first briefly review humor research with special reference to organization science. We then introduce the theory of social sharing of emotion (SSE), that is, the narrative framing of emotional work events in connection with the production of humor at the workplace. With the help of this theory we develop a model to clarify the process and the relevant antecedents and outcomes of humor in SSE at the workplace. We discuss in some detail the factors in our model in two phases of SSE. We contend that humor is a frequent product of SSE due to the specific social nature of the workplace. We conclude by suggesting future research directions pertaining to our model.

Emotional events are often molded in a humorous way in the course of frequent retelling after the event. An instructive example, in terms of our concerns in this theoretical chapter, appears in Linstead (1985) with an analysis of a particular case. A worker on a fruit-pie machine was left with a mutilated hand after an accident on the job. His amputated finger could not be found, and 4,000 pies were discarded. In the days and weeks that followed, his coworkers reinvoked the emotional event among themselves. Linstead identified comments, remarks, discussions, and jokes in which the emotional event was reframed in a humorous way. One coworker recalled, "I can't remember 'em all now, but when it happened there were loads of jokes about it. It sounds terrible, dun' it, but tha'd hear a new 'un every break. I wish I could remember 'em" (Linstead, 1985, p. 753). One such joke was, " 'They were going to get some 'finger-hunter' stickers made and pack them 4000 pies' (promotion boxes usually bore a sticker marked 'Bargain Hunter')" (Linstead, 1985, p. 754). As Linstead explained, humor was added to the emotional event by the workers in order to maintain their own status, competence, and independence, and to cope with their particular work environment. In the end the event was well recognized and well established in the sensemaking of the workgroup. What is striking about this example is the molding of a negative emotional event through the injection of humor. In addition to the social effects described by Linstead, humor seems to offer a means whereby the individual can talk about strong emotional events in the social sphere of work.

Repeated storytelling produced well-established narratives, and the development and enactment of such narratives are by no means uncommon in organizational settings (Boje, 1991; Czarniavska, 1997). What emerge are caricatures reflecting the culture and beliefs of an organization, often in the shape of insights arising in organizational life and conveyed in a fairly simple and humorous, although profound, manner (Hatch, 1997; Hatch & Ehrlich, 1993). It is the initiation and development of such narratives and the humor they contain that interest us in this chapter. Research on narratives and the way they develop in the stories has largely neglected the humorous element or has taken it for granted. We are intrigued by the way a humorous view of emotional events—what we could call "humor" in a broad sense—inserts itself into the everyday interactions of the members of an organization.

In recent years emotion, together with cognition, has become recognized as a persistent factor that can help us to understand organizational behavior in areas such as leadership, job satisfaction, employee well-being, and so on (Ashforth & Humphrey, 1995). From this growing interest, theories began to emerge about emotional labor, emotional intelligence, emotional events at the workplace, and various other related concepts (Ashkanasy, Härtel, & Daus, 2002b; Weiss & Cropanzano, 1996). In this chapter we explore the progression whereby emotional events become humorous narratives as a result of interpersonal and intrapersonal processes during the social sharing of those events.

Before going into detail about the way humor may be created and shared in narratives, we need to define and qualify some of the terms to be used in this chapter. *Emotion* as we understand it is short-lived, of considerable intensity, and directed toward an object, an individual, or a collective. It is regarded as a reaction to the experiencing of an event (Frijda, 1993). *Mood*, on the other hand, is seen as less intense, longer lasting, and less focused on a specific target. In this chapter, we adopt the concept of *emotional events* as described by Weiss and Cropanzano (1996). *Event* refers to a change in an individual's present experience, and our emphasis is on the emotional consequences of the event. For our basic framework we draw on social psychological research, but also make occasional forays into ethnographical or sociological terrain, where making sense of what has occurred takes precedence over the demonstration of benefits or drawbacks (Weick, 1995).

In the following pages, we first briefly review humor research, paying particular attention to organization science. We then introduce the theory of the social sharing of emotion (SSE), that is, the narrative framing of emotional work events (Rimé, 1995; Rimé, Finkenauer, Luminet, Zech, & Philippot, 1998; Rimé, Philippot, Boca, & Mesquita, 1992), and its connection with the production of humor at the workplace. With the help of this theory we develop a model to clarify the process of humor production and the relevant antecedents and outcomes of humor in SSE at the workplace. We then discuss in detail the factors in our model in two phases of SSE. We contend that humor is a frequent product of SSE at the workplace. We conclude by suggesting future research directions pertaining to our model.

HUMOR

The study of humor goes back more than 2,000 years. Interest in the topic has spread across disciplines such as philosophy, sociology, psychology, psychiatry, communications, and anthropology (Roeckelein, 2002). Despite centuries of widespread interest in the subject, the study of humor remains fragmented. This lack of concentration is particularly noticeable in management and organizational research. In a review of humor studies within the field of management, Duncan, Smeltzer, and Leap (1990) commented that this kind of research was in its infancy compared with its status in other disciplines such as sociology and that its scattered and sporadic nature is also reflected in the definitions that researchers have used in their studies.

The definitions of humor given by Roeckelein (2002) are concerned first and foremost with explaining of bodily fluids, second with temperament, and only after that with what we generally think of as "humor" today. This reflects the origin of humor in the philosophy of Ancient Greece. The Greek physician Hippocrates (460–370 BC) believed that an imbalance among the four bodily fluids or "humors" (blood, phlegm, black bile, and yellow bile) resulted in illness and pain. Galen (200–130 BC), the Greek physician and philosopher, later proposed that four basic "temperaments" (sanguine, phlegmatic, choleric/bilious, and melancholic) reflect the state of the four bodily humors more accurately. These Greek theories thus make a connection between physiological and psychological conditions. In medieval times humor was frequently considered to be indicative of ignorance and foolishness (Roeckelein, 2002). In modern colloquial language, however, the word *humor* is described in many different ways—for example, as a stimulus, a response, or a disposition. A sense of humor has become a very desirable trait and is regarded as part of a healthy personality. (It should be noted that these observations, especially that concerning the historical status of humor, may be particularly appropriate to Western society; Roeckelein, 2002.)

According to Martin (2000), humor has cognitive, emotional, behavioral, social and psychophysiological aspects. Lefcourt and Martin (1986) classified various theories of humor into three categories: arousal theories (e.g., Freud, 1928); incongruity theories (e.g., Kant, 1790/1914); and superiority theories (e.g., Hobbes, 1650/1994). The basic idea underlying *arousal theories* is that certain types of mirthful experiences can reduce tension and negative emotional energy that have built up over time. In particular, humor helps release energy associated with negative emotions and has been assigned a unique value due to its "liberating" and "elevating" effects (Freud, 1928). Freud was writing essentially about the self-deprecating and derisive kind of humor that transforms a negatively affective situation into a laughable one. He also claimed that the fundamental quality of humor consists in the belittling of a painful reality. In other words, humor occurs when a serious situation is viewed with a playful eye, so that it appears less grave. Since Freud's time, almost all theories of humor include the idea that a changed cognition in the experience of humor generates pleasure and laughter. According to *incongruity theories*, people perceive humor in the unexpected juxtaposition of two disparate ideas, concepts, or situations. There has been considerable debate about whether a solution to such incongruity is necessary to the individual's experience of humor (e.g., Nerhardt, 1976; Suls, 1972). Regardless of this debate, incongruity theories clearly indicate the importance of the perspective angle adopted in the humor-appreciation process. Finally, *superiority theories* can be traced back to the days of Plato (428–348 BC) and Aristotle (384–322 BC). But it was Thomas Hobbes (1650/1994) who introduced this approach into the existing theory, maintaining that laughter was born of a sense of superiority over the inferior quality of others or of oneself in the past. Further, this type of humor usually conveys a sense of aggression and hostility (Hobbes, 1650/1994). However, after reviewing research of the positive effect of humor on well-being (e.g., Levine, 1977; Mishkinsky, 1977), Lefcourt and Martin (1986) contended that even in the form of expressing superiority, humor does not signal an intention to put other people down, as much as a desire to raise their own self-esteem and personal efficacy.

In summary, different theories of humor converge in the common proposition that humor provides individuals with a chance to view a particular situation from a different angle, thus creating a sense of relief and control. Studies have recorded positive physiological effects stemming from humor, such as raising the threshold for physical discomfort (Zillmann & Stocking, 1976). Similar studies have elaborated also on the connections between humor/laughter and human anatomical/cerebral functions and development, and confirmed that humor is related positively to physical and emotional well-being (see Roeckelein, 2002).

With this in mind we have defined humor as the ludicrous or absurdly incongruous that is intended to induce laughter or amusement, often displayed in exaggeration or eccentricity (cf. Roeckelein, 2002). Humor can thus be reflected in objects or the manifestations of humor (e.g., cartoons or toys), as well as in different forms of communication and mental representation (stories, jokes, or songs). Our focus, however, is on verbal accounts in face-to-face communication, as this is the most personal and common occasion for the spontaneous production of humor.

When it comes to different kinds of humor, we adapt Fry's (1963) classification that differentiates between "canned," "situational," and "practical" jokes. Fry's classification is based on the joke's position within the context in which it is told. In this chapter we do not equate "humor" with "joke" because the latter is a form of humor, and is thus a narrower concept. Instead we extend and apply Fry's (1963) framework, in that we distinguish between canned, situational, and practical humor (see Fig. 8.1).

If humor is presented with little obvious relationship to any ongoing human interaction, it qualifies as canned humor. For example, people may recall and share a humorous story from a magazine or book in the middle of a conversation, in order to amuse and entertain. Situational humor originates in the ongoing interpersonal process. Situational humor is thus spontaneous and created on the spot, whereas canned jokes are known before they are told, often demonstrating the joke-teller's conscious intention to induce a sense of mirth and laughter in the audience. In contrast, practical humor is both intentional and spontaneous in that the joker intends the humor, but its content is not predetermined; rather, it develops as the interaction unfolds (cf. Fry, 1963).

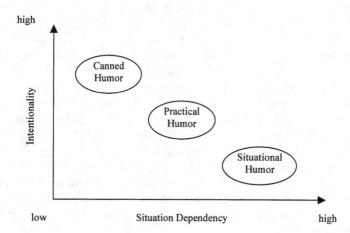

FIG. 8.1. Illustration of the relationship between situational, practical, and canned humor.

HUMOR AT THE WORKPLACE

Humor at the workplace has not received much attention among organizational scholars (exceptions include Collinson, 1988, 2002; Duncan, 1982; Duncan & Feisal, 1989; Duncan et al., 1990; Hatch, 1997; Hatch & Ehrlich, 1993). Because of the mirth that humor arouses and the lighthearted aura it often conveys, researchers tend not to take it very seriously. It is assumed that in organizations humor is a peripheral phenomenon, unrelated or only remotely related to such things as profitability, efficiency, staff turnover, job satisfaction, and so on, all of which clearly impinge on organizational effectiveness. Although in certain situations humor can be regarded as "good" and useful, few areas of organizational life actually call for it. Moreover, humor is an elusive concept that escapes precise definition; its widespread use and imprecise nature make it difficult to tie it down in models and theories. In reality, however, organization members come across humor almost daily in their work life. It can even be pretty pervasive, particularly in various types of organizational communication—live conversations, e-mails, written material, and so on—or attaching itself to certain objects or events.

Interest in humor, joking, and laughter at the workplace began to grow in the late 1950s and early 1960s (Duncan et al., 1990). The early researchers tended toward an ethnographic and sociological stance. Roy (1960), for example, reported his personal experience as a participant-observer in a small group of factory machine operatives. In an exploratory analysis he found that informal interactions, including humorous exchanges like "horseplay," helped to improve job satisfaction. In the few publications that began to call attention to humor at the workplace from the 1980s onward, humor was often defined in terms of stimulus, that is, something that can be interpreted as humorous, and response, usually laughter. Malone (1980, p. 357), for example, adopted Chapman and Foot's (1976) description of humor as "a process initiated by a humorous stimulus, such as a joke or cartoon, and terminating with some response indicative of experienced pleasure, such as laughter." The study of humor at the workplace has focused primarily on joking behavior in a group context (e.g., Duncan, 1982; Duncan et al., 1990). Here, humor has also been closely linked with communication in a group context and used interchangeably with "joke" (Duncan, 1982; Duncan & Feisal, 1989; Duncan et al., 1990). In addition, humor has been investigated as an artifact within the culture of an organization (Dandridge, Mitroff, & Joyce, 1980; Vinton, 1989).

Researchers generally seek to suggest ways in which management can foster humor with a view to improving the effectiveness of their organizations, although the feasibility of such an enterprise has not gone unchallenged (Collinson, 2002).

Although sociological, psychological, and ethnographic perspectives on humor have been adopted in previous management research, only rarely have the more theory-based psychological mechanisms been explored. Specifically, we believe that humorous accounts are created as individuals share emotional events with other members of their organizations. These events may then be spread further as one member passes them on to another, who in turn does the same, and so on. The humor contained in the original account is thus relayed, and probably modified by all these others as the sharing proceeds. Some of the humorous stories eventually become part of the organization's narrative corpus, its lore, reflecting certain characteristics of the organizational culture and introducing these to newcomers, as well as reverberating among the veteran members of the organization in a process of repetitive sharing. The emotional event thus provides the content and background for the production of humor. Hence, in this chapter we focus on the role of emotion in the creation and development of humorous narrated accounts.

SOCIAL SHARING OF EMOTION

The SSE Process

The social sharing of emotion (SSE) is conceptualized as an interpersonal process that occurs following the experience of some life event of emotional significance to an individual (Rimé et al., 1998). This line of research emerged from an interest in traumatic events, such as serious accidents, and the sudden death of a spouse (Rimé et al., 1992). People often have an urge to share their feelings and thoughts with others after the occurrence of some major negative life event. Rimé et al. (1992, 1998) argued that this phenomenon is not exclusive to major emotional events, but that it applies to daily emotional experiences as well. They identified five arguments for their own conjectures as to why social sharing occurs. Briefly, these are:

1. People share their experiences and emotional reactions in order to resolve ambiguous sensations arising from their emotions.
2. By putting an experience into words, people are able to organize the matter cognitively.
3. People seek to restore such beliefs regarding themselves as were challenged by the emotional occurrence.
4. Through sharing, people receive social support from important others, thus counteracting their own sense of insecurity.
5. Social sharing is a means whereby the collective can absorb and integrate individual affective experiences as well as developing and prescribing culturally acceptable interpretations (Rimé et al., 1998). SSE thus shows the properties that Weick (1995) noted to be essential for sensemaking in organizations.

Early studies of SSE used a procedure involving the recall of critical incidents (Rimé, Mesquita, Philippot, & Boca, 1991). Experimental studies involving the viewing of film excerpts were also conducted to address the question of memory bias and to corroborate the connection identified between emotional intensity and SSE in correlation studies (Luminet, Bouts, Delie, Manstead, & Rimé, 2000). Other studies were conducted for different age groups and across cultures and in relation to personality (see Rimé et al., 1998). The general conclusion was that SSE is a universal phenomenon that can be observed in both men and women, young and old, and across cultures. Most people share their experiences with someone else, if possible almost immediately after their occurrence, and they may continue sharing them with several receivers on more than one occasion (Rimé et al., 1991). A general positive relationship was also found between the intensity of the emotion and the frequency of social sharing (Luminet et al., 2000).

SSE at the Individual and Collective Level

To understand how SSE connects the individual and the collective levels it is important to make a distinction between two steps in social sharing. Primary social sharing of emotion (PSSE) is conceptualized as the basic form of sharing in which individuals repeatedly share their own experience with different receivers (Rimé et al., 1991). Secondary social sharing of emotion (SSSE) arises from the fact that hearing about an emotional event is itself an emotional event for those with whom the events have been shared. The receivers in PSSE may then share the heard story with other people, in much the same way they pass on rumors or gossip (Christophe & Rimé, 1997). We use *initiator* and *receiver* to refer to the two parties involved in sharing. The initiator is the one who shares the emotional event, and the receiver is the one with whom the experience is shared. In PSSE, the initiator is the one who experienced the emotional event and produces the humor. In SSSE, the initiator is the one who presents or reproduces the humorous slant they received in an earlier sharing. PSSE refers to "repeated reproduction" on the part of the individual who actually experienced the emotional event, whereas SSSE is "serial reproduction" of vicarious experience that comes with the relaying of information from A to B to C, and so on. PSSE focuses on the behavior of a single person who tells the same story repeatedly to one or more recipients. SSSE, on the other hand, focuses on a chain of individuals connected by the sharing of the same emotional event. Narratives, rumors, and gossip are common examples of the kind of thing reproduced in the SSSE.

One of the theoretical assumptions in explaining why SSE occurs is that people have a need to organize their emotional experiences cognitively (Rimé et al., 1998). Hence, sharing serves to process and complete emotional memory. Studies of shared and kept-secret memories (Finkenauer & Rimé, 1998) found that memories of unshared emotional events were associated with a more extensive search for meaning and a greater effort to get some order in one's mind about what had happened. In essence this is what Weick (1995) called sensemaking. The underlying idea of sensemaking is that reality is an ongoing accomplishment that emerges from efforts to create order and make retrospective sense of what occurs. One source and stimulant for sensemaking consists of the emotions that are elicited by significant interruptions of the everyday life of individuals (Weick, 1995, p. 46). In PSSE, individual sensemaking appears in the initiator as an explicit effort to tell a coherent story about an emotional event to the recipient and, implicitly, to themselves. The listener makes sense of the story as well, and the sensemaking activity persists throughout the process of SSSE (Rimé et al., 1998).

Consequently, the iterative process attributed to PSSE and SSSE leads to collective sensemaking, that is, the social construction of what is taken for granted as part of a shared reality (Berger & Luckmann, 1966; Weick, 1995). Collective sensemaking is inherent in social sharing, namely, in the "construction and dissemination of social knowledge on emotion" (Rimé et al., 1998). This is built largely on the receivers' processing of information and the subsequent SSSE. Receivers retain information about the shared event in light of their own emotion schemata (Shaver, Schwartz, Kirson, & O'Connor, 1987). These schemata contain simplified and easily accessible prior knowledge about particular emotions and related situations (cf. Rimé, 1995; Rimé, Philippot, & Cisamolo, 1990). The receiver highlights salient information in reference to his or her own schemata and organize it in ways that are compatible with his or her existing knowledge and expectations (Bartlett, 1932). In SSSE receivers retrieve from memory certain patterns from prior sensemaking, add details from the shared emotional event that fit their own knowledge, and pass it on to new receivers. During this recurring process of selecting, filtering, storing, and retrieving, pieces of emotional memories are added to the collective's reservoir of emotion knowledge (Shaver et al., 1987). And during this construction and reconstruction of the emotional event, diverse social schemata maintained by the various individuals involved and linked to the emotions in focus become aligned with one or a limited number of stereotypical conclusions. These are frequently expressed in a humorous story. For example, at Siemens AG there is a story about Werner von Siemens, the founder of the company and an immensely rich man, visiting the production plant one day. His contemporaries knew von Siemens as a brilliant engineer, but he was also feared as obsessed by accuracy and intolerant to ineffectiveness. He picked up a small piece of metal from the otherwise clean floor and showed it to an engineer. "Do you know what this is?" he asked. "A piece of metal," replied the intimidated engineer. "No," replied von Siemens, "this is *my* money" (Feldenkirchen, 1996). Werner von Siemens died in 1892, but the story is still told today. No one knows who started telling this story or how it has been transformed since it was first told, but somehow it became established as a humorous narrative in the Siemens culture, implying that waste should always be avoided. The event, probably in a form very different from its original one, remains as representing the collective's way of making sense of the relevant circumstances and emotions.

HUMOR IN SSE AT THE WORKPLACE

A large part of people's lives revolve around their work, the organizations they work for, and the people they work with. We can thus expect that a good deal of SSE is connected with events occurring in working life. Further, because colleagues at work know about the work processes involved and are implicitly interested in work events in the organization, they are also frequently the initiators and receivers of social sharing. As such SSE proves to be a common phenomenon in organizations (Meisiek, 2002; Rimé, personal communication, 2 March 2003).

Earlier field studies on humor at the workplace confirmed that humor is a frequent mode for communication at all functional levels of the organization (Collinson, 1988; Hatch, 1997; Hatch & Ehrlich, 1993; Linstead, 1985; Roy, 1960), which leads us to believe that it is presumably also an important ingredient in the process of SSE at the workplace and that it contributes to general sensemaking in organizations. This ties up with another observation, namely, that humor creates in those involved a sense of relief and of being in control.

The workplace has often been described as a place where the expression of strong emotion is widely regarded as inappropriate; unless it is officially sanctioned as part of the work role (Hochschild, 1983). Organizations do not expect their workforce to give way to emotion, either positive or negative, for fear that they might do something to harm the organization's policies or its culture (Ashforth & Humphrey, 1995). Consequently, organizations develop and maintain *display rules* as part of their culture, indicating the appropriate range, intensity, duration, and even the target of emotional expressions in certain given situations (Ekman & Friesen, 1969; Hochschild, 1983). It has been suggested, too, that this could lead to the repression of emotional displays that are regarded as inappropriate (Hochschild, 1983). However, as SSE theory tells us, emotion does demand articulation for sensemaking purposes (Rimé et al., 1998). Humor—which is generally regarded as an appropriate and beneficial ingredient in organizations (Collinson, 2002)—can thus be regarded as a useful mode for invoking emotional events in the complex social setting of the workplace. SSE also allows the person who shares the emotional event a chance to back away from the story, for example by adding, "I was just kidding. . . ." Moreover, humor offers a way of describing an emotional event that doesn't demand any direct empathy on the part of a receiver, which is particularly important when confiding in receivers that are not intimates. And apart from all this, emotional events that have been transformed into humorous stories are pleasant for people to hear and are more likely to be well received.

As regards the basic SSE process, an important observation is that people tend to share emotional experiences with close others, such as parents, family members, spouses, or close friends (Rimé et al., 1998). In an organizational setting, however, intimates may not be very numerous, such as their coworkers, which means that employees have to resort to sharing emotional experiences with people with whom they are unlikely to have such a close relationship. Sharing may then occur because of some common experience or mutual understanding of the background to the work events, or because employees are connected through some aspect of organizational life like their department or their functional area. A work setting thus provides both opportunities and constraints when it comes to the sharing of emotional experiences—which ones to share, how to share them, and where. The actual emotional events shared at work may of course be private as well as work related, but the latter can be expected to have more impact on subsequent organizational processes.

We propose next that emotional events can be transformed into practical humor and then into canned humor by way of PSSE and SSSE. Eventually they may crystallize into narratives that reflect the culture, history, and characteristics of the organization in question and of its employees. This proposition is addressed in this chapter by exploring the critical factors of the relationship between initiator and receiver, the emotions associated with an event, the organizational context, and the individual characteristics that encourage initiators to adopt a humorous approach in presenting a story to their receivers. Drawing on research into SSE and humor in organizations, Fig. 8.2 demonstrates the PSSE and SSSE process.

The process begins with the need felt by individuals to share an event that carries emotional significance for themselves. In the course of PSSE the initiator continues to process the emotional event cognitively and in doing so generates meaning. When an initiator launches the sharing with a view to presenting the emotional event in a humorous way, it may become possible to generate practical humor as the sharing evolves. In the course of this sharing the initiator and the receiver both have an opportunity to make sense of the emotional event. The initiator also gets a chance to go through the process over and over again and to revisit the meanings he or she has constructed and perhaps reconstructed over time. The receiver, on the other hand, may proceed to share the emotional event with other individuals within the organizations. The receiver retains the memory not only of what had happened to the initiator, but also the humor created during the PSSE. If the original humor is successfully conveyed, it is very likely to be retained in the organizational system, as repeated SSSE occurs and evolves as a humorous aspect of the narrative. However, although the emotional event may eventually become an example of

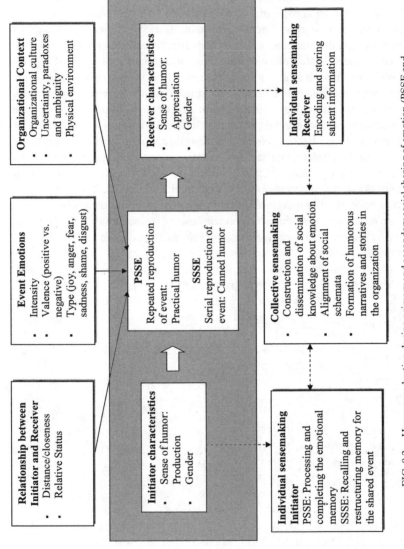

FIG. 8.2. Humor production during primary and secondary social sharing of emotion (PSSE and SSSE).

canned humor, the original story is likely to change in the process of the secondary sharing. As in the primary sharing process, the initiator and receiver both make sense of the emotional event in the course of sharing it, while also extending their understanding of the organization, the individuals concerned, and the particular situation involved. These memories are retained, and they help people who are exposed to them to make sense of their environment in the present and the future. It is also probable that several receivers may be able to share the same emotional events and their accompanying humor on several occasions. This labyrinth of mutual exchanges reinforces, and possibly alters or corrects, the way people remember and make sense of the emotional event, which in turn facilitates collective sensemaking in the organization. It is also likely that people are sharing is not a single emotional event but a whole emotional episode consisting of a series of emotional events around a common theme (Weiss & Cropanzano, 1996). Collective sensemaking can thus also be based on a chain of related events.

We next look at PSSE and SSSE separately, in order to discuss the specific circumstances under which humor relating to a shared emotional event may be produced. In other words we look at the antecedents of practical humor creation in PSSE and of canned humor production in SSSE.

HUMOR IN PSSE

Relationship Between Initiator and Receiver

Although most of us find at least some coworkers with whom we feel reasonably comfortable to "be ourselves" and whom we trust with our emotional experiences, we are rather more alert to the needs of self-presentation at the workplace than we are elsewhere (Bolina, 1999). Our motives for impression management may vary, depending on our goals and values. For example, if people want to rise quickly in the organizational hierarchy, they will seek to present themselves as competent and conscientious workers (Wayne & Ferris, 1990). They will then engage in various behaviors that convey such an image. Although it is usually assumed that humor helps to build up a desirable impression, because it is commonly interpreted as a favorable quality, it can backfire if used inappropriately. Thus an initiator has to consider the listener: Who is this person with whom they are sharing an experience, and does the relationship really allow for the expression of humor? Two attributes of the relation may be significant here: the distance/closeness between initiator and receiver, and their relative status in the organization.

Distance/closeness is regarded as a fundamental dimension of interpersonal behavior (e.g., Brown & Levinson, 1987; Spencer-Oatey, 1997). It is related to friendliness and affect or the degree of association. Hays's (1984) conceptualization of close and casual friendships can be used to tap this dimension (Spencer-Oatey, 1997). There are four behavioral contents that distinguish between close and distant relations: companionship, consideration, self-disclosure, and affection. Self-disclosure is related most closely to SSE. It pertains to disclosing or discussing information about oneself, to the exchange of ideas, facts, opinions, or confidences on any topic. This aspect of a close relationship corresponds to the SSE findings that emotional experiences are more frequently disclosed to intimate others rather than to strangers or to people of less importance to the focal individual at that particular stage in his or her life—an observation also suggesting that there is more freedom for self-disclosure in close relationships. However, because close relationships at work are rare, and because humor signals informality and reduces social distance (Graham, 1995; Sykes, 1966), closeness may be enhanced in primary sharing at the workplace by the introduction of humor into the exchange.

> Proposition 1: Due to their relative distance between coworkers, people are more likely to produce humor when they share an emotional event at the workplace than when sharing events with their personal intimates.

The *relative status* of the initiator and the receiver is another important aspect. Studies have shown that low-status individuals tend not to joke very much with those of higher status (e.g., Vinton, 1989). Hence, a big difference in status hampers the production of humor, and thus perhaps of SSE as well. In a study of humor in workgroups Duncan and Feisal (1989) reported that "solid citizens," that is to say, members of a group who possessed no formal authority and who were socially close to the group's rank-and-file members, were well received by the others in the group when it came to joking behavior. They could joke about the others and were among the favorite targets for other people's jokes, which suggests that they were liked and enjoyed special joking privileges. Lundberg (1969) found that people of similar status enjoyed themselves more when spending time exclusively with one another.

> Proposition 2: People are more likely to produce humor when sharing an emotional event with someone of equal or lower organizational status than when sharing with someone of higher status.

Event Emotions

Whether or not humor can be made out of an event, and the type of humor thus created may be affected by the intensity, the valence, and the type of the emotions associated with the event in question.

As noted earlier, SSE increases with the intensity of the emotional event. This observation has been corroborated by the results of studies of emotional secrecy in which Finkenauer and Rimé (1998) found that *intensity and valence* were not necessarily precursors of emotional secrecy. To the present authors' knowledge, no research has been done on the relationship between the intensity or valence of an emotion and the content, format, or quality of its sharing. However, it is reasonable to assume that the more intensive an emotion is, the more of its original perspective and framework will be retained in its social sharing compared with those of less intensive emotions. At the workplace, however, the expression of intense emotions may be hampered by the organizational display rules mentioned earlier (Hochschild, 1983). Thus, intense emotional events may be quickly converted into humorous narratives, to adapt them to the organizational context. This relationship between the intensity of emotion and the production of humor is also addressed in arousal theory (see Lefcourt & Martin, 1986). The basic idea underlying arousal theories is that, in the course of time, laughter can reduce tension and the buildup of energy (Freud, 1928). Thus a very intensive emotional experience at the workplace may be shared sooner rather than later and with lots of humorous comments. Further, the really intense emotions that may normally require a good deal of time and several iterations before they can be viewed in a different light (Rimé et al., 1998) will reappear sooner as an event in the production of practical humor in PSSE at the workplace. The valence of the emotions concerned may also influence the timing of the humor production—in that positive emotions delay the onset of this production for longer than negative emotions do (Linstead, 1985).

Proposition 3a: People are more likely to produce humor in PSSE at the workplace if they are sharing events of higher emotional intensity than when they are sharing events of less emotional intensity.

Proposition 3b: People are more likely to produce humor in PSSE at the workplace when they are sharing events of negative valence when they are sharing events of positive value.

Finkenauer and Rimé (1998) also found that emotional secrecy is correlated positively with events eliciting negative social emotions such as shame and guilt. An immediate implication of this in relation to the production of humor is that such emotions are probably less likely to become a subject of humor to begin with. And even if they were, the humor may be unintended, due to an underlying desire to avoid revealing socially inappropriate behaviors or thoughts.

Proposition 4: People are less likely to produce humor in PSSE at the workplace in relation to events that elicit negative social emotions such as shame and guilt.

Organizational Context

Context also affects the behavior of organizational members. Here we consider three types of contextual factors: uncertainty and ambiguity, organizational culture, and the physical environment.

Any *uncertain, paradoxical, and/or ambiguous* elements in an organization also have an impact on humor in PSSE at the workplace. Uncertainty often develops in the course of radical changes such as mergers and acquisitions, and it arouses strong emotions (Huy, 1999). The prevalence of emotional events in periods of organizational change encourages the primary sharing, thus also promoting the production of humor as a coping and sensemaking strategy. Hatch and Ehrlich (1993) also contended that when an organization is infused with paradoxes and ambiguity is particularly marked, humorous comments will flourish. Hatch (1997) identified irony in particular as a sign that employees are confronting contradictions. Observations like these suggest that an uncertain and ambiguous organizational environment provides a fertile ground for the production of humor in PSSE.

> Proposition 5: People are more likely to produce humor in PSSE at the workplace if the organizational environment is uncertain, paradoxical, and/or ambiguous.

Culture and language serve as a sense-giving backdrop for humor at the workplace. A joke, even one made with the best intentions, may not always be appreciated, due to differences in cultural values regarding the target or the style of the humor. In much the same way, ethnicity or language may have a significant impact on humorous behavior at work. Duncan (1982) asked, "Have you ever sat through a comedy in a foreign country and discovered that 'everybody is laughing but me'? Or, even worse, 'no one is laughing but me'?" In our model we consider organizational cultures favorable to humor. A strong humor culture encourages humor at the workplace. Some entrepreneurs such as the founder of Southwest Airlines recognize and promote a pro-humor culture (Quick, 1992). In this context, it has been proposed that humor can help to maintain an organizational culture (Linsted, 1985), and that humor can be an artifact or manifestation of a culture (Dandridge, 1986). In a culture of humor, organizational members believe that humor offers a desirable approach to daily activities. People are more conscious of humor and will act on this belief by creating humor in PSSE as they interact with others in the organization. In an organizational culture of humor, however, joking behavior may also be used as a cover for strong emotions. Buroway (1979) discovered that racial prejudice between Black and Caucasian workers was articulated in jokes on the shop floor. Because the production process demanded a degree of cooperation between workers, overt racial hostility had to be kept to a minimum and was therefore diluted by humor.

Proposition 6: People are more likely to produce humor in PSSE when the culture of their organization encourages humor at the workplace.

To our knowledge, researchers have not yet examined the relationship between the physical environment and humor at the workplace. But the physical environment may in fact contribute to the production of humor in PSSE, thus also enhancing a culture of humor. Davis (1984) identified three key elements in the physical environment: physical structure, physical stimuli, and symbolic artifacts. All three of these can affect people's perception of their environment and the way they interact with each other, which in turn will either encourage or discourage the production of humor.

People are more likely to interact with others who are physically close. Thus, workplaces whose physical structure leaves employees isolated or with little formal or informal contact with one another will restricts SSE and the chances it offers for producing humor. If on the other hand people are given more opportunities for meeting, they will have more time to develop relationships providing opportunities for humorous interaction (Davis, 1984). Within the physical structure, behavior is also affected by physical stimuli: the color scheme in the office (visual), the sound of the phone bell (audio), or the smell of the coffee brewer (olfactory). Most of the literature on physical stimuli focuses on the way the stimuli are manipulated in order to reduce distractions and to induce desired behaviors (Davis, 1984). Finally, symbolic artifacts are aspects of the physical environment that can direct interpretations of the social setting in a certain way. Office signs, carpeting, or type and style of furnishing, for example, can convey information about the organization and the people who work there (Davis, 1984). A workplace that is designed to be informal and enjoyable sends an implicit message to its occupants that a playful attitude is encouraged there, so that people feel more comfortable about making humorous comments, telling funny stories and laughing together with their colleagues. We believe that certain physical stimuli and symbolic artifacts may facilitate the production of humor.

Proposition 7: People are more likely to produce humor in PSSE if the physical environment at their workplace is favorable to interaction among the employees, providing pleasant stimuli and symbolic artifacts that encourage humor.

Individual Characteristics

Although the initiator may be inspired or stimulated by the receiver or by some factors of the situation, to imbue the narrative with a humorous quality, certain innate personal qualities help to also determine the possible importance of external conditions (Ross & Nisbett, 1991). In our model we consider two individual characteristics: sense of humor and gender.

A *sense of humor* is a distinct characteristic attributable to the individual. It makes a person more prone to convert emotional events into humorous stories, as well as making it easier for them to do so. A sense of humor can be regarded as a personality trait. The assumption is that there are stable differences between individual people as regards the extent to which they perceive, enjoy, and create humor (Lefcourt & Martin, 1986). However, a sense of humor is a multidimensional construct to which various meanings have been attached (Eysenck, 1972; Moody, 1978). Eysenck (1972), for example, suggested three subdivisions for the sense of humor concept, namely, the conformist, the quantitative, and the productive types. The first two refer to the extent to which an individual agrees with most other people about what is humorous, and to the frequency and immediacy of their laughter and smiles. Only the third type refers to the probability of a particular person perceiving a situation as humorous and amusing, and thus deriving humor from it (cf. Lefcourt & Martin, 1986, p. 22). Most sense of humor studies have started from individual differences in the appreciation of humor, such as a preference for particular types of humor (e.g., Eysenck, 1942, 1943; O'Connell, 1960; Redlich, Levine, & Sohler, 1951). We concentrate on the third meaning to emphasize the productive aspect of a sense of humor. In the course of PSSE, a strong sense of humor will predispose the initiator to convert an emotional event into a humorous story together with the receiver.

Proposition 8: An individual with a strong sense of humor is more likely than other people to produce humor when they share emotional events with others at work.

Studies have found *gender* differences in the appreciation and production of different types of humor (Collinson, 2002; Duncan et al., 1990; Lefcourt, 2001). Women in Western society seem to display a stronger tendency to appreciate and produce self-deprecating humor, whereas men prefer wit and jokes characterized by competition and aggression and often directed at others (Crawford & Gressley, 1991; Levine, 1976; Zillman & Stocking, 1976). In the workplace it can be expected that women may produce self-deprecating humor as a defense mechanism against stressful and disturbing events (Lefcourt & Martin, 1986). Self-deprecating humor allows people to laugh at themselves and to take things less seriously (Freud, 1928). Males at the workplace, on the other hand, tend to produce aggressive and competitive humor in connection with workplace events in which some coworker has behaved or responded in a foolish way (Collinson, 1988).

Proposition 9a: Females tend to produce self-deprecating humor in PSSE when sharing stressful work events.

Proposition 9b: Males tend to produce aggressive and competitive humor in PSSE when sharing work events that involve a colleague's behavior.

HUMOR IN SSSE

SSSE is similar to PSSE in its processes and many of its elements. Much of what has already been discussed is thus also valid for SSSE (see Fig. 8.2). However, because the initiator of SSSE has not experienced the shared emotional event personally, we can expect some differences in the nature of this kind of humor sharing. SSSE illustrates the way humorous descriptions of emotional events are developed to become well-established organizational narratives.

Sense of humor is again important to the initiator's reproduction of the humorous account (Lefcourt & Martin, 1986). However, because the initiator in SSSE has been a receiver in an earlier round of primary or secondary social sharing, the appreciation of humor is more likely to be relevant here than in its production. Only when a receiver has proved able to appreciate the humor shared earlier, as a receiver, will the person be able to share the humor that accompanies the description with a third party.

Proposition 10: People with a greater sense of humor are more likely to appreciate and to reproduce humor in SSSE at the workplace.

Similarly, *gender* differences in the appreciation of humor directly affect the retention of the humor first produced in the PSSE. A female receiver may not appreciate competitive and aggressive humor, so it is not very likely that she will then share it with someone else in a humorous form, which means that the practical humor generated in PSSE will not be preserved. On this part, a male receiver may not appreciate self-deprecating humor, which will thus be lost when the male receiver goes on to share the emotional event with someone else. The relation between the gender of the initiator, the type of humor, and the gender of the receiver may affect the choice of humorous mode: A male employee may avoid sharing aggressive humor with a female coworker, and a female employee may avoid sharing self-deprecating humor with her male colleagues (Zillman & Stocking, 1976).

Proposition 11a: Women are more likely then men to appreciate and subsequently reproduce self-deprecating humor in SSSE at the workplace.

Proposition 11b: Men are more likely than women to appreciate and subsequently reproduce aggressive and other-directed humor in SSSE at the workplace.

It can be posited that the relative impact of relationship and context may be different in SSSE. Relationships may be less important because the initiator is not the one who actually experienced the original emotional event. Over time the weight shifts toward contextual cues such as uncertainty and ambiguity, organizational culture, and the physical environment that are more likely to trigger the humorous elements in SSSE at the workplace. People may also engage in SSSE because they enjoy the humor and simply want to reproduce it.

Proposition 12: The influence of relational factors on the production of humor in SSSE is less than it is in PSSE, while the influence of contextual factors becomes greater.

In sum, the production of humor in PSSE may be a direct outcome of experienced emotional events, while the reproduction of humor in SSSE may be a direct outcome of an earlier sharing of experiences and of perceived features in the emotional events. The two stages of SSE occur in a work setting as follows. Employees experience emotional events at the workplace and share these with their coworkers, because the emotions associated with the events demand articulation for sensemaking purposes. As the employees proceed to share the experience, there are various factors—their work-based relationship with the receiver, the emotions associated with the experience, the organizational context, or their individual characteristics—that incline them to give a humorous spin to the narrative. Those receivers who appreciate the humor may then share the story socially with someone else in the organization. The receivers may also change the original story a little or give it a different humorous spin in order to adapt it to another conversational context. In this way some stories will withstand the trials of time and become well-known features of the organizational culture. They convey important aspects of organizational life in a lighthearted way that people can easily remember.

CONCLUSION

The purpose of this chapter has been to suggest a model of humor in the social sharing of emotion at the workplace. Building on prior humor research and the theory of SSE, and taking into account the specific social situation of the workplace, we have discussed the part played by humor in SSE in organizations on the one hand and, on the other, the part played by SSE in the development of humorous narratives in the organization. Our model unfolds in three steps: SSE is characterized as a theory for explaining why people share their emotional experiences in PSSE and SSSE at the workplace; PSSE is characterized as relying to a certain extent on the production of humor in organizations; stories from PSSE are transformed into organizational narratives through an iterative process of SSSE.

In organizational behavior research, humor has been widely regarded as an antecedent of emotion. It has been suggested that humor arouses emotions: joy, for example, in case the humor has been appreciated, or anger if it has been resented. Humor, thus, has been conceptualized as beneficial for the well-being and job satisfaction of the employees. This perspective seems to ignore the "ongoing" aspect of the presence of emotion in organizations. Consequently, our model aims to embed humor in the ebb and flow of emotional experiences at work, which means humor may be an outcome as well as an antecedent of emotions in organizations. Given the individual's need to articulate emotional events for sensemaking purposes and the collective's need for narratives as a "sensemaking currency" (Boje, 1991), as well as the specific social conditions at the workplace that imply relatively distant personal relationships, humor emerges as a powerful ingredient in communication at the workplace.

Sharing can occur via a telephone call, an e-mail, or a written note, but we assume that its main medium is face-to-face communication (Rimé et al., 1998). Further, although we have not directly addressed the many forms of sharing that occur—comic strips on the wall of a cubicle, ironic comments posted on a bulletin board, or artwork displayed in an office, for instance—all these and many more can be regarded as possible means of conveying affective reactions to certain events. Such things also serve to help individual people to comprehend the culture of their own organization, to learn about its norms and other people's attitude towards it. Situational humor as expressed in "horseplay" has not been considered in this chapter, as it has been identified primarily as a way of counteracting monotony or boredom and is irrelevant to our discussion on the impact of humor in organizations.

An entire emotional event can be presented as a joke, but under certain conditions it is only possible to take up certain aspects of a story, which cannot then be regarded as a complete story with a beginning and an end or as located in its own particular setting. The emotional event on which the account is based may have happened long ago, or just before it was told the first time. Or an experience may be hinted at, discussed, reshaped as a joke, and so on, without any attempt to present it as a complete story. It is not altogether clear how far such behavior can be regarded as an instance of SSE, but in the light of the theory just presented, it seems reasonable to regard it as covered by the model.

The intricacies of producing and retelling instances of practical humor make it unlikely that humor produced in the course of SSE will survive for long. Few such stories are likely to enter the corpus of organizational narratives, reflecting common grounds for the sensemaking of an event and its emotional outcomes. But when they do, they may be used to socialize and educate new employees, or as a way of strengthening bonds among the veteran employees through the frequent reiteration of emotional events. Humorous accounts of this kind can also venture beyond the borders of the organization, allowing outsiders a glimpse of various aspects of it. Humor can increase the cohesive nature of a group, or offer individual people a way of being able to talk about emotional events at work. At the same time, of course, humor serves to entertain, to strike a responsive chord in others, or to attract attention.

It seems to us that the social sharing of emotion, on which we base our ideas about the production of humor at the workplace, has not yet received much scholarly attention in organizations. We could perhaps say that it has been addressed indirectly in theories on informal communication. Certain findings from social psychology, however, encourage its use in seeking to explain organizational phenomena.

The model described in this chapter is based largely on research findings and theories developed in Western societies. Although SSE has been tested in both individualistic and collectivist cultures, theories of humor and related speculations have their roots in the individualistic world. Readers of this chapter should be cautioned about applying the same model in a collectivist context. Although we believe that the basic elements of humor—production, retention, and transformation—are likely to hold across cultures, the relation between the antecedents and production of humor may be affected by the presence of other social norms, values, or concepts of self. Social norms may dictate the amount of humor that can appropriately be shared, for example, or the kind of humor most suitable for sharing. We thus suggest that parallel studies should be conducted in both the individualistic and the collectivist type of culture, an undertaking that would contribute at the same time to cross-cultural humor research.

Although we have presented separate sets of antecedents for the production of humor in SSE, we do not deny that there may be interactive effects between them. Hence, certain factors in one category may interact with some factors in another, in this way affecting the production and reproduction of humor. At this stage of theory development we have concentrated on identifying certain factors and speculating about their possible general relationship with the phenomenon under study. Further refinement of the theory would necessarily have to build on empirical findings. A research program based on the present model could start by surveying and examining the correlation between all the antecedent factors proposed here and the creation of humor. Specific factors could then be focused and their relationship with the creation of humor tested. For example, the relation between the gender of the initiator, sense of humor, type of emotion, and the type of humor most likely to be created could be investigated by using a diary. It would be interesting to examine the survival of humorous stories produced in relation to an emotional event in relation to various characteristics of the initiator and receiver.

In brief, the intention of this chapter has been to introduce a general framework for addressing humor in SSE at the workplace and to propose some directions for research. Despite the limitations of the present approach, we suggest that humor and emotion research in organizational behavior seem to be more closely related than has been assumed in previous research. Further exploration of this relationship promises to extend the sensemaking paradigm and to contribute to social psychological research on emotions in organizations.

9

Understanding Cross-Cultural Negotiation: A Model Integrating Affective Events Theory and Communication Accommodation Theory

Mona White
Charmine E. J. Härtel
Debra Panipucci

This chapter attempts to bridge the gaps of strategic business negotiation, communication, and emotion in a cross-cultural context. In particular, we argue that miscommunications are "boundary-crossing mishaps," which are affected by the negotiator's understanding of the respective cultures (and cultural backgrounds) of the parties, negotiation skill, cultural differences, emotional awareness and regulation, negative affect, and discrepancy in convergence–divergence between the interactants. This chapter concludes that when too many hassles or mishaps occur, negotiation breaks down and the need to understand cross-cultural communication through alternative theoretical models arises.

We begin this chapter with a short case illustrating the effect of emotions and behaviors in cross-cultural negotiations.

In 2001, an Australian fertilizing company (AusFert[1]) employed a Chinese national in Australia to explore the possibility of exporting to the Chinese market. The company was already successfully exporting to American, Middle Eastern, and several European markets. Realizing that these markets are mature, the need for the company to grow into a new, possibly infant, market was recognized. After much consideration, the company decided on China.

Historically, the Chinese government had never allowed fertilizer importation and was just beginning to consider the possibilities of developing this avenue. AusFert's importation process began with obtaining an import permit in

---

[1]Not the company's real name.

China. This was a complex process as it required the establishment of a Chinese importing company (ChinFert[2]), which imported fertilizer from Australia. AusFert, however, was concerned that ChinFert might import other brands once the license was obtained, so it agreed to enter into a joint venture with an importing company in China to eliminate this possibility. AusFert drafted a contract with its Chinese alliance and proceeded to set a date for fertilizer to be purchased, as well as a quantity estimation for the next 3 years.

It wasn't long before problems began to surface. First, the shipment did not arrive on the due date, and AusFert began to realize that the possibility of receiving an order was remote. Aware of cultural sensitivity, AusFert approached an outside contact for advice. As soon as AusFert did this, however, communication with ChinFert ceased as ChinFert was insulted that the Australians were seeking outside advice. As a result, the Chinese began ignoring the contract, did not initiate any progress to obtain a permit, and did not engage in negotiation with AusFert. In addition, the Chinese negotiator was uncontactable both in Australia and in China.

Both parties believed that the other was to blame for the miscommunication, although it is evident that it was simply a matter of cultural differences and lack of understanding. According to AusFert, there was no explanation as to why the Chinese negotiator refused to communicate with them. After failing to establish any communication with the Chinese negotiator through "normal" channels, AusFert decided that communication would be established with the negotiator's parents.

Another problem that arose in the negotiation process was that the Chinese national, who lacked English-language skills, used an interpreter for all negotiations. However, the interpreter for her was a Chinese from Hong Kong and was excluded by AusFert, as it was assumed that "he was up to no good with her from day one." At the time of the communication breakdown, the interpreter was contacted directly by ChinFert and, like his client, refused to communicate. AusFert could not understand that the signing of the contract by AusFert's contact did not bind the contact to the delivery of orders on a certain date. The only option to complete the task was to discover the real reason for the communication breakdown.

By the time communication was established with the Chinese negotiator, the negative emotions were so strong that the Chinese national believed AusFert had no understanding of how the Chinese system worked and had completely discredited her effort and ability. She did not see fit to engage in any immediate communication. Her feelings also led her to believe that there was a conspiracy to undermine her role when ChinFert communicated with certain officials in Beijing without her knowledge. The effects of such negative

---

[2]Not the company's real name.

emotion resulted in both parties viewing the other as divisive, untrustworthy, uncooperative, and dishonest. ChinFert felt that, on this basis, no relationship existed and therefore there was no further need for communication. AusFert, however, felt that despite everything, there was a binding contract that needed to be honored.

The preceding actual case demonstrates how cultural differences can impact on felt emotions, the ability to detect others' emotions in a timely manner to avoid breakdown in negotiation and relationships, and the understanding of what steps need to be taken to repair the bad feelings the other party has. This chapter contributes to the understanding of the negotiation process by developing a cross-cultural negotiation model based on an integration of affective events theory (AET) and communication accommodation theory (CAT).

BOUNDARY CROSSING

Within today's global marketplace, it is inevitable that business interactions will continue to cross cultural boundaries. These boundaries are no longer purely physical but also include culture, religion, regulation, values and beliefs, social groups and circles, and unfamiliar emotions and communication methods (e.g., Ayoko, Härtel, Fisher, & Fujimoto, 2003; Phatak & Habib, 1996). Boundary crossing, which is the process of either uniting or separating people, is mediated through negotiation. This chapter aims to bridge the boundaries of strategic business negotiation, communication, and emotion in a cross-cultural context. Each of these three boundaries is discussed briefly, followed by a review of cross-cultural communication literature.

People use boundaries to achieve integration and separation from others, as a way of maintaining comfort zones (Petronio, Ellemers, Giles, & Gallois, 1998). They exist at the level of cultures as well as at the individual level. As such, during negotiation, people have a boundary they place between themselves and the other party and they evaluate the extent to which they need to tighten or loosen it. This boundary-crossing adjustment may be initiated by one or both parties to build the relationship. When boundaries are unattended to, miscommunication may occur (Coupland, Wiemann, & Giles, 1991, as cited in Petronio et al., 1998).

Miscommunication may occur when boundaries are too tight or when they are too loose. When they are too tight, the parties involved are not receptive to each other's definition of an affective event (Petronio et al., 1998). When boundaries are too loose, communication may cease altogether as the boundary is not salient and the parties are unsure of the appropriate behavior (Dayringer, 1998). Miscommunication will generally cause the tightening up of boundaries in all cultures when it is detected (Willemyns, Gallois, Callan, & Pittam, 1997).

The boundary-crossing process is achieved through negotiation. Negotiation is a frequent part of everyday life; thus, it is largely an unconscious process (Ferraro, 2002). Chang (2002) identified five negotiation style preferences: accommodation, collaboration, and withdrawal (cooperative), and competition and consultation (instrumental). Further, the dual concern model introduced by Rubin, Pruitt, and Kim (1994) portrayed negotiation style as a combination of high/low concern for the self and high/low concern for others.

The addition of differing cultures in the negotiation process adds further complexities. This is because the style of our negotiations is conditioned culturally, both consciously and unconsciously (Dayringer, 1998). Culture impacts on the way in which the parties think, feel, and behave (Casse & Deol, 1985). In terms of cross-cultural negotiation, Adler, Brahm, and Graham (1992) showed that the cooperative approach is more successful for both Westerners and Easterners when negotiating with each other. We assume this approach in our further discussion.

As shown, the process of boundary crossing in cross-cultural negotiations is dependent on the culture of the parties involved. In particular, cultural differences impact negotiation, with some cultures preferring to tighten the walls at the beginning and work toward loosening up when trust is built between parties, and other cultures preferring to start with very open boundaries and tighten these boundaries only when they feel threatened. Our focus, the Sino-Australian negotiation setting, involves these two opposing approaches to boundary crossing.

From a business perspective, the issue of boundary crossings involved in Sino-Australian negotiations is an important one. This is because the low success rate of foreign investments in China has been attributed, in part, to miscommunications (cf. Pye, 1982).

Both Hofstede (1980) and Trompenaars (1993) studied cultural differences between Westerners and the Chinese in their attempt to frame the behavioral patterns of the Chinese to ensure successful communication with their Western counterparts. Their research showed that certain patterns of behavior are evident within cultures. These patterns have been widely used within cross-cultural research and practice to train negotiators. Yet we argue that more is needed.

The Chinese culture is notably among the least understood and studied markets within the business arena (Zhang & Neelankavil, 1997). Therefore, this chapter attempts to bridge this gap through developing a theoretical framework for analyzing cross-cultural negotiation processes within Sino-Australian negotiations. Further, the framework developed represents a bounded-emotionality perspective of the negotiation process. This link between negotiation and emotion is discussed next.

EMOTION AND NEGOTIATION

Notwithstanding the fact that skill is an undeniable critical element in successful negotiations, negotiation is also affected, to a large extent, by emotion. Although not widely researched, emotional or affective reactions such as distress or anger are often experienced during the negotiation process (George, Jones, & Gonzalez, 1998), partly because of external and internal conflicts arising from the process of attitudinal structuring (George et al., 1998). When miscommunication occurs, it is likely to have a negative effect on negotiators, rather than a positive effect. This negative effect is likely to trigger the negotiators' subconscious, which may result in the negotiator displaying a defense mode or initiating the negotiation toward a negative emotion (Dayringer, 1998). Subsequently, the relationship between emotion and negotiation involves the impact of feelings or moods that people experience during cross-cultural negotiations (George et al., 1998).

Conflicts that take place during negotiations have an inherent affective component (Pondy, 1967), and distress or anger emotions are often experienced during the negotiation process (George et al., 1998). Further, these negative emotional reactions may continue to develop at an accelerated and accumulative pace—a pattern also known as a "negative spiral" (George et al., 1998). Fueled with negative emotions, negotiators may experience a negative spiral at different speeds, whereby there is little chance for that spiral to be broken by either party. Therefore, the negotiation result can be unsuccessful and can even terminate the possibility of future negotiations.

As with negotiation styles, culture impacts on the emotions experienced during the negotiation process. Studies have shown cultural differences in a range of emotional experiences including intensity, duration, and control of emotion (Matsumoto, 1993). Studies also conclude that cultures differ when judging other emotions (Matsumoto, 1993). As such, incorrect emotional judgments due to cultural differences will affect the outcome of a negotiation.

Behavior during the negotiation process is also affected by the emotions evoked. George and colleagues (1998) identified that an individual's behavior is as affected by the person's moods and emotions as by his or her attitudes and values. They suggested that there are two major emotional feelings during negotiation: positive and negative. However, we suggest that there may also be degrees of emotional uncertainty, with some factors during the negotiation process increasing the propensity for one's emotion to move in a positive direction, and others increasing the propensity to move in a negative direction. In other words, although the process of negotiation may begin positively, an "uncertain feeling" can emerge when either or both parties are not sure if the negotiation is heading in the agreed direction.

Toward the conclusion of the negotiation, negative feelings may emerge if the result is not satisfactory, and likewise, positive feelings may emerge if the result is satisfactory. Again, we argue for a third feeling, which appears between positive and negative, namely, the uncertain feeling.

The preceding discussion of cross-cultural negotiation shows that there are many points in a negotiation where an affective event can occur. According to affective events theory (AET), an emotional response flows from a particular type of event labeled as an affective event. These affective events are shaped by the environment in which interactions occur. The emotions that flow from affective events are in part a consequence of the event and in part a consequence of individual factors that shape the interpretation of the event. These emotions, in turn, impact on individuals' attitudes and behaviors.

INFLUENCE OF AUSTRALIAN AND CHINESE CULTURE ON NEGOTIATION

Cultural factors impact on whether negotiations begin with positive, negative, or uncertain feelings. For example, observations of Chinese–Australian negotiations suggest that Chinese negotiators have the tendency to start negotiating in a state akin to the uncertain feeling whereas Australians tend to start with a positive feeling (cf. Breth & Jin, 1991; Tung, 1991). Further, this uncertain feeling may also occur after negotiations have begun and neither party is certain of the direction of the negotiation, leading to a negotiation standstill. When negotiating with the Chinese, this type of ending may terminate the negotiation process or close avenues for future negotiations (Engholm, 1989; Pye, 1990).

In cross-cultural negotiation, cultural values play an important role in reaching an effective agreement. For example, Australians and the Chinese differ in their definitions of *value*. Therefore, the Chinese would not use the phrase "too expensive" because it suggests that one has not enough money to purchase the item, which negates the achievement of saving face. However, the Australian negotiator would have difficulty in understanding why the Chinese do not inform them of the prices that are too expensive and thus "save face." Pye (1982) supported this contention, commenting that Sino-American business negotiation misunderstandings are due largely to cultural differences and that joint-venture negotiations often intensify this problem further. Cultural difference in values, in effect, fuel the possibility of miscommunication. Cultural understanding is, therefore, an important moderator of the types of emotions flowing from misunderstandings in a cross-cultural negotiation and is depicted in our model (see Fig. 9.1).

Hall's (1976) theory of high- and low-context cultures is also helpful in explaining cross-cultural communication behaviors. In high-context cultures, such as in China, nonverbal or situational cues bear considerable importance (Stone, 2002), whereas the emphasis on time and formal documentation bears

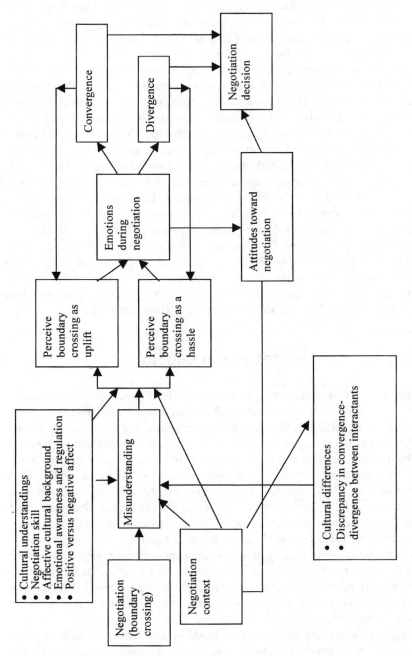

FIG. 9.1. Theoretical model of cross-cultural negotiation.

173

high importance in low-context cultures such as Australia. When negotiating between these two cultural groups, the group from the high-context culture requires a clearer interpretation of its negotiator's nonverbal signals. Failure to do so decreases the chance of a successful negotiation.

Culture also determines the negotiation strategy used by the parties involved. For instance, Chinese negotiation teams are often constructed with multiple layers of powerful people. This strategy is used to shift power from one person to the other, in the attempt to confuse other negotiators through role play. This shift may also be adjusted when a member of the team is entering a negative emotive state. Further, the Chinese society is a high power distance society (Hofstede, 1980), which means that subordinate persons converge more to the dominant persons rather than vice versa (Thakerar, Giles, & Cheshire, 1982). These features of Chinese negotiating norms contrast markedly with the features of Australian negotiations, making Sino-Australian negotiations undoubtedly difficult tasks (Shenkar & Simcha, 1987). It is no wonder that despite numerous attempts to develop successful negotiation relationships between the two cultures, studies in this area have not yet adequately addressed the dynamic character of the cultures involved. We next attempt to address this gap by first discussing culture and emotion, and then applying CAT to the Australian–Chinese negotiation process.

CULTURE AND EMOTION

Research has shown that cultures exert considerable influence over emotion through behavioral norms (Ekman, 1994; Friesen, 1972; Matsumoto, 1993). Awareness of this means that negotiators working in the cross-cultural context will not take the process of communication for granted but instead pay more attention to the processes employed and their potential emotional consequences.

There are several types of emotional effects that may influence the Sino-Australian negotiation process. The most pertinent one is a postdecision emotion that occurs when a decision is reached with strong emotions attached. This creates problems in negotiation, for instance, as our earlier scenario demonstrated; because the Chinese society is based on trust, as opposed to Western society's basis in legalities, the concept of being bound by a contract is less important in Chinese culture than abiding in accordance with one's emotions. In other words, the moral obligation was perceived by the Chinese as insignificant compared to one's emotion, especially when revenge was an added component.

Although great differences exist in expression and behavior, research suggests that the experience of basic moods and emotions tend to be universal (Ekman, 1994; Scherer, 1994, as cited in George et al., 1998). For example, crying, anger, and frustration are negative feelings that we have all experienced.

Difficulties arise during cross-cultural negotiation regarding the conversion of negative feelings to positive feelings. First, these feelings may occur when there is a misunderstanding. Moreover, the negative feelings are not detected by the other party. Second, the process of converting negative feelings to positive feelings is difficult, although not impossible. They may be overcome if the negotiator adopts the concept of "no hurt feelings." This suggests that no one party is at fault, and that business should continue as planned. Evidently, negative emotions can be controlled in this situation as the cause of the misunderstanding is not of paramount importance.

Further difficulties arise due to the terminology used in negotiations. For instance, there are often terms used by Australians that have no direct translation in the Chinese language, such as "to hold a grudge" and "no hard feelings." This indicates that the Chinese culture is lacking a process to convey verbally negative feelings. The only term used in China that is similar to this is *qing bie jian jue*, which translates as "please do not see it as odd." When it is used, it suggests that the Chinese person caused the misunderstanding. This confirms further Hofstede's (1980) power distance theory, which states that in Eastern cultures, the less powerful party is more likely to submit to the higher power party.

COMMUNICATION ACCOMMODATION THEORY IN SINO-AUSTRALIAN NEGOTIATIONS

In this section we extend communication accommodation theory (CAT) (Coupland et al., 1991; Giles, 1973) to detect positive and negative emotions in the communication process and in cross-cultural negotiations. This is achieved by drawing on George, Jones, and Gonzalez's (1998) model, which describes the affect of negotiators in cross-cultural negotiations. These authors identified negative emotional spirals as the major cause of unsuccessful negotiations. Further, unless the negotiators break out of the negative spiral, miscommunications or negotiation breakdowns are likely to result.

CAT is designed to examine the efficiency of communication (Petronio et al., 1998). In particular, it focuses on the convergence and divergence involved in speech communication. CAT is applied broadly in a number of areas, including convergence and divergence, cross-boundary communications, nonverbal communications, miscommunication, and integration of intergroup and outer-group communications (Petronio et al., 1998).

There are six levels of CAT, relevant to understanding problems in negotiation:

- Level 1: Discourse and meaning are inherently flawed although speakers are not likely to recognize the problem.

- Level 2: Strategic compromises or minor misunderstandings abound; there may be some awareness of miscommunication.
- Level 3: Miscommunication is typically attributed to the personal deficiencies of an individual.
- Level 4: Failure in conversational goal attainment, of which speakers are likely to be fully aware.
- Level 5: Intergroup considerations play the major role in miscommunication.
- Level 6: Sociostructural power imbalances.

The application of the CAT framework to Australian–Chinese negotiations can facilitate further the link between culture, emotion, and negotiation. Extending it to include emotions allows us to describe how a given negotiation process resolves.

Level 1 of CAT

The first level of CAT is concerned with the meaning and discourse, or cultural and language differences, in the use of the English language. Although English is becoming the international negotiation language, it is not used in the same way by everyone, and this can create a barrier to communication (Crystal, 2000). In other words, although Chinese and Australians speak English, they may not necessarily use the language in the same way (Crystal, 2000). When this issue is not recognized, miscommunication may arise, resulting in negotiation problems that may not be discovered until greater damage has surfaced.

Level 2 of CAT

The second level of CAT is primarily concerned with the minor misunderstandings likely to accumulate in cross-cultural negotiations, especially with the Chinese. When negotiators come from different origins, the potential for misunderstandings is even greater. Culture provides a perceptual filter that influences the way we interpret events (Adler & Rodman, 2000). Parties of different cultures begin the negotiation process testing many communication methods until a mutually understood method is established. This process is a fertile ground for misunderstandings, albeit mostly minor ones, and the accumulation of these misunderstandings causes negative emotions (George, Jones, & Gonzalez, 1998). For example, Chinese negotiators do not want to cause their counterparts hurt feelings and do not have any contingency plans for resolving such problems when they do occur. Although Australians are capable of saying "no hard feelings" or "no worries, mate" and continuing with the negotiation process, Chinese negotiators will not be able to forget the "hurt feelings." The accumulation of these hurt feelings throughout the process can become a large issue at a later stage of the negotiation, which is evident in the scenario presented at the beginning of this chapter.

Level 3 of CAT

The third level of CAT shows that individual differences have enormous potential to cause miscommunications. These personal differences influence people's communication pattern. Unless communication parties consciously are making allowances for such differences, miscommunication may occur.

Level 4 of CAT

The fourth level of CAT addresses the cultural differences which pose a barrier for negotiators in achieving the full awareness of misunderstandings. When negotiation occurs between high- and low-context culture groups, the interpretation of the negotiators' goals may differ dramatically from their actual goals. This is because the low-context group presents its evidence before its *conclusions* whereas the high-context group presents its conclusions before its *evidence* (Hall, 1976). These two contrasting ways of presenting information may cause some negotiators to mistake unimportant evidence as their counterpart's goals, thus missing the counterpart's actual goals, and vice versa. Unless the negotiators are trained or aware of such critical cultural differences, the miscommunication may not be detected and thus successful negotiation may be impaired.

Level 5 of CAT

Once boundaries are created, groups will remain within their boundary to avoid uncertainty (Petronio et al., 1998). Within Level 5 of CAT, these boundaries are used to keep nongroup members out and other group members in. According to Coupland and colleagues (1991), this involves regulating, aging, blurring, and coping with boundaries that often are fuzzy.

As Petronio and colleagues (1998) observed, "We fit in our environment by drawing lines around those things that are important to us, and then control them through rules." Yet we also recognize that to fit successfully within the environment, we must have enough flexibility within these boundaries to allow a degree of integration between ourselves and the world within which we live. Such boundary negotiation evokes emotions in ourselves and others, and requires emotional awareness and regulation (see Fig. 9.1).

Level 6 of CAT

The Australian culture is less structured and lower on Hofstede's (1986) power distance scale in comparison to the Chinese. In negotiation processes between these two cultures, Chinese negotiators are more likely to have an established team structure (cf. Breth & Jin, 1991). Further, Level 6 of CAT illustrates that Chinese negotiators have a power distance structure that facilitates decision making from the person with the most authority. When negotiating with one or two Australians, it is often difficult for the Chinese negotiator to determine how the power structure should be maintained and how to keep the balance of power for both parties (cf. Breth & Jin, 1991).

In summary, the CAT model predicts that speakers will be evaluated positively or negatively: Converging speakers will be evaluated positively, whereas divergers and maintainers will be evaluated as hostile and unfriendly (Hornsey & Gallois, 1998). When the style of negotiation is converted from convergence to divergence, it is also converted from positive to negative. At this stage, we propose that a negative emotion is likely to play a stronger role than a positive one (see Fig. 9.1), and it is at this point that the negotiation is likely to be guided toward a negative outcome (George et al., 1998). The first indication of this problem is the presence of ignoring or reducing (Dayringer, 1998) behaviors not coded among the nonverbal behaviors reported in Jones and colleagues' (1999) research. Therefore, these need to be added to CAT when applying it to the cross-cultural negotiation context.

The application of the CAT framework to Australian–Chinese negotiations can facilitate further the link between culture, emotion, and negotiation.

EXTENDING CAT FOR THE CROSS-CULTURAL NEGOTIATION CONTEXT: INTEGRATING AFFECTIVE EVENTS THEORY (AET)

The integration of AET in cross-cultural negotiations is beneficial because CAT in its current conceptualization fails to consider the role of affective events or emotional responses and their subsequent attitudinal and behavioral consequences.

Conversion and Diversion

Do all negotiators begin as converging speakers and convert to diverging throughout the negotiation (i.e., when they are ignored by their counterpart)? When negotiation occurs between people of the same culture, this changing process should occur at the same time due to a shared mental model of the negotiation process (cf. George et al., 1998). When the negotiation is between people of different cultural backgrounds (e.g., Australian and Chinese), the process may not occur at the same rate because of cultural differences and expectations (Eiteman, 1990). This could also precipitate misunderstanding as parties with less experience in cross-cultural communication will not be able to interpret this change (see Fig. 9.1). The hostility and the unfriendliness will be stimulated further by the change in the emotion and may possibly become a mixture of confusion and frustration, which again is vulnerable to misinterpretation or misunderstanding. This begins to form a circle of misunderstandings. Unless this circle is broken, the end result will be a total communication breakdown (see Fig. 9.1). Figure 9.1 demonstrates the many factors that contribute to misunderstanding, such as culture, emotions, and the negotiation context. Unless this circle of misunderstanding is broken, the negotiation process is unlikely to move on to the next stage of boundary crossing.

In applying AET, a negative misunderstanding result is likely to identify the boundary crossing as a hassle while a positive result is likely to identify the boundary crossing as uplift. At this stage of the negotiation, emotion levels are likely to change, and the flow of convergence or divergence from this point will, indeed, mark the end result of any negotiation process (see Fig. 9.1).

The likelihood of negative emotions arising in negotiations may be due simply to misunderstandings and conflicts. According to Trompenaars (1995), emotions and cultures are combined. Some cultures are affective (i.e., individualists), whereas other cultures are neutral (i.e., collectivists). People from affective cultures are likely to respond in a direct way whereas those from neutral cultures are likely to respond in an indirect way (Trompenaars, 1995). Thus, people from affective cultures express their emotions more than people from neutral cultures. There is also a tendency for those with norms of emotional neutrality to dismiss anger (Trompenaars, 1995), whereas those from affective cultures are likely to consider it a salient event. Thus, the level of affectivity of a culture is likely to determine whether an event is perceived as affective or not.

The display of any emotion has a strong impact on communication, especially during negotiation. For example, Chinese negotiators are less likely to display their negative feelings during negotiation. Even when the negotiation is terminated, the Chinese are often reluctant to provide any feedback in order to avoid the unnecessary display of emotions, whereas this characteristic is unlikely for Australian negotiators. Therefore, it is evident that emotional displays differ across cultures and contribute to miscommunication.

What Do Negotiators Affect?

According to George et al. (1998), there are three key sets of determinants that negotiators affect during cross-cultural negotiations: individual differences, cross-cultural differences, and contextual factors. These key determinants suggest that individual differences are likely to be affected by an individual's character, feelings, thoughts, and behaviors. These differences may exist both within and across cultures.

George and her colleagues (1998) identified further two major affective dispositions in the cross-cultural negotiation process: negative and positive affect. The diversity literature suggests that the former will negatively affect a negotiation process as well as the negotiating parties' decisions, whereas the latter will bring positiveness to the negotiation parties' decisions as well as a positive negotiation outcome (George et al., 1998). The second dimension of these individual differences is how preexisting cultural knowledge should influence one's decision-making process. In cross-cultural negotiations, an individual is prone to be guided by the existing schemas and to rely on them to make decisions (George et al., 1998). This proves the value of pretraining negotiators for a given cross-cultural context.

There are also three broad types of cross-cultural differences: differences in internalized cultural values and norms; cross-cultural differences in emotional expression; and cross-cultural differences in linguistic style (George et al., 1998). These are discussed next.

Differences in Internalized Cultural Values and Norms. It is believed that these internalized values and norms are likely to influence the moods and emotions negotiators experience. In cross-cultural negotiations, each party brings its own set of values and norms, and these are likely to differ between parties. Negative affect and distress is likely to result when these differences cause conflicts between the negotiation parties. The party that comes from an affective culture has a tendency for deeper distress, whereas the party from the neutral culture has a tendency to discount the emotional expressions of the other.

Cross-Cultural Differences in Emotional Expression. The cross-cultural differences in emotional expression suggest that different cultures express their emotions differently. Reserved negotiators express their feelings less, and this may be interpreted by their counterparts as uncertainty, thus causing misunderstanding, which potentially sways the negotiation toward a negative outcome. This example is prevalent in the Chinese culture. Australians, on the other hand, easily express their emotions. This is often interpreted by the Chinese as overenthusiastic and therefore is seen as signifying undeclared hidden benefits that the Australians may be gaining over the Chinese.

Cross-Cultural Differences in Linguistic Style. George and colleagues (1998) proposed further that cross-cultural differences in linguistic styles dampen negotiators' positive moods and emotions, and contribute to negative moods and emotions during negotiation. The differences in linguistic styles also create uncertainty for negotiators (George et al., 1998). In a typical Australian–Chinese negotiation, the Chinese will fully engage the interpreter (generally the interpreter is a colleague of the negotiation team) and have lengthy discussions with the person in Chinese during the negotiation. However, Australians tend to be uncomfortable with this method of negotiation. As Ting-Toomey and Oetzel (2001) noted, the use of "code-switching" by a bilingual person is a tactic engaged in to increase or decrease distance toward his or her native culture by switching languages (Billikopf-Encina, 2000). In business negotiations, this process of code-switching assists the previously discussed boundary-building process through the increase or decrease of culture distance.

The Chinese are also likely to engage in conversation when Australian negotiators are speaking, as they trust their interpreter to translate words and intentions, and would rather utilize the time to form strategies. Again, Australians are uncomfortable with this Chinese characteristic. The more frequently these behaviors occur, the more likely it is that Australians become uncertain and consequently develop negative feelings toward the Chinese.

DISCUSSION

Although cross-cultural differences in negotiation are increasingly becoming a topic of interest (Tse, Francis, & Walls, 1994, as cited in George et al., 1998), unfortunately, the empirical literature on cross-cultural negotiations is very limited (Fisher, 1990; Pruitt & Carneval, 1993, as cited in Pearson & Stephan, 1998). Past studies suggest that people use different negotiation approaches due to differences in their perceptions of the decision-making situation (George et al., 1998). Zhao (2000) suggested that this difference is due largely to the value difference in cultures. As such, cultural differences and the inability to bridge cultural gaps often lead to business negotiation failures (Swierczek, 1990). Without cultural knowledge, negotiation instruction on collaboration should not commence (Shell, 2001).

MANAGEMENT IMPLICATIONS

This chapter has illustrated that some misunderstandings are fertile ground for major miscommunications in the cross-cultural negotiation context. These misunderstandings, which may evoke negative emotions, can be cumulative, building to a point where negotiation fails. This challenge indicates that the selection of negotiators is extremely important. They must possess cultural understanding, negotiation skills, and be able to (a) anticipate and shift convergence–divergence in concert with the other parties, (b) moderate their affective cultural background appropriately (see Fig. 9.1), and (c) appropriately adjust their linguistic styles on the basic understanding of both cultures to adjust boundaries favorably. Negotiators should also given the opportunity to plan the negotiation process.

When negotiation personnel are selected, training in cross-cultural negotiation should take place using case studies of other negotiators in the given negotiation context. Further, negotiators need to understand the impact of high- and low-context contexts within Hofstede's interpretation of power distance (Hall, 1976) and that the fundamental differences in cultural communication styles may result in serious miscommunication. To avoid this occurring in the Sino-Australian negotiation context, Australian negotiators should be assessed according to their cultural backgrounds and, if necessary, be provided with the necessary training to work with their negotiating counterparts. The Chinese, on the other hand, should also emphasize the need for monitoring the negotiation process to detect misunderstandings and act on them as they occur. If negative emotion is detected by either party, the negotiation process should be interrupted and, if necessary, negotiators may be replaced.

CONCLUSION

We have argued that cross-cultural negotiations may involve crossing boundaries and that miscommunications can be viewed as "boundary-crossing mishaps." Such mishaps are affected by negotiators' understanding of the respective cultures of the parties, negotiation skill, affective cultural background, cultural differences, emotional awareness and regulation, positive and negative affect, and discrepancy in convergence–divergence between the interactants. When too many hassles or mishaps occur, the negotiation breaks down as depicted in Fig. 9.1. As we have shown, it is often the accumulation of many minor misunderstandings that breaks the negotiation process and the possibility of interacting successfully across cultures.

In this chapter, we integrated the CAT model and AET to develop a model that captures the role of emotion in Australian–Chinese cross-cultural negotiations. The model predicts that converging negotiators will be evaluated positively, whereas divergers and maintainers will be evaluated as hostile and unfriendly. This likelihood is increased by the differences between the two cultures. For example, certain nonverbal communications exhibited by the Chinese may be interpreted as divergence and therefore negativity is sensed in the process. Therefore, this may result in the beginning of a negative spiral (see Fig. 9.1).

Misunderstanding in negotiations act as affective events, which evoke perceptions of boundary crossing as a hassle rather than an uplift. The result is a negative effect on emotions during negotiation, which leads to a diverging communication style and increases negative attitudes toward the negotiation. The negative emotional spiral puts the negotiation decision at risk. What underlies successful negotiation, therefore, is cultural understanding and negotiation skill coupled with emotional awareness and regulation.

10

A Bounded Emotionality Perspective on Interpersonal Behavior in Organizations

Neal M. Ashkanasy
Wilfred J. Zerbe

The experience and expression of emotion is an essentially individual phenomenon (see chap. 6); however it is tightly bound within a social context. For example, the effects of emotion often become much more pointed when people are in groups. Interactions with others are a primary source of emotions; our relations with others serve to provoke, to help transfer, and to constrain emotions. These kinds of effects are reflected in the intragroup and intergroup situations that are the subject of the chapters in this section. Indeed, De Dreu, West, Fischer, and MacCurtain (2001) argued that group processes play a special role in developing emotion at this level of analysis. They described group interactions as a process of emotional incubation, where group members come to their group with a set of feelings and emotional expectations that are tested and then developed or diminished, depending on other group members' reactions. The resulting group-level emotional tenor then infuses the whole group, creating what De Rivera (1992, p. 197) referred to as group "emotional climate" (see also Barsade, 2002; Kelly & Barsade, 2001).

In the first chapter in this section, Matthew Grawitch and David Munz tackle the difficult issue of the role of individual affect in problem-solving workgroups. They present a model where individual and group affect norms influence each stage of ostensibly rational problem solving. The model, which they call GAPS (Group Affect in Problem Solving), includes four stages: problem identification; brainstorming; solution development; and implementation. At each of these stages both individual and group affect are influenced by the problem-solving process, with group affect becoming more influential over individual members' affect as the group matures. Distinctive features of the model are that it covers both positive and negative emotion, and includes reciprocal influences between the individual and the group problem solving process. Although yet to be tested, the model that these authors propose is the first to provide a comprehensive explanation of the nexus between affect and problem-solving in groups.

In chapter 8, Stefan Meisiek and Xin Yao address the manner in which emotions are promulgated in groups, through an original theory of social sharing of emotion (SSE) based on humor. In this model, humor is not something light and easily dismissable—as it so often is, outside the model. Instead, it is an essential tool that people at work use to deal with everyday affective issues, and to share experiences. In this model, humor is not just related to positive affect—it also provides a powerful medium for employees to deal with the negative things that happen to them, including strongly negative issues such as the death of a friend or colleague. Meisiek and Yao provide a thoughtful set of propositions concerning both the antecedents and the consequences of humor, including identifying the special roles of "canned", "practical", and "situational" humor, and the role of gender.

In the final chapter in this section, Mona White, Charmine Härtel, and Debra Panipucci consider intergroup issues, with a focus on what they refer to as "boundary crossing." Dealing specifically with cross-cultural communication in the context of strategic business negotiation, they identify in particular miscommunications in this context as "boundary-crossing mishaps." They argue that these mishaps are affected by numerous factors, including negotiators' understanding of the respective cultures of the parties, negotiation skill, affective cultural background of the parties, cultural differences, emotional awareness and regulation, negative affect, and discrepancy in convergence–divergence between the parties. Based on Weiss and Cropanzano's (1996) affective events theory, they propose that negotiation ultimately breaks down because of an accumulation of these mishaps. The theory is applied in the specific context of Chinese–Australian negotiation.

The three chapters in this section provide but a glimpse, however, of the topic of emotion in groups and teams. Indeed, we believe that this is perhaps the most underdeveloped arena for future research in the role of emotions in organizational behavior. From the perspective of bounded emotionality, the three chapters are especially convincing. It is clear from these authors' writing that emotion plays a central role in the way teams function, both endogenously and exogenously. Perhaps the most intriguing of the contributions, however, is Meisiek and Yao's. Here we see that humor, so often dismissed as unimportant, may be an important component of social cohesion in groups. In their model, the emotional relief of humor serves as the quintessential ingredient of group belongingness, and also as a release for negative events that beset group members from time to time. The practical and research possibilities of these ideas are, to our knowledge unexplored to date.

Mumby and Putnam's (1992) formulation proposed bounded emotionality as an alternative to bounded rationality. For them, bounded emotionality represented an emancipating organizing principle, based on a feminist reading of organizations, that stood in opposition to those underlying traditional, male-centered, rationally based organizations. It is not that they saw traditional organizations as unemotional, but rather that in traditional organizations emotions are managed for instrumental means. Indeed, they saw the concept of emotional labor as part of the organizational control inherent to traditional organizations. They proposed instead that organizations "be identified with work feelings rather than emotional labor" (p. 477): work feelings that are spontaneous and emergent rather than organizationally controlled, based on interrelatedness rather than used as commodities, meaning-centered rather than organizationally ascribed, and based on practical rather than instrumental reasoning. The chapters in this section are centered in traditional organizations, and although they adopt a tolerant view of the role of emotions in organizations, they implicitly adopt a more or less instrumental view of organizational emotions. Emotions thus serve as means to ends, such as effective problem solving, group harmony, and the outcomes of negotiations. On the one hand, then, bounded emotionality suggests that at the very least we need to acknowledge our assumptions as to the presence of instrumentality among the subjects of our research. Mumby and Putnam would advocate that ideally we would be open to alternative ways of conceiving organizations and become advocates for less instrumental forms of organizing (or forms that have different instrumentalities, i.e., aimed at achieving community rather than profit).

On the other hand it may be that bounded emotionality represents merely an alternative means of control, as Martin, Knopoff, and Beckman (1998) suggested. In their study of the Body Shop, an organization that was characterized by many of the features of a "feminist" organization, they found evidence for markers of bounded emotionality, but also found that organizationally and interpersonally ascribed emotional labor was alive and well, and that at times the expectation on employees to be free with their emotions was equally coercive. In short, and as the chapters in this section make plain, the interplay of individual, organizational, and interpersonal influences on emotions creates a complicated puzzle, for which we are only just beginning to make sense of the nature of the elements, much less the dynamics that connect them.

IV

ORGANIZATIONAL PROCESSES, STRUCTURE, AND DESIGN

11

A Reconceptualization of the Emotional Labor Construct: On the Development of an Integrated Theory of Perceived Emotional Dissonance and Emotional Labor

Robert S. Rubin
Vicki M. Staebler Tardino
Catherine S. Daus
David C. Munz

A close examination of the emotional labor literature reveals a myriad of conceptualizations contributing to a current state of theoretical disorientation. The purpose of this chapter is to clarify the nature of the construct and specify a more unified research model. To maximize theoretical clarity, the present model separates behaviors, emotional states, and situational demands. In addition, we suggest that the construct of *perceived emotional dissonance* is an important mediator between situational demands and emotional labor behavior, thereby disentangling the emotional state from behavior.

Recently, the construct of emotional labor has garnered a great deal of scholarly interest in the organizational literature (cf., Ashforth & Humphrey, 1993; Ashforth & Tomiuk, 2000; Brotheridge & Grandey, 2002; Brotheridge & Lee, 1998, 2002; Fisher & Ashkanasy, 2000a; Grandey, 2000, 2001, 2003; Kruml & Geddes, 2000; Mann, 1999; Pugliesi, 1999; Schaubroeck & Jones, 2000; Tews & Glomb, 2000; Wharton & Erickson, 1993). Along with the enthusiasm generated by such interest has come the rapid development of multiple theoretical frameworks. Although some aspects of these frameworks converge, many are quite theoretically discrepant. Consequently, these various conceptualizations have created confusion and have left researchers in a conceptual quandary regarding how best to understand the construct.

More specifically, current conceptualizations of emotional labor have confused or often treated as equivalent, two theoretically distinct constructs: One construct is a *subjective state* (experience) resulting from organizational requirements/norms regarding emotional expression, and the other is the *moti-*

vated behavior undertaken to manage or regulate the subjective state. We propose, as have others (Mann, 1999; Wakefield, 1989), that it is conceptually necessary to separate emotional states from behavior. Thus, we contend that separating the state (as experienced) from behavior (broadly defined) will increase the theoretical clarity and ultimate utility of the emotional labor construct.

THEORETICAL COMPONENTS
OF THE EMOTIONAL LABOR CONSTRUCT

Although diverse in nature, the previous conceptualizations of emotional labor can be roughly collapsed into three categories: (a) those that conceive of emotional labor as an emotional state arising from organizational or social norms and requirements; (b) those that suggest emotional labor consists of the behaviors undertaken to manage an implied or explicit emotional state (*Note*: "behavior" implies action and/or reaction, some of which may be unobservable, such as self-talk or cognitive reappraisals); and (c) those that consist of states, behavior, and/or situational factors. Most common, however, are conceptualizations that combine two or more of these categories within a single construct. For example, Morris and Feldman (1996) defined emotional labor as consisting of five dimensions, four of which are situational factors (frequency, duration, variety, and intensity of emotional display) and one of which is an individual state (emotional dissonance). Others have proposed similar definitions (Morris & Feldman, 1997; Rafaeli & Sutton, 1989; Sutton, 1991). Recently, Schaubroeck and Jones (2000) commented that the emotional *state* of dissonance (similar to Morris & Feldman, 1997) was the most similar in concept to their construct; however, their definition seems to also include situational factors ("in order to meet the demands of the job"), emotional states ("the experience of workers"), and behavior ("to suppress negative and express positive"). Mann (1999) defined the construct as having three dimensions: (a) expectations or rules about emotional display, (b) emotional suppression, and (c) emotional faking. As she implied, the first dimension represents a situational component and the second and third dimensions represent behavioral components. She remarked, "The last two dimensions incorporate the conflict idea, since emotions can only be suppressed or faked because of a discrepancy between expected and felt emotion" (p. 354). Thus, Mann's (1999) conception involves a behavioral reaction to a state of conflict.

One of the earliest conceptualizations of emotional labor (in the organizational literature) by Ashforth and Humphrey (1993) narrowed the scope considerably by defining emotional labor as "the act of displaying appropriate emotion" (p. 90). They added, "We prefer to focus on *behavior* rather than on the presumed emotions underlying behavior." Further, they explained that their definition "decouples the experience of emotion from the expression of emotion" (p. 90). Thus, they made a clear distinction of identifying emotional labor as a behavior versus an emotional state.

Although these formulations of emotional labor are certainly relevant and highly related to the construct, the collective consequence of these conceptualizations has been theoretical and practical confusion. Alicia Grandey (2000, 2003) developed a comprehensive model of emotional labor, defining emotional labor as an act rather than an emotional state and specifying situational factors and outcome variables. In particular, Grandey conceptualized emotional labor as the emotion regulation process enacted *in response* to situational cues such as service interaction expectations (frequency, duration, variety, display rules) and emotional events. Emotional regulation is undertaken to meet organizational demands felt by individuals, and can be achieved through "surface acting" (regulating expression) and "deep acting" (regulating feelings) (Hochschild, 1983). Thus, Grandey has separated the situational factors, such as display rules, from other parts of the emotion regulation process. We modify and extend her conceptualization by specifying the nature of an emotion state—perceived emotional dissonance—and expand the notion of emotional labor as *one possible* behavioral response to the state of perceived emotional dissonance.

TOWARD A RECONCEPTUALIZATION
OF EMOTIONAL LABOR

We employed Wakefield's (1989) framework of levels of explanation to disentangle the emotional labor construct. His model makes distinctions between distal explanations of behavior (e.g., primary traits such as the extraversion and intelligence) and more proximal levels of explanation (e.g., specific psychological states such as emotion and cognition). Pertinent to our discussion is the distinction between what he termed the *intentional state*, or what is going on within the person, and the actual behavior being performed, called the *motivated act*. Again, motivated acts are broadly defined such that the behaviors employed are not always visible to others, such as cognitive reappraisal. Wakefield used the term *motivated act* to make the distinction between unmotivated behaviors/actions such as automatic responses, and motivated or volitional behaviors/actions. He explained that because of its proximity to behavior, "intentional states form the reasons for actions, and therefore, explain behavior" (p. 335). Thus, intentional states are the best predictors of motivated acts within a given context. Current models of emotional labor have confused and/or merged the intentional state experienced by an individual with the motivated act or behavioral response to that intentional state. Wakefield's framework suggests that a given emotional state should influence behavior, but is necessarily distinct from the behavior.

Certainly we are not the first to argue that confusing the state and behavior may be theoretically unfavorable. Although we used Wakefield's model to guide our thinking delineating the emotional state from the motivated act, others have made similar distinctions in studying emotion constructs (cf. Weiss & Cropanzano, 1996). For example, Mann addressed the challenges presented by current emotional labor theory, stating, "The emphasis [of previous theory] thus ranges from the internal effort on the one hand, to the external behavioral display on the other. But which part is 'emotional labor'?" (p. 348). To date, the distinction between states, behaviors, and situational factors remains unspecified in the emotional labor literature.

Proposed Model

We believe that an additional construct is necessary to conceptually clarify the literature and provide the critical link between the situational demands and state conditions, and the outcome, behavior or act. This alternate and intervening construct is needed to disentangle the response to the organizational requirements before emotional labor is undertaken. One such construct that has been examined in the literature is that of dissonance. We conceive of this dissonance as a *perceived emotional state representing the dissonance between felt emotion, and emotion that is perceived to be required* and contend that it arises from situational demands combined with individual differences. Emotional labor in the form of surface acting or deep acting, then, is *one possible motivated response* to a psychological condition of high perceived dissonance. In Fig. 11.1, we offer our proposed model, and we next discuss the theoretical conceptualizations of each section. We begin with a discussion of dissonance, emotional labor, and their relationship, and then move to a discussion of situational factors, individual differences, and outcomes.

The Affective State of Perceived Emotional Dissonance

As mentioned earlier, we conceive of perceived dissonance as a disconnect between emotions that are genuinely felt and those that are required for the situation (Middleton, 1989). We place a high importance on this state of dissonance because we believe perceived dissonance to be a necessary precursor to emotional labor. A relatively recent but well-supported theory of job satisfaction, affective events theory (AET; Weiss & Cropanzano, 1996), underscores the critical nature of affective states as precursors to outcomes such as job attitudes and behaviors. Similarly, we consider perceived dissonance to be the affective state necessary for the behavioral response of emotional labor. There have, however, been a number of dissonance constructs (e.g., emotive disso-

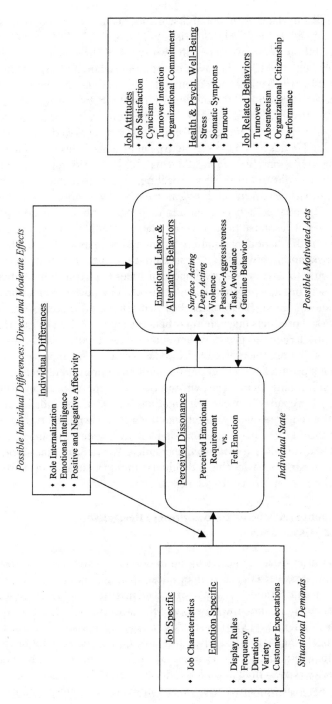

FIG. 11.1. Proposed research model of perceived emotional dissonance and emotional labor.

nance, emotional deviance, emotional dissonance) utilized in emotional labor research (Kruml & Geddes, 2000; Morris & Feldman, 1997; Zerbe, 2000). Our review of the literature shows generally two types of dissonance: (a) dissonance experienced prior to the behavior of emotional labor, and (b) dissonance experienced after this behavior has occurred. Zerbe (2000) attempted to provide some clarity surrounding the dissonance construct by distinguishing between these two types. Specifically, he described one type of dissonance as, "the degree of mismatch between felt emotions and displayed emotions, or *faking*" (p. 202). He described the second type of dissonance as "the mismatch between expressed emotions and local norms" (p. 202). Although both forms of dissonance are valid and intuitively appealing, only a mismatch between *felt emotion* and *normative requirements for emotional display* captures a purely affective state. Dissonance between felt and displayed emotion (or faking) requires a behavioral response to an affective state. Note that this type of dissonance (faking) *is* the "labor" of emotional labor and reflects a process whereby one experiences an affective state and is motivated to deal with it.

Thus, in order to separate clearly emotional states from motivated behavior, we define dissonance as a purely affective state occurring prior to emotional labor. Morris and Feldman (1996) remarked that "It should require little emotional *labor* to sell products one genuinely believes in" (p. 992). Thus all things being equal, the larger the gap between genuine felt emotion and those required for the situation, the greater perceived dissonance. Again, note that dissonance is not a product of conflict between felt emotions and objective organizational requirements per se (i.e., written rules or supervisor instructions); rather, it is a discrepancy between felt emotions and what the individual *perceives* to be the required display. Much like the well-known literature on cognitive dissonance, emotional dissonance is likely to create psychological discomfort that individuals are *motivated* to reduce. We believe that emotional labor *is* the motivated behavior that individuals employ in an attempt to reconcile their feeling of emotional dissonance.

Emotional Labor: A Motivated Behavioral Response to Perceived Dissonance

We argue that individuals typically engage in one of two strategies for dealing with a situation of perceived dissonance. These strategies are similar to Hochschild's (1983) and Grandey's (2000) mechanisms for *managing* emotional demands, but do not include the appraisal of the affective state (perceived dissonance). The first behavioral strategy for managing perceived dissonance, "surface acting," is accomplished when an individual simulates emotion that is appropriate for the situation. An example of surface acting would be when a customer service representative smiles and acts warmly in the face of an abrasive and disrespectful customer who churns up feelings of anger and resentment. The expression of positive emotion is fitting for the customer-service context, but negative emotion is being experienced.

A second strategy for managing perceived dissonance is through the process of "deep acting," in which the individual endeavors to experience the emotion that is appropriate for the situation. In this case, the individual is actually changing the feeling experienced prior to the behavior by changing the underlying causes, or the mental construction of the feeling state (e.g., cognitive reappraisal). Changing the feeling can occur by evoking or suppressing an emotion, or through trained imagination (Hochschild, 1983). For example, a ticket counter agent may imagine himself successfully completing transactions and noticing the smiles on customers' faces. As Grandey (2003) implied, deep acting may require advanced emotional regulatory skills.

In sum, Hochschild claimed that surface acting can be likened to compliance, while deep acting strategy can be likened to conversion. Both strategies can be adaptive (i.e., allow for productive performance) in terms of dealing with perceived dissonance. Over the long term, deep acting should be more adaptive in that it allows the individual to internalize a role, and thus *reduce the level of perceived dissonance* (as shown by the feedback loop in Fig. 11.1). Regardless of adaptability, both strategies are based on the notion of *acting*—that is, manufacturing a substitute for the emotion one genuinely wants to display. Thus, surface and deep acting may temper perceived dissonance, but are unlikely to eliminate completely the source of the motivation to act, or perceived dissonance.

Extending Hochschild's typology, Ashforth and Humphrey (1993) noted that there are instances in which the sanctioned emotion corresponds to the felt emotion, as is ordinarily the case in medical emergencies. Ashforth and Humphrey (1993) and Tews and Glomb (2000) classified this match between genuine emotion and the situational requirements as a third and important way of accomplishing emotional labor. Yet, note that we propose that if one does not perceive dissonance, one will not be motivated to engage in behaviors that might be described as emotional labor. Regardless of the organization's normative requirements, if one does not experience dissonance, there will be no motivation to *act*, to "put on a face", and thus, no emotional labor—the emotional display will be genuine. If an employee is required by the organization to act pleasantly, and he or she does not perceive this to be emotionally taxing, there will be no necessity for him or her to "act" pleasantly. In fact, a match between organizational requirements and felt emotion may even facilitate or emotionally energize an individual to display particular emotions and would most likely appear to be effortless. Taken together then, perceived dissonance and emotional labor represent the entire emotion regulation process as Grandey (2000) discussed; however, our framework separates situational factors, emotional states, and behaviors: Perceived dissonance is the perceptual state of appraisal of the situational factors, and emotional labor is the behavioral strategy chosen to manage the dissonant state.

As noted, we view emotional labor as one potential and typical response to perceived dissonance. There are then, multiple other strategies for reconciling the state of perceived emotional dissonance, including withdrawing from the task or interaction completely (e.g., hanging up on a customer); becoming hostile or aggressive (e.g., raising one's voice); becoming violent (e.g., physically attacking a customer); or using passive-aggressive behavior (e.g., acting polite during the interaction and then sabotaging a customer's order afterward). These behaviors, however, are unlikely to be viewed by the organization as constructive and representative of appropriate protocol or policy and therefore, are likely to be punished or at least heavily discouraged. Because both emotional labor strategies (surface acting and deep acting) are attempts to produce organizationally desired and rewarded behavior, they are likely to be the strategy of choice utilized by individuals attempting to reduce perceived emotional dissonance, while reaping organizational benefits and rewards (e.g., promotions). Thus, depending on the situational requirements, the actual behavioral display could be positive or negative (e.g., A debt collector must be intimidating and downright hostile at times to be successful). Although this chapter does not directly address at length the numerous possible responses beyond labor, we do present some of them in the model to emphasize their potential importance in future research. Thus, Fig. 11.1 is illustrative, not exhaustive.

Situational Demands of Perceived Dissonance

As stated earlier, our premise is that much of the early work on emotional labor is descriptive of an emotional state influenced by a variety of factors. Given the proposed model, our attempt here is to identify situational demands that impact perceived dissonance and thus indirectly impact emotional labor. We discuss two categories of situational demands we believe largely contribute to the perception of dissonance and subsequent emotional labor. As the model depicts, these situational demands are comprised of (a) *job-specific demands*, including characteristics of the job, and (b) *emotion-specific demands*, including emotional characteristics of the job, display rule norms, and a special case of display rules, customer expectations. Interestingly, these variables have all appeared in prior research on emotional labor; however, many have actually been labeled as dimensions of the emotional labor construct (e.g., display rules and frequency of emotional display), and not as situational factors. Our view is that these important variables work together to create the critical environmental stimuli that may lead to an appraisal of perceived dissonance, and subsequent emotional labor acts.

Job Characteristics. Humphrey (2000) suggested that the critical psychological states resulting from job characteristics (Hackman & Oldham, 1975) clearly impact affective conditions like job satisfaction and thus they should strongly impact secondary work behavior ("behavior that is influenced by the work task, but not actually part of the task," p. 239) including emotional displays. He further argued that job characteristics influence the social context of the work environment. Thus, job characteristics are powerful contextual factors that contribute to an individual's affective state. In our terms, the affective state of perceived emotional dissonance should similarly be impacted by job characteristics.

To date, research on emotional labor and job characteristics has focused primarily on job autonomy. For example, Morris and Feldman (1997) reported a negative relationship between autonomy and emotional dissonance. Pugliesi (1999) explored the relationship between emotional labor and certain characteristics of the job among university employees. She found negative correlations between emotional labor and job characteristics such as control (autonomy) and complexity (skill required, level of challenge, variety and intrinsic interest) of the job. Other research yielded similar results (Rafaeli & Sutton, 1989; Wharton, 1993). Yet beyond skill variety and autonomy, very little research exists linking other job characteristics to emotions. However, given the effects found for autonomy, we argue that other job characteristics might impact perceived dissonance similarly. For example, individuals who experience a high degree of meaningfulness via skill variety, task identity, and task significance are likely to experience a more positive psychological state (Humphrey, 2000). This state should positively influence individuals' emotional appraisal of their work situation and lead to lower perceived emotional dissonance, or at least make it easier to maintain a positive emotional state. Similarly, high responsibility (autonomy) and knowledge of results (feedback) from the job should lead to a lesser degree of perceived emotional dissonance.

Display Rule Norms.   Display rules can be conceptualized as societal, occupational, and organizational norms that provide structure for service transactions (Ashforth & Humphrey, 1993; Ekman, 1973a; Rafaeli & Sutton, 1989). Display rules serve to regulate the type of sanctioned expression in a given situation, as well as the degree to which it is expressed. In an organizational service setting, display rules are often highly explicit to ensure consistency of service. Additionally, display rules are found in all types of organizational communication, including handbooks, performance appraisals, and new employee orientation classes. For example, at the Ritz-Carlton hotels, employees are required to memorize service credo cards, which explicitly state what is meant by service, and which all employees carry on their person at all times. One service "basic" reads, "Smile—We are on stage. Always maintain positive eye contact. Use proper vocabulary with our guests (e.g., "Good morning", "Certainly" and "My pleasure")." Service employees are "on stage" in the sense that these display rules require employees to become actors (Grandey, 2001), acting out organizationally required emotions that may not be congruent with their own personal emotions.

Empirical research demonstrating a link between display rules and emotional labor has provided mixed results. For instance, Hochschild (1983) found that explicit display rules for flight attendants heavily impacted their behavior on the job. In contrast, Morris and Feldman (1997) found that the explicitness of display rules was negatively related to the frequency of emotional labor. These differences are most likely due to the discrepancies in conceptualizations of the construct. As we mentioned, it is important to disentangle the stimulus (e.g., the organizational context) from an individual's internal state (e.g., the felt experience). Our model suggests that an incongruence between the desired emotional expression required by the organization and the felt emotion of the individual creates an experience of perceived dissonance. Therefore, highly explicit display rules would exacerbate the importance of sanctioned emotional expression and create a larger gap between required and felt emotion. Thus, the less latitude employees have (i.e., the more explicit the display rules) in expressing their own felt emotions in lieu of organizationally sanctioned emotion, the greater is the possible perceived dissonance.

Customer Expectations.   Schneider and Bowen (1999) asserted, "By concentrating on [customer] needs, we have an opportunity to delve more deeply into the customer's internal states to offer managers insights about how to create customer delight, as well as how to avoid customer outrage" (p. 38). In addition, they highlighted multiple needs customers expect to receive from service transactions that contribute to positive organizational outcomes, including keeping promises and commitments, help when needed, and friendliness, honesty, and politeness. Similarly, Zeithamal, Parasuraman, and Berry (1990) found that customer evaluations are a function of 10 dimensions, including responsiveness, courtesy, credibility, access, communication, and understanding (in Ashforth & Humphrey, 1993, p. 91). Clearly, customer needs and criteria for good service are laden with emotional content (e.g., "Greet every customer with a smile"). Thus, customer expectations are a special and highly salient type of display rule.

For example, a customer can easily interpret a simple sigh exuded by a customer service agent to mean "I don't care about you—I want to go home," when in fact the agent may simply be tired. Recently, Pugh (2001) found a positive relationship between the display of positive emotion by bank employees and customer positive affect. Similarly, Daus (2001) found converging evidence from a laboratory experiment where expression of positive emotion contributed to higher evaluations of performance for waiters/waitresses. This research confirms what organizations have intuitively known for years—positive employee displays satisfy customers. Organizations are increasingly advertising and educating their customers about this relationship, and customers now approach service exchanges with clear expectations for what good service should look like (e.g., Delta Airline's slogan, "We love to fly and it shows").

Thus, for some organizations, customers will have incredibly high service expectations, including expectations for how employees will display emotions. These expectations often are built into the fabric of the organization and serve as yet another source of information about how employees should behave in customer service interactions. Yet the paradox is that this may be taxing to employees because organizations that promise customers consistent top-notch service thereby increase the emotional requirements of their employees. We therefore propose that customers' expectations will be positively associated with the perceived dissonance of employees.

Emotional Job Characteristics.   Service-role jobs vary considerably across industries and job categories. Logically, these jobs also differ in their emotional characteristics, or the specific type and level of emotional expression inherent in the job itself. These specific emotional characteristics of the job may lead to variance in how an individual actually feels on the job. Therefore, we include them in our model as predictors of perceived dissonance. Three emotional job characteristics that have appeared in prior research are the *frequency of emotional display or interaction, duration of emotion display or interaction*, and *variety of emotions required*. Again, these have previously been presented as dimensions of the emotional labor construct (Hochschild, 1983; Morris & Feldman, 1996, 1997). We separate them from the behavior of emotional labor as Grandey (2000) did, and extend her work to conceptualize them as precursors to perceived dissonance.

Frequency of emotional display or interaction can be defined as the rate of emotional displays or interactions between service providers and clients (Grandey, 2000; Hochschild, 1983; Morris & Feldman, 1997). Some jobs inherently require higher frequencies of emotional displays than others. For example, a cashier at a busy fast-food restaurant may be required to serve hundreds of people in one shift, whereas a concierge at a small hotel may only service a handful of people in a day. In their study of supermarket cashiers, Rafaeli and Sutton (1990) found that during particularly busy hours, cashiers displayed fewer positive emotions. Other research has shown both positive (Brotheridge & Lee, 1998) and negative (Grandey, 1999) relationships between frequency and emotional labor. Note that these studies did not measure the impact of frequency on the emotional state, but rather the impact of frequency on behavior, which may explain the inconsistent findings. The state should impact behavior more strongly than contextual circumstances (Wakefield, 1989). Therefore, for any particular job, the greater the frequency of emotional display required, the more likely it is that an individual will experience a higher degree of perceived emotional dissonance.

Duration of emotional display or interaction is generally referred to as *duration*. Service interactions that are relatively short tend to follow a scripted interaction schema (Rafaeli, 1989) and require less emotional effort. As the duration increases, so does the level of emotional effort required to go beyond the social script in order to comply with organizational demands. Back to our previous example: The cashier at the fast-food restaurant may on average spend about 3 or 4 minutes with a customer, whereas the concierge at the hotel may spend upward of 10 to 15 minutes working with a customer planning entire outings. Thus, the concierge's job requires him or her to engage in positive emotional displays for more extended periods. Long durations could lead to a feeling of heightened perceived dissonance if in fact the discrepancy between what the job requires from the concierge and how he or she feels is too great. Thus, we propose that the longer the duration of interaction, potentially the greater is the amount of perceived dissonance.

Certain jobs require a greater *variety of emotions* to comply with organizational requirements. For example, some occupations "often require frequent changes of emotions that are displayed: positive emotions to build enthusiasm, negative emotions to support discipline and neutrality of emotions to demonstrate fairness and professionalism" (Morris & Feldman, 1996, p. 992). In the theatrical arts, actors often talk about "range" in reference to the ability to play a wide variety of characters and across multiple genres (e.g., slapstick comedy vs. Shakespearean theater). Similarly, service employees are often called on to express a wide range of emotions in order to successfully perform on the job. Some of these emotional expressions may even contradict one another. For example, an employee might force a smile while communicating a tough policy issue to a customer in a firm voice. Few researchers have explored this idea empirically, but there are similar theoretical conceptions (Grandey, 2000; Wharton & Erickson, 1993). Our proposition is that jobs requiring a wide range of emotions and/or multiple emotions to express simultaneously have a greater impact on one's emotional state than jobs requiring only a few emotions to be expressed. Much like cognitive load, perceived dissonance could increase under such circumstances.

The situational demands just outlined seem to contribute to an individual's overall affective state. Clearly, a single property may not produce a significant change in the emotional state; however, the cumulative effect contributes to the experienced state. Thus, it should be acknowledged that although the main effect of any single antecedent may impact perceived dissonance (positively or negatively), the potential interactions are likely to yield more complex types of relationships and may strengthen, weaken or nullify the main effects.[1]

The Direct and Moderating Effect of Individual Differences

In this model, perceived dissonance mediates the relationship between situational demands and emotional labor. All things being equal, a number of indi-

---

[1]We thank Blake Ashforth for bringing this important point to our attention.

vidual difference variables could potentially influence the amount of perceived dissonance experienced, thereby impacting subsequent emotional labor and concomitant outcomes. In other words, some individuals might never experience a high degree of perceived dissonance whereas others might be plagued by it, even given identical antecedent conditions. It follows logically then that individual differences may also differentially affect the emotional labor process. In all, individual difference variables might influence the perceived dissonance–labor relationship. Directly, individual differences may impact the amount of perceived dissonance one experiences and the type and level of emotional labor undertaken. Individual differences may also moderate the relationship between situational demands and perceived dissonance, as well as the relationship between perceived emotional dissonance and emotional labor. We next use examples of individual differences from the extant literature to illustrate some of these potential pathways of influence.

Role Internalization. Role internalization or identification denotes the degree to which individuals identify with the job (or job values). Ashforth and Humphrey (1993) asserted that role internalization is a potential outcome of compliance with display rules over time. Morris and Feldman (1997) confirmed that assertion, demonstrating that longer duration of emotional labor results in greater internalization of role expectations. We do not disagree with this perspective; however, there may be a case for role internalization as an individual difference variable directly influencing perceived dissonance. Specifically, individuals who have internalized their career role as a "customer service" employee are likely to experience less perceived dissonance than individuals who have career identities in opposition to service. For example, an individual who has worked for multiple years in one service company may accept a job in a similar service company, multiple times within the same industry. Although each job is different, he or she is likely to incur similar role expectations on the new job and may have already internalized the standard industry display expectations. For instance, the task requirements of department-store sales clerks may be substantially different in terms of procedures, but rather similar in terms of customer service. Thus, the individual begins to view "customer service agent" as a career descriptor, much as an accountant (or other professional categories) might, and internalizes or transforms into the role. For these individuals, emotional expression is not a chore but rather second nature; it *is* what they do. Recently, Ashforth and Tomiuk (2000) further delved into this construct empirically, and proposed that role internalization leads to an experience of "deep authenticity" whereby "one's emotional expression or display is consistent with the display rules of a specific identity that one has internalized (or wants to internalize) as a reflection of self—*regardless of whether the expression genuinely reflects one's current feelings*" (p. 195). According to these authors, deep authenticity should lead to either no emotional dissonance (our construct of perceived dissonance) or, at worst, low emotional dissonance (when the temporary affective state is incongruent with normative requirements). Therefore, we propose that role internalization should buffer the effect of situational demands, as well as directly impact perceived dissonance, leading to less perceived dissonance.

Emotional Intelligence.   Another construct that would seem intuitively to influence directly perceived dissonance is emotional intelligence. Emotional intelligence focuses on an individual's ability to both interpret emotional information (both internal and external) and manage it in an adaptive manner. Most importantly for the discussion of emotional labor, emotional intelligence (through mood maintenance) is an ability that allows people to better regulate their emotions compared to others (Ciarrochi, Chan, & Caputi, 2000; Mayer, Caruso, & Salovey, 2000; Mayer & Salovey, 1997). Mayer and colleagues (Mayer et al., 2000; Mayer & Salovey, 1997; Salovey & Mayer, 1990) argued that emotional intelligence has four important components. First, it involves the ability to perceive and appraise emotion, both verbally and nonverbally. For example, emotionally intelligent individuals are better at accurately identifying various emotional expressions on individuals' faces (Ekman, Friesen, & Ancoli, 1980), as well as at appraising emotional content in art or music, than nonemotionally intelligent individuals. This ability would seem vital for jobs where reading emotions of customers and clients is a critical precursor to interacting with them effectively.

Emotional intelligence also consists of the ability to assimilate emotions into perceptual and cognitive processes. Thus, emotionally intelligent individuals are better able to be flexible when planning, to generate more creative solutions, and to redirect attention and motivation (e.g., directing feelings away from trivial problems toward those of higher priority) (Mayer et al., 2000; Mayer & Salovey, 1997). Thus, the emotionally intelligent customer service agent should be better able to maintain focus during particularly busy times, allowing for creative and emotionally appropriate responses to impatient customers.

Third, emotional intelligence consists of the ability to reason about and understand emotions. A person with this higher level ability would have the capacity to understand, for example, how emotions progress from one to another (Mayer, 2001; Mayer et al., 2000). It would certainly seem to be an asset for a customer service agent to be able to recognize when and how frustration in a customer could lead to anger, which could progress to rage.

Finally, emotional intelligence involves the ability of regulation or management of emotion in oneself and in others. This is perhaps the key ability involved in emotional labor. The central mechanism for regulating emotions is mood manipulation. In the self, individuals are generally motivated to maintain or prolong pleasant moods and curtail unpleasant moods—"mood maintenance" and "mood repair," respectively (Isen, 1985). An emotionally intelligent customer service representative who recognizes her own and her customers' moods may be able to utilize the information to better serve her customers. For example, if she knew she was in a bad mood, she might try extra hard to avoid displaying this to her customers (Berkowitz, Jaffee, Jo, & Troccoli, 2000). As such, this ability inherently involves emotional expression that encompasses empathy (Ciarrochi et al., 2000; Fox & Spector, 2000; Hogan, 1969; Mayer et al., 2000; Mayer, DiPaolo, & Salovey, 1990). Empathetic responses lead to genuineness and appropriate behaviors, whereas a lack of empathy leads to ill-mannered behaviors. Empathy, then, is critically important in jobs that tend to require emotional labor.

Highly emotionally intelligent individuals are likely to experience less perceived emotional dissonance, based on their ability to effectively interpret and regulate their own and others' emotional states. Emotional intelligence may directly and indirectly influence the type of emotional labor undertaken and skill at emotional labor. In fact, recent research (Jordan, Ashkanasy, & Härtel, 2000) indeed demonstrated a significant moderating relationship of emotional intelligence on emotional labor. Thus, we propose that emotional intelligence abilities will directly affect perceived emotional dissonance, as well as moderate the perceived dissonance–emotional labor relationship.

Positive and Negative Affectivity. Positive and negative affectivity (PA/ NA) have particular relevance to our model. According to Watson (2000), "Affective traits/temperaments provide a 'set point' that is characteristic for each individual but differs across individuals. Mood varies around this set point" (p. 18). Given that this set point is variable across individuals, PA/NA may directly influence the amount of perceived dissonance an individual experiences. A person who is higher in positive affectivity may perceive less dissonance across situations. Generally, persons high in positive affectivity perceive things more positively, and persons high on negative affectivity generally perceive things more negatively. Recent research has focused on the role of positive and negative affectivity as a moderator of situation-response relationships (Munz et al., 1996; Williams, Gavin, & Williams, 1996). Specifically, PA and NA are assumed to substantively affect other variables and their relationships through perceptual, temperamental, and instrumental processes. For example, to the degree that employees with high NA perceive more stringent display rules (perceptual), have stronger negative reactions to internal and external stimuli (temperamental), and behave to evoke environmental reactions (instrumental), then NA will moderate the perceived dissonance–labor relationship. Similarly, Abraham (1999) suggested that individuals high in negative affectivity tended to experience a conflict between expressed (positive) and felt (negative) emotions in organizations that demand the expression of positive emotions. She found that negative affectivity moderated the relationship between emotional dissonance and job satisfaction, whereas it mediated the relationship with emotional exhaustion.

In all, we believe that individual differences augment the understanding of the perceived dissonance-emotional labor process. The three individual differences highlighted in our model were used to illustrate the importance of individual difference variables in this process. Clearly, there are a wide range of individual difference variables that might be intuitively hypothesized (e.g., self-monitoring, public vs. private self). Future research is critical to establish the relevance and role of individual differences and their direct and/or indirect effects.

Individual and Organizational Outcomes

There is little doubt that emotions play out in various ways and are deeply embedded in organizational life. As such, research on emotions has been concerned with important individual and organizational constructs (e.g., job satisfaction, stress, burnout, organizational justice) that have strong direct and indirect effects on organizational success (Nord & Fox, 1995).

Our model suggests that there are a number of significant individual and organizational consequences of high perceived dissonance and subsequent emotional labor. It is important to note that in the short term, organizations may clearly benefit from individuals engaging in emotional labor; however, over time individuals may become increasingly emotionally exhausted, which could lead to a family of deleterious behaviors (e.g., burnout and performance) or, in extreme cases, a choice to employ a less appropriate strategy (e.g., workplace violence).

In other words, we recognize that the next subsection paints a rather gloomy scenario such that engaging in emotional labor in the long term leads to primarily deleterious outcomes and that *all* service employees will incur negative outcomes. This is not entirely our intention. Clearly, there are satisfied, authentic, lifelong employees who exist in service roles. Indeed, there are some positive effects that may emerge in the short term. However, based on our definition, the lifelong service employee is unlikely to be experiencing significant and prolonged periods of emotional dissonance. Individuals who are engaging in emotional labor behavior do so because they *labor* to reconcile a dissonant state. Thus, if one does not experience this dissonance, one will not be required to act incongruously with one's own genuine feelings and thus it is *not laborious* to act. As mentioned earlier, individual differences or situational demands that buffer or eliminate these effects or an interaction of the two may contribute to low perceived emotional dissonance.

Our discussion of outcomes covers three general categories, some of which are interrelated and include job-related attitudes and behaviors, physical and psychological well-being, and withdrawal behaviors. The following is not intended to exhaust every potential direct or indirect outcome of emotion management or emotions at work, but to focus on those outcomes most closely related to emotional labor as identified in the extant literature. Others have provided broader reviews beyond the scope of this chapter (cf. Mastenbroek, 2000b).

Job-Related Attitudes and Behaviors. A number of job-related attitude and behavior outcomes of emotional labor have been offered in the literature (Ashforth & Humphrey, 1993; Grandey, 2000; Morris & Feldman, 1996, Pugliesi, 1999). Many have suggested that emotional labor negatively impacts job attitudes such as job satisfaction and organizational commitment (Grandey, 2000; Hochschild, 1983). Some, however, point to potential benefits, arguing that emotional labor allows individuals to gain a sense of control over their work environment (Wharton, 1993) or allows for increased enjoyment (Ashforth & Humphrey, 1993). To date, there have been mixed findings regarding job attitudes, which may be attributable to the various operationalizations of emotional labor (Grandey, 2000). Given that many job attitudes are highly affective in nature (Weiss & Cropanzano, 1996), we contend that perceived dissonance and subsequent labor may lead to negative job attitudes (all things being equal). Thus, an individual who experiences a great deal of perceived dissonance and engages in emotional labor to reconcile the dissonance might feel like he or she is not being "true" to him- or herself. In the service role, where employees often are asked to "put the customer first," one's own feelings about one's job situation are secondary. As Hochschild (1983) suggested, this continuously felt inconsistency is likely to lead to a negative appraisal of one's job circumstances. For example, Hochschild (1983) related accounts of flight attendants who resented the notion of the "customer is always right," especially when the customer was clearly not right. Other research has supported this. Pugliesi (1999) found that among university staff, emotional labor decreased job satisfaction. Therefore, we propose that long-term emotional labor will decrease job satisfaction and would have a similar impact on other job attitudes such as organizational commitment and turnover intention. Indirectly, then, emotional labor might lead to other negative consequences, such as turnover, as a result of these negative attitudes (Griffeth, Hom, & Gaertner, 2000). Further, as evidenced by Hochschild, we propose that long-term emotional labor will similarly increase employee resentment or cynicism, which has also been shown to have detrimental effects in organizations (Bommer & Rubin, 2001; Reichers, Wanous, & Austin, 1997).

Individuals experiencing a high degree of perceived emotional dissonance and engaging in emotional labor might feel as if their emotional resources are depleted or overloaded. When struggling to draw on their own emotional resources to "put on a happy face," employees' willingness to display extrarole behaviors such as coming to the aid of a coworker or resolving interpersonal conflicts (Podsakoff, MacKenzie, Paine, & Bachrach, 2000) should decrease. This idea is consistent with the emotional regulation literature indicating that individual performance tapers off when one is forced to spend resources regulating one's own emotions (Gross & Levenson, 1997; Muraven, Tice, & Baumeister, 1998). In general, individuals who experience high perceived dissonance and respond via surface acting or deep acting will be less likely to go the "extra mile" on the job. Again, we depart from other researchers such that the relationships just described hinge on an individual experiencing perceived dissonance and choosing to engage in emotional labor. For individuals who have internalized their role to a great degree and do not experience perceived dissonance, we would not expect our model to predict attitudes or behaviors. We do not mean to suggest that a lack of perceived dissonance and subsequent emotional labor will lead to satisfaction and other positive behaviors. There are, of course, multiple pathways to job attitudes and behaviors. Our focus here is on how emotional labor might produce these outcomes.

Physical and Psychological Well-Being. As Grandey (2000) remarked, "Emotional labor may result in good organizational performance, but may have consequences for the employee's health" (p. 107). Long-term emotional labor efforts may lead to an increase in stress and reported physical and psychological strain. Hochschild (1983) suggested that long-term emotional labor would lead to a host of dysfunctional behaviors that impact individual well-being, including excessive drinking, drug use, and sexual dysfunctions. For example, Schaubroeck and Jones (2000) showed that individuals who perceived a greater demand to express positive emotions (i.e., contributing to dissonance) on the job reported a greater number of somatic symptoms. Grandey (2000) also suggested that emotional labor might lead to increased individual stress over time. Stress has a long history of study in management demonstrating its direct, negative relationship with job attitudes (e.g., job satisfaction), as well as long-term physical (e.g., heart disease) and mental health (e.g., depression) consequences (Matteson & Ivancevich, 1987). Yet here too there are mixed findings. For instance, Zerbe (2000) found that emotive dissonance (similar to our conception of perceived dissonance) was not associated with employee psychological well-being (as measured by dimensions of burnout). However, Pugliesi (1999) found that emotional labor was strongly and positively related to job stress and increased psychological distress. Again, these differences are possibly due in part to the range of operationalizations of emotional labor.

One important potential consequence of long-term emotional labor is that of burnout, which has been characterized by emotional exhaustion, depersonalization, and diminished personal accomplishment (Jackson, Schwab & Schuler, 1986; Maslach, 1982) primarily arising from stress. Burnout is a common syndrome found most often in helping professions such as nursing, social work, and customer service and has been shown to have deleterious effects on both the individual and the organization (Cordes & Dougherty, 1993). There is growing evidence showing a positive relationship between emotional labor and burnout, often captured via the emotional exhaustion dimension of burnout. Hochschild (1983) argued that individuals who engage in deep acting strategies should experience more exhaustion because they become emotionally involved with the customers they serve. Brotheridge and Grandey (2002) did not find support for this hypothesis, showing a positive association between surface acting and emotional exhaustion but no relationship between deep acting and emotional exhaustion. Similarly, others found little support for Hochschild's contention (Brotheridge & Lee, 1998; Kruml & Geddes, 2000). Kruml and Geddes (2000) showed that individuals experience more stress by faking emotion (rather than genuinely expressing what they feel), thereby demonstrating a potential link to burnout. Morris and Feldman (1997) found a positive relationship between emotional labor and emotional exhaustion among debt collectors, military recruiters, and nurses. Thus, it seems that emotional labor has a potentially dangerous cascading effect (beginning with stress) on individuals who engage in it long-term.

Suppression of emotion has also been shown to have harmful effects on health, as well as psychological well-being and adjustment (Balswick, 1988; Berry & Pennebaker, 1998; Brotheridge & Grandey, 2002; Feshback, 1986; Gross, 1998b; Labott & Martin, 1987). In contrast, inhibition of negative emotional expression in the context of the workplace, such as avoiding an emotional outburst, generally speaking has been *conventionally regarded* as a positive characteristic. In other words, organizations generally want their employees to suppress negative emotional expressions. Yet again, research has demonstrated several negative individual and organizational consequences of inhibition of negative emotions, including decrements in problem solving, personal growth, and job satisfaction (French & Bell, 1990). Also, Gross (1998b) and Gross and Levenson (1997) addressed the effects of inhibition and suppression of emotion on the individual. Although there have been mixed findings, the data seem to suggest that faking emotion, regardless of the strategy employed, is harmful to the individual. Thus, individuals who experience high perceived dissonance may be in a "catch 22," whereby expressing emotions that are incongruent with display rules leads to negative outcomes (e.g., poor performance ratings), yet conforming to display rules (via emotional labor) leads to other negative outcomes (e.g., burnout).

Given the logic just presented, the relationship between emotional labor and performance is not altogether straightforward. On one hand, there is evidence that performing emotional labor strategies (either through surface acting or deep acting) leads to good customer service interactions (Daus, 2001; Pugh, 2001). In other words, the employee is able to successfully cope with the perceived dissonance he or she experiences by "acting" out his or her role in accordance with the display rules for the job and thus performs well (i.e., the customer is satisfied). On the other hand, insincerity of emotional display may be detectable by customers (Rafaeli & Sutton, 1987), leading the customer to believe the employee is "faking" the smile or simply going through the motions. Further, emotional labor is related to burnout, and there is evidence building that burnout, particularly emotional exhaustion, is negatively related to performance (Cordes & Dougherty, 1993; Wright & Bonett, 1997). Grandey (2000) suggested that the type of emotional labor strategy employed (i.e., surface acting or deep acting) will differentiate between good and bad performance. For instance, she asserted that surface acting, whereby the employee fakes the emotional display, would lead to poor performance based on customers' sensitivity to genuine expression. Deep acting, whereby the employee truly adopts the required emotional display as his or her own, should lead to good performance. We agree with this perspective but propose that a temporal element is important to consider. Long-term deep acting in which the person is able to truly feel and express the emotion required may lead to poor performance over time. A Broadway actor performing his or her 550th musical show is more likely to experience burnout than when he or she did the first 50 shows. If he or she has truly internalized the role (i.e., "become" the character), however, and less emotional energy is expended, the actor may be able to avoid complete burnout.

Withdrawal Behaviors. Individuals who experience sustained perceived dissonance over time in service roles and respond via surfacing acting or deep acting could begin to withdraw as a way of escaping the persistent emotional burden they perceive. Hulin and colleagues conceptualized withdrawal behavior as a family of *adaptive* behaviors that help individuals avoid the work circumstances (Hulin, 1990; Hulin, Roznowski, & Hachiya, 1985). Their model (Hulin et al., 1985) categorized withdrawal behaviors into four families: (a) behavioral intentions to increase non-job outcomes, such as using work time for personal tasks; (b) behavioral intentions to reduce job inputs, such as taking long breaks or talking with coworkers about non-business-related topics; (c) behavioral intentions to reduce work role inclusion, such as absenteeism, tardiness, or quitting; and (d) behavioral intentions to change the work role such as unionization or transfer attempts. Thus, in the short run, individuals may take refuge from the *labor* of emotional labor in the form of taking longer breaks or leaving a workstation unattended; however, in the long run this might lead to more significant behaviors such as turnover or requests for transfers. This argument seems to warrant merit. For instance, Grandey (1999) found a positive relationship between turnover intent and emotional labor, which may suggest that the high turnover rates observed in service industries (e.g., hospitality and call centers) may be in part due to emotional labor.

Continuous regulation of emotion may lead an employee to believe he or she is working in the wrong environment, and thus the employee becomes motivated to find a better match (Grandey, 2000), or even burns out before he or she recognizes the poor match.

As stated, emotional labor may impact emotional exhaustion and job satisfaction, which in turn might influence withdrawal behaviors (Hulin, 1990). Some research has supported this notion. For example, Abraham (1999) found emotional dissonance resulted in withdrawal intention indirectly through job dissatisfaction, whereas others have found that emotional exhaustion predicted turnover through job satisfaction (Babakus, Cravens, Johnston, & Moncrief, 1999). Wright and Cropanzano (1998) found that emotional exhaustion led to turnover among 52 social welfare workers. Given the logic just described, we propose a positive relationship between emotional labor and withdrawal.

CONCLUDING REMARKS

In an increasingly customer-driven and "branded-service" market, the topic of emotional labor is likely to garner increased attention by academicians and practitioners alike. To date, the conceptual status of the construct is, at best, "muddy." Empirical research based on a variety of differing conceptualizations has contributed to this confusion. Our intent here was to propose a research model that might provide some conceptual utility and ultimately make a contribution to the empirical literature. Specifically, we attempted to make four important contributions to the literature and our understanding of the construct:

1. We argued that theoretical confusion has stemmed largely from a myriad of conceptualizations that defined emotional labor as an emotional state, a behavior, or both.
2. We attempted to disentangle the construct by offering an intervening construct we called *perceived emotional dissonance*.
3. We clarified the definition of emotional labor as strictly a behavioral strategy (one of many possible) used to appropriately (i.e., within the guidelines of acceptable organizational behavior) respond to reduce the experienced emotional state.
4. We stated that an individual must experience perceived emotional dissonance for him or her to be motivated to engage in emotional labor.

Härtel and Zerbe (2000) noted, "No theoretical framework has been put forward that identifies the crucial contextual features of organizations upon which emotional experience varies" (p. 216). The present model may directly address some of their expressed concern. Specifically, disentangling the potential situational demands from the state and behavior should provide more clarity regarding the selection of variables that are true dimensions of the construct from those that exist outside the construct. However, the present model does not in any way attempt to explain the dynamic complexity of emotional labor. In Fig. 11.1 we include a feedback loop between perceived dissonance and emotional labor to highlight the notion that this is, in all likelihood, a *highly dynamic* process. For example, engaging in deep acting may reduce the amount of perceived dissonance one experiences and therefore in turn may influence one's emotional labor strategy in the future. Thus, although we still believe that a dissonant state must exist for an individual to engage in emotionally laborious acts, we recognize that this relationship may be more complex than the rather linear model we present. However, in order to "see the forest through the trees," we felt some simplification was required to maximize theoretical clarity.

Future Research. Because it was beyond the scope of this theoretical chapter, we have not discussed *how* to measure perceived dissonance and/or emotional labor. Recently, there have been great advancements made in developing measures (e.g., Tews & Glomb, 2004), which have highlighted both the complexity and challenge of operationalization in this area. The model presented here may be useful in propelling, or at least supplementing, current measurement development efforts in the near future. Regardless of whether the reader agrees with the viability of our perspective, measurement and subsequent empirical work in this area would benefit greatly from clear explication of the theoretical underpinnings of the construct.

Additionally, because our intent was to present a reconceptualization of the emotional labor construct, we by no means claim to have tapped the entire domain of potential factors that surround emotion management in the workplace. Other authors have called for examination of broader issues in relation to emotional labor. For example, Ashforth and Humphrey (1993) suggested a number of emotion variables, on multiple levels, that have been recognized as critical elements in motivation, leadership, and group dynamics that may influence the emotional labor process. In addition, they called for future research that focused on other professional roles and settings beyond service. Grandey (2000) discussed the importance of examining coworker and supervisor support as a moderator of emotional labor. Further, *Emotions in the Workplace* (2000), edited by Ashkanasy, Härtel, and Zerbe, and *Emotion in Organizations* (2000, 2nd ed.), edited by Stephen Fineman, cover a broad range of emotion issues in workplace research. Clearly, there are a number of moderators and mediators that would fit nicely with the proposed model. Undoubtedly, there is still a great deal of work to be done in this area. In short, we hope the described model realized some of our goals and will provide utility for those involved in emotions in organizations research.

ACKNOWLEDGMENTS

The authors thank Blake Ashforth, Theresa Glomb, and Ron Humphrey for their helpful comments on previous drafts and presentations of this chapter. A version of this chapter was presented at the 17th Annual Conference of the Society for Industrial and Organizational Psychology, Toronto, Canada.

12

Toward Understanding Emotional Management at Work: A Quantitative Review of Emotional Labor Research

Joyce E. Bono
Meredith A. Vey

In this chapter, we cumulate the results of empirical research on the predictors and outcomes of emotional labor. After a discussion of the definitions and operationalizations of emotional labor, we use meta-analytic techniques to obtain estimates of the associations between emotional labor and organizational display rules, burnout, physical symptoms, personality, and job characteristics. We discuss these finding and their implications for future research on emotional management in organizations, with a focus on the ubiquity of emotional regulation, the role of personality, and ways that organizations can buffer the negative effects of emotional labor on their employees. We conclude with a brief discussion of the implications of emotional labor research for employee selection, job performance, and organizational success.

A customer service representative who loses his or her temper with a customer would be considered "unprofessional;" as would a funeral director who is perky and bubbly with grieving clients. Behavior in organizations is profoundly influenced by organizational norms and rules. Emotional behavior is no exception. Organizational rules and norms for emotional behavior are communicated to employees through both formal means, such as selection, training, evaluation, and incentive systems, and informal means, such as social influence and pressures. Many organizations encourage employees to exhibit only a narrow range of emotions while at work, such as expressing only cheerfulness when interacting with customers, or suppressing their irritation with a difficult coworker in the name of professionalism. However, as human beings, we can experience a wide range of emotions in a given workday. In order to comply

213

with organizational requirements, many employees must suppress their true emotions or manipulate their emotional expressions. Employees experiencing discordance between felt and required emotions can suppress their genuine emotion, pretend to feel the required emotion (surface acting), or change their emotions to match their organization's display rules (deep acting; Ashforth & Humphrey, 1993; Brotheridge & Lee, 2002; Grandey, 2000). This emotional regulation at work was termed *emotional labor* by Hochschild (1983). In the 20 years since Hochschild's (1983) study, emotional labor researchers have focused their energy and attention on further defining the emotional labor construct, exploring possible operationalizations of emotional labor, and identifying possible antecedents and outcomes of emotional labor.

This chapter has two main objectives. The first objective is to quantitatively review the emotional labor literature. Toward this end, the history of the emotional labor construct and its definitions and operationalizations is reviewed. Also, relationships between emotional labor and its proposed predictors and outcomes are quantitatively synthesized, using Hunter and Schmidt's (1990) "bare-bones" meta-analytic techniques. After this descriptive and quantitative review of the literature, we turn to the future of emotional labor research. Our second objective is to use what we have learned from the quantitative review to advance emotional labor research. We identify several areas of concern with current emotional labor research and a number of areas ripe with possibilities for future research.

THE EVOLUTION OF EMOTIONAL LABOR

Reichers and Schneider (1990) proposed that scientific constructs evolve following a predictable sequence of three developmental stages: (a) concept introduction/elaboration, (b) concept evaluation/augmentation, and (c) concept consolidation/accommodation. During the initial concept introduction/elaboration stage of construct development, researchers and theorists work toward legitimizing a new construct or a construct recently borrowed from another field. Papers are written to disseminate information about the concept and to present data, with the construct as an independent or dependent variable, as evidence that the construct reflects a legitimate phenomenon. If the concept survives the first stage, the second stage of concept evaluation/augmentation begins. In this state, critiques of early papers and disagreements over how to properly define and operationalized the concept arise. Hopefully, these criticisms and debates lead to augmentation of the concept, through the development of improved measures, the introduction of possible moderating and mediating variables, and the utilization of advanced methodologies. The last stage of construct development, according to Reichers and Schneider, occurs when debate and controversy over the construct has ebbed. By this last stage, one or two key definitions and operationalizations have garnered common acceptance, and there is consensus as to the predictors and outcomes of the construct. During this stage, comprehensive meta-analyses are conducted and research efforts focused on the concept abate.

The construct of emotional labor is a relatively new one. Introduced by Hochschild (1983) approximately 20 years ago, emotional labor has been the topic of numerous book chapters, journal articles, and conference proceedings. Emotional labor researchers and scholars have focused their energy and attention on further defining the emotional labor construct, by identifying antecedents, emotional regulation strategies, and outcomes of emotional labor. Many of the journal articles and book chapters written on emotional labor have been theoretical in nature, proposing and revising definitions, operationalizations, process models, predictors, and outcomes of emotional labor. To date, fewer than 30 journal articles have been published on the topic, with fewer than half of those articles presenting data.

The construct of emotional labor seems to have survived its infancy, however. The legitimacy of emotional labor as a construct has been enhanced by research on organizational display rules, emotional management at work, and the possible deleterious outcomes of emotional labor. Findings from both qualitative and quantitative studies of employees from bill collection agencies, restaurants, universities, hospitals, airlines, and even Disneyland suggest that some organizations and jobs prohibit the free expression of emotions (Abraham, 1998; Adelmann, 1995; Brotheridge & Grandey, 2002; Cropanzano, Weiss, & Elias, 2004; Diefendorff & Richard, 2003; Morris & Feldman, 1997; Rafaeli & Sutton, 1989; Sutton, 1991; Van Maanen & Kunda, 1989). In some service jobs, employees are expected to express positive emotions to promote goodwill and spending. In contrast, bill collectors may be required to display negative emotions (anger, irritability) in an effort to gain debtor compliance (Sutton, 1991). Ekman (1973b) used the term *display rules* to refer to social norms regarding the appropriate experience and display of emotions. Perhaps more importantly, research has also revealed that employees do regulate their emotions to conform to organizational display rules by suppressing the emotions they genuinely feel and faking emotions they do not feel (Brotheridge & Lee, 2002; Erickson & Ritter, 2001; Glomb, Miner, & Tews, 2002; Grandey, 2003). Finally, researchers have couched the need to learn more about emotional labor in terms of preventing the possible negative effects of such emotion work. Individuals holding jobs involving emotional labor have reported both work-related stress and emotional exhaustion (Brotheridge & Grandey, 2002; Brotheridge & Lee, 2002; Erickson & Ritter, 2001; Grandey, 2003; Holman, Chissick, & Totterdell, 2002; Kruml & Geddes, 2000; Morris & Feldman, 1997).

Clearly, a number of researchers have deemed emotional labor to be a topic worthy of research and inquiry. Thus, the construct of emotional labor has survived the first stage of concept evolution, the concept introduction/elaboration phase. Few researchers and theorists would argue with the idea that employees in many jobs feel required to regulate their emotional expressions at work. Agreement on how to define and operationalized emotional labor, however, has not been reached. The emotional labor literature is thick with discussion of how to best capture the phenomenon of emotional labor through definition and operationalization. Thus, emotional labor now seems to be struggling through the throes of construct adolescence or concept evaluation/augmentation.

DEFINITIONS AND OPERATIONALIZATIONS

In Table 12.1, we provide a list of the definitions of emotional labor that have emerged over the last decade. Although researchers and theorists are in general agreement as to the importance of increasing our understanding of emotional labor, subtle differences in definitions and operationalizations of emotional labor have led to disagreement and confusion (Cropanzano et al., 2004;

TABLE 12.1
Recent Definitions of Emotional Labor

Source	Definition
Hochschild (1983)	"The management of feeling to create a publicly observable facial or bodily display; emotional labor is sold for a wage and therefore has *exchange* value."
James (1989)	"The labour involved in dealing with other people's feelings, a core component of which is the regulation of emotions" (p. 15).
Ashforth and Humphrey (1993)	"The act of displaying the appropriate emotion (i.e., conforming with a display rule" (p. 90).
Morris and Feldman (1996)	"The effort, planning, and control needed to express organizationally desired emotion during interpersonal transactions" (p. 987).
Pugliesi (1999)	"The performance of various forms of emotion work in the context of paid employment. . . . Emotion work (or emotional management) refers to various efforts to manage emotional states and displays" (p. 126).
Zapf, Vogt, Seifert, and Isic (1999)	"The emotional regulation required of the employees in the display of organizationally desired emotions" (p. 371).
Grandey (2000)	"May involve enhancing, faking, or suppressing emotions to modify the emotional expression . . . in response to display rules for the organization or job" (p. 95).
Kruml and Geddes (2000)	"What employees perform when they are required to feel, or at least project the appearance of certain emotions in order to produce, for insurance, 'excellent customer service' " (p. 177).
Glomb, Miner, and Tews (2002)	"The effort expended in expressing appropriate emotions and not expressing inappropriate emotions on the job, as defined by role requirements" (p. 4).
Zammuner and Galli (2003)	"Emotion regulation that occurs within work contexts."
Diefendorff and Richard (2003)	"The management of emotions as part of the work role."

Grandey, 2000). Hochschild (1979, 1983) is credited with first conceptualizing emotional labor as emotional management at work by defining emotional labor as "the management of feeling to create a publicly observable facial and body display" (Hochschild, 1983, p. 7). She went on to note that although emotional management can occur at work or in a private context, emotional *labor* refers to emotional management that is "sold for a wage" (p. 7). Furthermore, she stated that emotional labor "requires one to induce or suppress feeling in order to sustain the outward countenance that produces the proper state of mind in others." Thus flight attendants must display a calm and friendly demeanor so that airline passengers feel welcome and safe. According to this emotional labor as emotional management viewpoint, employees conform to organizational display rules by manipulating their emotional displays and maybe even emotional states, if their genuine emotions are discordant with organizational display rules. A key element to the emotional labor as emotional management approach is dissonance. In this approach, emotional labor, or the management of emotions, takes place when the individual must express emotions that he or she does not actually feel.

According to Hochschild (1983), employees can manipulate their emotions by utilizing three main emotional management strategies: suppressing genuine emotion, surface acting, and deep acting. The suppression of genuine emotions might involve hiding one's irritation with a customer or coworker. Surface acting involves faking or pretending to feel the emotions required by organizational display rules, and deep acting describes the act of trying to actually change one's emotional state to match the organizationally required expressions. A customer service representative who plasters on a fake smile to comply with the organization's cheerful display rules while experiencing negative emotions on the inside would be surface acting. A customer service representative who actually tries to actually change his or her negative emotional state to a positive one in order to genuinely feel and experience cheerfulness would be deep acting.

Taking a more behavioral approach to emotional labor, Ashforth and Humphreys (1993) defined emotional labor as "the act of displaying the appropriate emotion (i.e., conforming with a display rule)" (p. 90). The aim of this approach is to focus on observable behavior, not internal feelings or emotional states. Thus, emotional labor can be operationalized as the expression or display of certain prescribed emotions. For Ashforth and Humphreys, it is the observable emotional behavior in response to organizational display rules, rather than any internal dissonance between experienced and expressed emotion, that is key. The advantage of this approach is its focus on observable behaviors. However, by focusing only on behavior, rather than emotional management, we are left without a theoretical link between emotional labor and proposed outcomes, such as stress or burnout. Why would we expect that smiling would be stressful, unless the smile was not a genuine expression of happiness?

In a third approach to emotional labor, Morris and Feldman (1996) defined emotional labor as "the effort, planning, and control needed to express organizational desired emotion during interpersonal transactions" (p. 987). Their definition is quite similar to Hochschild's (1983), in that both are focused on emotional management and the expression of prescribed emotions. Morris and Feldman expanded Hochschild's definition in two ways. First, they suggested that emotional labor occurs even when employees are asked to display emotions they genuinely feel, as the appropriate *expression* of the genuinely felt emotion may be prescribed by the organization. For example, happy Walmart employees must be certain to express their happiness with appropriate smiles or greetings, which may require effort for employees who might naturally express their happiness in a more exuberant fashion (e.g., singing or hugging). Morris and Feldman also expanded the emotional labor concept by identifying four dimensions that affect the experience of emotional labor: the frequency of interpersonal interactions, attentiveness (the intensity of emotions expressed and duration of the interactions), variety of emotions required by the interactions, and emotional dissonance (discrepancy between felt and expressed emotions). Thus, the nature of a job, or the nature of the interactions required in a job, plays a role in defining emotional labor. Morris and Feldman's approach contributed to our understanding of emotional labor by pointing out that emotional labor is not a dichotomous variable (an employee is performing emotional labor or not). They focus our attention on the factors that influence the degree or intensity of the emotional labor. Some researchers have taken this perspective to an extreme, by operationalizing emotional labor as job demand or job characteristics (Wharton, 1993), thus confusing the antecedents of emotional labor with emotional labor.

As is clear in Table 12.1 (with the exception of Ashforth & Humphreys, 1993), there is general agreement that emotional labor involves managing emotions at work in order to conform to norms and expectations for emotional displays. In our examination of empirical studies, however, we find less agreement on the appropriate way to measure or operationalize emotional labor. Operationalizations of emotional labor found in the empirical studies identified for this review are presented in Table 12.2. The majority of studies have indeed operationalized emotional labor as emotional management or regulation. These studies explore deep and surface acting, emotional suppression, emotive effort, and dissonance. However, other operationalizations have been used alone or in combination with emotional management. As seen in Table 12.2, some researchers have operationalized emotional labor as the existence of and/or compliance with display rules. However, the mere existence of display rules does not necessarily mean employees are engaging in emotional labor. Other researchers have operationalized emotional labor or in terms of role requirements, such as Hochschild's classification of jobs or Morris and Feldman's (1996) frequency, intensity, duration, and variety of interactions re-

TABLE 12.2
Operationalizations of Emotional Labor

	Emotional Labor Operationalization		
	Emotional Management	Display Rule Existence and Compliance	Role Requirements
Wharton (1993)			X
Adelmann (1995)	X	X	X
Morris and Feldman (1997)	X		X
Abraham (1998)		X	
Pugliesi (1999)	X	X	X
Zapf et al. (1999)	X	X	X
Kruml and Geddes (2000)	X		
Schaubroeck and Jones (2000)		X	
Zerbe (2000)		X	
Erickson and Ritter (2001)	X		
Brotheridge and Grandey (2002)	X		X
Brotheridge and Lee (2002)	X	X	X
Davies and Billings (2002)	X		X
Glomb, Miner, and Tews (2002)	X		
Holman et al. (2002)	X		
Grandey (2001)	X		
Zammuner and Galli (2004)	X		
Grandey (2002)	X		
Glomb and Tews (2004)	X		X

Note. X indicates which operationalization of emotional labor was used in the article. Articles are listed in chronological order by publication date.

quired in the job. Although these job characteristics may be important antecedents of emotional labor, they do not define the psychological processes involved in emotional labor. One of the advantages of using meta-analytic techniques in conducting our review is that we will be able to shed light on the issue of whether the way in which emotional labor is operationalized is associated with the results found in a particular study. Thus, in the next section, we summarize what is known about the predictors and outcomes of emotional management at work.

A QUANTITATIVE REVIEW: WHAT DO WE KNOW ABOUT EMOTIONAL LABOR?

Purpose and Method

The purpose of our quantitative review is not to prematurely rush emotional labor into the final stage of Reichers and Schneider's (1990) model—concept consolidation/accommodation. The topic is not mature enough for a comprehensive meta-analysis to definitively estimate the associations between emotional labor and its antecedents and consequences. Instead, this quantitative review is intended to guide and inspire further emotional labor research through its construct evaluation/augmentation stage, by examining what we know about emotional labor thus far. Through this quantitative review, we can examine which predictors and outcomes seem to have clear relationships with emotional labor, which do not, and which have yet to be empirically investigated. These initial "bare-bones" meta-analyses simply summarize the early research on predictors and outcomes of emotional labor across studies, removing the statistical effects of sampling error. Furthermore, they allow us to compare results across operationalizations.

We located emotional labor studies in three ways; searching PsychInfo, examining references and citations in articles and book chapters, and requesting working papers or those in press from authors who had published empirical work on emotional labor. We identified 18 articles (listed in Table 12.2 in the emotional management column) with data linking the emotional labor with any of its hypothesized predictors and outcomes. Only studies reporting correlations (or the information necessary to calculate correlations) were included in our analyses. Studies that reported only significant correlations were excluded from the analyses, unless all the correlations relevant to our study were significant. If a study included more than one correlation from the same sample (e.g. if a study contained multiple measures of dissonance), the correlations were averaged.

Using Hunter and Schmidt (1990) "bare-bones" meta-analytic techniques, we estimated sample-weighted mean correlations across studies and a standard deviation of those estimates for each of the relationship for which we found at least two empirical studies (or two samples). We also computed 80% credibility intervals. Credibility intervals estimate variability of the *individual* correlations in the population of studies. Thus, a credibility interval that does not include zero indicates that at least 90% of the correlations reported are greater than zero (or less than zero, in the case of a negative correlation).

In accordance with our review of emotional labor definitions, our analyses are confined to emotional labor operationalizations that conform to the emotional labor as emotional management approach. Four operationalizations met this criterion: emotional dissonance, deep acting, surface acting, and emotional labor performance. Most emotional dissonance measures of emotional labor asked employees to self-report *dissonance between their emotional displays and their actual emotional states*. For the most part, deep acting scales tap the extent to which individuals attempt to *change their internal emotional states* to match that of the required emotional display. In contrast, surface acting scales measure the extent to which an individual attempts to *fake the expected emotion*. Measures of emotional labor performance assess *how well individuals regulate their emotions* when dealing with customers (Diefendorff & Richard, 2003; Grandey,

2002, 2003). These emotional performance ratings consist of supervisor and coworker ratings of employees' emotional regulation when dealing with customers; they are not merely ratings of emotional expression.

Predictors of Emotional Labor

Although researchers have been active in exploring the negative outcomes of emotional labor, somewhat less attention has been paid to the predictors, or antecedents, of such emotional regulation. We found two or more studies that examined the following predictors: organizational display rules, job characteristics (control, autonomy, routinization), social support (coworker and supervisor), and individual differences (gender, positive and negative affectivity, and self-monitoring). When enough studies were available, we examined the associations between emotional labor and predictors (and outcomes), based on how emotional labor was measured (dissonance, deep and surface acting, or emotional performance). It is important to note that although the overall estimates in Tables 12.3 and 12.4 represent data from independent samples (we averaged multiple estimates from a single sample where necessary), the analyses by measurement type (e.g., dissonance or surface acting) are *not* independent of each other or of the overall estimate (though the data within each analysis does represent data from independent samples). That is, a correlation used in the deep acting analysis will also be used in the overall analysis (labeled *All* in Tables 12.3 and 12.4).

The existence and explicitness of organizational rules with respect to emotional behavior (display rules) has been the most frequently explored predictor of emotional labor. Indeed, as shown in Table 12.3, a positive association between emotional labor and display rules was found (r_{corr} = .15). However, the credibility interval included zero, indicating that in more than 10% of the studies, the association between display rules and emotional labor was negative. Examination of the various emotional labor operationalizations is informative. Positive associations and credibility intervals that did not include zero were found for display rules, deep and surface acting, and emotional performance (r_{corr} = .32, .26, and .07, respectively). The association between display rules and emotional dissonance was also positive (r_{corr} = .12); however, the credibility interval included zero. Thus, employees who perceive explicit display rules are more likely to engage in emotional regulation, via surface and deep acting (though these associations are not large), but do not necessarily experience more emotional dissonance.

When examining job characteristics, we found that when employees perceive autonomy in their jobs, they are less likely to report experiencing emotional dissonance (r_{corr} = –.20). Similarly, the more routine the job, the greater is the emotional dissonance (r_{corr} = .16). This may be because individuals who can limit or shorten interactions with customers or coworkers or manage the

TABLE 12.3
Predictors of Emotional Labor

	n	k	r_{corr}	SD_r	80% CV
Display Rules					
Emotional dissonance	1,417	5	.12	.14	−.07 to .30
Deep acting	521	3	.32	.07	.23 to .41
Surface acting	521	3	.26	.12	.10 to .41
Emotional performance	437	3	.07	.00	.07 to .07
All	2,090	9	.15	.13	−.02 to .32
Job Control and Autonomy					
Emotional dissonance	1,764	6	−.20	.06	−.28 to −.12
Job Routineness					
Emotional dissonance	1,159	3	.16	.00	.16 to .16
Supervisor and Coworker Support					
Deep acting	583	2	.13	.11	−.02 to .27
Surface acting	583	2	−.14	.03	−.17 to −.10
All	583	2	−.03	.10	−.16 to .10
Positive Affectivity (PA)					
All	501	2	−.13	.06	−.21 to −.05
Negative Affectivity (NA)					
All	501	2	.19	.08	.09 to .28
Self-monitoring					
Deep acting	386	2	.10	.03	.06 to .14
Surface acting	386	2	.26	.00	.26 to .26
Gender					
Deep acting	501	2	−.06	.00	−.06 to −.06
Surface acting	501	2	−.01	.00	−.01 to −.01
All	501	2	−.01	.00	−.01 to −.01

Note. k, Number of independent samples; r_{corr}, n-weighted mean correlation; CV, credibility interval calculated using formulas in Whitener (1990). There is no *All* category for self-monitoring because some nonsignificant correlations between self-monitoring and emotional labor variables in this study (Zammuner & Galli, chap. 15, this book) were not reported. Thus, an overall emotional labor result would be inflated.

timing of these interactions (due to greater job control) may not need to engage in emotional labor as frequently. Employees with a high degree of job control may be able to change tasks or otherwise limit interactions with customers if they are not feeling the required emotion. However, it should be noted that Abraham (1998), in a study that was not included in Table 12.3 results because it did not report zero-order correlations, did find a positive association between job autonomy and emotional dissonance. We cannot tell

TABLE 12.4
Outcomes of Emotional Labor

	n	k	r_{corr}	SD_r	80% CV
Emotional exhaustion					
Emotional dissonance	2,376	11	.30	.06	.22 to .39
Deep acting	751	3	.14	.09	.03 to .26
Surface acting	955	7	.36	.10	.24 to .49
All	2,948	14	.28	.08	.18 to .38
Depersonalization					
Emotional dissonance	916	4	.24	.13	.07 to .42
All	1,152	5	.23	.12	.08 to .39
Personal accomplishment					
Emotional dissonance	916	4	.06	.12	−.09 to .21
All	1,152	5	.02	.12	−.13 to .18
	Physical Complaints				
Emotional dissonance	916	4	.36	.00	.36 to .36
	Job Satisfaction				
Emotional dissonance	2,172	7	−.37	.12	−.52 to −.21
Deep acting	515	2	−.03	.11	−.17 to .11
Surface acting	515	2	−.34	.06	−.41 to −.26
Emotional performance	320	2	.10	.00	.10 to .10
All	2,492	9	−.30	.18	−.53 to −.06
	Self-Esteem				
Emotional dissonance	508	3	−.05	.04	−.10 to .00
	Role Internalization				
All	798	2	−.32	.13	−.49 to −.15
	Turnover				
Emotional dissonance	408	1	.35	—	—
	Role Ambiguity				
Emotional dissonance	408	1	.35	—	—
	Role Conflict				
Emotional dissonance	408	1	.02	—	—

Note. k, Number of independent samples; r_{corr}, n-weighted mean correlation; CV, credibility interval calculated using formulas in Whitener (1990).

whether this is an anomaly of Abraham's study or sample, or whether including the other variables in the regression explains her results.

No clear conclusions can be reached about the relationship between social support and work and emotional labor. In the two studies that reported zero-order correlations between social support and deep and surface acting, we find that employees who report surface acting do not report strong social support. Although the relationship is in the opposite direction for deep acting (those who report deep acting report having strong social support), both associations are quite small and the credibility interval for deep acting includes zero. Abraham (1998) also examined social support as a moderating variable between emotional labor and job satisfaction. Her results are discussed in the outcomes section.

As predictors of emotional labor, individual differences have received less attention than have situational characteristics such as organizational display rules or job characteristics. We found two studies each that examined positive and negative affectivity, self-monitoring, and gender. Positive affectivity was negatively related to emotional labor ($r_{corr} = -.13$), and negative affectivity was positively related to emotional labor ($r_{corr} = .19$). Self-monitoring was positively associated with both deep and surface acting ($r_{corr} = .10$ and .26, respectively). Gender was unrelated to emotional labor. Thus, the few studies located suggest that individual differences do influence emotional labor. More research is needed to shed further light on the nature of the relationship between individual differences and emotional labor.

Outcomes of Emotional Labor

Many emotional labor scholars and researchers have hypothesized that the strain of emotional regulation negatively affects employee physical and psychological well-being (see Grandy, 2000, for a process model). We found at least two empirical studies addressing each of the following outcomes of emotional labor: emotional exhaustion, depersonalization, personal accomplishment (these three are components of Maslach and Jackson's [1981] burnout syndrome), physical complaints (e.g., headaches), role internalization, self-esteem, and job satisfaction. We also found a single study that examined turnover intentions, role conflict, and role ambiguity. In Table 12.4, we present estimates of the relationship between emotional labor and these outcomes. Overall, the associations between emotional labor and its outcomes are somewhat larger and less variable than those found between emotional labor and the predictors.

Results in Table 12.4 support the notion that emotional labor is associated with poor physical and psychological health. With respect to Maslach and Jackson's (1981) burnout syndrome, we found that irrespective of the operationalization, emotional labor was associated with emotional exhaustion ($r_{corr} = .30$) and depersonalization ($r_{corr} = .23$) but not personal accomplishment ($r_{corr} = .02$). Employees who reported engaging in emotional labor also reported more physical complaints ($r_{corr} = .36$).

With respect to job attitudes, we found a less clear picture. Employees engaged in emotional labor reported lower role internalization ($r_{corr} = -.32$), indicating that they were less likely to identify with and be committed to their jobs.

In general, the association between emotional labor and job satisfaction was also negative ($r_{corr} = -.30$ when all operationalizations were combined). However, the specific operationalization of emotional labor mattered for job satisfaction. Our results indicate that both emotional dissonance and surface acting were associated with decreased job satisfaction. However, for deep acting, the correlation was small ($r_{corr} = -.03$) and the credibility interval included zero. Furthermore, both studies that examined emotional performance found a *positive* link between emotional labor and job satisfaction. However, in this study reports of emotional management were provided by colleagues, who may have focused more on the expressions of emotion than the regulation of emotion. Only one study (Zerbe, 2000) examined the relationship between emotional dissonance and turnover ($r = .35$), role ambiguity ($r = .35$), and role conflict ($r = .02$). More research is needed to clarify the nature of emotional labor's impact on job attitudes.

There were a few additional studies focused on outcomes of emotional labor that are not included in Table 12.4 because they did not report correlations between emotional labor and either a predictor or outcome. These studies linked predictors (display rules) and outcomes (job stress and job satisfaction) of emotional labor, without measuring emotional labor directly. Results of these studies are consistent with a model in which display rules lead to emotional labor (dissonance or acting), which in turn leads to outcomes such as job stress or dissatisfaction. Pugliesi (1999) found that, across multiple measures, display rules were positively associated with both job stress (mean $r = .40$) and psychological distress (mean $r = .37$) and negatively associated with job satisfaction (mean $r = .28$). Schaubroeck and Jones (2000) found that display rules (demands to express positive and suppress negative emotions were correlated with physical symptoms (mean $r = .36$). When they examined organizational identification and job involvement, however, they found small positive associations with demands to express positive emotions ($r = .14$ and .13, respectively) and slightly larger negative associations with demands to suppress negative emotions ($r = -.23$ for organizational identification and $r = -.18$ for job involvement).

Wharton (1993) operationalized emotional labor as having one of the jobs Hochschild (1983) identified as involving high emotional labor demands. Therefore, we did not include her data in our Table 12.4 analyses. Using this broad, rough measure of emotional labor, she found that emotional labor was positively associated with job satisfaction but did not find an association between emotional labor jobs and emotional exhaustion. Her results should be interpreted with caution, as it is likely that the emotional labor demands of jobs vary by organization.

Finally, we identified three studies examining outcomes of emotional labor that reported only the results of multiple regressions or path analysis (Abraham, 1998; Adelmann, 1995; Kruml & Geddes, 2000). As they did not report zero-order correlations, these studies were not included in Table 12.4. More-over, some of their findings are consistent with Table 12.4 results and some are not. For example, Kruml and Geddes (2000) found that dissonance was positively associated with emotional exhaustion and depersonalization but deep acting was negatively associated with these outcomes. However, these re-sults cannot be clearly interpreted as they represent *partial* correlations. Thus, they represent the association between the variables of interest after control-ling for all other variables in the equation. Abraham (1998) reported that dis-sonance was positively association with emotional exhaustion (consistent with Table 12.4 results). She also found that dissonance was positively associated with job satisfaction, but the relationship was moderated by social support. If social support was high, emotional labor and job satisfaction were positively related. However, when social support was low, emotional labor and job satis-faction were negatively related. Finally, Adelmann (1995) found a positive as-sociation between emotional labor and job attitudes (satisfaction and commit-ment). Again, it is important to keep in mind these are partial correlations and zero-order correlations were not reported in this study. Because of the small number of studies in our analyses, the possibility that the differences we find in the emotional labor–job satisfaction link across studies and samples is as likely to be due to sampling error as they are to be due to true moderating ef-fects of the way emotional labor was measured.

WHAT HAVE WE LEARNED AND HOW CAN WE USE THIS INFORMATION?

Perhaps the most striking conclusion that can be reached from our analysis is that the variables studied by emotional labor researchers do *not* have strong associations with perceptions of emotional labor. Indeed the strongest association we found for predictors was $r = .32$ (display rules and deep act-ing) and the average correlation between emotional labor and the predictors was $r = .13$. The results for outcomes are a bit stronger with a high of $r = .36$ (emotional dissonance and physical complaints) and an average of $r = .22$. Nonetheless, the combined results of these empirical studies can serve as a guide for future research.

With respect to the predictors of emotional labor, the most obvious hypoth-eses (and the most empirically tested predictor hypothesis) is that when orga-nizations demand that employees express certain emotions and suppress oth-ers, employees will either change their emotions, suppress emotions they genuinely experience, or fake emotions they do not feel. Hence, we find it somewhat surprising that the relationship between organizational display rules and reports of emotional labor is modest at best ($r_{\text{corr}} = .32$ and .26 for deep and surface acting, respectively, r_{corr} = .12 for emotional dissonance, and r_{corr} = .15 for all measures of emotional labor combined). The whole premise underlying theory and research on emotional labor is that when organizations demand certain emotions, employees perform emotional labor, which may be damaging to physiological and psychological health. Yet we do not find a strong association between organizational demands and employees' perceptions of emotional labor.

There are several possible explanations for this finding, including poor measurement of these variables. It would be plausible to assess organizational display rules by asking a representative of the employees' organization (e.g., human resources [HR] professional) about formal guidelines for emotional expression in order to obtain more "objective" measurement. However, display rules (or social norms for emotional expression) may exist completely independent of such formal guidelines. Thus, is seems appropriate to use self-reports of display rules and emotional labor. Nonetheless, we encourage research focused on the construct validity of both display rules and emotional labor.

If measurement is not the problem, do our findings imply that employees rarely accept or comply with emotional demands made by organizations? Alternatively, do our results suggest that emotional management at work is widespread and ubiquitous and thus occurs in the presence and in the absence of organizational display rules? We suspect the latter may be true. Goffman (1959), in his now classic book on the presentation of the self, argued that individuals routinely adapt their self-presentations (including emotional displays) to the norms, expectations, and demands of the social situations they encounter. Providing support for this notion is research by Gross, Feldman-Barrett, and Richards (1998, as cited in Gross, 1998b), who reported that 9 of 10 undergraduate students reported altering their emotions about once a day (and could provide examples of when they did so). Moreover, Tomkins (1984) reported that adult emotions are almost always regulated. Indeed, although emotional labor researchers rarely link their work to the impression management or social influence literature, we know that individuals in organizations regularly and voluntarily use impression management techniques (such as ingratiation, which includes the faking and suppression of emotions) to obtain jobs, raises, promotions, and better performance evaluations. A recent study (Higgins, Judge, & Ferris, 2003) documented the success of these efforts, especially during employment interviews. Moreover, in an experience sampling study, in which they assessed emotional labor several times a day for about 2 weeks, Glomb et al. (2002) found a general trend in the aggregate data toward emotional suppression at work. That is, employees tended to report feeling emotions more often than those emotions were expressed. Thus, it may be that emotional regulation at work is a simple, routine reality of work life.

Why Continue to Research Emotional Labor?

Even if this is true—that emotional labor is routine—there are several reasons why researchers might remain interested in studying emotional labor. First, although we are reluctant to engage in excessive comparison of effect sizes (given the small number of studies in our analysis), we do note that the strongest display rule–emotional labor association is with deep acting ($r_{corr} = .32$). When employees try to change their emotions in response to organizational demands, they may no longer perceive emotional dissonance after their emotions have changed. Furthermore, it is possible that the amount of emotional labor required in a job is very high during the learning stages and levels off at some point in time, once employees adapt to the job. When employees understand that *cheerful* is the appropriate work emotion for a particular job, perhaps they make emotional adjustments at the start of the work day and thus find no need to manage emotions throughout the day. Studying the experience of emotional labor over time—especially contrasting the experiences of new and experienced employees—is an important area for future research. Indeed, experience sampling methodologies like that used by Glomb et al. (2002) are becoming more and more important for the study of emotions in general.

Another important area of research, in our view, is the effects of changing emotions, or deep acting, for work purposes. On the one hand, there is a great deal of psychological research documenting the negative physiological and cognitive effects of emotional regulation in general (see Gross, 1998b, for a review) and emotional suppression in particular (e.g., Gross & Levenson, 1993; Richards & Gross, 1999). Yet there is also evidence that changing emotional expressions can actually alter emotions (e.g., moving facial muscles into a smile position is associated with a feeling of cheerfulness; see Gross & Levenson, 1993, for a brief review of this literature) Thus, even when employees surface act (e.g., smiling when they are not happy), they may actually become more cheerful. If performing emotional labor actually changes employees' emotions, are they at some point no longer performing emotional labor? Clearly, it is time for emotional labor researchers to move beyond single-point-in-time studies of the correlates of emotional labor. We believe that the advances of the next decade will come from a combination of tightly controlled laboratory experiments that simulate emotional labor and from longitudinal and experience sampling studies that follow the experience of emotional labor in as it occurs and over time. Furthermore, although research like that of Gross and colleagues (see Gross, 1998b, for a comprehensive review of the literature on emotional regulation) is critical in informing emotional labor research, much of what is known about the effects of emotional regulation has been learned in the lab from experiments of short duration. There is much progress yet to be made in our understanding of the process and effects of sustained and repeated emotional regulation.

A second reason emotional labor research deserves ongoing attention is that the strongest association we found in our analyses was between emotional management and physical complaints (r_{corr} = .36). An association of this size—between emotional management and physical health—deserves our attention. Furthermore, we found fairly consistent positive relationships between emotional labor and psychological distress (e.g., emotional exhaustion and depersonalization). In the following paragraphs we discuss two issues. First, we deal with our concern that correlations between emotional labor and negative outcomes, such as headaches, emotional exhaustion, and depersonalization, may be spurious. Second, if our argument that emotional management at work is routine and ubiquitous is correct and emotional labor is causally related to outcomes such as reduced job satisfaction, stress, burnout, and physical complaints, then it is critical for us to gain a better understanding of the characteristics of individuals and work environments that moderate the association between emotional management and these outcomes. We discuss this in a following section.

Examination of Table 12.4 would lead anyone concerned with occupational health to take a second look. Although none of the associations we report are large, the outcomes of emotional labor are not positive for employees. Hence, it is a bit unsettling that none of the studies we examined could address issues of causality. The assumption of much emotional labor research is that emotional regulation *causes* depersonalization, emotional exhaustion, and stress. However, it is possible, even plausible, to argue that the association between these variables is not causal. Rather, they may be spuriously correlated due to the influence of personality.

Individual Differences and Emotional Labor

Personality has played only a small role in emotional labor research to date, and researchers have not always been clear or explicit about how personality should be linked to emotional labor. Yet there are several theoretical and empirical reasons to believe that personality traits, such as positive affectivity (PA) and negative affectivity (NA; or related traits such as extraversion and neuroticism) may play a key role in emotional labor. First, two studies we reviewed found that personality was associated with perceptions of organizational display rules (Diefendorff & Richard, 2003; Schaubroek & Jones, 2000). For example, Schaubroek and Jones (2000) reported that employees who scored high on NA also reported that their organizations had display rules for the suppression of negative emotions. In contrast, those high in PA were less likely to perceive such demands. Second, results in Table 12.3 show that employees who score high on NA are more likely to experience emotional labor than those who score low. Third, it has been well established in the research literature that NA is positively associated with the types of negative outcomes studied by emotional labor researchers (stress, physical complaints, emotional exhaustion; Watson, 2000). Linking these three research findings, it seems plausible to us that the positive correlations between emotional labor and outcomes may be entirely a function of NA and its effects on the other variables. In our view, research focused on this issue represents some of the more urgent and important future research for emotional labor researchers. Does emotional regulation at work cause the negative outcomes reported in Table 12.4? If so, does emotional labor have these negative effects on all or only some employees? For example, it might be that when the emotions an employee is asked to display personality-congruent emotions (e.g., cheerfulness for an extravert), employees do not experience negative outcomes. Furthermore, some personality traits (e.g., low neuroticism) may buffer employees from the negative effects of emotional labor due to the link between the trait and effective coping. These are all important questions for future research, in which personality might play a leading role.

Environmental Factors

In addition to personality as a buffer of the emotional labor–negative outcome link, we are also interested in characteristics of jobs, leaders, or organizations that might also serve to buffer employees from the ill effects of emotional management. For example, Abraham (1998) found that social support moderated the emotional dissonance–job satisfaction link. When employees reported strong social support, emotional labor was positively associated with job satisfaction. However, when there was little social support, this link was negative. This is a provocative results that deserves replication and theoretical development. Why and how does social support buffer the negative effects of emotional labor?

We are also intrigued by the role that control may play in the experience of emotional labor. In Table 12.3, we report that job control is negatively associated with the experience of emotional labor. We suggested earlier that this link might mean that employees with high job control are likely to have more control over their interactions with customers, both in terms of timing of those interactions and in terms of rules about the appropriate expression of emotions. However, we also think perceptions of autonomy and control in the work environment—beyond formal characteristics of the job—might be important to emotional labor researchers. As we noted earlier, we suspect that emotional management at work may be more widespread than is currently recognized. If this is true, we are puzzled about why emotional management at work would be expected to have more negative effects than the emotional management that most adults engage in throughout every aspect of their lives. We suspect that perceptions of autonomy and control play a role. For example, we may choose not to be grumpy with our bosses or our spouses because we value these relationships. In such a situation, we are likely to feel a sense of choice or autonomy in managing our emotions. In contrast, when our employer tells us not only what emotion to feel but how to express that emotion so the company can make a profit, we are likely to feel externally controlled.

There is a growing body of literature that demonstrates how perceptions of autonomy and control influence attitudes, behavior, and well-being. Research on self-determination theory (Ryan & Deci, 2000) and the self-concordance model (Sheldon & Elliot, 1999) demonstrates that when individuals feel they are the authors of their own actions (e.g., an employee decides to do something nice for the boss), and when they are engaging in activities that are consistent with their own personally held values and interests (e.g., a father who suppresses feelings of frustration with his children because he values their individuality), they exert more effort, are more satisfied, and experience a greater sense of well-being. We think an empirical examination of the link between emotional management, perceptions of autonomy and control, and outcomes, such as job satisfaction and emotional exhaustion, would be interesting. We do not mean to imply that employees must be given full control over the expression of their emotions. Research on perceptions of autonomy and control in the lab (Deci, Eghrari, Patrick, & Leone, 1994) shows that when individuals are given a meaningful rationale for *why* they should do something, they are more likely to feel a sense of autonomy. This finding was replicated in a business simulation and in a natural work environment (Bono & Judge, 2003). Bono and Judge (2003) found that when leaders focused on the meaning of the work, employees reported having more autonomous work goals. Thus, organizations might buffer the negative effects of emotional labor by talking with employees about why and how their emotional expressions are linked to the goals and mission of the organizations, rather than simply instructing them to smile.

Organizational Considerations

Because the purpose of this volume on emotions in organizations is to advance our understanding of organizations through emotions, we turn now to a discussion of research issues with an organizational focus (e.g., performance, training, selection). With respect to performance, it is surprising that organizations seem to assume—without empirical evidence—not only that happy, smiling employees are good for business, but also that the business gains that accrue from happy, smiling employees outweigh the negative outcomes examined in this review. This is especially ironic given that the only study to explore the association between smiling employees and sales (Sutton & Rafaeli, 1989) found a weak, *negative* relationship. Recent work by Pugh (2001), however, documented some positive effects of employees' emotional displays for the organizations. Pugh examined the link between employees' emotional expressions (greetings, smiles, and eye contact) and customer attitudes, finding a positive association between them. Clearly, there is a need for more research on this topic. Although rigorous examination of the cost/benefit ratio of emotional labor for organizations (and employees) may not be feasible, it is important that organizations and researchers consider both the costs of emotional labor and its benefits to organizations and their customers.

Assuming for the moment that happy, smiling employees do contribute in some way to organizational success, there should also be a link between emotional labor and individual job performance. This is an important issue for the selection of employees into service jobs. Are personality traits like self-monitoring associated with the ability to adapt emotions to the situation? If so, would individuals high in this trait be better job performers in service jobs? Perhaps it would be best for organizations and individuals if organizations selected those individuals who naturally experience and express positive emotions (e.g., PA or extraversion) or those individuals who like to cooperate with others and prefer to avoid conflict (e.g., agreeableness). Barrick and Mount's (1991) meta-analysis shows that extraversion is linked to job performance for jobs that require interpersonal skills.

CONCLUSION

In interpreting these results, we offer a few final comments. First, it should be noted that Tables 12.3 and 12.4 represent data from only 11 studies (16 independent samples). Of these studies, 3 studies and 6 samples are from conference papers or working papers. On the one hand, the value of our review is to get these data quickly into the hands of other emotional labor researchers. However, in doing so, it is important to recognize that our results are based on a small number of studies, some of which have not yet been subjected to peer review.

Second, we note that most studies that went into this review, and the emotional labor literature in general, are field studies of employees working mostly in service jobs. Despite our call for rigorous experimental research and longitudinal and experience sampling studies earlier in this chapter, we consider the number of field studies to be a strength of this literature. However, given our views about the frequency of emotional management in daily life and work, we do not consider it a strength of the literature that most studies were conducted in service setting. If one is concerned with formal emotional display rules, the service setting is ideal. However, it would be informative to replicate some of this research in settings where the target of the emotional labor is not the customer. Even though Hochschild's (1983) seminal work was in a service setting (flight attendants), her definition focused on emotional management for a wage. This is a broad definition, and our knowledge about the frequency and effects of emotional labor might benefit from tests of our theories in non-service settings.

In conclusion, it is clear from our review that rapid advances are being made in emotional labor research. The number of recent empirical articles—half completed in the past year—attests to this fact. Moreover, our review suggests that the results of these studies provide us with an excellent guide for future research. There is much yet to learn about the how and when employees experience emotional labor and the nature of its determinants and consequences.

13

The Interaction Effect of Emotional Intelligence and Emotional Labor on Job Satisfaction: A Test of Holland's Classification of Occupations

Chi-Sum Wong
Ping-Man Wong
Kenneth S. Law

Although emotional intelligence has been a popular concept in the media, there have been few scientifically rigorous studies designed to examine its roles in the workplace. Following the exploratory evidence provided by a recent study, the study reported in this chapter replicated the finding that emotional intelligence and the nature of job requirement (i.e., emotional labor) have an interacting effect on job satisfaction. Using a sample of 307 respondents from six different jobs, this interaction effect was confirmed. Furthermore, this study argues that the nature of job requirement could be estimated from Holland's occupational model. Results supported this argument. Implications for future career and human resource management research concerning emotional intelligence are discussed.

Emotional intelligence (EI) has been an emerging topic for psychological, educational, and management researchers and consultants in recent years. In general, EI has been defined as the ability to perceive, understand, and manage one's emotions (Salovey, Hsee, & Mayer, 1993; Salovey & Mayer, 1990). Although lacking solid research supports, proponents of the EI concept argue that EI affects people's physical and mental health as well as career achievements (e.g., Goleman, 1995). Some emerging leadership theories also imply that emotional and social intelligence are even more important for leaders and managers because cognitive and behavioral complexity and flexibility are important characteristics of competent leaders (Boal & Whitehead, 1992). However, up to now, there has been little empirical evidence in the literature about the relationship between EI and job outcomes such as performance and job satisfaction. There are at least three major reasons for such lack of empirical evidence. First, as a new construct, scholars have not adopted a uniform domain of the EI construct. Political sensitivity, social awareness, service orientation, achievement drive, and some other personality dimensions have been argued as part of EI by some authors (e.g., BarOn, 1997), while other scholars confine EI to the domain of one branch of social intelligence (see, e.g., Mayer, Caruso, & Salovey, 2000). Second, because different domains of the construct are being used, a simple and psychometrically sound EI measure that can be used practically in management studies has not been developed. Third, there is no conceptual framework that defines the role of EI in the area of management and its relationships with job outcomes.

In response to these deficiencies in the literature, Wong and Law (2002) derived specific hypotheses concerning the relationship between EI and job outcomes. These were based on Mayer, Caruso, and Salovey's (2000) theoretical view that EI could be viewed as one facet of intelligence and from the conceptual framework of Gross's model of emotional regulation (Gross, 1998a, 1998b). Specifically, they hypothesized that the relationship between EI and job outcomes would depend on the nature of job requirements. Borrowing the concept of emotional labor from Hoschild (1983), they argued that if the job required incumbents to present a particular form of emotion regardless of their true emotions (i.e., high emotional labor requirement), the relationship between EI and job outcomes would be stronger. After clarifying the domain of EI and developing a 16-item EI measure, Wong and Law (2002) provided exploratory evidence supporting their hypotheses.

There are two main purposes of this chapter. Firstly, we extend and build on Wong and Law's results concerning the interaction effect between EI and emotional labor on job satisfaction. To provide a stronger test of the interaction between EI and emotional labor, it is necessary to control for the most common predictors of job satisfaction, which was not done in the Wong and Law study. Also, to further illustrate the authenticity of the interaction effect, we compare the interaction between EI and emotional labor on job-related outcomes (job satisfaction) and a nonjob outcome (life satisfaction). Life satisfaction is chosen as the nonjob outcome because it has been shown repetitively that EI has a main effect on life satisfaction (see, e.g., Ciarrochi et al., 2000; Martinez-Pons, 1997; Wong & Law, 2002). Although the interaction between emotional labor and EI should have significant effects on job satisfaction, this interaction effect on life satisfaction should be insignificant.

Second, the concept of EI would have greater relevance in management and vocational psychology research if it can be extended to a well-established occupational model. Some researchers in vocational psychology have called for more studies concerning the role of emotions in career theories (e.g., Kidd, 1998). Because Wong and Law argued that job nature would moderate the relationship between EI and job outcomes, it is very likely that this relationship would also differ among occupations. If this relationship can be systematically examined in a well-established occupational model, it would help to advance our understanding of career counseling, selection and training for various occupations. In this chapter, we apply Holland's model of occupational interest and use it as a proxy for the emotional labor of the job.

In the following discussion, we first briefly summarize the domain of EI and the occupational model that may be relevant to the differential relationships between EI and job outcomes. Then an empirical study is reported that tested the applicability of the occupational model to explain the differential relationships between EI and job satisfaction.

DOMAIN AND MEASURES OF EMOTIONAL INTELLIGENCE

Emotional intelligence has its roots in the concept of "social intelligence" first identified by Thorndike in 1920. Salovey and Mayer (1990) were among the earliest to propose the term EI to represent the ability of a person to deal with his or her emotions. They defined EI as "the subset of social intelligence that involves the ability to monitor one's own and others' feelings and emotions, to discriminate among them and to use this information to guide one's thinking and actions" (p. 189). In response to writers who expanded the domain of EI to personality traits and other psychological concepts, Mayer and Salovey (1997) attempted to confine its domain to a human's ability in dealing with emotions. These emotion-handling abilities are composed of four distinct dimensions:

1. *Appraise and express emotions in the self (self emotional appraisal)*. This aspect of EI concerns one's ability to be aware of and to be able to express one's emotions in various forms. People who have high ability in this area will sense and acknowledge their emotions before most other people do.

2. *Appraise and recognize emotions of others (other's emotional appraisal)*. This aspect of EI concerns one's ability to be aware of and sensitive to the emotions of other people. People who have high ability in this area will be able to acknowledge and understand others' emotions quickly and accurately.

3. *Regulate one's emotions in the self (regulation of emotion)*. This aspect of EI concerns one's ability to evaluate and monitor one's emotions. This refers to an individual's ability to repair unpleasant moods while retaining pleasant ones. It also describes a person's ability to control his or her negative emotions and prevent them from developing into destructive behaviors.

4. *Use one's emotions to facilitate performance (use of emotion)*. This aspect of EI concerns one's ability to make use of one's emotions by transferring or transforming these emotions in order to facilitate one's performance.

The definition of the construct of EI just given has several advantages. First, as we continue to argue that EI is one branch of social intelligence, this definition of EI makes it clear that it is one form of human intelligence (Gardner, 1993). Second, this definition of EI addresses an erroneous view of the EI construct in the past—that EI is only a mix of well-established constructs. This erroneous view of EI led Davies, Stankov, and Roberts (1998) to draw the conclusion that EI is elusive and is a combination of personality traits. Under the four-dimensional view just shown, EI is an ability facet, which is conceptually distinct from other well-established and researched human characteristics such as personality, needs, and achievement drive. The final advantage of this four-dimensional view of EI is that it allows formal testing of the psychometric properties of measures designed to capture the underlying multidimensional EI construct (Law, Wong, & Mobley, 1998).

There is very limited empirical evidence of the impact of EI on job outcomes. Theoretically, employees with a high level of EI are those who can understand, master, and utilize their emotions and can, therefore, master their interactions with others in a more effective manner. Based on a work–family relations framework, Wharton and Erickson (1995) argued that emotional management affects individual consequences such as work–family role overload and work–family role conflicts. Mayer, Caruso, and Salovey (2000) showed that EI is positively related to empathy, life satisfaction, and parental warmth. Using Gross's model of emotion regulation (Gross, 1998a, 1998b), Wong and Law (2002) showed preliminary evidence that EI was positively related to job satisfaction. Therefore, employees with a high level of EI are those who understand their emotions, are able to regulate them, and are able to use them in a constructive way to enhance job performance. The continual presence of positive emotional states of the employees should also lead to positive affect toward their job. As a result, they should have both a higher level of general satisfaction as well as satisfaction toward their job. Based on these findings, we propose:

Hypothesis 1.   Emotional intelligence is positively related to life satisfaction.

Hypothesis 2.   Emotional intelligence is positively related to job satisfaction.

EMOTIONAL LABOR AND HOLLAND'S MODEL OF VOCATIONAL CHOICE

Kidd (1998) argued that traditional theories of occupational choice and career development were largely driven by the assumption of rationality in behavior at work. As such, the roles of feelings and emotions such as anger, worry, enthusiasms, hurt, and so forth are rarely elaborated in any detail in career theories

(p. 277). This may due to the fact that these theories are largely applied to fresh graduates entering employment for the first time. However, as more and more employees and job seekers experience redundancy or are unemployed, with need to find a job of different nature due to economic restructuring, the role of emotions may become more important to career theories.

By applying the concept of emotional labor, Brotheridge and Grandey (2002) attempted to investigate differences among occupations. Their results suggested the existence of a hierarchy of emotional labor expectations, with human service professionals reporting the highest levels of frequency, variety, intensity, and duration of emotional display and expectations for control over emotional expressions. Thus, it appears worthwhile to further investigate the role of emotions among occupations. Unfortunately, Brotheridge and Grandey did not incorporate their findings in existing career theories. In this section, we review the concept of emotional labor and examine how this can be incorporated in a well-established model of vocational choice.

In the economics literature, many scholars view employee emotions as a commodity provided by the employees in exchange for individual rewards (see, e.g., Hochschild, 1983; Morris & Feldman, 1996, 1997; Sutton, 1991). On top of the traditional mental labor and physical labor, they argue that there is a third type of labor, emotional labor, which can be offered by employees in exchange for a wage or salary. According to this view, *mental labor* refers to the cognitive skills and knowledge as well as the expertise that can be offered by the employees. *Physical labor* refers to the physical efforts of employees to achieve organizational goals. *Emotional labor* refers to the extent to which an employee is required to present an appropriate emotion in order to perform the job in an efficient and effective manner. Examples of jobs requiring a high level of emotional labor are those of restaurant waiters, bank tellers, and flight attendants. These jobs require employees to be amiable. Even if they are in bad mood, they have to regulate their emotions in order to achieve high performance. In contrast, the emotional labor of auto mechanics would be quite low. They have very infrequent interaction with customers and spend most of their work time dealing with machines. As a result, there is not a strong requirement from the job that they need to regulate their emotion. Subsequently, scholars studying emotional labor have argued that the extent of emotional labor required may vary across occupations.

Wong and Law (2002) argued that the emotional labor of the job would moderate the EI–job satisfaction link. In particular, for jobs with high emotional labor, EI would have a strong impact on job satisfaction, whereas if the job required low emotional labor, the relationship between EI and job satisfaction would be less significant. This chapter further extends Wong and Law's argument. First, we argue that it would be a better test of the interaction effect if we could control for major variables affecting the outcome variable, namely, job satisfaction. Second, we compare the interaction effect of EI and emotional labor on job satisfaction as well as life satisfaction. Life satisfaction refers to the " 'global' well-being, that is, happiness or satisfaction with life-as-a-whole or life in general" (Andrews & Robinson, 1991, p. 61). Theoretically, emotional labor is a job characteristic, which should not interact with EI in affecting overall life satisfaction. As a result, the interaction effects of EI and emotional labor on life satisfaction should be insignificant, while their interaction effects on job satisfaction should be significant. Finally, we also use Holland's model of vocational choice as an operationalization of emotional labor in this study.

Holland's model of vocational choice (Holland, 1959, 1985) has been one of the most widely chosen models used to describe an individual's career interests and classification of occupations (Borgen, 1986; Brown & Brooks, 1990). This model prescribes individuals' career interests toward six types of occupations, which lie at the vertices of a hexagon: realistic (e.g., plumber and machine operator), investigative (e.g., mathematician and computer programmer), artistic (e.g., artist and designer), social (e.g., teacher and social worker), enterprising (e.g., managers and salesperson), and conventional (e.g., clerks and accountant). For this reason, it is sometimes referred to as the RIASEC model (using the first letter of each career types in their specified order). The basic argument in Holland's theory is that "people search for environments that will let them exercise their skills and abilities, express their attitudes and values, and take on agreeable problems and roles" (Holland, 1985, p. 4). Consequently, realistic people seek realistic environments (or jobs), social people seek social environments, and so forth. Another important feature of Holland's model is the concept of calculus that specifies the relationship within and between types or environments. Holland argued in the calculus assumption that the six types can be ordered as the vertex of a hexagon, in which the distances between the types are inversely proportional to the theoretical relationships between them. In other words, the "distance" between a realistic job and a social job is three times the distance between a realistic job and an investigative job. Similarly, the distance between a realistic job and an artistic job is double the distance between a realistic job and an investigative job.

According to Holland's (RIASEC) model, social jobs would have the highest level of emotional labor because they (a) involve a lot of interpersonal interactions and (b) require incumbents to serve their clients or customers in some form of appropriate manner. For example, educational occupations such as teachers and social workers must be able to present the appropriate type of empathic emotion when they are interacting with their students and clients. In contrast, realistic and investigative types of occupations involve less interpersonal interaction and there is much smaller demand on the incumbents to present an appropriate emotion when performing their jobs. In agreement with Hochschild (1983), occupations with high emotional labor are mostly jobs in service industries that require substantial amount of interpersonal interaction. Thus, it is reasonable to argue that the relationship between EI and job outcomes is strongest for social jobs. In addition, according to the calculus assumption of Holland's (RIASEC) model, the strength of this relationship will decrease according to the distance of the particular occupation type from the social type. That is, this relationship will be similar for the adjacent types (i.e., artistic and enterprising) and will be weaker than the social type. The relationship will also be similar for the alternate types (i.e., investigative and conventional), and in turn weaker than the adjacent types. Finally, the relationship will be weakest for the opposite type (i.e., realistic). As a result, we proposed:

Hypothesis 3.   The effects of emotional intelligence on job satisfaction is dependent on the emotional labor of the job. Specifically, the higher the emotional labor of the job, the stronger would be the effects of EI on job satisfaction.

Hypothesis 4.   Following Holland's model of vocational choice, the effects of emotional intelligence on job satisfaction would be highest for social types of jobs. The effect sizes of the EI–job satisfaction relationship for different types of jobs follow Holland's calculus assumption.

Hypothesis 5.   The effects of emotional intelligence on life satisfaction are independent of the emotional labor of the job.

METHODS

Sample and Sampling Procedure

The sample of this study came from two sources. The first source was union members of five types of job. The five jobs included bus driver (realistic), computer programmer (investigative), art designer of advertising companies (artistic), shop manager of retailing shops (enterprising), and clerks (conventional). In total, 300 questionnaires were given to the union and 218 valid responses were returned, representing a response rate of 72.7%. However, because there are no social jobs in the union, our second sample source was teachers of two secondary schools. One hundred and ten questionnaires were sent to all the teachers of two schools and 89 valid responses were returned, representing a response rate of 80.9%. Thus, the final sample consisted of 307 respondents (46 bus drivers, 103 clerks, 17 computer programmers, 9 art designers, 43 shop managers, and 89 secondary school teachers). The average age was 37.5 years with a standard deviation of 8.2. Fifty-one percent of the people in this sample were male and 62.6% were married.

Measures

Emotional Intelligence. The 16-item measure developed by Wong and Law (2002) was adopted in this study. This scale was carefully developed according to the definition of the four dimensions with acceptable factor structure, reliability, and convergent and discriminant validities with other measures of EI, general mental abilities, and Big Five personality dimensions. Furthermore, both Wong and Law (2002) and Law, Song, and Wong (2002) showed that EI measured by this scale has predictive validities on life satisfaction, job performance, and job satisfaction in multiple samples.

For this scale, each EI dimension was measured by four items. A sample item of the first dimension of "self emotional appraisal" is *I really understand what I feel*. A sample item of "uses of emotions" to facilitate performance is *I would always encourage myself to try my best*. A sample question of "regulation of emotions" is *I can always calm down quickly when I am very angry*. A sample question of "other's emotional appraisal" is *I have good understanding of the emotions of people around me*. Internal consistency reliabilities (i.e., coefficient alphas) for the four EI dimensions of self emotional appraisal, other's emotional appraisal, regulation of emotion, and use of emotion for this sample are .87, .92, .89, and .93, respectively.

Emotional Labor. In this study, the 5-item measure from Wong and Law (2002) was used to measure the emotional labor of a job. A sample item is, *To perform my job well, it is necessary for me to hide my actual feelings when acting and speaking with people*. In a sample with 149 supervisor–subordinate dyads, the coefficient alpha of this scale was .88 and the job incumbent's ratings according to this scale had high convergence with supervisory ratings ($r = .77$; Wong & Law, 2002). Internal consistency reliability was .84 for this sample.

Proxy of Emotional Labor by Holland's Occupational Model. To test the importance of EI in various occupational types, we created a second proxy measure of emotional labor according to Holland's (RIASEC) model. As argued before, social type of jobs would probably have the highest level of emotional labor because these jobs have the greatest requirement of social interaction. Following the calculus assumption of Holland's (RIASEC) model, the order of emotional labor will thus be social, its adjacent types (i.e., artistic and enterprising), its alternative types (i.e., investigative and conventional), and its opposite type (i.e., realistic). Thus, this proxy measure of emotional labor was coded as follows: The social type (i.e., secondary school teachers) was coded as 4, its adjacent types (i.e., art designers and shop mangers) were coded as 3, the alternate types (i.e., computer programmers and clerks) were coded as 2, and the opposite type (i.e., bus drivers) was coded as 1.

Job Satisfaction. The four items from the Job Diagnostic Survey (Hackman & Oldham, 1975) that measured satisfaction with the work itself were adopted in this study. These items asked respondents to evaluate the extent of their satisfaction from four dimensions of performing their jobs (including, e.g., the amount of personal growth and development and the feeling of worthwhile accomplishment). To be more comprehensive, we added one item asking for respondents' satisfaction with the overall job content. Internal consistency reliability of these five items was .89.

Life Satisfaction. The nine items constructed by Campbell, Converse, and Rodgers (1976) were adopted to measure an individual's life satisfaction in this study. Items of this scale were pairs of opposite adjectives (e.g., *interesting* vs. *boring, enjoyable* vs. *miserable*) with a 7-point Likert-type scale of numbers between them. Respondents were requested to circle the number that best described their feeling toward their lives. Internal consistency reliability was .94 for this sample.

Organizational Commitment. Because respondents worked for various organizations, it was necessary to control their attitudes toward their organization in examining their level of job satisfaction. Six items measuring the affective commitment to the organization, developed by Meyer, Allen, and Smith (1993), were adopted in this study. An example of an item is, *I really feel as if this organization's problems are my own.* The response format was a 7-point Likert-type scale. Coefficient alpha of the six items was .92.

Job Characteristics. Job characteristics are one of the most important factors affecting job satisfaction (Fried & Ferris, 1987; Loher, Noe, Moeller, & Fitzgerald, 1985). Thus, it is necessary to control this predictor of job satisfaction. The three items used by Wong (1997) were adopted in this study. These items were: *The content of my job is complicated and complex, My job is very challenging,* and *The scope of my job is quite large.* Internal consistency reliability is .79 for this sample.

Demographics. The demographics of respondents were also statistically controlled to avoid confounding results. Respondents were required to give their age and tenure by open-ended questions. Education level, gender, and marital status were measured by multiple-choice items.

Analysis

Hierarchical regression was conducted to test the main effect of EI and the interaction effect between EI and emotional labor on job satisfaction and life satisfaction. Specifically, the control variables, EI and emotional labor, were entered into the regression equation first. The product term of EI and emotional labor was entered in the last step to examine the significance of change in R-squared. To test for the utility of Holland's occupational model in predicting the differential importance of EI in various occupations, the proxy measure of EI calculated from the Holland's model was used to replace the emotional labor measure in the hierarchical regression. Finally, to ensure that this result is applicable to job-related criterion, life satisfaction was used as the dependent variable to test for the interaction effect of EI and emotional labor.

RESULTS

Descriptive statistics and correlation among variables are shown in Table 13.1. The univariate correlation coefficients between EI and job satisfaction ($r = .36, p < .01$) and EI and life satisfaction ($r = .30, p < .01$) are moderately high. Therefore, both Hypotheses 1 and 2 are supported. EI has significant effects on both job satisfaction and life satisfaction, and the effects of EI on job satisfaction and life satisfaction are of similar magnitude.

Before conducting the hierarchical regression analyses, we conducted a confirmatory factor analysis on the 16-item EI measure to cross-validate its factor structure and the assumption of an underlying second-order EI construct behind the four dimensions. The measurement model included the four respective items of each dimension specified as the indicators for each dimension, as well as the four dimensions specified as the indicators of an underlying second order EI construct. Using the LISREL 8 package (Jöreskog & Sörbom, 1993), the fit of this model is very reasonable ($\chi^2 = 356.65, df = 100$, SRMR = .074, TLI = .92, CFI = .93, IFI = .93). These goodness-of-fit indices, together with the internal consistency reliabilities for the four dimensions, provide further evidence of the psychometric soundness of this 16-item EI measure.

Results of the hierarchical regression are shown in Table 13.2. Columns 1 and 2 show the regression results when job satisfaction and life satisfaction are regressed on the predictor variables. The first column shows that the incremental R^2 of the interaction term between EI and emotional labor in predicting job satisfaction is significant ($\beta = .64; p < .05$) after controlling for all other variables. The second column shows the regression results when life satisfaction is used as the dependent variable. As expected, this interaction term is not significant when life satisfaction is used as the dependent variable. Finally, columns 3 and 4 of Table 12.2 show the regression results when emotional labor is proxied using Holland's model of vocational choice. Results of these two regression analyses are almost exactly the same as columns 1 and 2. Therefore, it is clear that emotional labor moderates the EI–job satisfaction relationship, but does not moderate the EI–life satisfaction relationship. Thus, Hypotheses

TABLE 13.1
Descriptive Statistics and Correlation Among Variables

	Mean	S.D.	1	2	3	4	5	6	7	8	9	10	11
1. EI	4.98	.88	1.00										
2. EL	4.78	1.01	.46**	1.00									
3. JS	4.40	1.19	.36**	.37**	1.00								
4. LS	4.51	1.14	.30**	.19**	.39**	1.00							
5. OC	4.30	1.34	.34**	.26**	.62**	.25**	1.00						
6. JC	4.64	1.28	.37**	.41**	.61**	.35**	.38**	1.00					
7. Age	37.49	8.21	.30**	.17**	.11	-.01	.31**	.20**	1.00				
8. Tenure	10.54	7.84	.22**	.07	.07	.06	.15*	.19**	.52**	1.00			
9. Edu	4.43	1.57	.15*	.20**	.15*	.26**	-.09	.20**	-.13*	-.00	1.00		
10. Gender	.49	.50	-.07	.03	.01	.10	-.08	.02	-.13*	-.07	.05	1.00	
11. Married	.63	.48	.25**	.13*	.11	-.04	.24**	.19**	.54**	.35**	-.12*	-.13*	1.00

Note. EI, emotional intelligence; EL, emotional labor; JS, job satisfaction; LS, life satisfaction; OC, organizational commitment; JC, job characteristics; Edu, education level; Married, marital status. For gender, male is coded as 0 and female as 1. For marital status, single is coded as 0 and married as 1.
$*p < .05. **p < .01.$

TABLE 13.2

Results of the Regression Analyses Testing the Interaction Effect

	EL Measured by Employees' Responses						Holland's Proxy as EL Measure					
	(1) Job Satisfaction			(2) Life Satisfaction			(3) Job Satisfaction			(4) Life Satisfaction		
Independent Variables	β	ΔF	ΔR^2	β	ΔF	ΔR^2	β	ΔF	ΔR^2	β	ΔF	ΔR^2
Tenure	-.05			.03			-.06			.01		
Gender	.04			.10			.02			.07		
Age	-.07			-.09			-.07			-.09		
Married	-.03			-.10			-.04			.16		
Edu	.11	3.20**	.06**	.16*	3.53**	.07**	.10	3.21**	.06**	.07	3.54**	.07**
JC	.40**			.21**			.40**			.06**		
OC	.48**	138.65**	.49**	.17*	15.30**	.10**	.49**	138.72**	.49**	.05*	15.38**	.10**
EI	-.30			-.15			-.18			.18		
EL	-.34	1.62	.01	-.50	4.48**	.03*	-.60*	1.09	.00	-.26	7.26**	.05**
EI × EL	.64**	4.84*	.01*	.69	3.06	.01	.62**	5.04*	.01*	.04	.01	.00
Model R^2	.57**			.21**			.57**			.21**		

*$p < .05$. **$p < .01$.

246

3 and 5 are supported. Hypothesis 4, which expected there to be differential impacts of the moderating effect of emotional labor on the EI–satisfaction relationship, is also supported.

To further examine differences across occupations, Table 13.3 presents the means and standard deviations of EI, emotional labor, and job related variables for the respondents from the six jobs. In general, the mean scores appear to support our expectation about differences among occupations with the exception of bus drivers. For example, teachers and shop managers have the highest levels of EI and emotional labor, whereas other occupational groups have relatively low levels on these two variables. The unexpected results of bus drivers may due to two factors. First, bus drivers in this sample are relatively older than respondents in other occupational groups. As a set of emotion-handling abilities, older people should master these abilities better (Mayer, Caruso, & Salovey, 2000). As shown in Table 13.3, the mean age of bus drivers in this sample is about 5 years older than other groups. This difference is statistically significant in a t-test ($t = 3.44, p < .01$). Second, the bus companies in recent years have emphasized their services to the customers. Thus, although the main duty of bus drivers is still driving the bus (i.e., operating a machine), bus drivers may have perceived a higher level of emotional labor when this study was conducted.

DISCUSSION

The study reported in this chapter serves two main purposes. First, it empirically investigates the interaction effect between EI and emotional labor on job satisfaction. Although EI has become a popular concept, there is relatively little scientific evidence concerning its impact on job outcomes. This study provides evidence that EI interacts with emotional labor in affecting job satisfaction. Furthermore, to ensure that the interaction found in this study did not happen by chance, we controlled for other antecedents of job satisfaction and contrasted this interaction effect between job satisfaction and life satisfaction. Clear support was found that EI, as an interrelated set of abilities, will interact with the nature of the job, that is, emotional labor, in affecting job outcomes.

The second purpose of the reported study was to follow recent studies in vocational psychology concerning the role of emotions in career theories. Specifically, we attempted to apply Holland's occupational model to further understand the role of EI and emotional labor on various occupations. We argue that the concept of emotional labor can be incorporated to Holland's classification of occupations. Specifically, social types of occupations should have the highest level of emotional labor and thus Holland's classification can be used as a proxy measure of emotional labor. Results of our hierarchical regression show that the same conclusion concerning the interaction effect of EI and emotional labor can be drawn using this proxy measure. With few exceptions, the mean

TABLE 13.3

Mean Scores (Standard Deviations) for EI, EL, Job and Life Satisfaction,
Organizational Commitment, and Job Characteristics Across the Six Occupations

Job	EI	EL	JS	LS	OC	JC	Age
Teachers ($n = 89$)	5.17 (.81)	4.94 (.80)	4.57 (.97)	4.91 (1.00)	4.30 (1.42)	5.07 (.93)	39.26 (6.77)
Shop managers ($n = 43$)	5.14 (.76)	5.32 (.81)	4.85 (1.40)	4.80 (1.26)	4.53 (1.34)	5.00 (1.38)	36.71 (7.29)
Art designers ($n = 9$)	4.90 (.97)	4.76 (1.17)	5.09 (.83)	4.79 (.78)	4.51 (1.06)	4.81 (.80)	28.67 (4.42)
Programmers ($n = 17$)	4.99 (.65)	4.73 (.81)	3.94 (1.26)	4.22 (.71)	3.43 (1.19)	4.06 (1.43)	33.24 (6.62)
Clerks ($n = 103$)	4.72 (1.00)	4.40 (1.16)	3.99 (1.06)	4.32 (1.07)	4.01 (1.19)	4.15 (1.27)	36.26 (8.57)
Bus drivers ($n = 46$)	5.07 (.79)	4.81 (.97)	4.57 (1.35)	3.92 (1.25)	4.99 (1.29)	4.75 (1.42)	41.29 (8.95)

levels of emotional labor and EI for the six jobs included in this study are also consistent with our expectation from calculus assumption of the model. These findings support our argument and the applicability of Holland's model in understanding the role of EI in different occupations.

There are at least five implications for future research and human resource practitioners. First, although there has been a lot of discussion about the importance of EI in the popular press, both the conceptual framework and scientifically rigorous empirical evidence concerning its relationship with job outcomes are scarce. By defining EI as a set of interrelated abilities to deal with emotions, it is possible to use the common conceptual framework concerning the interaction effect between individual abilities and job nature in affecting job outcomes. Results of the reported study in this chapter provide further evidence supporting this argument. Thus, more scientific and rigorous research on this construct would be worthwhile.

Second, the study reported in this chapter is the first attempt to hypothesize and test the role of EI in various occupations based on a well-established occupational model. Results indicate that the role of emotions can be incorporated in Holland's career model. Not only does the level of emotional labor differ among the occupations specified by Holland's model, the calculus assumption is also applicable to conceptualize the extent of differences among various occupational environments. This conclusion should be regarded as preliminary because this study did not control for the characteristics of incumbents in the six jobs. For example, the bus drivers in this sample are older than other respondents and this makes the EI level for them unexpectedly high, and the sample size for some jobs (e.g., art designer and programmer) may be too small. Future research may use more rigorous control in order to further validate this conclusion.

Although the results may be preliminary, they are encouraging and may lead to important implications in both the conceptual development of career theories and practical application of human resource selection. For the development of career theories, it appears possible that the role of emotions can be incorporated in existing models. It may not be necessary to develop completely new theories in responding to the changes in demand of career counseling. A more efficient way for vocational psychology researchers to examine the role of emotions may be to review the present career theories and try to incorporate the element of emotions in these theories. For human resource selection, the element of emotional labor may need to be examined in job analysis and EI may be used as a selection variable for jobs with high emotional labor. For employees, EI may be an important consideration in one's career choice and development. For human resource practitioners, EI may be used in selection and placement decisions for jobs with high emotional labor. Thus, more studies in this line of research concerning the roles of EI and emotional labor in career theories and human resource selection should be worthwhile.

The third implication of this study for future research and human resource practitioners concerns the role of EI on job types. Although we argue that the six job types used in this study are representatives of their respective occupation type according to the Holland's model, variations should exist among jobs within the same occupation group. It is necessary to examine jobs in more occupations prescribed by Holland's model in order to ensure that the calculus assumption is really generalizable to most of the occupations. For applications in career counseling and human resource selection, it is also necessary to examine as many occupations as possible. Thus, future research should further investigate the roles of EI and emotional labor for more jobs both across and within occupational groups.

The fourth implication is that common method variance may be a problem for this study. This should be better addressed in future research. However, as the main purpose of this chapter is to investigate the interaction rather than direct effect, and the interaction term was entered into the regression equation after controlling for all other variables, this issue may not be critical for the reported study in this chapter. However, it is worthwhile for future research to use a non-self-report EI measure to examine its effect on job outcomes.

Finally, the simple correlation between emotional labor and job satisfaction is positive. This is somewhat counterintuitive because emotional labor is basically a form of restriction on job incumbents' expression of their true feelings. With greater restriction, the chance that the job incumbent will have negative feelings towards his or her job may increase. However, after controlling for job characteristics, the relationship is negative. This is probably due to the positive correlation between emotional labor and job characteristics. It is well known in the job design literature that trade-offs exist. That is, when we enrich the job characteristics of a job to increase its motivational value, some unavoidable negative consequences may result (see, e.g., Campion, 1988; Wong & Campion, 1991). Results of the study reported in this chapter indicate that when jobs are enriched, their emotional labor may be increased as well. Future research may further examine the exact relationship among job characteristics, emotional labor, and job satisfaction.

ACKNOWLEDGMENT

The work described in this chapter was supported by a grant from the Research Grants Council of the Hong Kong Special Administrative Region (project CUHK4038/00H).

14

The Relationship With Patients: "Emotional Labor" and Its Correlates in Hospital Employees

Vanda L. Zammuner
Cristina Galli

The nature and extent of emotion regulation and its psychophysical consequences were studied in a sample of 150 Italian hospital workers. Their self-reports showed that they performed emotional labor by (a) surface acting, expressing job-required emotions, and (b) deep acting, trying to actually feel required emotions; (c) they also frequently felt emotional consonance. The significant relationships that surface acting and emotional consonance had with burnout dimensions, and the mediating role on the frequency, nature, and effects of emotional labor played by personal and job variables, such as empathic concern and "relational" time spent with hospital patients, were among the main results.

Health care employees, that is, doctors, nurses, and to some extent technicians, who work in hospital structures must daily take care of patients and their relatives, and must pay attention to their contingent psychological, social, or physical problems: for example, listen to their complaints, deal with their suffering, pain, anger and helplessness, and deal with death-associated issues. Such interactions imply that health care workers have a constant emotional involvement with customers/patients and, as a consequence, are often burdened with negative feelings such as anxiety, fear, embarrassment, and, possibly, the despair their "clients" feel.

Nowadays, in times when the overall level of health care structure quality needs to be certified, there is a growing consciousness that the relationship the structure has with its customers needs to be improved. This awareness gets translated in many countries, Italy included, in concrete actions whose goal is to *make a patient's hospitalization period more "human"*, as it were, starting with the acceptance-at-the-hospital phase, through residence at the structure, to the discharge moment, when the sick person leaves the hospital. Hospitals are thus conceived as services that, beyond fulfilling their therapeutic mission, care for their customers by paying attention to the quality of the relationship patients have with health-care operators. In sum, the overall adequacy of the therapeutic system is evaluated not only in terms of quality of medical care proper but also as regards its ability to establish satisfactory relationships with customers. To the latter end, employees are required to express both affective neutrality (symbolized, for instance, by the white uniforms hospital workers wear), and involvement and commitment toward their customers, establishing positive human contacts with them: listening carefully to their queries, making them feel at ease, reassuring those who are anxious. In fact, the very first help action performed by health care personnel toward customers, that of listening to patients' problems, is at the same time the very first opportunity to convey the message that the structure is able to supply an appropriate "answer" to the problem/question they have. A fundamental aspect of the workload of hospital workers is thus monitoring the relationship they establish with patients, how they shape their communication with them, so as to achieve the required quality, not unlike what happens in most interpersonal relationships.

As Hochschild (1983) discovered, the *emotional style* with which one offers a service is an integral part of the service itself, so much so that business organizations try to govern and control it by means of (more or less explicit) expression rules that dictate what emotions must be expressed. Such emotion-related job-role requirements are a crucial rather than a sporadic aspect of working roles in many so-called "helping professions," that is, in service jobs that imply employee–customer interactions, such as in hospital, school, bank, and public office jobs. The most general hypothesis of this study was that emotion-related job-role requirements trigger *emotion regulation processes*, whose nature, frequency, and consequences in turn contribute to defining, individually and socially, life quality parameters. For instance, not conforming to emotional demands might induce dissatisfaction, lower self-esteem, and burnout in employees, and induce employee-client conflict, complaints to the organization, and so forth. A specific hypothesis was that hospital workers (similarly to other service employees, but possibly to a more demanding extent given the peculiar nature of their working context) as part of their job role are asked to comply with the organization's emotion-style requirements. Thus, if the worker, when interacting with a customer, feels emotions that are *discrepant* with job-required emotions, he or she ought to engage in regulatory processes to express the prescribed emotions. If workers engage in such regulatory processes, from the organization's viewpoint they are emotionally competent. Such emotional compliance, however, as we discuss next, is associated with preconditions (e.g., the worker must be aware of a discrepancy state, and be able and motivated to engage in regulatory processes), as well as to psychophysical consequences.

Additionally, this chapter (as part of a larger research project; e.g., Zammuner & Canato, 2000; Zammuner, Lotto, & Galli 2002), aims to help ground the well-known concept of "emotional labor," explored mainly within the sociological tradition, within the framework provided by emotion theories, especially in relation to emotion-regulation concepts. This theoretical gap between traditionally distinct fields of inquiry has, however, lessened in very recent writings (e.g., Ashkanasy, Härtel, & Zerbe, 2000; Fisher & Ashkanasy, 2000), which also testify to the upsurge of interest in the emotions, and underlying processes, that we experience in relation to that important part of life that we spend *at work*.

EMOTION REGULATION AND EMOTIONAL LABOR

The Emotional Labor Concept

We discuss emotion regulation as it occurs within work contexts. Hochschild (1983), a sociologist, originally addressed this issue and termed *emotional labor* the regulation performed by employees in work-setting contexts requiring employees' interactions with customers. Her theoretical approach very much drew on Goffman's (1959) dramaturgical impression-management perspective. Hochschild's emotional labor construct was meant to capture the fact that, in many kinds of service jobs, employees *must* manage their feelings and their emotional expressions so as to meet their employer's *feeling* and *display rules*, defining what emotion a person ought to feel and express to others (Ekman, 1972, 1984; Hochschild, 1983). In a customer-oriented service society, where products provided to clients are at least in part intangible, organizations do need to focus greater attention on the quality of their services, including the quality of customers' interaction with service providers. As several studies confirm, customers' evaluations of interpersonal aspects of their interaction with service providers contribute to defining their judgments of service quality; this evaluation, in turn, tends to reflect employees' feelings about their job and their organization (e.g., Pugh, 1998; Rafaeli & Sutton, 1987). Organizations may explicitly instruct or train workers about their job emotional requirements, control the quality of employees' emotional service performance, and reward or "punish" them accordingly.

However, not all service sectors, nor all job roles in them, require emotional labor to the same extent and frequency, nor do they require employees to display emotions of the same nature. For instance, medical personnel (e.g., nurses) have to express positive emotions most of the time (e.g., hope, encouragement, joy) and empathize with patients' feelings and worries, as well as, at times, display negative emotions (e.g., anger at a patient for not following medical prescriptions); front-line employees, such as receptionists and bank-counter workers, typically are required to express positive emotions (e.g., friendliness); "control-role jobs" (e.g., workers' supervisors, bill collectors) might need to alternate between negative, in-control emotions such as anger, contempt, and indignation, and positive emotions such as encouragement, pride, and satisfaction (e.g., Best, Downey, & Jones, 1997). In sum, the specific nature of a service sector, and that of a job role, are likely to be crucial variables in predicting various aspects of the required, and performed, emotional labor.

Emotional Labor as a Process of Emotion Regulation Within Work Contexts

In this chapter we use the term *emotional labor* to refer to emotion regulation that occurs within work contexts. However, as stated earlier, to better understand the construct itself, possibly defining it more precisely, we think it is necessary to conceptualize it with reference to the very concept of emotion regulation, both in general and in specific terms—that is, in relation to a number of distinct regulation aspects that need to be considered when studying emotional labor.

For emotion theorists, emotion regulation is "part and parcel" of the emotion process (see especially Frijda, 1986), potentially activated at any of its phases, such as when an event is to be *appraised* as good or bad for oneself, or a felt emotion is judged for its personal *significance*, or its degree of personal or contextual *legitimacy*, or is to be *expressed* to others. In other words, assuming that an emotion is a multicomponent process (Scherer, 1984), regulation can, in principle at least, influence every *component* of the emotion experience: appraisal, physiological reaction, facial expression, and so on. Regulation may moreover influence the antecedent of an emotion (e.g., when a person avoids an event known to cause in him or her an unwanted emotion), and its consequences (e.g., when a person refrains from engaging in a vindictive behavior). Regulation of the felt emotion, or of its expression, is called for when the emotion conflicts with known internalized norms, or with contextually salient ones, or when a person experiences a dysphoric emotion.

Distinct Aspects of Emotion Regulation

In the social sciences, emotion regulation processes are referred to by a variety of terms, including emotional control, emotion inhibition, self-regulation, self-control, emotion-focused coping, and, as already noted, emotional labor (for theoretical reviews and empirical data, as well as for a discussion of aspects that here cannot be touched on, see, e.g., Campos, Campos, & Barrett,

1989; Ekman, 1972; Frijda, 1986, 1999; Gross, 1999; Gross & Levenson, 1993; Keltner & Gross, 1999; Lazarus, 1991; Mesquita & Frijda, 1992; Pennebaker & Hoover, 1986; Russell, 1991; Saarni, 1993; Salovey et al., 1993; Zammuner, 1995, 1996, 2000a). This terminological variety points to differences not only in what "objects" distinct disciplinary traditions select to study, and with what theoretical or applied concerns they do so (e.g., consider the coping and stress traditions; see Gross, 1998), but also in how the process is conceptualized, overall reflecting the complexity of regulation issues. What we focus on, and how we conceptualize it, will bring forward this or that aspect of regulation. It is therefore important to specify what regulation "aspects" we need to consider when studying emotional labor, a *contextualized* regulation process. We next simply list the most crucial aspects, supplying hypothetical and simplified examples of health care employees' regulatory actions, or regulation-related evaluations, in their interaction with a patient *P*:

- *Regulation object(s)*, namely, *what* is being regulated. Regulation may act either (a) on a felt ("inner") emotion, in relation to this or that emotion component, including how the emotional event is appraised (e.g., "*P* did not mean to be rude to me"), or one's level of autonomic arousal, or (b) on its outward, visible expression, including the facial or verbal expression of the emotion.

- *Regulation motivation*, namely, *the extent to which a person is motivated* to regulate his or her emotions, in general, or in a specific circumstance (e.g., "I am not the kind of person who gets upset for such a little thing"; "*P* is in great pain; I must be patient with him").

- *Regulation motives and goals*, namely, what causally triggers regulation, and what is/are the *target result(s)* that (consciously or not) a person tries to achieve when regulating an emotion (e.g., "If I start getting angry this early, I shall get crazy by lunch time!").

- *Regulation norms*, namely, the norms that prescribe what is to be regulated, when, how, and why. Job-related norms typically include *feeling rules* (e.g., "You have to be understanding with people who are in pain"), and *display rules* (e.g., "You cannot show that you are angry at *P*"), and constitute a (more or less overlapping) subset of the *emotion norms* that are defined according to existing sociocultural values.

- *Regulation processes per se*, namely, both *how regulation* operates to achieve its goals vis-à-vis a specific emotion (or component of it), and with *what effects*; automatic and voluntary regulation processes include, for instance, breathing deeply to calm down; smiling, or trying to appraise the event differently (e.g., as a challenge rather than as a threat) to feel better; and redirecting attention to event aspects that one can cope with, rather than to those one feels helpless about.

- *Psychophysical resources in regulation*, namely, what resources a person needs in order to activate, maintain, and sustain regulation effort, and to what extent they are available to him or her at a given moment in time, or in general (e.g., a stressed worker, or an ill person, might not have sufficient resources to engage in regulation).

- *Regulation costs*, namely, what *psychophysical costs* are associated with regulatory efforts: For example, frequent, prolonged, or difficult to activate, sustain, and enact regulation processes might induce health risk-conditions, such as stress, fatigue, burnout, and heart problems.

RISK AND PROTECTION FACTORS
IN THE WORKING LIFE OF HOSPITAL STAFF

Burnout

In recent years job-related stress in a variety of jobs, and its consequences, have received increasing attention. Research has found evidence for a number of major job stressors, including inadequate staffing, work overload, and, for hospital workers in particular, emotional demands made by patients, and problems associated with being constantly faced with death. Among the potentially negative consequence of chronic exposure to such job stressors, *burnout*, defined as "a syndrome ... that occurs frequently among individuals who do 'people work' of some kind," especially resulting from contact with people who are suffering (Maslach & Jackson, 1981, 1984), and caused by a prolonged period of high stress levels, has received perhaps the greatest attention (Lee & Ashforth, 1996). Burnout is characterized by physical and emotional exhaustion, depersonalization (cynicism), and a low sense of personal accomplishment (work realization, job satisfaction). Although a review of the literature reveals considerable agreement about burnout effects (e.g., impaired health conditions; leaving the stressful work environment), there is considerable disagreement about its causes. A central hypothesis of this study (and of the mentioned parallel ones; e.g., Zammuner & Canato, 2000) was that specific kinds of emotion regulation can be, under specific conditions, subjectively taxing, dysfunctional, thus contributing to cause burnout.

Self-Monitoring and Self-Consciousness

The likelihood that an employee will adhere to organizational emotion-norms, and with what consequences, might be mediated by a number of personality characteristics. For instance, a person who is motivated to behave in socially appropriate ways would be attentive to the environment, and would try to react in adequate ways to environmental features that cue context-adaptive behaviors. Snyder (1974), describing a personality type that tends to adapt to his or her environment, defined *self-monitoring* as "self-observation and self-control guided by situational cues to social appropriateness." High self-monitors are very concerned with the image they present to others and hence frequently scan their social environment for feedback regarding their own behaviors. In contrast, low self-monitors evaluate the appropriateness of their own behavior by attending to internal cues; they therefore tend to be more true to themselves, relying on their own feelings and attitudes to guide their behavior in different situations. High self-monitors perform better than low self-monitors in boundary-spanning roles that require attending to frequent and varied social cues as regards "desired" behaviors; they thus can be expected (Doucet, 1998; Morris & Feldman, 1996) to display greater compliance with organizational norms, feeling rules and display rules included, than low self-monitors. Because they are likely to pay greater attention to others' emotions, and be more "emotionally responsive," regulating their own emotions to meet others' needs (Doucet, 1998), they ought to perform emotional labor more easily and with greater contextual adequacy. These hypotheses were investigated in this study in terms of two distinct constructs: *self-consciousness* (Fenigstein, Scheier, & Buss, 1975), construed as the extent to which the person directs his or her attention to the self, and *self-monitoring*, conceptualized as the behavioral component of self-consciousness (Forzi, Arcuri, & Kodilja, 1987).

Empathic Concern and Perspective Taking

Empathy, a two-dimensional construct comprising a *cognitive* capacity to take others' perspective, to know what another person is feeling, and empathic concern, the *affective* sensitivity to others' feelings and concerns, "feeling what another person is feeling" (Levenson & Ruef, 1992; Redmond, 1989), is likely to play a crucial role in health care job roles that imply interactions with patients (needless to say, it is an essential ingredient, a crucial feature in defining the quality of most interpersonal transactions). Empathic individuals are more likely to be *emotionally responsive* to others, feeling and/or expressing greater emotional consonance with their interactants; for example, an empathic health care employee will adapt his or her felt and/or expressed emotions to those of the patient.

Positive and Negative Affect

To what extent employees endorse organizational emotion norms, and with what consequences, might be mediated by the nature of emotions a worker experiences at his or her job (e.g., their hedonic tone), and by their relative frequency. For instance, if a worker often feels pleasant emotions (e.g., pride, calmness, joy), then he or she is less likely in need of regulating them than if he or she feels unpleasant ones (e.g., fear, anger, sadness; felt emotions to some extent define the "affective climate" of one's job). We expected felt emotions on the one hand to be a causal variable in emotion regulation, in particular as regards its frequency and kind, and on the other hand to vary in relation to both job-role variables (such as employees' typical workload in terms of number of interactions with patients per day) and psychological variables. In particular, felt emotions might (indirectly) index job satisfaction (as an antecedent of its evaluation, and as a measure of its affective aspects; Brief & Weiss, 2002), burnout, and life satisfaction. In sum, felt emotions were expected to be both causal inputs to other psychological processes, and the result of various kinds of events as subjectively appraised.

Life Satisfaction

If emotion regulation has relevant consequences for the individual, as we hypothesize, then it ought to influence subjective evaluations of well-being. Felt emotions, as stated earlier, do measure well-being, but do so in relation to one rather "fluctuating" aspect of it. To assess well-being at a more global level we asked employees for an overall *life satisfaction* evaluation. Previous studies (e.g., Diener, Emmons, Larsen, & Griffin, 1985; Pavot & Diener, 1993) showed that life satisfaction correlates negatively with dysphoric emotions, and positively with positive emotions; in other words, measurements of life satisfaction, positive affect, and negative affect tap dimensions of well-being that are in part independent (Lucas, Diener, & Suh, 1996). Life satisfaction level can be construed as a summary index of antecedents and consequences of emotion regulation.

HYPOTHESES

Felt Emotions and Emotional Expressions as Regulation Objects, and Emotional Consonance

Emotion regulation might be expected to work on either of two "complex" objects:

1. *Emotion expression* vis-à-vis a patient, expression that occurs vocally and/or face-to-face; this process was called *surface acting* by Hochschild (1983), in that the person simply *acts* as though he or she feels the context-required emotion (e.g., smiling to an annoying patient; putting on an happy mask even though one is terribly sad).

2. *Felt emotions*: Hochschild called this process *active deep acting*, assuming that it involved "pumping emotions up" to actually feel the required

job-congruent emotions, which can then be expressed in the service interaction.

If workers are at all suited for their job, and/or their job role is not too demanding, their felt emotions ought to be congruent with job requirements quite often, making regulation unnecessary because workers can simply express their *"genuine emotions"* (Ashforth & Humphrey, 1993; somewhat misleadingly, job-congruent emotions were referred to by Grandey, 1998, and Hochschild, 1983, as the result of *passive deep acting*). In our opinion, *emotional consonance/dissonance* is best construed as a dimension defining whether, and to what extent, felt emotions call for the activation of regulatory processes: job-congruent emotions denote *consonance*, and job-incongruent emotions indicate *dissonance* (see also Grandey, 1998; Hochschild, 1983; Morris & Feldman, 1996; *dissonance* indicated instead extent of genuine emotions for Kruml & Geddes, 1998a). In sum, as specified later in greater detail, surface and deep acting were hypothesized to be independent dimensions of emotion regulation, acting on different objects, and thus indirectly measuring the nature of the activated process. Emotional consonance was expected either to exhibit a negative relationship with the regulation dimensions, or to be unrelated to them.

Hypothesis 1A.   Health care workers experience, to a greater or smaller extent, consonant, job-congruent emotions that do not need to be regulated, as well as job-incongruent ones that require regulation.

Hypothesis 1B.   Emotional labor is performed by activating different regulation processes that act on different objects, namely, *surface acting* and *deep acting*, expected to be independent dimensions.

Hypothesis 1C.   The two regulation dimensions might hold relations of a different nature with *emotional consonance*. More specifically:

Hypothesis 1Ca.   Regulation dimensions are negatively correlated with emotional consonance: frequent job-congruent emotions ought to imply infrequent regulation processes.

Hypothesis 1Cb.   Regulation dimensions are unrelated to emotional consonance; feeling job-congruent emotions does not prevent a worker from experiencing at times job-incongruent emotions that need to be regulated.

Hypothesis 1D.   *Surface acting* and *deep acting* might exhibit either one of two opposite-direction interrelations, due to the effect(s) of *mediating variables*:

Hypothesis 1Da. *Surface acting* and *deep acting* are positively related to
each other; for example, a highly realized worker will perform one or the other kind of emotional labor as required, and allowed, by the context.

Hypothesis 1Db. *Surface acting* and *deep acting* are negatively related to
each other; for instance, if a worker has (too) many interactions with patients, surface acting, *ceteris paribus*, might
become the only *available* regulation option, thus possibly
causing emotional exhaustion, depersonalization, and
lowering the worker's level of job satisfaction. These psychological effects would in turn imply that "deeper" regulation is less likely, for example, because it requires psychological resources unavailable to the worker.

Felt Affect, Emotional Dissonance, Regulation Processes, Psychological Effort, Psychophysical Costs, Affect, and Life Satisfaction

During the time spent at work, workers are likely to feel a variety of emotions.
As stated, emotional labor might be engaged in when felt emotions are *dissonant* with job requirements, a discrepancy state of affairs that might be due to
personal causes, job-related ones, or both. A central hypothesis in our approach is that emotion regulation implies a certain amount of *psychophysical
effort*, and therefore a *psychophysical cost*, with significant implications for
workers' psychological well-being (as measured, e.g., by felt burnout, frequency of negative emotions, and life satisfaction). As the original names of
emotion-labor dimensions suggest, surface acting was hypothesized to be a
"shallow" regulation process, not very costly, in that it needs *not* act on a
worker's "true" emotions, whereas deep acting was hypothesized to be more
effortful (Hochschild, 1983). Note, however, that to obtain their desired "product," expressing job-congruent emotions, *both* processes imply an emotionally
effortful *dual task*: temporarily suppressing or masking a job-incongruent *felt*
emotion (e.g., anger with an annoying patient), *and* expressing a job-congruent one (e.g., smiling at the annoying patient) in surface acting; suppressing a job-incongruent *felt* emotion (e.g., anger with an annoying patient) *and*
feeling a job-congruent one that can then be expressed, in deep acting. Therefore, in principle we cannot expect surface acting to be a "better" regulatory
process, that is, less psychologically costly, than deep acting, nor vice versa
(from the organization's viewpoint, it is indifferent what process is activated,
provided the worker expresses the required emotion).

Hypotheses about how the two regulation processes are likely to differ in
terms of their psychological preconditions and effects can, however, be specified by taking into account further variables (the hypotheses stated next were

tested and overall supported in parallel studies; e.g., Zammuner & Canato, 2000; Zammuner et al., 2002). For instance, surface acting might be the only, or most frequently activated, regulation process a worker engages in when his or her job role is unsatisfying or stressful; therefore, it might be the psychologically "worst" process to the extent that it reflects a "bad" job condition. On the other hand, deep acting might reflect a psychologically "good" job condition, in that only workers who feel happy about their job, and are "emotionally energetic," have sufficient motivation and psychological resources to regulate their emotions when necessary; in turn, successful deep acting makes workers feel well, more realized in their job, and so forth. To use a metaphor, frequent surface acting might trigger a vicious circle, whereas deep acting triggers a virtuous circle.

Hypothesis 2Aa. Emotional consonance is positively related to work realization, positive affect, and life satisfaction.

Hypothesis 2Ab. Emotional consonance is negatively related to emotional exhaustion, depersonalization, and, possibly, negative affect.

Hypothesis 2Ba. Surface acting is positively related to emotional exhaustion, depersonalization, and negative affect.

Hypothesis 2Bb. Surface acting is negatively related to work realization, positive affect, and life satisfaction.

Hypothesis 2Ca. Deep acting is positively related to work realization, positive affect, and life satisfaction.

Hypothesis 2Cb. Deep acting is negatively related to emotional exhaustion and depersonalization, and, possibly, to negative affect.

Personal and Personality Variables

Age and *gender* were the personal sociodemographic variables expected to be most relevant. Age might indirectly predict burnout, via its association with job-related variables such as job experience (see later discussion). Gender, given the requirements of gender roles, was expected to be a more crucial variable (Fischer, 2000; Greenglass, 1995; Hochschild, 1983; Wharton, 1993; Wharton & Erickson, 1995; Zammuner, 2000a). Because of the interpersonal orientation requirements of their gender, women might be both more motivated and accustomed than men are to regulate their dysphoric emotions vis-à-vis other people (especially so-called "powerful" ones such as anger), and do so with greater expertise. Regulatory processes, moreover, might be facilitated by women's greater *empathy* with others' emotions, enabling them to feel contextually appropriate "genuine emotions" more frequently than men do, and perhaps with greater intensity. We expected workers' marital status and number of children to be variables that might be relevant mostly in connection with gender roles. For instance, we can make two competing (but simplified) hypotheses about a woman who is married and has one or more children (i.e., has a family to care for, emotionally as well as in other ways): To the extent that she identifies with her traditional role, her emotion regulation "practice" at home will carry over to her work context, enabling her to easily perform whatever regulation kind is necessary, whenever necessary; or, vice versa, she might inadequately regulate her emotions (e.g., displaying job-incongruent emotions, or doing surface acting) because, due to her "double" role, she suffers from burnout, or feels unsatisfied about her job, and so forth. As regards the personality variables expected to mediate emotion regulation, high self-monitors were expected to regulate their own emotions more than low-level ones to meet others' demands; likewise, high self-conscious individuals were expected to experience greater emotional consonance because of their greater skill at managing their own emotions, in particular by activating deep regulation. As already stated in connection to the gender variable, empathic people easily understand others' state of mind and tune in to their experiences, and thus are both less likely to be in need of regulating their own emotions in order to sympathize with others', and more likely to regulate them if necessary.

Hypothesis 3A.   Age is positively related to the negative dimensions of burnout.

Hypothesis 3B.   Women show higher empathy levels than men do, experience emotional consonance more frequently than men do, and more often regulate their job-incongruent emotions.

Hypothesis 3C.   Self-monitoring is positively related to emotional labor, in terms of surface and/or deep acting.

Hypothesis 3D.   Self-consciousness is positively related to emotional consonance and deep acting.

Hypothesis 3E.   Empathy is positively related to emotional consonance and deep acting.

Hypothesis 3F.   High self-conscious and high self-monitoring individuals show high empathy levels too.

Job-Related Variables

In addition to job-related psychological variables such as job satisfaction (measured by the work realization component of burnout and, more indirectly, by the nature of felt affect, as discussed earlier), we expected emotion regulation to be influenced by several organizational job-related variables, including job role (e.g., doctor vs. nurse) and nature of job role. The latter is actually a compound variable, indexed especially by the typical frequency and duration of patient interactions the role requires, by the time the employee spends "interacting" with patients—that is, in relational activities of talking with, and listening to, patients (as opposed to, e.g., administering them a medicine, feeding them, etc.)—and by the kind of department (e.g., reanimation, anesthesiology, medicine) where the employee works (the latter might correlate with patients' pathology seriousness, and therefore with frequency and duration of patient interactions, and with relational time). Job experience, measured in terms of amount of time workers spent in their present job role (at the present hospital/unit, or elsewhere), is a further relevant variable in that it may define workers' "expertise," including the extent to which they have learned how to cope with dissonant emotions. Finally, although organizational norms about emotional labor (i.e., its expected kind, frequency, and "intensity") were not measured directly in this study, we did ask employees to report whether they had received organizational norms training, and to evaluate its usefulness. Because we expected these variables too to exhibit a complex pattern of relationships, we mention next only a few of the hypotheses about organizational variables, the most straightforward ones; we specify other relevant hypotheses in the Results section.

Hypothesis 4A.   A worker's (frequency and kind of) emotional labor performance is worse with a higher number of patient interactions per day.

Hypothesis 4B.   A worker's (frequency and kind of) emotional labor performance is worse with a shorter duration of such interactions.

Hypothesis 4C.   A worker's (frequency and kind of) emotional labor performance is worse the shorter relational time that the worker spends with patients.

Other Variables

The study considered a few other variables, including social desirability of workers' answers, as a control variable, a control question measuring workers' attitudes toward control of emotional expression, and workers' sense of belonging to their department versus the hospital. These variables, and the hypotheses related to them, are described in the Results section.

METHOD

Experimental Measures

Data were collected by means of a self-report questionnaire, conceived, as stated, on the basis of a theoretical analysis of relevant literatures (e.g., on burnout). It contained several questions, related to personal and job information variables, such as age, job role, frequency and duration of interactions workers had with patients, and so on, as earlier specified. The main psychological variables were measured by six experimental rating scales, taken from previous studies carried out with English-speaking subjects and usually somewhat adapted to the study purposes, especially as regards question wording (in two cases, as detailed later, scales had already been translated and used with Italian speaking subjects). More specifically, in addition to emotional labor (measured by a 10-item scale by Grandey, 1998, an adaptation of a measure developed by Brotheridge and Lee, 1998), the questionnaire measured burnout, frequency and intensity of felt affect, self-monitoring and self-consciousness, empathic concern and perspective taking, and life satisfaction (see the Results section for details about the measures). To try to avoid memory biases, employees were asked to answer each of the mentioned scale thinking about the last 2-week period. Finally, a short social desirability scale was used to control for biased self-report answers.

Subjects and Procedure

Questionnaires were administered to medical personnel of the various departments of a hospital in a northern region of Italy. A total of 150 employees, 30% males and 70% females, working as doctors (22%), nurses (66%), and technicians (12%), completed the questionnaire (out of 260; the mean return rate was 57.7%; more specifically, it was 61% for nurses, 40% for doctors, 85% for technicians). Employees were mostly in their 30s (age range 23–65 years; mean age 35), had at least 13 years of education (64%; 24% had a university degree), were married and/or lived with a partner (70%), and about half of them had children (49.3%).

Data Analysis

Subjects' answers to personal and job-related questions, and their scale ratings, were analyzed in various ways (e.g., chi-square statistics; correlation and analyses of variance for interval scale ratings; regression analyses) as detailed in the Results section. Before testing differences between subject groups, and the relationships among variables, each administered scale, given that its original format and construct had been developed and/or tested with a different cultural population than the one tested in this study, was subjected to a factorial analysis (employing the Varimax rotation method when more than one factor was extracted). Whenever the factor analysis showed that one or more items had negative loadings on a factor, item scores were reversed before computing mean factor scores. As we show in the Results section, the results we obtained in the factorial analyses mostly confirmed the original solutions (notable exceptions, as well as main results, are reported later). Relationships between variables were first analyzed by computing their degree of association, using Pearson's r; correlation values are reported in Table 14.2. Relationships among variables were further tested in a series of univariate analyses of variance; results are reported in Tables 14.3 and 14.4. Finally, the relationships between variables were tested in a set of multiple regression analyses; results are reported in Table 14.5. The main results we obtained are summarized in Fig. 14.1.

RESULTS

This section is organized as follows. The first three subsections report specifications and results about each construct/variable that was measured in the study, reporting main factor analysis results for each scale, and subjects' scores on each measured variable. The next subsection reports results on psychological correlates of emotional labor, whereas the fifth subsection reports on the effects that job-related and personal variables have on emotional labor, and on other psychological measures. Results obtained in a series of regression analyses performed to test hypothesized relationships are finally reported in the last subsection.

Dimensions of Emotional Labor

The results obtained from the factorial analysis of subjects' ratings on the emotional labor scale (see Table 14.1 for item content, factorial loadings, and explained variance; see Table 14.2 for mean factor scores), overall supporting Hypotheses 1A–D and 2A–C, showed the existence of three independent factors, as hypothesized: Surface acting and deep acting constitute dimensions of emotional labor proper, whereas emotional consonance indicates the extent to which emotion regulation is necessary. Surface acting was measured by four items (e.g., *Put on a "mask" in order to express the right emotions for the job*), that express different forms of "shallow" regulation, that is, simply complying with job-congruent display rules of emotion; it explained the highest variance. The emotional consonance factor loaded significantly two items (e.g., *React to customers emotions naturally and easily*). Finally, deep acting, the dimension of intrapsychic regulation attempts, explained the least amount of variance and was measured by two items (e.g., *Try to actually experience the emotions that I must show*). One scale item, *fake good mood*, was plurifactorial. Mean hospital workers' scores showed that they felt consonant, job-congruent emotions quite frequently. Despite this generally "positive" emotional profile, employees did report, although not very frequently, that they experienced emotional dissonance too, as evidenced by their performing both surface acting, the "shallow" emotion regulation, and deep acting, the in-depth regulation, the

TABLE 14.1
The Emotional Labor Scale: Items and Factorial Loadings

Items	Item Number	Factor Loading		
		I SA	II EC	III DA
Put on a "show" or "performance"	SA1-17			.76
Put on a "mask" in order to express the right emotions for the job	SA2-24	.72		
Just pretend to have the emotions I need to display for my job	SA3-6	.70		
Put on an act in order to deal with customers in an appropriate way	SA4-20	.67	(−.24)	(.21)
Fake a good mood	SA5-16	.64	(.40)	(−.37)
Try to actually experience the emotions that I must show	DA1-22			.76
Work hard to feel the emotions that I need to show to others	DA2-21	.55		
Make an effort to actually feel the emotions that I need to display toward others	DA3-12	.75		
React to customers emotions naturally and easily	EC1-13	(−.26)	.77	
Easily express positive emotions to customers/ clients as expected for my job	EC2-3		.79	
R^2 or percentage of variance explained: total 57.9		29.0	15.7	13.2

Note. SA, surface acting; EC, emotional consonance; DA, deep acting; item number, in the Italian version, and in the original scale by Grandey (1998).

latter more frequently than the former. The extent to which emotional labor was related, directly or indirectly, to the psychological, personal, and job-related variables hypothesized to be relevant, that is, the extent to which it had significant implications for employees' psychophysical well-being, is discussed later, after reporting, in the next two subsections, details about the measurement of each variable, and a summary of obtained results.

Measures of Burnout, Affect, Self-Monitoring and Self-Consciousness, Empathic Concern and Perspective Taking, and Life Satisfaction, and Employees' Scores

Burnout was measured by the Maslach Burnout Inventory (MBI; Maslach & Jackson, 1981), a 22-item scale, using a 1–5, *never–often* rating scale. Many studies (e.g., Byrne, 1993; Evans & Fischer, 1993; Maslach & Jackson, 1984), including several Italian replications (e.g., Pierro & Fabbri, 1995; Sirigatti, Stefanile, & Menoni, 1988), showed burnout to have a three-dimensional structure, namely, *emotional exhaustion, depersonalization,* and *work realization* (also called job satisfaction). In our study we used an Italian version, vali-

TABLE 14.2

Mean Scores on, and Significant Correlations Between, Main Subjective Dependent Variables, and Independent Organizational Variables

	DP	WR	EXH	PAf	CAf	NAf	LS	SA	DA	EC	SM	SC	EmC	PT	SD	Pt/D	Dur	RT
Depersonalization DP	****																	
Work realization WR	-.41c	****																
Emotional exhaustion EXH	.49c	-.42c	***															
Positive affect PAf	—	.23b	—	***														
Calm affect CAf	—	.34c	-.26b	.25b	***													
Negative affect NAf	.21a	—	.33c	—	—	***												
Life satisfaction LS	-.17a	.38c	-.36c	.39c	.34c	-.31c	***											
Surface acting SA	.39c	—	.27b	—	.21a	.16a	—	***										
Deep acting DA	—	—	—	—	—	—	—	—	***									
Emotional consonance EC	-.30c	.40c	—	.19a	—	-.18a	.24b	—	.14t	***								
Self-monitoring SM	-.25b	.14t	—	—	—	.16a	.17a	.28b	.20a	.20a	***							
Self-consciousness SC	-.25b	28c	—	—	.21a	—	.17a	—	.20a	.21b	—	***						
Empathic concern EmC	-.43c	.25b	—	.21a	.25b	—	.21b	—	.19a	.33c	—	.23b	***					
Perspective taking PT	-.21b	.16t	—	—	.26b	-.22b	.28b	—	—	.33c	—	.18a	.37c	***				
Social desirability SD	-.24b	.34c	-.18a	—	—	—	—	—	—	.32c	.20a	.22b	.39c	.35c	***			
Patients/day Pt/D	—	—	—	—	—	—	—	—	.16t	—	—	—	—	-.15t	—	***		
Duration Dur	—	—	—	—	—	—	—	—	-.15t	—	—	—	—	—	—	-.37c	***	
Relational time RT	-.29c	26c	-.25b	—	—	-.29c	—	-.19a	-.15t	.27c	-.27c	—	.15t	.26c	—	—	.25b	***
R^2 or percentage of variance	9.6	8.1	28.6	24.8	17.5	12.3	69.5	29.0	13.2	15.7	20.3	17.9	32.8	10.2	25.7			
Mean scores	1.88	3.55	2.55	3.34	3.39	1.84	4.33	1.97	2.54	3.85	2.90	4.89	4.70	4.11	3.51	2.79	2.33	2.64

Note. Significance probability level: $^t p < .10$; $^a p < .05$; $^b p < .01$; $^c p < .001$. The symbol — indicates lack of significance. Please refer to notes for more information.[1]

[1] Department type was recoded on the basis of duration of patient interaction, and hospitalization time. Employees with short-time durations were from the x-ray department, laboratory of analyses, transfusion center, or emergency departments; employees of medium-length duration were from the surgery, physiotherapy, maternity, pediatrics, or neurology departments; and employees of long-time duration were from the reanimation, anesthesiology, psychiatry, or medicine departments.

The duration of patient interactions was calculated as the average duration of patient interaction, with the intervals of 1–5 minutes, 6–10 minutes, and 11–60 minutes.

Relational time was calculated as the average quantity of time that employees spent in relational activities with patients, with intervals of less than 30 minutes, about 1 hour, about 2 hours, and 3 hours or more.

Frequency of patient interactions per day were recoded under the intervals of 1–5 interactions, 6–15 interactions, 16–20 interactions, and 21–60 interactions.

Depersonalization (DP) and work realization (WR) were measured on the Maslach Burnout Inventory; 1–5, *never–always* scale. EXH, 7-item scale; DP, 7-item scale; WR, 7-item scale.

Positive affect (PAf), negative affect (NAf), and calm affect (CAf), were respectively measured by 4, 3, and 2 items, inspired by the Panas test; for each emotion (e.g, happiness) subjects reported its frequency, on a 1–5, *never–always* scale.

Life satisfaction (LS) was measured on a 5-item scale, 1–6, *disagree–agree* scale. A sample item is *My life conditions are excellent.*

Surface acting (SA), deep acting (DA), and emotional consonance (EC) were measured as subscales of an original 10-item Emotional Labor Scale; 1–5, *never–always.*

Self-monitoring (SM), self-consciousness (SC), were measured by 7-item scale and 6-item scales, respectively, where 1 = *disagree–6(7)agree.*

Empathic concern (EmC) was measured on a 6-item scale; perspective taking (PT) was measured on a 4-item scale; and the subscale of the Interpersonality Reactivity Index (Davis, 1980), was measured on a 1–6 *false–true* scale.

Social desirability bias (SD) was measured on a 5-item scale, adapted from the 8-item short version of Marlow and Crowne's SD scale, with 0–5 *false–true* scale.

dated with a large sample of Italian subjects working in the "helping professions" (Pedrabissi & Santinello, 1988; Sirigatti & Stefanile, 1992; Sirigatti et
al., 1988), shown to have good psychometric characteristics (e.g., the internal
coherence of the emotional exhaustion subscale was .87), and a factorial structure quite similar to that obtained with North American subjects. Given the
different population sample tested in this study, a new factorial analysis was
nonetheless carried out. The results (see Table 14.2) confirmed the original
three-factor structure (but not all original items loaded the hypothesized
subscales; each dimension was measured in our study by seven items).

Affect was measured by an 11-item scale, inspired by the Panas test (Watson, Clark, & Tellegen, 1988). For each emotion (e.g., joy), subjects reported
its frequency in the last 2 weeks, on a 1–5, *never–always* scale; subjects were
also asked to report its intensity, on a 1–5, *almost nul–extremely intense emotion* scale (except, of course, when they reported never feeling a given emotion). Watson et al. (1988), administering the 20-item (10 positive and 10 negative) Panas test to both students and employees of a university, obtained two
relatively independent factors, positive affect and negative affect; correlation
between them varied from –.12 to –.23. The factorial analysis of the 11-item
scale in the present study showed the existence of three factors, explaining a
quite high portion of total variance (see Table 14.2). Positive affect was measured by four items, namely, *joy, love/affection, excitement,* and *pride/sense of
satisfaction. Calm (deactivated) affect* was measured by two items, namely,
calm and *quietness* (peacefulness; *tranquillità* in Italian). Finally, *negative affect* was measured by three items, *shame/guilt, fear,* and *sadness.* Two items,
anger and agitation, had a double nature (loading on both the deactivated and
the negative factor) and were therefore not considered in subsequent analyses.
Half of the sample had been asked to think about "the last two weeks in general, excluding the work context," whereas the other half was asked to "think
about the work context." The results showed that this experimental instruction influenced only calm reported emotions, somewhat more frequent (.25
mean difference) when employees "excluded" the work context.

Self-Monitoring and Self-Consciousness. Self-monitoring and self-consciousness were measured by a 14-item, 1–6 *disagree–agree* scale, developed by
Forzi et al. (1987), combining in a single instrument, the Self-monitoring Scale
(Snyder, 1974), and the Self-consciousness Scale (Fenigstein et al., 1975), thus
tapping both the behavioral and the self-perception dimensions of self-
monitoring. Eight items form the self-monitoring subscale (e.g., *It is because I
like to get along well with others, and to be appreciated, that I tend to be what others expect of me*), and six items the self-consciousness scale (e.g., *I try to understand myself*). The results we obtained supported the original bifactorial scale
structure (only one self-monitoring item was found to be bifactorial and excluded from subsequent analyses), and its good psychometric properties.

Empathy. To measure empathy we used two subscales of the Interpersonal Reactivity Index (Davis, 1980, 1983; Italian version by Bonino, Lo Coco, & Tani, 1998), namely, the Perspective Taking Scale, measuring the person's cognitive ability to adopt others' point of view (composed of six items, e.g., *I believe there are two sides to every question and I try to look at both of them*), and the Empathic Concern Scale, measuring the person's emotional reactivity, that is, his or her tendency to feel sorry, worry, and warmth toward others who go through disagreeable experiences (composed of seven items, e.g., *I often have tender, concerned feelings for people less fortunate than me*). Answers were given on a 1–6, *false–true* scale. The obtained results (see Table 14.2) supported the two-factor structure of the original scale (except for three bifactorial items, one related to empathic concern, and two to perspective taking; we did not consider them in subsequent analyses).

Life Satisfaction. This was measured by a five-item Satisfaction with Life Scale, developed by Diener et al. (1985; Diener, 1984; Suh, Diener, Oishi, & Triandis, 1998), on a 1–6, *disagree–agree* scale. The items (e.g., *My life conditions are excellent*) ask for a global evaluation of life quality, focusing on the cognitive component of subjective well-being. The factorial analysis of employees' ratings confirmed the original one-factor solution, explaining a very high portion of total variance (see Table 14.2).

Employees' Mean Scores. Results (see Table 14.2) showed that on average, health care employees felt sufficiently realized in their job, not much depersonalized, but somewhat emotionally exhausted; they reported relatively frequent positive and calm emotions, and infrequent negative ones; they were characterized by higher levels of self-consciousness than of self-monitoring, and higher levels of empathic concern than of perspective taking; and they defined in positive terms their life satisfaction.

Employees' Features on Job-Related Variables

This section reports results obtained from the analyses of employees' answers to job questions, and in relation to their sociodemographic background (see Tables 14.2 and 14.4 for mean original frequencies, recoded values of the variables, and correlation and analyses of variance results).

Frequency and Duration of Interactions With Patients, Relational Interaction Time, Job Role, Department, Sense of Belonging, and Training. Before we report the results related to interactions with patients, let us note that its duration is a difficult-to-measure variable when using subjective estimates, because people might interpret the question differently. For instance, someone might include the time spent in health care actions not associated with a communicative exchange, not implying an actual relational contact (e.g., the time an employee spends in caring for a patient in the reanimation chamber, when a dialogue with the patient is impossible); or some might include in the evaluation interactions during which the amount of actual relational contact varies (as when a doctor is taking the blood of a donor, or medicating a patient); when such variations occur, they might be perceived differently by different employees. It is for this reason that we operationalized the interaction variable asking employees two evaluations, in this order: (a) relational time, the "daily amount of time spent on average in relational activities of talking with, and listening to, patients," that is, actual dialogue, and (b) interaction duration, the average duration of a single interaction with a patient. Answers about relational time showed that the sample varied: 16.7% of employees reported less than 30 minutes, 30% about 1 hour, 23.3% about 2 hours, 28% 3 hours or more. They reported, further, a mean of 20 interactions with patients per day ($SD = 13.03$), each lasting for 16.32 minutes ($SD = 12.77$). After a close inspection of the obtained results, the original frequency and duration of interaction values were recoded into new ones, descriptive of differential frequency ranges (see Table 14.4). Job role, that is, whether subjects worked as doctors, technicians, or nurses, was, not surprisingly, positively related to education level ($r = .92, p < .001$), as well as to age ($r = .50, p < .001$). Doctors (61% of them were men) reported a greater amount of relational time (i.e., in activities of talking with, and listening to, patients) than either nurses or technicians (job role and relational time were correlated, $r = .20, p < .05$). As regards employees' *sense of belonging* to the department where they worked, rather than to the hospital organization in general, the results showed a generally high involvement level with the department (mean score = 4.63, on a 1–6, *false–true* scale), an involvement that was higher for those associated with their present department for at least 3 years (for 3–8 years, 30%; over 8 years, 29%) in comparison to those whose association time was less than 3 years (35%; respectively, 4.98 and 4.77 vs. 4.11, $F = 4.19$). Finally, only 35% of the employees reported that they had received a specific client-interaction training that they (98%) judged to be useful. We return to these results later, when discussing the correlates of emotional labor.

Psychological Correlates of Emotional Labor Dimensions

Correlation Results

As regards emotional consonance, results (see Table 14.2) supported in part Hypothesis 1Cb, in that emotional consonance showed a marginally significant tendency to be positively associated with deep acting, whereas it was not associated with surface acting. As expected (Hypothesis 2Aa), workers who reported higher emotional consonance were characterized by a higher work realization and life satisfaction, and reported more frequent positive affect. Congruently with this positive profile, this worker group reported a lower depersonalization level and less frequent negative affect (Hypothesis 2Ab); consonance was instead unrelated to emotional exhaustion, contrary to expectations, but positively related with self-consciousness (Hypothesis 3D), and both empathic concern and perspective taking (Hypothesis 3E).

Surface acting correlated (see Table 14.2) positively with both depersonalization and Emotional exhaustion (Hypothesis 2Ba), whereas, contrary to Hypothesis 2Bb, it was unrelated to work realization, positive affect (and calm affect too), and life satisfaction. Surface acting was positively related to self-monitoring too (Hypothesis 3C).

Finally, as regards deep acting, the results (Table 14.2) showed that, against predictions (Hypotheses 2Ca, 2Cb), it was not significantly associated with burnout dimensions, life satisfaction, and positive and negative affect. It did display instead a positive correlation with calm affect, thus indirectly supporting in part Hypothesis 2Cb, and with self-monitoring, self-consciousness, and empathic concern (as stated by Hypothesis 3C, 3D, and 3E).

Social Desirability Biases

As mentioned in the Method section, to test for potential self-report biases, an eight-item version of the Social Desirability Scale (Marlow & Crowne, 1961; Italian version by Manganelli Rattazzi, Canova, & Macorin, 1999), rated on a 0–5, *false–true* scale, was used. A factorial analysis showed that five items could be retained (25.7% variance explained), all of which dealt with the attribution to the self of positive traits, such as *No matter whom I am talking to, I am always a good listener*, *I have never deliberately said something that hurt someone's feelings*, and *I am always willing to admit it when I make a mistake*. Social desirability correlated positively with emotional consonance, burnout, and other psychological variables too (see Table 14.2 for correlation results and the sample's mean, actually quite high, and Table 14.3 for mean values in association to specific variables).

Results of Analyses of Variance, With Social Desirability as a Covariant

To test differences between groups controlling for self-report biases, social desirability was assumed as a covariant in subsequent analyses of variance in which we assumed the variable hypothesized to differentiate between groups as the independent variable, after recoding the original (interval, or categorical) scores of each variable into two or more categories (on the basis of its score distribution, or by taking the sample mean as a cut-off point; see Tables 14.3 and 14.4 for main results).

TABLE 14.3
Subjects' Means on Psychological Variables as a Function of Dichotomized
Personality and Emotional Labor Variables, and F Values Associated
With Significant Differences Between Subgroups

| | Self-Monitoring | | |
	Low n = 78	High n = 68	F
Negative affect	1.73	1.97	9.01[b]
Surface acting	1.80	2.19	11.55[c]
Deep acting	2.34	2.72	3.31[t]
Social desirability	3.35	3.69	6.85[c]

| | Self-Consciousness | | |
	Low n = 66	High n = 81	F
Deep acting	2.22	2.77	6.04[a]
Perspective taking	3.93	4.26	3.06[t]
Social desirability	3.38	3.62	3.34[t]

| | Empathic Concern | | |
	Low n = 72	High n = 75	F
Depersonalization	2.06	1.72	8.17[b]
Positive affect	3.19	3.47	4.51[a]
Deep acting	2.28	2.77	5.73[a]
Self-consciousness	4.72	5.04	4.22[a]
Perspective taking	3.83	4.38	7.76[b]
Social desirability	3.25	3.75	15.86[c]

| | Perspective Taking | | |
	Low n = 75	High n = 72	F
Depersonalization	2.04	1.72	6.60[a]
Calm affect	3.18	3.60	4.08[a]
Emotional consonance	3.70	4.03	3.37[t]
Self-consciousness	4.74	5.03	3.40[t]
Empathic concern	4.39	5.02	10.91
Social desirability	3.24	3.79	19.83[a]

| | Surface Acting | | |
	Low n = 77	High n = 73	F
Depersonalization	1.72	2.05	12.75[c]
Emotional exhaustion	2.43	2.68	4.74[a]
Emotional consonance	3.96	3.76	5.12[a]
Self-monitoring	2.68	3.13	10.65[b]

(Continued)

272

TABLE 14.3
(Continued)

| | Deep Acting | | |
	Low n = 78	High n = 67	F
Calm affect	3.25	3.52	4.11[a]
Self-monitoring	2.79	3.03	3.85[t]
Self-consciousness	4.80	4.98	3.02[t]
Empathic concern	4.56	4.79	4.70[a]

| | Emotional Consonance | | |
	Low n = 58	High n = 92	F
Depersonalization	2.11	1.74	15.79[c]
Work realization	3.33	3.68	22.30[c]
Positive affect	3.11	3.48	10.00[b]
Life satisfaction	3.99	4.52	5.58[a]
Surface acting	2.10	1.91	3.16[t]
Deep acting	2.25	2.71	4.33[a]
Empathic concern	4.38	4.90	8.07[b]
Perspective taking	3.77	4.33	10.10[b]
Social desirability	3.28	3.65	7.64

Note. Significance probability level: [t] $p < .10$; [a] $p < .05$; [b] $p < .01$; [c] $p < .001$. Social desirability entered as covariant in the analyses of variances. Only variables that were significant in themselves (independently of the significance of the covariant) are reported here.

Emotional Labor.   The obtained results overall confirmed the correlation trends reported above. More specifically, focusing first on the three emotional labor dimensions (see Table 14.3, right-hand column), workers who felt higher levels of emotional consonance reported greater empathic concern, perspective taking, work realization, life satisfaction, and felt positive affects more often; they also performed deep acting more frequently, and felt less depersonalization. Congruently with the results just reported, workers characterized by a low frequency of surface acting felt less emotional exhaustion and depersonalization than those obtaining high scores, and reported, moreover, lower levels of self-monitoring and greater emotional consonance. Finally, workers who reported more frequent deep acting showed greater empathic concern, higher levels of self-monitoring and self-consciousness, and more frequent calm affects. The latter results seem to indicate that when deep regulation is engaged in, the worker actually manages *to feel* the contextually required emotions, which can then be expressed. The greater emotional consonance brought about by the worker's successful attempt to feel the "calmness" appropriate to the patient-interaction is in turn functional to his or her well-being, and, in an indirect fashion, might induce him or her to focus on the positive self-perception that is associated with less agitation and higher tranquility. Workers who performed deep acting more frequently than their colleagues were, in general, characterized by a better "psychological job status."

Personality Variables. The results obtained as regards personality variables (see Table 14.3, left-hand column), in addition to confirming those already reported in relation to emotional labor, overall indicated on the one hand that the two empathy dimensions, namely, empathic concern and perspective taking, were significantly related to each other, and on the other hand that both were associated with self-consciousness (Hypothesis 3F). In addition, high-level empathic concern was associated with lower depersonalization and more frequent positive affect, whereas high perspective taking was associated with lower depersonalization and more frequent calm emotions. In other words, empathy seems to be a main predictor of well-being.

Attitudes Toward Control of Emotional Expression. Employees' attitudes might define the extent to which they perform emotional labor, or the kind of activated regulatory process. The analyses of employees' answers to a single question that measured (on a 1–6, *false–true* scale) such attitudes, namely, *In the relationship with patients, in order not to risk both one's professionalism, and the clinical results, one needs to be able to have self-control and emotional distance*, showed, congruently with some of the results just reported, that high surface-acting employees obtained higher control scores than low surface-acting ones (respectively, mean 4.10 vs. 3.47; $F = 5.45$); furthermore, a more pronounced control attitude characterized high self-monitors in comparison to low self-monitors (respectively, mean 4.31 vs. 3.32; $F = 14.68$).

Effects of Personal- and Job-Role Variables on Emotional Labor, and on Other Psychological Measures

Gender. Recalling that women were expected to engage more than men both in emotional labor, as well as to feel emotional consonance more often (Hypothesis 3B), a major finding was that men and women did *not* actually differ in their scores on any of the three labor dimensions. Men and women differed instead in their empathic concern, in the direction implied by gender roles, with women reporting higher scores than men (respectively, mean 4.81 vs. 4.44; $F = 5.74$; Hypothesis 3B). Men and women differed also in their well-being self-assessment scores, again in the direction implied by gender roles: Women reported a greater level of emotional exhaustion (respectively, 2.66 vs. 2.33; $F = 6.77$), more frequent negative affect (respectively, mean 1.92 vs. 1.64; $F = 6.36$), and more frequent positive affect (respectively, mean 3.40 vs. 3.18; $F = 2.76$). Gender did not significantly influence other psychological variables that we tested.

Age, Marital Status, and Number of Children. As regards effects associated with the age variable (after recoding its values to obtain three groups: young [23–30 years], intermediate age [31–40 years], and "older" employees [41–65 years]), the results showed that the youngest group reported positive affect more frequently than the other groups (respectively, 3.57 vs. 3.28 and 3.07, $F = 5.83$), whereas the intermediate-age group reported the highest perspective taking score (respectively, 4.45 vs. 3.89 and 4.13, $F = 5.55$). Two marginally significant effects were also obtained, with intermediate-age employees reporting higher work realization (partially supporting Hypothesis 3A), and both intermediate-age and older employees reporting more frequent calm affect. A single and marginally significant effect was observed as regards the number of children variable: employees with children exhibited lower emotional exhaustion than those without (respectively, mean 2.45 vs. 2.66, $F = 3.20$). Finally, marital status values were not associated with any significant differences in emotional labor dimensions, nor in other psychological variables.

Job Role, Job Experience. Job role was not a very informative variable per se (see Table 14.4); it was associated with two significant effects only: nurses were characterized by the lowest emotional consonance and perspective taking, technicians obtained the highest emotional consonance and emphatic concern, and doctors were characterized by the highest perspective taking. Job experience (measured in terms of number of years the employee had been working) was found to have a similar low-explanatory value; it obtained a positive correlation with perspective taking ($r = .17, p < .05$), and a negative association with positive affect ($r = -.25, p < .01$) that was most frequent in the "youngest" employees, with up to 4 years of experience (mean = 3.58), and least frequent in the "oldest" ones, with more than 12 years (mean = 3.12; 4–12 years of experience: mean = 3.32; $F = 4.73$). These results mostly coincide with those, reported above, obtained in relation to the age variable. In other words, age is a proxy and sufficient measure of job experience (as measured in this study).

Frequency and Duration of Patient Interactions, Relational Time, and Department Type. To test the effects of assumedly crucial job-role variables, namely, frequency and duration of patient interactions, and relational time, a set of analyses of variance was carried out on recoded scores (see Table 14.4). The results indicated that job-role variables contribute to explain employees' scores on psychological variables (e.g., emotional labor, life satisfaction), but did so in varying magnitude and fashion; moreover, their interpretation in terms of causal direction is not straightforward as regards emotional labor. More specifically, the lowest frequency of patients per day (1 to 5) was marginally associated with the least frequent deep acting; likewise, surface acting was

TABLE 14.4
Subjects' Means on Psychological Variables as a Function
of Job-Role Variables, and F Values Associated With
Significant Differences Between Subgroups

	Department Type			
	Short Patient Interactions $n = 36$	Medium Patient Interactions $n = 68$	Long Patient Interactions $n = 46$	F
Depersonalization	1.96	1.70[1-3]	2.08	6.60[b]
Work realization	3.44	3.72[1-3]	3.39	8.22[c]
Calm affect	3.64	3.45	3.11	2.57[t]

	Job Role		
	Nurses	Technicians	Doctors
Emotional consonance	3.75	4.26[1]	3.98	4.99[b]
Empathic concern	4.65	5.15[1]	4.61	2.70[t]
Perspective taking	3.98	4.31	4.41[1]	3.39[a]

	Duration of Patient Interactions		
	1–5 minutes $n = 25$	6–10 minutes $n = 39$	11–60 minutes $n = 69$
Life satisfaction	3.99[2]	4.67	4.26	3.60[a]

	Relational Time				
	Less than 30 minutes $n = 25$	About 1 hour $n = 45$	About 2 hours $n = 35$	3 hours or more $n = 42$	F
Depersonalization	2.02	2.06	1.83	1.63[1-2]	5.13[b]
Work realization	3.35	3.49	3.57	3.70	2.17[t]
Emotional exhaustion	2.79	2.67	2.57	2.28[1-2]	3.50[a]
Negative affect	2.04	2.01	1.77	1.59[1-2]	4.85[b]
Surface acting	2.11	2.12	1.86	1.80	2.46[t]
Emotional consonance	3.64	3.67	3.97[2]	4.09[1-2]	4.25[b]
Self-monitoring	3.26	3.03	2.83	2.61[1]	3.68[a]
Perspective taking	3.80	4.02	4.02	4.48	2.37[t]

	Frequency of Patient Interactions per Day				
	1–5 interactions $n = 17$	6–15 interactions $n = 40$	16–20 interactions $n = 27$	21–60 interactions $n = 47$	F
Depersonalization	2.03	1.65[3]	2.04	1.88	3.28[a]
Deep acting	1.62	2.65	2.48	2.56	2.22t
Perspective taking	3.87	4.55[1]	4.06	4.10	3.77[a]

Note. Significance probability level: [t]$p < .10$; [a]$p < .05$; [b]$p < .01$; [c]$p < .001$. The superscript symbol indicates the subjects' groups for which the difference between mean scores is significant. Job role: 1 = nurses, 2 = technicians, 3 = doctors. Please refer to notes at end of Table 14.2 for more information.

greatest, and emotional consonance lowest, when relational time was short, that is, 1 hour or less, indirectly supporting Hypotheses 4A–C. In the same direction are the results showing that employees who interacted with not too many patients per day (i.e., 6–15; but not those interacting with 1–5 patients per day only) reported higher perspective taking and lower depersonalization levels (they also reported a marginally more frequent surface acting). Significantly or marginally significantly greater perspective taking, emotional consonance, and work realization, and less depersonalization, emotional exhaustion, self-monitoring, negative affect, and surface acting were reported by employees who spent the longest time (3 hours or more) in relational activities (as expected, duration was positively related to relational time, and negatively related to frequency of patients per day (see Table 14.2); frequency of patients per day and relational time were instead unrelated to each other), thus supporting Hypothesis 4D. Employees interacting only very shortly with patients reported, finally, the least life satisfaction. Altogether, these results suggest that a "rich" relationship with the patient is beneficial for employees: When they spend longer times meaningfully interacting with patients (a job feature that necessarily implies a limited number of interactions), they react to them and their needs more easily, without much effort, experiencing emotional consonance more frequently.

As stated earlier, each hospital department is characterized by somewhat different working tasks, working rhythms, frequency and duration of patient interactions, and, finally, typical seriousness level of the pathologies it deals with. It is thus likely to be a salient variable. Indeed, as reported earlier in this section, employees felt greater involvement (sense of belonging) with their department than with the hospital. After carefully inspecting the available data, we recoded the 13 departments in which employees worked into three categories, labeled, for simplicity, *short*, *medium*, and *long* patient interaction (see the upper part of Table 14.4). Recoding was done on the basis of both typical interaction duration and patients' hospitalization time, itself related to patients' pathology seriousness (information on the latter two variables was collected in pretest talks with employees). The results of a set of analyses of variance (with social desirability as covariant) showed significant effects on burnout—namely, employees working in a "medium" department type reported lesser depersonalization and greater work realization. Department had no significant effects on emotional labor. Further analyses of covariance were carried out after regrouping departments into short and long relational time: In the first group (which included x-ray, laboratory of analyses, neurology, reanimation, anesthesiology, and medicine), employees were likely to spend in relational activities at most 1 hour per day, whereas in the second (which included emergency, physiotherapy, maternity, pediatrics, psychiatry, transfusion center, and surgery) they were likely to spend up to more than 3 hours per day. Results showed that in long-relational-time departments, workers had a better psychological profile, that is, felt less depersonalized (1.81 vs. 1.98, $F = 2.95$) and emotionally exhausted (2.47 vs. 2.70, $F = 3.44$), and felt more frequent calm (3.51 vs. 3.24, $F = 2.96$) and positive affect (3.44 vs. 3.20, $F = 3.54$).

Training Effects on Emotional Labor. Employees who reported having had a specific patient-interaction training judged it useful, as reported earlier in this section. This result might be due to social desirability biases (e.g., "the hospital paid for the training, it must be useful!"), as well as to implicit self-theories that presuppose a positive change if the person spent effort (or time) in an activity ("since I was trained, it must have been useful!"). An alternative hypothesis, however, is that if employees consider training as a formation opportunity offered to them by their organization, then training might really influence their ability, and perhaps their very motivation, to comply with organizational emotion norms. If the training was adequate, employees might therefore engage in patient interactions of better quality and display a greater ability in adopting (the presumably clearly stated) normative behavior criteria, feeling in turn more adequate in meeting their job role demands. Analyses workers' surface acting and deep acting as a function of training (yes vs. no) showed that group's surface acting did not differ, whereas trained employees reported more frequent deep acting than untrained ones (respectively, 2.88 vs. 2.34, $F = 4.78$). One could argue that the training simply made employees more aware that "serious" emotion regulation was expected of them, inducing them to report performing deep acting somewhat more frequently than their untrained colleagues. This argument, however, is discredited by the finding that trained and untrained employees did not differ in self-consciousness scores. In sum, training seems helpful, but, because group differences concerned only one kind of regulation process, although the most "effective" one, this conclusion is at present only tentative, a working hypothesis to be explored by further studies.

Emotional Labor Dimensions, Their Antecedents, and Their Correlates: Regression Analyses

To better understand the complex constellation of influences on employees' emotional labor, and on their perception of their life quality, as well as to verify the relative contribution that each main tested variable had in the effects previously reported, four sets of separate regression equations were tested. The results, discussed in more detail next, are reported in Table 14.5, and the most important ones are graphically summarized in Fig. 14.1.

Relationships Between Job-Role Variables, Emotional Labor, and Burnout. A first set of three regression analyses focused on job-role variables (job role, duration and frequency of interactions, relational time, and department

TABLE 14.5

Job-Role Variables and Personality Variables as Predictors of Emotional Labor and Burnout Dimensions; Job-Role Variables, Personality Variables, Emotional Labor, Burnout, and Affect as Predictors of Life Satisfaction; and Beta Weights Obtained in Regression Analyses (Methods: Stepwise Sp), and Related R^2, Adjusted R^2, and F Values

	Surface Acting Beta	Deep Acting Beta	Emotional Consonance Beta	Depersonalization Beta	Work Realization Beta	Emotional Exhaustion Beta
Job role	—	—	—	—	—	—
Frequency of patient interactions/day	—	.22[a]	—	—	—	—
Duration interaction in minutes	—	—	—	—	—	—
Relational time	—	.27[b]	.31[c]	-.31[c]	.25[b]	-.24[b]
Department type	—	—	.10	.09	.06	.19[a]
R^2	.08	.08	.10	.09	.06	.10
Adjusted R^2	.07	.07	.09	.09	.05	.08
F	12.22[c]	5.33[b]	13.13[c]	12.89[c]	7.85[b]	6.75[b]
Self-monitoring	.28[c]	.20[a]	—	—	—	—
Self-consciousness	—	.15[t]	—	-.16[a]	.24[b]	—
Empathic concern	—	.19[a]	.23[b]	-.39[c]	.19[a]	—
Perspective taking	—	—	.25[b]	—	—	—
R^2	.08	.08	.16	.21	.11	—
Adjusted R^2	.07	.06	.15	.20	.10	—
F	12.22[c]	5.83[b]	13.91[c]	19.18[c]	9.58[c]	—

Life Satisfaction

	Beta
Positive affect	.39[c]
Emotional exhaustion	-.28[c]
Negative affect	-.25[b]
Self-monitoring	.17[a]

$R^2 = .35$, Adjusted $R^2 = .33$, $F = 16.24^c$

Note. Significance probability level: [t]$p < .10$; [a]$p < .05$; [b]$p < .01$; [c]$p < .001$. The symbol — indicates lack of significance.

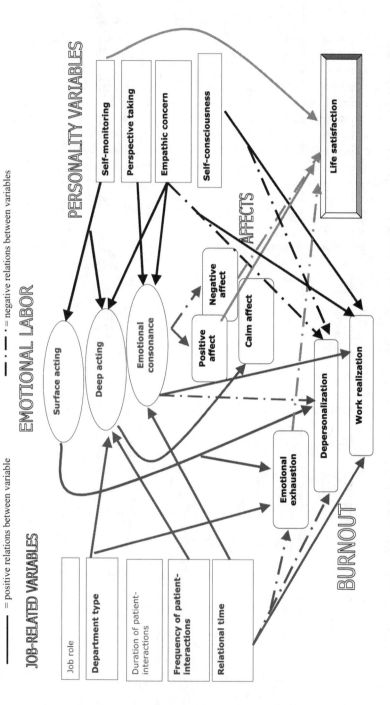

FIG. 14.1. Emotional labor and its correlates. Relationships between variables (regression analyses).

type recoded into three categories) as predictors of each emotional labor dimension, entered as the dependent variable (see the left-hand top section of Table 14.5). The results confirmed, overall, those previously reported. More specifically, no job-related variable predicted surface acting, whereas frequency of interactions and, to a greater extent, department type, significantly contributed to explain deep acting; finally, relational time was a good predictor of emotional consonance. In other words, the frequency of patient interactions is not a stressor per se. What matters more is the *quality* of work as regards the nature of interactions with patients, itself related to the department type where employees work: Together these variables define the likelihood that regulatory processes need to be activated, and that, if employees experience emotional dissonance, they will deal with it by means of intrapersonal regulation.

A second set of three equations, which tested the specific contribution of job-role variables as predictors of each burnout component, showed that relational time predicts work realization, and "protects" employees from depersonalization and emotional exhaustion; the latter is predicted by department type, too (see the right-hand top section of Table 14.5). These results confirmed, from a different viewpoint, those obtained in the first set of equations, namely, the psychological importance that the "quality" of interactions with patients has for workers, quality that depends on the extent to which employees have the possibility to develop a "human relation" with patients by means of relational activities.

Relationships Between Personality Variables, Emotional Labor, and Burnout. A third set of six regression equations tested the four personality variables that were measured as predictors of each emotional labor, and burnout, component. The results (see the middle section of Table 14.5) showed that empathic concern and perspective taking predicted emotional consonance. Self-monitoring was the only significant predictor of surface acting, whereas deep acting was significantly predicted by empathic concern, self-monitoring, and, marginally by self-consciousness. Self-consciousness and empathic concern significantly predicted work realization too, and (especially the former) "protected" workers from depersonalization. Finally, no single personality variable was a good predictor of emotional exhaustion (recall that negative affect, frequent surface acting, infrequent calm affect, low relational time, and female gender were the variable values, besides depersonalization and lack of work realization, positively associated with it; see Tables 14.2 and 14.3, and earlier discussion).

The Most Important Predictors of Life Satisfaction. A last regression equation tested to what extent life satisfaction was predicted by the most important tested variables, namely, each job-role variable (job role, frequency and duration of interactions, relational time, and department type recoded into three categories), self-monitoring and self-consciousness, empathy dimensions, each of the emotional labor variables, burnout, and by affect, entered at a predefined step in the order just mentioned, with the social desirability variable entered in the final step. The results (see the bottom part of Table 14.5) showed that four variables significantly predicted employees' evaluation of their life satisfaction, altogether explaining a good percentage of the variance (adjusted R-square $= .33$). Positive affect, (lack of) emotional exhaustion, and (lack of) negative affect were the most important predictors, but self-monitoring obtained a sizeable significant effect too. The "comprehensive" picture obtained with this last equation indicates that global life satisfaction is a judgment that is very much emotional in nature, and, more specifically, is defined not only by the "absence" of ill states, evaluations, and feelings (an absence indicated by the negative association it had with emotional exhaustion and negative affect), but also by the "presence" of positive aspects, such as actually feeling hedonically pleasant emotions (positive affect), and possessing the skill to react (i.e., performing, behaving) in adequate ways when salient cues indicate the need to comply with contextual constraints (self-monitoring). Needless to say, the life satisfaction judgment is just the tip of the iceberg, a concise, summarylike pointer to an underlying complex network of variables, that is, those "implied," associated with, the variables on which life satisfaction is directly anchored, as shown by the results reported in this and the previous sections.

DISCUSSION AND CONCLUSION

The set of results that were obtained in this study, carried out with Italian hospital employees, showed (see Fig. 14.1 for a synthesis) that emotion regulation processes, measured by the emotional labor multidimensional construct, contribute in crucial ways to the psychophysical well-being of employees who work in health care professions that imply interactions with patients. (Obviously enough, emotion regulation is important as regards the "objective" quality of the interactions employees have with their patients, as such quality contributes to define the extent to which the hospital meets its goals, but in this study we were not concerned with this issue per se.)

    The obtained results showed that the scale we employed to measure emotional labor (taken from Grandey [1998] and translated into Italian [Zammuner & Canato, 2000] for use with Italian subjects) is effective in discriminating between a consonance dimension, measuring the extent of "appropriate," job-prescribed felt emotions that do not require regulation, and a regulation–activation dimension, measuring extent of masking or modifying felt emotions in order to express "appropriate" ones. The scale is instead less apt in discriminating between the two regulation modalities it purports to measure, namely, surface and deep acting, the "shallow" and "deep" regulation kind, failing especially to adequately test deep acting (measured by one item only out of the three that composed the original subscale [see Results section, and Table 14.1], and by a second item originally belonging to the surface acting subscale). Results obtained in this study, and in parallel ones with Italian workers performing service jobs in different sectors (e.g., schools, banks, public offices; see Zammuner, 2000b; Zammuner & Canato, 2000; Zammuner & Galli, 2002; Zammuner et al., 2002), indeed showed that "migration" to a different dimension (subscale) of individual items supposed to define each of the three dimensions (subscales) in the original scale, and/or item bidimensionality, and/or item irrelevance, is a frequent phenomenon. In sum, the employed emotional labor scale presents the hypothesized three-dimensional structure; however, the structure is unstable as regards what items measure the two regulation modalities, especially deep acting. The obtained results thus raise questions about the differentiation between the two modalities, certainly at the operational level, and, more importantly, at the theoretical level too. Future studies therefore will need to address with greater attention questions such as what kind(s) of intrapersonal regulation people activate in work settings, what is the best way to operationalize this process, and what is most un/likely to trigger this type of regulation.

Not withstanding the limitations just mentioned, the reported results showed that emotional labor has crucial implications for employees' well-being, in that it has significant relationships with burnout level, with hedonic quality of felt emotions and their arousal level, and with life satisfaction more generally. The results lead us to conclude, in agreement with conclusions put forward in related studies (e.g., Hochschild, 1983; Kruml & Geddes, 1998a, 1998b; Zammuner et al., 2002), that interpersonal emotion regulation in work settings implies an emotional effort, that is, the activation of cognitive-emotional processes that use psychological energies, resulting in a psychophysical cost (indexed by burnout, negative affect, dissatisfaction, etc.). An important finding, coherent with our hypotheses, was the result that the two regulation modalities, surface acting and deep acting, tend to influence in different ways the psychological variables that were measured. In particular, workers who reported higher surface acting frequencies felt greater emotional exhaustion and depersonalization than those who reported lower scores, whereas workers who reported a high frequency of deep acting felt calm emotions more often. We might conclude that frequent surface acting is a psychologically "unproductive," dysfunctional regulation process in that, instead of reducing emotional dissonance (between the felt and the prescribed emotion), it aggravates it because the worker expresses an "untrue," "false" emotion (dissonant with the felt one), causing distress and psychological ill-being. Instead, the worker's activation of deep acting, a process of intrapsychic regulation whose goal is to feel the context-required emotions, not only is effective in reducing emotional dissonance but facilitates the ongoing social exchange, making it both subjectively more pleasant, and more in line with the organization's prescriptions; therefore, deep acting is functional to the worker's well-being because of its implications for his or her role as a worker. In sum, as we metaphorically stated earlier, frequent surface acting triggers a vicious circle, whereas deep acting triggers a virtuous circle.

The obtained results supported furthermore the hypothesis that emotional labor "activates," and is the result of, a complex net of direct and indirect links with other variables, including objective ones, such as job-role requirements (e.g., typical number of patients per day an employee interacts with), personality ones, such as empathic level and self-monitoring skills, and psychological ones, such as burnout, and how people feel about their life in general, that is, how much satisfied they are with it. Let us recall in particular the significant role of empathic concern, the emotional dimension of empathy, in predicting not only emotional consonance and the likelihood of deep acting, but also personal well-being at work, as indexed by less depersonalization, greater work realization, and more frequent positive emotions. The cognitive aspect of empathy, that is, perspective taking, although covarying with empathic concern and highly associated with calm emotions, emotional consonance, and high self-consciousness level, was instead a less crucial variable. Coherently with these results, the activation of regulatory processes, and more generally workers' well-being, were not much predicted by the job variables that characterized workers' "institutional" role (e.g., being a doctor vs. a nurse; having little or much job experience), whereas they were highly influenced by the quality of employees' relationships with patients, as defined by the time workers actually spent in relational activities with them, the kind of department where they worked, and the typical number of patient interactions they had per day (the latter findings have to be interpreted recalling both that job role and relational time were positively related [see Results] and that 66% of the employees we tested were nurses).

In conclusion, the results of this study showed that to try to understand emotional processes in work settings we need to take into account a complex network of variables. This complexity is not surprising, considering that in one's job one spends quite a sizeable portion of one's life. Further, one's job is the source (as we saw) of quite a variety of emotion-related processes, states, and consequences, including the processes of emotion regulation, the psychophysical states of emotional exhaustion, the self-fulfilling sense of work realization, and the frequency of pleasant emotions like joy, pride, and calm, or of negative ones, like anger and shame. The extent to which, and the reasons why, employees feel "inappropriate" emotions, perform emotional labor, and the nature of the regulation processes they try to implement (i.e., acting on one's emotions vs. controlling one's emotion expressions so that they fit job-required ones) were shown to have implications that reach well beyond the "here and now." That is, the implications of emotional labor go beyond the fact that its extent and nature contribute to determining how customers judge quality service, or how the employer perceives and judges the quality of an ongoing interaction, and thus the quality of his or her employee's job performance. As we indeed found, emotional processes directly or indirectly very much influence life satisfaction judgments, the "summary" evaluations that are anchored, when positive, both on "absence" of ill states (such as negative emotional states, and exhaustion feelings), and "presence" of positive, well-being markers (such as pleasant emotions, and context-sensitive skills and behaviors).

Although our study showed quite clearly that emotion regulation is a very important aspect of health-care jobs that imply interactions with clients, it did not, and could not, address all relevant issues, nor, because of its method, did it obtain results that can be interpreted with confidence in terms of cause–effect relationships. Future studies are thus needed to further explore, and validate, the effects and the causes of emotion regulation, as regards both the aspects that we did consider in the study, and others that might be hypothesized to be potentially relevant, such as differences between job roles characterized by specific demands, or between work contexts varying in terms of the norms they prescribe to their employees, or in terms of the extent to which they try and enforce employees' adhesion to those norms (these questions were addressed in part in parallel studies; e.g., Zammuner, 2000b; Zammuner & Canato, 2000; Zammuner et al., 2002). The present study, finally, did not directly address the possibly very important issue of cultural differences in processes, causes, contexts, and consequences of emotion regulation. This is thus a main question that needs to be addressed in further studies. However, cross-cultural comparisons are possible to the extent that there exist consensual measures, and associated constructs, to be used. When this study was planned and carried out, such shared "instruments" were not available. The present study was meant to be a contribution also to that aim.

ACKNOWLEDGMENTS

We thank Daniele Monzani, who collected the data and contributed in the data preliminary analyses, as part of the requirements for his thesis in psychology (academic year 1999–2000). The study was financed by a Start-Up Project grant of the University of Padova, 1999. Preliminary results of this study were presented at the 4th Congress of the Social Psychology Section, AIP, Palermo, Italy, September 2001.

15

A Bounded Emotionality Perspective on Work Characteristics

Wilfred J. Zerbe
Charmine E. J. Härtel

The proposition that behavior in organizations is characterized by "bounded emotionality" has at least a couple of notable implications. The first implication, most obvious and many times overstated, is that organizations are settings that evoke and exhibit emotional thoughts and behavior in addition to more cognitive ones. Second, however, is the implication that our emotionality is bounded. Like the bounds on rationality in decision making posed by external conditions (like the availability of perfect information) and internal conditions (like human information processing capability), internal and external factors serve to bound human emotionality. The chapters in this section each consider how the emotional labor of employees is shaped by external factors such as the characteristics of the work they perform, and organizational expectations, as well as by internal factors such as personality.

Organizational scholars have traditionally approached the study of the nature of jobs in a highly rational way. Jobs are seen to have objective features or characteristics that give rise to consequences, with the relationship between characteristics and their effect perhaps moderated by the characteristics of the observer. The classic example of this is Hackman and Oldham's (1975) job characteristics theory (JCT). Within JCT, emotions are at best a minor, tangential part and at worst absent and excluded. In its original formulation, for instance, the core job characteristics of skill variety, task identity, and task significance were specified as determinants of "experienced meaningfulness," which in turn and together with "experienced responsibility" and "knowledge of results" resulted in work satisfaction among other outcomes. Affective events theory (Weiss & Cropanzano, 1996) would argue that, at best, experienced meaningfulness and work satisfaction are evaluative judgments about one's work rather than experienced affect.

More recently emotions have crept into reformulations and elaborations of JCT. Pekrun and Frese (1992), and Saavedra and Kwun (2000), for example, articulated how objective job characteristics result in the experience of affective states, such as mood and specific emotions. Notably, they considered emotions only as a consequence of work, rather than as something as a characteristic of the work that employees do. Humphrey (2000) suggested that the link between job characteristics and outcomes like job satisfaction should influence emotional display. Research that has studied the relationship between traditional job characteristics has generally found that the greater the autonomy employees enjoy, the lower is the emotional dissonance they feel (e.g., Morris & Feldman, 1997; Pugliesi, 1999). Seemingly, the greater the choice employees have about how to react to jobs, the more they are able to align their behavior with their true feelings. Parker, Wall, and Cordery (2001) proposed an elaborated model of work design that included "emotional demands" such as the requirement for emotional labor in their list of expanded work characteristics, in recognition of the changing nature of work, particularly in the service sector.

The authors in this section would agree that emotions are a central feature of work and that any taxonomy or system of characterization of work must include the question of the extent to which emotions are demanded by jobs. At the same time, they build on the fundamental structure of work characteristics research, which poses that jobs have features that create employee reactions, moderated by individual and organizational characteristics, and result in consequences for workers and firms.

In the first chapter in this section, Rubin, Tardino, Daus, and Munz argue that in order to clarify the study of emotional labor it is important to separate constructs that capture the subjective state that may result from organizational demands for emotional expression from the motivated behavior that results. They describe how studies examining emotional labor have confused the experience of employees with the behavior they choose to manage their experience. For example, if emotional labor is defined as encompassing both rules about emotional display as well as emotional display itself, then it confounds experience and behavior. To untangle this confounding they propose a model that distinguishes between situational demands, the state of individuals in those situations, possible motivated acts, and possible outcomes. Further, they make plain that situations or jobs make both emotion-specific and non-emotion-specific demands on employees. In order, however, for research on the effects of such demands to make the greatest contribution to our understanding of emotional labor, Rubin et al. argue that we must begin with clear and unambiguous definitions and operationalization of our constructs.

In a similar vein, in their introduction to the second chapter in this section, Joyce Bono and Meredith Vey relate the sequence proposed by Reichers and Schneider (1990) as describing the development of scientific constructs. They argue that the construct of emotional labor has survived the first stage of "concept introduction/elaboration" and is presently experiencing the critiques and debates inherent in the second stage, "concept evaluation/augmentation." Like Rubin et al., Bono and Vey lament the disagreement in the field about how emotional labor should be defined and the presence of conflicting operationalizations of the construct. Their approach to this problem is to undertake a meta-analysis of the limited number of studies of emotional labor to date, in order to determine the associations between emotional labor and such variables as job characteristics, display rules, effects of employees, and possible moderating effects. From this they identify implications for future research and present practice. Indeed, the strength and patterns of associations across studies that they estimate reveal more questions to be answered than have as yet been addressed. Although on the one hand they conclude that emotional labor has effects that make it an important area of study, they also raise the problem of possibly spurious relationships due to the simultaneous effect of personality variables, and the effect of critical moderating variables such as social support that may change the direction of an effect. Bono and Vey identify a wealth of important research questions for future study and through their synthesis have helped create order out of disparate results.

One of the promises of meta-analysis remains unfulfilled, however. Bono and Vey point out that meta-analysis can "shed light on the issue of whether the way in which emotional labor is operationalized is associated with the results found in a particular study." Despite the dramatic differences among the studies in how emotional labor was operationalized, the very limited number of studies they had to work with presumably prevented them from exploring measurement effects. Indeed, they incorporated studies in their meta-analysis that both conformed with and violated the Rubin et al. proscription to separate the measurement of situational demands and the states that they give rise to. Perhaps it will be possible to explore such measurement effects in the future, with a larger body of work from which to draw, and in so doing bring some empirical light to bear on the question of how emotional labor ought to be measured.

In the third chapter in this section, Wong, Wong, and Law demonstrated the relationships between job characteristics, emotional labor, and individual differences by examining the moderating effect of emotional labor on the relationship between emotional intelligence and job satisfaction. Like the authors of other chapters in this section, Wong et al. view emotional labor as a job characteristic. Moreover, by classifying the five types of jobs of workers in their study according to Holland's model of vocational choice, Wong et al. also obtained an external indicator of the degree to which jobs required emotional labor, thus avoiding possible bias associated with the use of only a single source of data. The similarity between the pattern of results for the self-reported emotional labor measure and the external vocational choice measure is striking. Interestingly, however, Wong et al. report that increased emotional labor is associated with greater job satisfaction, contrary to other studies. Further, when job characteristics were controlled for, the relationship was negative. Wong et al. conclude that job enrichment may increase employee's emotional labor. Clearly the case can be made for both positive and negative relationships between job characteristics and emotional labor. For example, increasing task autonomy may provide employees with the freedom to self-regulate their emotional display and feeling. Conversely, increasing task identity may restrict this ability. One answer to this dilemma lies in examination of the way that Wong et al. measured job characteristics. Specifically, they measured job complexity and scope. Thus, what they found was that as jobs became more challenging, employee emotional labor increased. Alternatively, how emotional labor is defined and measured may play a part in how it relates to job characteristics. Wong et al. appear to have focused on the role-required suppression of emotion. First, as Rubin et al. would argue, this definition confounds organizational expectations and employee behaviors and, as we show next in the discussion of the next chapter, it does not address the question of whether the suppression represented deep acting or surface acting.

The final chapter in this section, by Vanda Zammuner and Cristina Galli, reported the results of a comprehensive study of the correlates of emotional labor among hospital workers. Like the results of Bono and Vey's meta-analysis (within which the Zammuner and Galli chapter was included), Zammuner and Galli demonstrate the relationships among job-related variables, worker reactions, personality variables, and employee well-being. Although they relied on responses from employees as their only data source, Zammuner and Galli did assess the effect of objective job characteristics, such as the frequency and duration of employee interactions with patients, and the kind of department in which employees worked. Their overall finding of greatest well-being among employees who had fewer but longer interactions with patients and who engaged in deep acting rather than surface acting hearkens back to the proposition in JCT that it is the experienced meaningfulness of jobs that results in greater job satisfaction. Employees who experience numerous, fleeting interactions in which they pretend to feel the emotions they are supposed to, and who work in departments that serve only to support those that represent the core function of the organization, engage in what Zammuner and Galli call an "unproductive, dysfunctional regulation process."

The four chapters in this section make a strong case for the continuing value of research on the determinants and effects of emotional labor. It is evident that it has important effects for organizations and individuals in them. At the same time, it is also evident that we know far too little about the complex web of relationships among the factors that serve to bound the emotional reactions of employees to their jobs. This is due, in part, to the inherent complexity of this phenomenon and to the interplay of internal and external factors (cf. Härtel, Hsu, & Boyle, 2002). It is also due, however, to the liability of newness present in what is still a very young and immature subset of a young and immature field of study. This newness is manifested in differences in method, specifically in definitions and operationalizations such that it is almost impossible to draw clear conclusions about relationships among constructs.

The third and final stage in Reichers and Schneider's (1990) sequence for the development of scientific constructs is "concept consolidation/accommodation," which Bono and Vey describe as happening when a few key definitions and operationalizations are commonly accepted and there is consensus on the predictors and outcomes of the construct. Clearly we are not at this stage yet in the study of emotions in organizations, much less emotional labor. In order to progress to this stage we need to pass through the messiness of concept evaluation/augmentation. If one thinks of this process as one where the fittest definitions and measures survive, then the evolution of the construct is served by both kinds of studies that are exemplified in this chapter: empirical studies that propose new measures or operationalizations or use old ones in new ways, and so expand the variety in our study, and qualitatively and quantitatively meta-analytic studies that serve to sift and weed, and so bring us closer to understanding the bounds on our emotionality.

V

ORGANIZATIONAL CHANGE AND CHANGING ORGANIZATIONS

16

Emotion Management to Facilitate Strategic Change and Innovation: How Emotional Balancing and Emotional Capability Work Together

Quy Nguyen Huy

For organizations faced with the stress of strategic change to improve declining performance, skillful management in all areas is required. Without the emotional touch, executives may find it difficult to bring about strategic renewal. Anxious, fearful employees cannot devote their full attention to their current tasks and have little inclination or capacity to gain new knowledge and skills. Resentful and angry employees may engage in covert sabotage. Depressed and sick employees increase the burden of work on peers who are already overwhelmed (Noer, 1993). All of these emotion-related conditions slow and even thwart organizational learning and strategic renewal.

Skillful emotion management is necessary because, for many people, work not only provides the economic compensation that provides for their material needs, but also defines who they are and how they view themselves, that is, their identity and self-esteem (Ibarra, 1999). Anxiety about not having a meaningful job often causes shame, sadness, hopelessness, and depression among people, and can result in major deterioration in work productivity, effectiveness, and innovation (Dougherty & Bowman, 1995).

Unfortunately, thoughtful management of employees' emotions during strategic change processes is little understood and even less systematically practiced in organizations. Many organizations have been designed formally as emotional vacuums and display, at least on the surface, unemotional and instrumental business logic, that is, operational efficiency and financial effectiveness (Weber, 1947). Although this mode of management may produce satisfactory performance in machinelike bureaucratic organizations and allow, at best, modest innovation in slowly changing environments, I suggest that skillful emotion management is necessary to create organizational contexts that foster innovation and rapid change. This requires emotion-aware managers systematically to allocate organizational resources to develop procedures related to emotion management. Skillful enactment of these procedures constitutes the organization's emotional capability. Such a collective capability mobilizes aggregate emotion management efforts from many people and allows the organization to transcend the need for having a large number of individuals with superior emotional intelligence.

This chapter is organized as follows. First, I discuss why strategic change can arouse strong emotions and some of the emotions that matter to the realization of disruptive organizational change. Second, I introduce the concept of emotional balancing of radical change and continuity to discuss emotion management related to change agents—the people proposing and conducting the change—as well as change recipients, that is, people affected by the proposed change. Too much change driven by agents could lead to organizational chaos, whereas too much attention to recipients' continuity could lead to modest change or organizational inertia. Adaptive change requires emotional balancing. Third, I elaborate how recipients' emotions can be managed during strategic change through the concept of emotional capability. Emotional capability refers to organizational emotion management actions that addresses specific emotions aroused during strategic change. Appropriate enactment of emotional capability enhances the odds of renewed organizational innovation and renewal. Fourth, I suggest one key organizational group that is particularly positioned to perform skillful emotion management, middle managers, as opposed to senior executives. I conclude with implications for future research in the area of emotion management in organizational change.

WHY IS STRATEGIC CHANGE EMOTIONAL?

Strategic change refers to a qualitative change in an organization's capabilities (Ginsberg, 1988). This change is often accompanied by a fundamental change in the firm's philosophy, supported by shifts in other organizational dimensions, such as structure, systems, and personnel, to preserve alignment. Strategic change not only causes a pervasive redistribution of resources and power but also demands a "paradigm shift" that challenges members' basic assumptions about the organization (Reger, Gustafson, Demarie, & Mullane, 1994). These assumptions define intersubjective reality and provide a way of dealing with ambiguous, uncontrollable events (Schein, 1992). Organization members are emotionally invested in these nonnegotiable assumptions that shape their cognitive structures for sensemaking and meaning giving. Challenging this source of cognitive and emotional stability represents an attack on core identity and thus triggers strong defense mechanisms, such as anxiety and defensiveness (Schein, 1992).

Core identity refers to the central, enduring, and distinctive values of the organization that many employees have personally identified with (Dutton & Dukerich, 1991). If recipients view the proposed change as opposing these values, the emotional arousal becomes more intense than that caused by a lack of cognitive understanding of change. Oppositional concepts are likely to trigger feelings of anger and fear (Reger et al., 1994). Because strategic change arouses strong emotions, I discuss how emotions influence employees' thinking and behavior as they affect the realization of such change.

EMOTION LINKS TO COGNITION AND ACTION IN RESPONSE TO CHANGE

Emotions and change are intertwined because emotions are not aroused by the presence of favorable or unfavorable conditions, but rather by actual or expected changes in these conditions (Frijda, 1988). Emotions enable people to reorder priorities as situations change, allowing them to take actions they believe will enhance their chances of survival, and permit them to set long-term goals when choices involve incomplete data or incommensurate alternatives (Damasio, 1994). Emotions also help people make a leap of faith and face the challenges of major change (Westen, 1985; Zajonc, 1980).

Change arouses emotions that motivate action responses. Emotions focus people's attention on an event and prompt the search for adaptive actions. Lazarus's (1991, 1993) emotion theory suggests that this involves a two-stage appraisal process. First, through primary appraisal, people evaluate the significance of a new event in relation to their own goals and concerns. If they appraise the potential consequence as beneficial, pleasant emotions are aroused. However, they experience unpleasant emotions if they appraise the consequence as potentially harmful. Emotions can lead to paralysis because of fear, although they often generate a readiness to act (Frijda, 1996). Emotions serve first as relevance detectors, focusing people's attention on change events, then as motivators of action. Second, potential action response is determined through secondary appraisal, whereby people evaluate their own capabilities for dealing with a relevant change event. If they believe they have adequate resources, they are more likely to respond actively. Otherwise, they may adopt a passive/avoidance approach, which is sometimes interpreted as a form of resistance to change (Lazarus, 1993; Huy, 2002).

Emotions aroused by strategic change are not only felt at the personal, idiosyncratic level. Faced with a change event, a large number of employees in different work roles can collectively experience certain shared group emotions. Individual emotions converge into group emotions through several mechanisms. First, employees who share a common organizational culture have similar beliefs, leading to similar appraisals and ways of feeling (Schein, 1992). Second, a group translates tendencies into collective expressions more easily than individuals acting alone, because group membership boosts people's feelings of power by making them feel bolder through anonymity (Barsade & Gibson, 1998). Third, emotional contagion could be at work. Individuals could unconsciously respond to others' emotional displays by imitating and exaggerating them. The perceived threats involved in strategic change increase needs for affiliation, particularly among people who believe they are confronting the same situation (Gump & Kulick, 1997). Group members identify strongly with one another and experience each other's emotions, for synchrony conveys empathy. The group's emotional charge amplifies through mutual interaction that promotes group cohesion and continuity (Hatfield, Cacioppo, & Rapson, 1992). In this regard, organizational groups can express shared emotions and act upon them.

I now introduce two emotion-based organizational concepts and elaborate how they work with each other: emotional balancing and emotional capability. Emotional balancing involves the emotion-management behavior of two distinct organizational groups: change agents and change recipients. Practicing emotional balancing brings about positive organizational adaptation and avoids the extremes of organizational chaos and inertia. Emotional capability then focuses on change recipients and elaborates how recipients' emotions should be managed to facilitate major change and innovation.

EMOTIONAL BALANCING

Emotional balancing refers to a group-level process juxtaposing emotion-related actions intended to drive change while inducing a sense of continuity in a group of people (Huy, 2002). My field research suggests that balancing is necessary because too many and too rapid change risks generate chaos, while too little and too slow change risks create inertia (Huy, 2002). Methods for my field research have been described in more detail elsewhere (Huy, 2002). Findings from this research have since been validated with research conducted with over 20 large-profit as well as nonprofit organizations world wide. Some of these findings are published in Huy (2001).

Emotional balancing entails, at the organizational level, (a) the change agents' commitment to champion and pursue change projects and (b) organizational attending to the emotions of recipients to restore some operational continuity. Different organizational members can play different roles, however. Some people may choose to play the role of change agents who propose radically new ways of doing things, whereas others may focus on attending to organizational continuity and employees' emotions. Put differently, the emotional balancing model I propose does not require all influential employees to display a high level of emotion management skills. The aggregation of various emotion management actions performed by different groups of people and facilitated by the organization's procedures, resources, and training could help develop an enabling emotional climate that facilitates adaptive change. Furthermore, although the presence of a very large number of supporters of change is obviously desirable, this may not be critical to start a strategic change. Many successful major changes seem to have been initiated by a small group of people and then to have been diffused (Rogers, 1995). Because strategic change can elicit very different intense emotions in change agents and recipients, it helps to understand the psychological mechanisms that elicit these emotions.

Psychological Mechanisms of Emotions Related to Change and Continuity

People have at least two motivational foci. When they are focused on change (or growth), people are driven by development needs and seek to bring their behaviors and self-conceptions in line with how they would like to be; eagerness or ensuring gains dominate their behavior. On the other hand, when they are continuity (or security) focused, they seek to align their actual selves with their duties and responsibilities.

At the risk of oversimplifying, I use the circumplex model of emotions to explore categories of emotional states that people experience during strategic change. The circumplex model is akin to an emotional compass (see Fig. 16.1), in which emotions are categorized along two dimensions (Larsen &

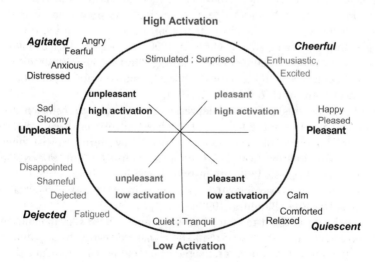

FIG. 16.1.   Circumplex model of emotions. Adapted from Larsen and Diener (1992).

Diener, 1992). One dimension reflects the hedonic valence (pleasant-un-pleasant), and the other refers to the intensity of arousal or action readiness (high vs. low activation). Together, the four bipolar dimensions produce eight emotion categories that capture a large range of emotional experiences (Bartel & Saavedra, 2000). Thus, the hybrid category of pleasant high-activation emotions includes enthusiasm and excitement, whereas pleasant-low activation emotions include calm and comfort. On the other hand, unpleasant high-activation emotions include anger, anxiety, and fear, whereas unpleasant low-activation emotions include disappointment, shame, or dejection.

As shown by the 45-degree axes in Fig. 16.1, the emotions of change-focused people vary along a cheerful–dejected axis, whereas those of continuity-focused people vary along an agitated–quiescent axis. These four hybrid categories reflect the operation of two evolutionarily adaptive motivational systems (Watson, Wiese, & Vaidya, 1999).

The first system motivates people to seek change; the second motivates people to seek continuity and security and act as change recipients. Enthusiastic change agents who are also distressed recipients of another change initiative could, however, experience a wide range of conflicting emotions and experience uncomfortable emotional ambivalence. Treatment of ambivalence is beyond the scope of this chapter.

Change Agents' Emotions

To create the necessary emotional energy that helps people envisage ambitious change and persist in adversity (Kanter, 1983), change agents seek to enhance pleasant high-activation emotions (e.g., enthusiasm) and reduce unpleasant low-activation emotions (e.g., dejection). As previously discussed, strategic change often challenges organization members' identity, roles and privileges, thus triggering anxiety (Argyris, 1990). Anxiety, in turn, can degenerate into depression, which blocks all learning efforts as people perceive that they cannot achieve valued outcomes and are pessimistic about potential improvement in their situation (Schein, 1996).

To fight against this anxiety and depression, people seek to restore peace of mind, which comes from the belief that one has control over threats that may arise, either by changing objective circumstances or by altering the psychological impact of the situation (Mischel, Cantor, & Feldman, 1996). For example, medical research suggests that patients who have illusory beliefs that they can exercise partial control over their treatment enjoy important psychological and physiological benefits (Bandura, 1997).

Emotional commitment to change provides agents with stamina and hope to persevere in change efforts and reduces premature despair from potentially disappointing outcomes. Moreover, people who feel they can influence the direction of change are likely to feel more confident about their own future. After committing to a goal, people will normally pay selective attention to information relevant to its realization and generally evaluate its consequences positively (Gollwitzer, 1990). This shields them from the distractions of competing alternatives and paralyzing self-doubts (Kuhl & Beckmann, 1985). Research also suggests that perceptions of personal control are related positively to maintaining the effort devoted to challenging tasks, such as the pursuit of ambitious change projects (Aspinwall & Taylor, 1997). People who display low emotional commitment to major change projects are likely to have a difficult time competing with highly committed peers for scarce organizational resources (Huy, 2002).

But how would people on the receiving end of change agents' actions feel? I now explore change recipients' emotions and their underlying mechanisms.

Change Recipients' Emotions

Employees affected by strategic change may feel powerless and fatigued about change and, as a result, neglect to perform the mundane but critical organizational routines that serve the needs of key constituencies, such as paying staff salaries, delivering good customer service, and ensuring safety and quality in production. Organizations need to mitigate the extreme effects of too much change and chaos by focusing managers' attention on the importance of maintaining operational continuity in their own work groups (Huy, 2002).

As I alluded to previously, the second motivational system (seeking continuity) mediates the threat avoidance withdrawal behaviors typical of coerced change recipients who likely experience emotions in the upper left and lower right quadrants of Fig. 16.1. These recipients seek to attenuate unpleasant high-activation emotions (e.g., fear, anger) and enhance pleasant low-activation emotions such as calm (Schein, 1996).

The organization needs to display emotional sensitivity behaviors that distinguish, repair, and manage the emotions of change recipients. This requires managers to attend to their subordinates' emotional responses to achieve some emotional equanimity in their employees' work and private lives. Attendance to employees' private lives is crucial to enhancing their receptivity to strategic change, because during such disruptive change, employees tend to be less concerned about the organization's new strategy than the potential effects of the new strategy on their personal and family welfare. This arouses strong emotions that need to be attended to achieve beneficial organizational outcomes, which I illustrate in the next section.

Organizational Outcomes Related to Emotional Balancing

In my field study, I found that managers' aggregate emotional balancing actions facilitated two important organizational outcomes: development of new skills and operational continuity (Huy, 2002). From employees' experience in doing change projects, learning to change seems to represent, at the aggregate organizational level, one of the major benefits of change. Through "learning by doing," certain organization members developed a more refined embodied understanding of the necessary skills involved in major, rapid change. These change skills included, for example, process mapping and reengineering, project management, employee downsizing and relocation, outsourcing routines, customer segmentation, statistical analyses related to work processes, and emotion-attending to highly stressed employees. They gradually built new skills by applying and adapting to their own work context a variety of change tools that had been relatively new to them. Besides getting acquainted with the technical and human elements involved in change knowledge and skills, veteran employees learned to interact with executives and external consultants and appreciated the exposure to new ways of doing things, such as aggressive marketing, quick competitive responses, taking more risks in fast action, and the importance of cash and profits.

With regard to operational continuity, certain middle managers' attention to work details and subordinates' emotions contributed to a smooth downsizing in certain work units. By working with union representatives to soften downsizing and relocation hardships on recipients, managers reduced the likelihood of extreme responses. Powerful unions had threatened management with sabotage and strikes to protest downsizing, but very few of these actions occurred. Managers' emotion-attending behaviors dampened in part employees' anger and fear, emotions that could spread and amplify through the dynamics of emotional contagion. Some continuity in providing products and services allowed the organization to maintain some of its revenue-generating capability, thus providing part of the needed cash to fund more than 100 change projects (Huy, 2002).

My research also suggests that inadequate attention to recipients' emotions can lead to underperformance in outcomes even if change agents' commitment to realizing operational efficiency and manpower savings are strong (Huy, 2002). Similarly, weak commitment to change in a high-pressure strategic change context or when emotions are not attended to can lead to workgroup inertia or chaos, thus resulting in deteriorating workgroup performance. This suggests that emotional balancing is particularly important for major change that requires both strong commitment to pursuing change and, minimally, some moderate acceptance from recipients to integrate the change while maintaining some of their traditional but still important tasks (e.g., serving customers).

In summary, emotional balancing involves broad categories of emotion management actions related to change agents (e.g., emotional commitment to the proposed changes) and recipients (e.g., the need to attend to their emotions). I now elaborate the concept of emotional capability, which specifically describes more textured emotion management actions that attend to recipients' emotions.

EMOTIONAL CAPABILITY

At the organizational level, emotional capability refers to the organizational ability to acknowledge, recognize, monitor, discriminate, and attend to emotions at both the individual and the collective levels (Huy, 1999). This ability is built into the organization's habitual procedures for action, otherwise known as routines (Nelson & Winter, 1982), which reflect the collective knowledge and skills demonstrated in local contexts to manage emotions related to strategic change. Organizations that develop procedures related to emotion management and provide systematic training on this subject to employees reduce the need to rely on the innate competence of individuals' emotional intelligence and their variable individual initiatives. In this respect, an organization's emotional capability can be far greater than the sum of the emotional intelligence of its more mobile individual members (Huy, 1999). Building emotion management skills among a large number of employees with various levels of emotional intelligence is likely to require a long-term, sustained organizational effort (Goleman, 1995). Because organizations have finite resources and need to prioritize their developmental activities, a gradual development of emotional capability seems necessary.

I next elaborate the various emotion management action routines that constitute an organization's repertoire of emotional capabilities: experiencing, reconciliation, identification, encouragement, liberation, and playfulness. Figure 16.2 summarizes how the various emotion management routines described below influence the three change dynamics of receptivity, mobilization, and learning, discussed in Huy (1999).

Sympathy and the Capability for Reconciliation

Sympathy represents a less demanding emotional process than empathy, because it refers to the ability of an individual to feel for the general suffering of another, with no direct sharing of that person's experience (Goleman, 1995). Expressing sympathy in strategic change involves emotional reconciliation, that is, the process of bringing together two seemingly opposing values or goals people feel strongly about (Huy, 1999). Genuine efforts expended toward achieving a new synthesis and understanding increase receptivity to proposals for change.

To achieve this new synthesis, Albert (1984) suggested that change agents present change as a juxtaposition of additions and deletions. If change can be framed and accepted by the recipients as an addition or an expansion of existing values, it is easier for employees to accept it. The more continuity is perceived to exist between the past and the future, the less the change is regarded as radical. In one case study of the merger between two large organizations with different value systems (Ramina & Huy, 2002), for example, managers or-

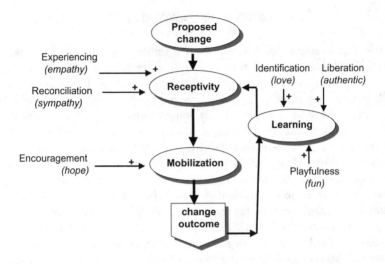

FIG. 16.2.   Developing emotional capability in organizations. Adapted from
Huy (1999).

ganized formal sessions with employees from both organizations. Each company group was asked first to articulate the traditional ways of doing (norms
and values) that they would like to keep and those they would like to abandon.
Then the results were shared with the other group. Employees discovered,
much to their surprise, that the norms they valued and those they were less
proud of were very much alike. A sense of continuity between the two cultures
was thus established, and there was a shared understanding to delete certain
negative elements of each culture.

However, to the extent that certain valued elements from the past must be
deleted, mourning may help ease the transition. Change agents who ignore the
mourning period and rush the organization through this meditative phase risk
a backlash, as happened to distressed AT&T employees in the post-breakup
phase (Moses, 1987). AT&T faced the government's decision to break up the
million-people-strong institution into smaller units known as Baby Bells
(Tunstall, 1985). These employees were proud of their company's achievements, values, and history and could not fully understand or accept the forced
breakup of a great American institution. The physical aspect of the massive
structural breakup was implemented quickly. However, executives in the post-
breakup phases were eager to move on to a new phase and cut down on emotion management of their employees. The mourning period was curtailed.
This resulted in lingering widespread emotional stress among employees and
caused major organizational damage, as an internal report on AT&T employees written by a psychologist revealed:

We have very "disturbed" managers. Managers who are forced to make work force reduction decisions without any guidance, training, or support are becoming cynical. . . . Open hostility is surfacing as never before and its focus is toward the company rather than toward the competition or the marketplace where such energies can be productively channeled. The amount of suppressed, covert hostility lurking just below the surface in many people is truly frightening. Unfortunately, much of the frustration, anger, and depression is taking its toll on the non-work lives of our people. . . . At the same time, we have noted a marked increase in symptoms of depression among managers we have studied. Today's survivors are often disillusioned, frustrated, bitter, and, most of all, lacking in hope. (Moses, 1987, pp. 35–36)

What happened to AT&T employees? Bridges's (1980) work on personal transition suggests careful management in all three phases of transition, that is, "endings," then "neutral zones," and finally "new beginnings. These phases seem to have been ignored in managing AT&T employees' emotions. In the endings phase, organization members recognize that "positive feelings toward past situations cannot be replicated in the future." In the neutral zone, people feel disoriented (the past is no longer appropriate but the future direction is not yet clear). Managing actively the transition between the ending phase and the neutral zone is important. Members will need sufficient time to reflect on the past and develop new perspectives for the future. They have to come to terms with issues such as what went wrong, why it needs changing *now*, and thinking about the new beginning. The time allotted to mourning should be adequate, neither too long nor too short. The organization has to encourage shared meaning construction about the proposal for change, and people should be helped to find their new roles in the new order (Bridges, 1986).

Change agents who rush the rest of the organization through this meditative, seemingly unproductive phase of allowing people properly to work through their emotions could suffer recipients' backlash, as happened in the case of AT&T. In summary, emotional reconciliation are translated through a combination of emotion management actions, such as organizing one-to-one listening to any concerns that recipients feel uncomfortable voicing in public; empathetic rather than judgmental response; attending to recipients' personal and work-related concerns, especially when these are caused by the change process; organizing mourning sessions for cherished values that are no longer appropriate while extolling values that have been preserved; and organizing regular small-group meetings to inform as well as to listen to recipients' feedback on both task and emotional needs.

These activities require different levels of skills, sensitivity, and specialized training and should be shared among many managers and their support staff. Sharing is necessary because individualized emotion management can become taxing on a manager's time and stamina if he or she has to personally attend to the emotional needs of every employee in a large group (Huy, 2002). However, for a demonstration of sympathy to be appreciated by change recipients, an overarching climate of emotional authenticity has to present, as is discussed next.

Authenticity and the Capability of Liberation

At the organizational level, the emotional capability of liberation refers to an organization's ability to facilitate the variety of authentic emotions that can be legitimately displayed (and felt) during a strategic change process. Under major stressful change, employees are likely to experience emotional dissonance if they are only allowed to express a narrow range of emotions. Emotional dissonance is the internal conflict generated between genuinely felt emotions and emotions required to be displayed in organizations (Morris & Feldman, 1996; Wharton & Erickson, 1993).

Display of positive emotions tends to be encouraged whereas display of negative ones is sanctioned, as the latter are feared to cause poor group performance (cf. Jehn, 1997). For example, during a process of strategic change, the chief operating officer of one company I studied sent a confidential memo to all managers stating that "expressions of cynicism [about change] will not be tolerated. We are in positions of leadership and must display enthusiasm at all times [to everyone]."

Curtailing a full range of emotional display may be viable in a slow change environment, as it speeds up execution by reducing hesitation and doubt. Nevertheless, emotional suppression can impair collective learning during strategic change. Under major change, it may be more productive for managers to relax emotional display rules and express more authenticity in order to restore some continuity in their subordinates' lives. To protect themselves, however, managers may strategically choose to observe traditional rules in their dealings with certain superiors—executives who still frown upon intense emotional displays, especially unpleasant ones.

The routine of emotional liberation to encourage authentic emotional displays needs to be activated to increase receptivity to change. People may resist change for nonwork-related reasons yet feel compelled to invoke a work-related rationale because the latter is deemed more legitimate (Huy, 2002). To illustrate, in my field research, certain managers had to relocate their staff and maintain the operating objectives of revenue generation and service quality. These actions were taken in the context of a massive downsizing effort to centralize work locations and cut costs. Their customer service employees claimed they were reluctant to reorganize customer service because it did not make sense from a business strategic perspective. More astute line managers discovered, however, that the invoked business reasons often acted as a cover for employees' concerns for their families' welfare. For example, one manager realized that half of the relocated people were mothers with young children and that the longer commuting time for them would be exhausting and not sustainable.

Another manager organized emotion management for separate small groups of 20 to 40 recipients. Employees were encouraged to verbalize in small groups (outside the scrutiny of their superiors) their feelings about how change had affected them. Then managers invited each group to make a drawing about how the change felt collectively, and they displayed the drawings around the room. There were drawings of anxious-looking people in lifeboats, of caravans lost in the desert, big thunderstorms. It was only then that individual people started to realize how similar their feelings were, and they started to laugh and joke about them. A facilitator showed them Bridges's (1980) transition model and explained that it was normal and common to have these feelings (Huy, 2002). The sessions encouraged emotional authenticity by liberating employees to experience a wide range of emotions and to surface and accept their deep feelings.

The sessions were also therapeutic in that they elicited low-activated pleasant feelings such as calm and sympathy and attenuated unpleasant emotions such as fear and helplessness. Mild pleasant emotions like calm can facilitate problem solving. Calm people are more likely to make associations among ideas and to see more complex relations than do people in an agitated state (Isen, 2000). Conversely, excessive agitation and emotional demands on recipients can lead to emotional numbness and low sensitivity to new ideas and experimentation (Morris & Feldman, 1996). It follows that the more organization members feel free to display authentic emotions during strategic change, the higher the level of learning is likely to be (Huy, 1999, 2002). The less they feel free to display authentic emotions during strategic change, the higher are the emotional dissonance and the proportion of employees disabled by burnout, and the lower is the learning.

Although display of empathy, sympathy, and authenticity can help enhance recipients' receptivity to change, mobilizing people for collective action to realize ambitious change goals seems to require the arousal of another important emotion, hope.

Hope and the Capability of Encouragement

The emotional capability of encouragement refers to an organization's ability to instill hope among all of its members during a strategic change effort. Hope refers to the belief that a person has both the will and the means to accomplish goals; hope buffers people against apathy and depression and strengthens their capacity to persist under adversity (Snyder et al., 1991).

Organizational actions that arouse hope among employees include establishing meaningful change goals; creating small wins to rekindle optimism and self-confidence; frequent and cheerful interaction between change agents and employees; uplifting ritual devices, such as rousing speeches and award ceremonies; and a compelling strategic vision (Ashkanasy & Tse, 2000). The higher the degree of encouragement to instill hope among all organizational members, the higher the degree of collective mobilization is likely to be (Huy, 1999). In the more successful cases in my study, change agents aroused hope and action by promoting wide participation of, and active consultation with, recipients right from the beginning of the planned change. They developed some enthusiastic supporters in recipient groups, who, in turn, championed their cause inside their respective units in language that their local peers could relate to. As a result, they achieved a wider receptivity for the proposed change and voluntary cooperation in adapting the change to the specific local conditions to make it work better (Huy, 2002).

While hope can facilitate collective mobilization, it may also promote group think (Janis, 1972) and action devoid of adaptive creativity. Consequently, innovative change actions require the arousal of another emotion, fun.

Fun and the Capability of Playfulness

Fun results from the motivated search for pleasant experiences and aesthetic appreciation (Salovey & Mayer, 1990). It fuels intrinsic motivation, which is necessary for creativity (Amabile, 1988). From a neuropsychological perspective, fun permits the rapid generation of multiple images so that the associative process is richer. A happy person engages more often in exploratory behavior, which is necessary for creative discovery. By contrast, neurologists have found that sadness slows image evocation, thus narrowing the associative process and reduces creativity (Damasio, 1994).

Playfulness refers to the organizational ability to arouse fun in employees to create a context that encourages experimentation and tolerates mistakes during strategic change (Huy, 1999). Fun here does not just refer to the superficial process of telling jokes, office parties, or sports events, which provides some temporary release but bears little effect on work creativity and innovation (Csikszentmihalyi, 1997a). "Deep fun" as opposed to superficial fun is accompanied with the experience of flow or timelessness involved in intense activities (Csikszentmihalyi & LeFevre, 1989). It represents an intense state of consciousness in which one's entire affective, cognitive, and physical resources are totally invested in the task at hand. Mountain climbers, motivated artists, and researchers are likely to experience this state when they are totally immersed in their tasks and lose their sense of time (Csikszentmihalyi, 1997b).

Organizational actions that elicit deep fun and timelessness in a work context combine establishing tasks with clear goals, optimal challenges, and frequent feedback; allowing employees autonomy in tasks that require creativity; developing meaningful work (i.e., work that is compatible with a person's preferences and values); and reducing pressures and distractions on employees (Mainemelis, 2001).

Once an innovative spirit has been (re)kindled in the organization, managers should work hard at maintaining it and retaining innovative employees. Beyond satisfactory economic incentives, which are unlikely to elicit or sustain people's intrinsic motivation in the long run, managers could develop emotional rewards that would create in their employees a strong sense of identification with, and loyalty to, their organization, thus leading to the sustained innovation that allows organizations to produce distinctive products and services ahead of their competitors.

Love and the Capability of Attachment

The process of attunement, in which emotions are accepted and reciprocated, elicits love; unconditional and sustained love is often exemplified in the relationships between parents and children (Goleman, 1995). At the organizational level, the emotional capability of attachment represents the collective behavior of organization members, expressing their deep identification with the organization's core values (Dutton, Dukerich, & Harquail, 1994). In order to maintain a sense of identity, individuals have to feel a basic level of security and comfort, which can be achieved through attachment to symbolic objects (e.g., teddy bears for children; professional identity, clothing, houses for adults) that bridge a person's internal and external worlds (Winnicot, 1965).

The deeper the change targets' positive attachment to an organization's identity (core values), and the more the proposed change is evaluated as incongruent with that identity, the more resources are needed to promote receptivity to the proposed change (Huy, 1999). Individuals identify more strongly when their organizational identities evoke positive affects, but disengage themselves if organizational identities are conducive to negative affects (Harquail, 1998). The stronger the significance of the current identity, the more intense the emotions will be. This suggests that building emotional attachment to the organization's renewed values and goals in the later stages of strategic change is important.

There are at least two organizational actions that elicit attachment to organizations: first, socially desirable actions that enhance employees' external recognition and self-esteem (e.g., protection of environment, charitable causes, innovative achievements), and second, actions that demonstrate that the organization cares about the long-term development and welfare of its employees and their significant others, such as career development, education, and medical, pension, and family benefits. Emotional identification can be reinforced through personnel selection, socialization, and retention.

To summarize, emotional balancing works in tandem with emotional capability in that emotional balancing addresses general management of different broad categories of emotions experienced by change agents and recipients. Emotional capability further specifies discrete emotions experienced by change recipients and how they should be managed in an orderly manner to bring about major change and innovation.

During strategic change, there is a group of organizational actors that seems singularly better situated and equipped to perform more effectively emotion management actions than other groups, namely, middle management (Huy, 2001, 2002). Consequently, the role of middle management is discussed next.

EMOTION MANAGEMENT: THE CONTRIBUTION
OF MIDDLE MANAGERS

Consistent with the literature on middle management, I define middle managers as people who are two levels below the CEO and one level above the first-line supervisor (Floyd & Woolridge, 1996; Kanter, 1983). Large organizations tend to have many hierarchical levels of middle managers, so one senior middle manager in the line groups could act as a "general manager in the middle" and be in charge of 200 to 5,000 front-line workers (Uyterhoeven, 1989). This manager has hierarchical authority over junior middle managers, who in turn supervise a number of line supervisors overseeing professionals and workers.

The literature on middle managers has documented their proactive contribution to organizational innovation mainly in incremental change contexts. In such slow change contexts, the resource allocation mechanisms are assumed to be relatively stable, while the organization's strategy is evolving gradually (Burgelman, 1983). Middle managers are then motivated to act under familiar incentives and structurally pre-designed reward systems. The more successful agents are the individuals who can manipulate and maneuver within the complex web of explicit rules and informal interactions (Kanter, 1983). For example, middle managers mediate vertically between the strategic and operational levels by acting as linchpins between executives and front-line workers and by balancing conflicting demands (Westley, 1990). They also mediate horizontally by facilitating diffusion and integration of knowledge across departments and locations (Bartlett & Goshal, 1987). Middle managers implement by synthesizing strategic and operational details, infusing data with meaning, championing new issues, and influencing how executives interpret them (Guth & McMillan, 1986). By providing slack resources and sheltering initially illicit experimentations, they facilitate surprising innovations outside the scope of deliberate strategy (Burgelman, 1983, 1994). Many of these functions would also be useful in implementing radical change.

Yet in planned strategic change, middle management's roles and contributions are seen as much weaker (Tushman & Romanelli, 1985). The literature tends to deemphasize the role of middle managers and to portray them in a relatively self-effacing role as compared with executives. Most normative models of strategy tend to accord middle management a supporting role at best (Shrivastava, 1986); executives are advised to reduce equivocality so that middle managers can act on clear instructions.

Middle management has often been singled out as the primary organizational group that resists strategic change (Biggart, 1977). Executives view middle managers as part of the inertial systems and barriers to change that need to be co-opted, sidelined, or disposed of, especially if attempts at co-optation fail. This implies that for change to spread, putting newcomers in influential executive positions to initiate radical change is only the first stage of a sweeping personnel change process (O'Neill & Lenn, 1995). Consequently, middle managers have been portrayed as deenergized and emotionally stricken in the face of the overwhelming power of turnaround executives (Noer, 1993).

My field research suggests, however, that it was middle managers, rather than senior executives, who took on the essential role of emotion management, including emotional balancing, to help achieve successful strategic change (Huy, 2001, 2002). Middle managers were able to devote more time to internal company issues than were the executives, who had to attend to multiple external institutional demands. Middle managers were generally closer to their front-line workers than executives and, therefore, more attuned to their employees' needs. Emotion management must be highly appropriate in order to be effective, so middle managers were more suitable than executives. One must be close to a particular individual or group to recognize that not everyone feels the same type of emotion with the same intensity at the same time in response to the same event (Huy, 1999). This suggests that middle managers could be key loci for emotion management during strategic change.

Further, in my study, I found that a number of middle managers formed a self-emerging social support group that attended to employees' emotional needs in an organization supposed to function on instrumental, unemotional routines. This social support group provided an emotional buffer against, and a repair unit for stressful events and thus facilitated continuity (Stroebe & Stroebe, 1996). Other managers emerged as intrapreneurs, applying emotion management to drive change, and this relaxed the unrealistic requirement that influential organizational actors had to support and drive change (Kotter, 1995). Thanks to this diversity in the emotion management patterns that shape emotional balancing, these middle managers (in aggregate) created emotionally capable organizational groups that adapted positively to change without requiring a majority of influential individuals to be emotionally intelligent (Goleman, 1995).

As previously mentioned, the emotional balancing model I am proposing in this chapter does not require all middle managers to play an exemplary role in their organizations. Although the presence of a very large number of supporters of change is desirable, it may not be critical to start a strategic change. Generally, it is a small group of people who initiate major change, and who diffuse it gradually to a growing number of adherents, Consequently, careless downsizing of middle management means that whatever skills these veteran managers have gained in incremental change are unavailable when the organization implements strategic change.

CONCLUSION AND RESEARCH IMPLICATIONS

In this chapter, I have discussed how emotion management is critical to successful realization of strategic change. Strategic change tends to arouse strong emotions because it (a) upsets existing personal privileges, personal comfort, and self-esteem derived from work and (b) alters organizational values many employees personally identify with. Intense negative emotions, such as anxiety, fear, and anger, can lead people to resist the change and sabotage it. Consequently, recognizing the range of emotions and attending to them is critical to sustained successful change.

First, I have discussed the concept of emotional balancing as a broad concept addressing organizational change and continuity. Emotional balancing can facilitate adaptive change by recognizing the emotions of two groups of organizational actors: change agents and change recipients. Change agents have to manage their own emotions related to the pursuit of change (enthusiasm, emotional stamina) that allow them to persist in their change efforts. But for adaptive change to occur, some maintenance of operational continuity is also necessary to keep the organization running and serving its existing customers. It is thus critical to attend to recipient employees' emotions elicited by too much disruptive change. How to attend to recipients' emotions was then elaborated in the concept of emotional capability.

Building emotional capability involves developing systematic organizational action routines that attend to recipient employees' emotions caused by major change; it includes at least six different types of action, which over the long run build the organization's capabilities: the capability of experiencing that expresses empathy, reconciliation that expresses sympathy, liberation that creates a context of emotional authenticity, capability of encouragement that arouses hope, playfulness that arouses deep fun or timelessness, and the capability of identification that arouses organizational attachment or loyalty.

I have also suggested why and how middle managers could be one of the key agents of change and innovation. Based on my field research (Huy, 2001, 2002), I found that some middle managers were capable of acting as change agents because they had entrepreneurial ideas they had not been able to sell and implement previously. Other middle managers facilitated change by attending to operational continuity: They attended to work details and subordinates' emotions.

Continuity in providing products and services allowed the organization to maintain some of its revenue-generating capability during strategic change, thus providing part of the needed cash to fund change projects.

The ideas advanced in this chapter contribute to three research streams: research on organizational change, the social psychology of emotion, and middle management. I now elaborate these contributions and conclude by suggesting avenues for future research.

CONTRIBUTIONS

This chapter contributes to the strategic change literature by proposing emotional balancing and emotional capability as two promising emotion-based theoretical lenses to use in examining the challenges of implementing strategic change. The literature on strategic change has often focused on executives. This study suggests that a richer knowledge of strategic change can be achieved by including other actors. It reveals that there were a number of middle managers, many of them veterans, who were willing and able to initiate, lead, and implement changes even under very stressful conditions.

The chapter also contributes to the literature on the social psychology of emotion. First, it links microemotions to macro-organizational and strategic phenomena. Radical change is strategic because its outcome affects the life chances of an organization. Although building on some of the insights of the emotional intelligence literature, such as emotional awareness and repair, this chapter suggests a complementary path to organization theorists interested in including emotion in their research. The current skepticism about measuring emotional intelligence and associated undersubstantiated grandiose claims (cf. Salovey, Bedell, Detweiler, & Mayer, 2000) should not discourage organization scholars from studying emotions. In addition to or in lieu of personality and individual-level emotion constructs, one might consider studying the aggregation of emotion-related expressions and actions at the social group level. These group-level emotion constructs could also be studied as organizational phenomena.

Emotional balancing and capability rely on observable behavioral constructs. I suggest that beyond self-reported questionnaires and lab experiments that have advanced our knowledge on emotion, the study of emotion in work organizations can be enriched by a repertoire of measurement tools that complement each other. Emotional arousal in natural work settings and, more importantly, the organizational consequences of such emotional arousal and management thereof can be studied in a number of different ways—both objective and subjective. For instance, development of emotional capability in general may be measured by the proportion of organizational resources allocated to emotion-attending activities such as budget, specialized support groups, training, or executive time. Emotional identification can be measured using the turnover rate of workers and through various measures of cultural strength. Emotional reconciliation can be measured by the time change targets spend in the grieving process and the time change agents and recipients spend together to develop a cultural graft.

In addition, the overt nature of emotion-related behaviors lends itself more easily to outsider observation and assessment (and thus to enhanced construct validity) via triangulation of interviews, surveys, company reports, and ethnographic research in natural settings, all of which allow researchers to validate and enrich participants' self-reports (see Huy, 2002). The proposed emotion management constructs lend themselves to multimethod research and triangulation, thus enhancing validity and reliability.

FUTURE RESEARCH

The limitations of the studies reported in this chapter reveal potential for future research. First, emotional balancing involves management of four groups of emotions in the quadrants of low-high activation and pleasant-unpleasant hedonic valence (see Fig. 16.1). Within each of these four groups, discrete emotions can be quite different in terms of what people experience (e.g., anger is distinct from fear, disappointment is different from depression). This suggests that the antecedents and consequences of discrete emotions can also differ. Future research on emotional balancing should go beyond the effects of groups of emotions to tackle the effects of discrete emotions (cf. Izard & Ackerman, 2000). Emotional capability with its focus on certain discrete emotions represents only a preliminary step toward greater specificity.

Second, the organizations that are involved in the research reported in this chapter tend to be large and bureaucratic ones in which little attending to emotions before strategic change was implemented. Future research can explore individual differences that led some managers to emphasize emotions related to change and others to focus on attending to recipients' emotions. Future research could tease out the effects of organizational conditions from individual competencies in predicting attention to recipients' emotions versus emotional commitment to change behaviors.

Third, this chapter suggests that emotional balancing and capability are likely to widen and deepen the learning of managers involved in strategic change. Future research could flesh out the underlying organizational and psychosociological mechanisms that facilitated such cognitive learning processes. Emotional balancing may enhance certain kinds of organizational learning such as trial-and-error learning. Balancing continuity and radical change can be alternatively studied as balancing exploitation and exploration in organizations. Learning organizations may be those that systematically develop "emotional capability" routines that arouse certain mildly pleasant emotions such as interest and fun that favor creativity and attachment to work (Huy, 1999; Isen, 2000).

Emotional balancing and capability may also be useful for other forms of organizational change that are less extreme than radical change, such as continuous change. Brown and Eisenhardt (1997) found that continuous-change organizations applied time-paced "semistructures" balancing mechanistic and organic activities. Time-related pressures could cause a high level of emotional excitement and agitation among employees (Perlow, 1999). Many innovative employees have played the role of change agents when promoting their new ideas and acted as recipients to defend their achievements from threats of cannibalization, and so could experience the full range of emotions (Kanter, 1983; Burgelman, 1994). Burns and Stalker (1994) found that the abnormally high levels of emotional stress inherent to the success of many organic, innovative organizations and firms that were exciting places to work could also be harmful and exhausting for their employees. The protracted emotional hardship in dealing with relentless uncertainties and ambiguities made employees yearn for some stability and, in part, led certain organic firms to become more mechanistic in the long run. Appropriate emotional balancing and capability could help increase innovators' emotional resilience and could sustain the pace of continuous change.

The challenge of sustaining beneficial continuous change raises another issue. Would developing emotional balancing and capability in organizations vary according to organizational age and employee turnover? In large and established organizations with a long history, people (including middle managers) who attend to recipients' emotions generally had a long tenure and knew many of their subordinates well, and this might explain in part their voluntary efforts to attend to their subordinates' emotions. In young companies, such as dot-com startups, where many employees expect short tenure or share few, if any, core organizational values, people may be less likely to expend extraordinary personal efforts over a long time to attend to colleagues' emotions when faced with adversity. Future research could validate whether and how emotional balancing emerges in young organizations undergoing stressful change, and whether emotional capability can be developed in such transient contexts.

It is also unclear what kinds of emotional balancing and capability might be developed during strategic change in flatter or networked organizations and who might be willing and able to do it. The majority of the employees in these organizations will be front-line workers or professionals rather than experienced personnel managers. It is possible that emotional balancing and capability and thus organizational adaptation in these organizations might depend mainly on individuals' skills and predispositions. This raises the hypothesis that organizations that tend not to value emotional awareness, such as certain engineering or financial trading companies, may have less emotional resilience and adaptive capacity under strategic change than organizations that value it more, such as The Body Shop (Martin, Knopoff, & Beckmann, 1998).

Despite growing evidence showing that downsizing middle management may reduce organizational flexibility and innovation (Dougherty & Bowman, 1995; Floyd and Woolridge, 1996; Huy, 2001), executives still appear to make this a frequent practice (Wysocki, 1995). If downsizing precedes change, whatever skills veteran managers may have gained in incremental change are therefore unavailable when the organization implements radical change. The possibility that there might be a number of effective middle managers in organizations who could facilitate major changes through emotion management invites us to reconsider an important issue: Blanket dismissal of the role of middle managers in strategic change and careless downsizing of middle management ranks risks throwing the baby out with the bathwater and damaging one of the key levers of organizational renewal. Until we explore further the role of middle managers in strategic change, we will not know the long-term costs of that damage.

17

Managing Emotion: A New Role for Emergent Group Leaders

Anthony T. Pescosolido

This chapter proposes a new role for group leaders, the role of managing group emotion. This new leadership role suggests that individual group members are perceived as leaders by others when they provide direction and guidance during times of ambiguity, particularly when this guidance involves the display of appropriate emotional responses to unsettling events. An individual is perceived as a leader by making an interpretation of the emotional response that would best serve the group's needs, and then modeling that response for the other group members. By modeling an emotional response to the situation, the leader resolves ambiguity and provides the group with the direction needed for action. At they same time, this leadership action can increase group solidarity by creating both shared emotion and shared action within the group. The idea of leadership as the management of group emotion is not tied to one specific individual, but rather is a leadership action that can be performed by different group members at different times. The emergence and success of any individual as group leader is subject to several conditions, such as the group context, group norms, and individual skills and abilities.

For thousands of years, people have known about the importance of effective leadership. Numerous leaders from throughout history have written treatises on how to be effective as a leader, including individuals such as Alexander the Great, Marcus Aurelius, Lao Tsu, and St. Ignatius of Loyola. If you were to go to the business management section of your local bookstore, you would find a number of books written in modern times that focus on the phenomenon of leadership. Indeed, a recent query on Amazon.com resulted in a list of over

13,000 titles and five subcategories that were associated with the term "leadership." Whether we read "how to" books by various experts, or biographies of successful leaders from industry, politics, or the military, it appears that many of us inherently know how important the skills and abilities of leadership are to our own lives.

However, one thing that many of these titles seem to have in common is that they look at the "great ones" among us. If we want to read about leadership, we read about people who are seen as leaders by many people. Consequently, we read about people at the highest levels of political, corporate, military or service careers. We may read about political leaders such as Mohatma Gandhi, Winston Churchill, and Abraham Lincoln; military leaders such as Joan of Arc, Robert E. Lee, or Napoleon; corporate leaders such as General Electric's Jack Welch, Virgin Group's Richard Branson, and The Body Shop's Anita Roddick. Unfortunately, this type of reading doesn't help most of us, as most of us are not heads of state, of large military organizations, or of well-financed corporations. Although it may be very interesting to know the steps that Jack Welch took over the years to make GE a more profitable company, this doesn't help us unless we are also in the position of running a multi-million-dollar concern.

For most of us, leadership opportunities do not appear in the corporate boardroom or its equivalent in other arenas. For most of us, leadership opportunities appear in our day-to-day environments, whether with our coworkers, our friends, or our families. Consequently, our attempts at leadership should not be based so much on the model of an executive mandate, as they should be based on models of relationship and interpersonal effectiveness. This suggests that our concern with leadership should not be based on "formal leadership," that which is held by executives and is backed up by executive power, but rather on "emergent leadership," that which arises informally within a group of people as they go about performing a shared task.

Emergent leaders can be defined as group members who exhibit initiative and have influence over other group members (De Souza & Klein, 1995; Hollander, 1961). They hold no legitimate authority or power; they hold no control over organizational rewards or punishments. Instead, they acquire authority from group members who give away some of their own control because they believe the emergent leaders provide value to the team (Druskat & Pescosolido, 2003).

A growing body of research has recently begun to examine the role of informal or emergent leaders within groups (DeSouza & Klein, 1995; Druskat & Pescosolido, 2003; Hollander & Offerman, 1990; Neubert, 1999; Nygren & Levine, 1996; Pescosolido, 2001; Smith & Foti, 1998; Taggar, Hackett, & Saha, 1999; Wheelan & Johnston, 1996). This interest in emergent or informal leaders can be attributed partially to the recent rise in self-managing work teams (SMWTs) (Lawler, 1998) and the consequent need for leadership to emerge from within groups rather than being imposed on them externally (Beekun, 1989; Cohen, Ledford, & Spreitzer, 1996; Druskat & Kayes, 1999).

To date, research on emergent group leaders has focused on either the conditions that allow an individual to emerge as leader (e.g. personality traits and behaviors) (Druskat & Pescosolido, 2003; Taggar, Hackett, & Saha, 1999) or on the effects of emergent leader behavior on the group (e.g. group goals and group efficacy) (DeSouza & Klein, 1995; Pescosolido, 2001). Little research has focused on the role that emergent leaders play within groups, and on whether that role is different from the role(s) played by formal leaders either within or external to groups.

This chapter develops the idea of emergent leaders playing the role of an "emotional manager" for the group. I propose that one form of emergent leadership is to help group members resolve and make sense of ambiguous events by modeling particular emotional reactions to those events. Consequently, the emergent leader is able to set the "emotional tone" for the group, and to influence how group members will interpret and react to events that impact the group. I also suggest that although formal leaders may engage in the management of group emotion, this is of particular importance to the informal or emergent group leader. This is because informal leadership is essentially a process of influence (Hollander, 1961) and because leaders who emerge from within the group do not have access to formal organizational punishments and rewards to shape behavior.

This chapter attempts to describe group emotional management and how it occurs within a group. It then draws on qualitative descriptions of several emergent leaders in action to demonstrate how informal leaders manage group emotion, as well as to illustrate the conditions that facilitate this type of informal leadership. The chapter concludes with a further description of the role of emergent leaders as managers of emotion, and some theoretical and practical implications of the proposed theory.

EMERGENT LEADERS AS MANAGERS
OF GROUP EMOTION

Various theories of leadership have had components (e.g., behaviors or traits) that are linked to the display and management of emotions (Ashkanasy & Tse, 2000; George, 1995; Westley, 1991). For example, Bales's early studies of group interactions (Bales, 1950; Bales & Slater, 1955) identified two emergent leaders within the group; one was primarily task focused and the other was primarily socioemotionally focused. Trait-based theories of leadership include traits such as emotional balance, interpersonal skills, social nearness, and maintenance of group cohesion, all of which have a socioemotional component (Bass, 1990). The emotional aspect of leadership recognized in the trait-based research often focuses on the promotion of positive feelings and cohesion within the group, and the control of the expression of negative feelings (Bass, 1990). As such, the leadership trait literature raises the issue of the management of group emotions by examining how leader personality traits influence the expression of emotions within groups.

Behavior-based theories of leadership also raise the issue of the management of group emotion. The Ohio State University leadership studies identified the behavior factor of consideration for group members (Bass, 1990). Similarly, the Michigan State University studies identified the factor of employee-oriented behavior (Kahn & Katz, 1960). In both cases, the leader is described as engaging in behaviors that affect the emotions of group members. For example, these leaders take a personal interest in group members, identify more with the concerns of group members, make special efforts to put group members at ease, and often express appreciation of group member efforts (Bass, 1990; Kahn & Katz, 1960). Charismatic theories of leadership are also linked to the emotions of group members as they emphasize emotion, values, and the importance of leader behavior in "making events meaningful for followers" (Boas, 1999). However, none of these theories address the specific question of how the group leader affects the overall "group emotion" (Kelly & Barsade, 2001), and the effect that this can have on group processes and performance.

The majority of leadership research has focused on formal, established leaders within groups and organizations (Wolff, Pescosolido, & Druskat, 2002). However, research has begun to focus on the role of emergent leaders within groups (DeSouza & Klein, 1995; Druskat & Pescosolido, 2003; Neubert, 1999; Pescosolido, 2001; Taggar et al., 1999; Wolff et al., 2002). Emergent leaders can be defined as group members who exercise influence over the group (Hollander, 1961, 1964, 1985). The key distinction between emergent leaders and formal, established leaders is that emergent leaders do not have formal organizational authority or power; rather, they lead by influencing group processes, beliefs, and norms (DeSouza & Klein, 1995; Druskat & Pescosolido, 2003; Pescosolido, 2001).

I propose that a key role for these emergent leaders of groups is that of the manager of the group's emotion. Although the role of emotion in organizational studies has long been neglected (Ashforth & Humphrey, 1995; Fineman, 1993a), its role in organizational phenomena has begun to be the subject of analysis and inquiry (Ashakansy & Tse, 2000; Barsade & Gibson, 1998; Druskat & Wolff, 1999; Fineman, 1993a; George, 2000; Goleman, 1995). Although various theories of leadership have had components related to the display and control of emotion, previous research and theory has failed to articulate fully the role that emotion plays in group leadership. Past leadership theory has focused more on individual attributes and behavior, for example, leadership styles (Bass, 1990), or abilities such as communicating a vision (Yukl, 1999), or a leader's charisma (Boas, 1999), than on the role the leader fills in the group. Jones (2001) highlighted the difficulty of focusing on the traits and behaviors of individuals when he stated that leadership "occurs only when followers believe they have found in some individual a solution to the problems that confront them" (p. 763). This suggests that a given group may require very different and distinct traits and behaviors from its leadership over time. The idea of the leader acting as the manager of group emotion is offered in this spirit: that the group leader interprets ambiguous situations and models an appropriate emotional response, thereby solving immediate problems of ambiguity and expression that the group needs to confront.

When an ambiguous event occurs within a group context, group members often look to the group leader to help make sense out of that event (Hollander, 1961). They may turn to the group leader for a variety of reasons: The leader may serve as a parental figure for the group (Freud, 1922), the leader may have the greatest amount of knowledge and experience (Yammarino, 1996), the leader may have the greatest understanding of the larger organization and its likely behavior (Yammarino, 1996), or the leader may be the individual who is the most reassuring and has the most positive relationships with other group members (Hollander, 1964). In any case, the group leader models an emotional response to the situation, illustrating what an "appropriate" reaction would be. This allows group members to interpret and express their own emotional reactions in an otherwise ambiguous situation. The emergent leader's reaction is considered "appropriate" by group members and is used as a model for their own reaction primarily because of the "idiosyncrasy credits" held by the emergent leader (Hollander, 1964). Idiosyncrasy credits are allotted to those who contribute to the group's primary task and show loyalty to group norms. Hollander (1964) found that these idiosyncrasy credits enabled leaders to deviate from group norms, giving them the opportunity to bring about innovation and shape group behavior.

I propose that group leaders manage group emotional responses by first empathizing and identifying with the collective emotional reaction of group members, and understanding what factors in the situation are causing these reactions. Then they craft a response to the situation causing the emotional reaction, and communicate their response to the group both verbally and by taking action. In this way the leader is able to address the situation and set the emotional tone for other group members to adapt their own emotional responses, and thus their future behavior.

Several theoretical perspectives on leadership suggest that certain conditions will enhance the ability of an individual to "step forward" and assume a leadership role for a period of time. These perspectives then give us a starting place to help predict how to determine who will step forward as a leader within a group, and how and when that will happen.

Fiedler (1967) was the first to propose that leadership success was dependent not only on the behaviors of the leader, but also on other situational factors within the group and its environment. He theorized that there were three factors that impacted the necessary "leadership style" (task oriented or relationship oriented) for success in any given situation. These three factors were: (a) the degree to which group members trust and respect the leader (leader– member relations), (b) the positional power and formal authority of the leader (position power), and (c) the degree to which the task and individual assignments are routine or standardized (task structure). These three factors could be combined into eight different categories, each of which would describe a particular leadership style that would lead to success (Fiedler, Chemers, & Mahar, 1977). Looking at Fiedler's three factors, we can see that the first two (leader–member relations and position power) are closely related to our concept of emergent leadership. Remember that our definition of an emergent leader is a group member who has influence (brought about by trust and respect, or leader–member relations) without having formal authority (position power). Therefore, there are two of Fiedler et al.'s (1977) categories that provide the conditions of emergent group leadership: (a) when there are strong leader–member relations, low position power, and high task structure, and (b) when there are strong leader–member relations, low position power, and low task structure. Fiedler et al.'s (1977) model predicts that in the first of these two situations, when there is high task structure, a leader is best off employing a task-oriented style, meaning that the leader should focus on setting goals, developing new performance strategies, and giving performance feedback to group members. However, in the second situation, where there is low task structure, a leader is better off employing a relationship-oriented style, meaning that the leader should emphasize a concern for group member feelings, building trust, and creating a cohesive group. In other words, leaders in this second situation are more productive when they engage in the management of group emotions.

Although a formal leader in an ambiguous situation could rely on his or her formal authority (position power) to take control of the situation, an emergent leader must rely on persuasion and modeling rather than "giving orders." Similarly, an emergent leader when faced with a clear, routine situation simply needs to keep the group focused on the task at hand. However, when an emergent leader is faced with an ambiguous, unclear situation, his or her ability to identify the group's emotion, understand the factors causing this emotion, and model an appropriate response to the situation allow them to lead the group through the situation as best as possible.

Proposition 1: Emergent leaders are more likely to engage in the management of group emotion when the group receives ambiguous performance feedback from relevant stakeholders.

Several leadership theorists have suggested that a leader's success is dependent on the degree to which his behavior conforms to the expectations of the group members. Leadership, particularly emergent leadership, is a two-way construct; group members do not follow an informal leader who does not provide value in ways considered acceptable to the group (Hollander, 1961; Steiner, 1972). Hollander (1964) developed the term *idiosyncrasy credit* to refer to the leeway that emergent leaders are given to deviate somewhat from group norms in order to further progress toward the group goal. Idiosyncrasy credits are given to a group leader (or indeed to any group member) as an informal reward for providing value to the group in the past. In other words, the more you have proven your loyalty and your value to the group, the greater leeway you have to break "group norms," the informal rules and codes that govern group behavior. For example, although a rookie baseball player in his first professional season would be expected to be on time for every practice, attend all team meetings, and never argue with a team coach, a veteran player who had contributed many seasons of high performing play would not be faulted for showing up 15 minutes late for batting practice, or voicing his disagreement with a decision made by the coaching staff. He is able to do this by drawing on the pool of idiosyncrasy credits that he has built up over his years of serving as a productive member of the team. However, Hollander (1964) argued that this is a finite pool of "credit," and a group member can exhaust it by drawing on it too often (e.g., consistently showing up late for practice), or by drawing too much at once (e.g., engaging in physically violent behavior when the coaching staff makes a decision the player does not like). Consequently, although emergent leaders have earned sufficient "credits" to deviate from established group norms when they need to, if they try to depart too far from group norms they may be stripped of their leadership role and ostracized from the group (Hollander, 1964). Therefore, although emergent leaders enjoy a greater degree of freedom than do other group members, they are still limited in their behavior by what the group feels is acceptable and appropriate.

However, when we talk about emergent leaders as managers of group emotion, we must discuss not only the interactions between leaders and groups, but also the interaction between groups and the expression of emotions. Expression of emotions within a group has been suggested as a key factor in overall group development (Bennis & Shepard, 1956), as impacting persuasion within a group (Mackie, Asuncion, & Rosselli, 1992), and as a key indicator of psychological safety within a group (Edmondson, 1999).

The expression of emotions within the context of the group is expected to be a very important aspect of an emergent leader's ability to manage group emotion. If emotion is not directly expressed by individual group members, then emergent leaders are not able to identify emotional responses or look for their causes. From this it follows that more frequent expressions of emotion within the group will lead to more frequent experiences of a leader engaging in the management of group emotion.

Proposition 2: Emergent leaders will be more likely to engage in management of group emotion when the group has developed norms that allow and encourage the expression of emotion within the group context.

Two of the more recent trends of leadership research focus on what is known as *transformational leadership* and *charismatic leadership* (Robbins, 2003). In transformational leadership, the leader is focused on inspiring followers to grow and develop in a manner that helps to achieve the mission of the organization (Bass, 1990). In other words, transformational leaders focus on their followers and try to understand the goals and desires of an individual follower, and then use the information to encourage them to achieve the goals and desires in a way that creates the greatest utility to the organization. This is often contrasted with *transactional leadership*, which is characterized by a contractual relationship and the idea of a leader utilizing promises of reward and punishment to produce the needed behavior. In the research tradition of transformational leadership, the primary tool of the leader is his or her ability to understand followers' hopes and dreams, and link them to the organizational mission and to organizational productivity. The research tradition associated with charismatic leadership, on the other hand, suggests that the primary tool of the leader is his or her ability to articulate a compelling vision of the future that attracts and motivates people to work to achieve this vision (Robbins, 2003). This vision, combined with the leader's willingness to engage in unusual or even risky behavior to achieve the vision, creates the essence of a leader's "personal charisma" (Bass, 1990).

Both of these research traditions are usually focused on formal, rather than emergent, leadership (Boas, 1999). However, they are both equally applicable to the phenomenon of emergent group leadership, as both focus on how leaders interact with followers on an emotional level to create a working group. In transformational leadership, one of the key components is the leader's ability to understand his or her followers' hopes and dreams, and to be able to incorporate those hopes and dreams into a set of goals that furthers the organization's mission (Bass, 1990). This is accomplished at least in part by the leader's use of empathy, the ability to understand what another person is feeling and what is causing this particular emotional reaction. Some research has already begun to demonstrate and explain the importance of empathy as a key trait for the success of emergent group leaders (Wolff et al., 2002).

The body of research on charismatic leadership is equally applicable to emergent group leaders. As we define emergent group leaders as "group members who have influence over other group members," the inevitable question then is, "influence members to do what?" This question is answered through an emergent leader's charisma, his or her ability to combine unusual, attention-getting behavior with a clearly articulated and compelling mission. Charisma helps to illustrate the direction in which the emergent leader wishes to take the group. This, when combined with the empathy that is often implied in discussions of transformational leadership, provides a potential basis for who will stand forth as an emergent leader. When an individual assures group members that he or she holds their interests at heart (empathy) and can incorporate those interests into a clear vision for the future (charisma), then group members will cede more of their individual control and autonomy to that individual, and the process of leadership emergence begins (Hollander, 1964).

Proposition 3: Emergent leaders who exhibit both charisma and empathy will be more likely to engage in the management of group emotion.

METHODOLOGY

The incidents described in this chapter were observed during a field study on the emotional dynamics of groups (Pescosolido, 2000). The fieldwork encompassed observation and whole group critical incident interviews with 20 different groups. A theoretical sampling procedure was used as described by Strauss and Corbin (1995) to identify two types of groups to which the author had access, and also to maximize the opportunities to provide rich, descriptive material for theory development. The two types of groups were either semiprofessional jazz music groups (meaning that although the groups were paid for their performances, members held full-time jobs to meet their financial needs), or they were collegiate rowing crews. Although the jazz groups ranged in size from four to eight members, the rowing crews consistently had nine members (eight rowers and a coxswain). It was expected that the use of these groups would allow observation of emotional situations within a group context, along with the factors led to the expression of emotion within a group and how expressions of emotion were resolved.

All of the groups were observed for at least one complete practice or performance session, lasting from 2 to 4 hours. During the group observation periods, extensive notes were taken regarding which group members took initiative, which ones were treated with respect, how group members talked about incidents that might affect their task performance, and how they expressed emotion within the group context. Each group also participated in a whole-group interview afterward where they described a "critical incident" in their group's life together (Druskat & Pescosolido, 2003; Flanagan, 1954; Motowidlo et al., 1992; Ronan & Latham, 1974). Specifically, the group members were asked to describe, in great detail, a recent experience where they "all felt that the group clicked." Group interviews lasted from 45 to 90 minutes. During the critical incident interview, the interviewer limited his questions to those necessary to draw out more detail about the incident. Subsequently the interviewer was limited to asking questions such as: "What led up to the event?" "Who did and said what to whom?" "What happened next?" "What were you thinking or feeling at that moment?" "What was the outcome?" Although the critical incident interview method provides a retrospective account of behavior and thoughts, validity and reliability of event descriptions are strong (Motowidlo et al., 1992; Ronan & Latham, 1974) because the interviewer probes for highly detailed responses. Several groups (dependent on the group's availability and willingness to continue) were observed for multiple practice/performance sessions, and were subsequently involved in multiple group interviews.

The interview transcripts and field notes regarding group member behavior were analyzed to identify examples and illustrations of a group leader acting as the manager of the group's collective experience of emotion. These examples are discussed next to add further description and explanation to this previously overlooked role of the group leader.

DISCUSSION: DETERMINANTS
OF MANAGING GROUP EMOTION

There are several factors thought to influence an emergent leader's ability to influence group emotions. These factors fall into three main categories: the group's context, the group's "norms," and the leader's skills and abilities. The following section describes how each of these factors influences a group leader's ability to manage group emotion. Each category is supported by examples that illustrate this influence process.

Group Context

When an ambiguous event occurs within a group context, group members often look to the group leader to help make sense out of that event (Hollander, 1961). As discussed previously, they may turn to the group leader for a variety of reasons. In any case, the group leader models an emotional response to the situation. This allows other group members to make sense of and express their own emotional impulses in an otherwise ambiguous situation.

> Proposition 1: Emergent leaders are more likely to engage in the management of group emotion when the group receives ambiguous performance feedback from relevant stakeholders.

An example of the group leader helping other group members make sense out of an emotionally ambiguous situation occurred with one of the jazz groups that was observed. It was relatively early in the evening's performance and the group was playing very well to a small audience. Although the audience had been demonstrative of its appreciation of the group's performance at the very beginning of the performance, it had begun to grow very quiet. The musicians reacted to this, by looking at each other more frequently, casting glances that appeared to express concern. They also became less vocal with each other during this period. After several minutes, the trumpet player stepped forward for a short solo. During this solo he exuded a strong sense of confidence, demonstrated by the expression on his face and the style of his playing. This confidence rapidly caught on with the other group members, who began to once again look out toward the audience, talk with each other as they were playing, and seemed to regain the confidence with which they had started the performance.

In later discussions about their performance, group members indicated that they had been very aware of that time period in the performance as being a critical part of their overall success for the night. When asked what had happened, group members revealed that they had been unsure how to interpret the audience's growing silence. As one member expressed, "We weren't sure if they liked it, or if they didn't like it, you know? Usually, when folks like the music, they tell us. They start clapping or moving or calling out—but these folks, they just went quiet. We didn't know what to think!" Later on, a different group member expressed the opinion that the trumpeter "really knows how to read an audience," and that consequently, his behavior in the conduct of his solo piece gave comfort to the other group members. "We could see that he wasn't upset about the situation. And you know he can tell when an audience is with you and when they aren't. So when Bobby stepped out like that, well I could just tell from the way he did it that he thought everything was just fine."

In this case, the group was faced with an ambiguous response from the audience. The stillness on the part of the audience could have been interpreted as being a result of either great interest in and appreciation of the group's performance, or a lack of those same things. The group trusted the trumpeter to interpret the audience reaction and model an appropriate response to that reaction. Clearly, he had a large amount of influence over the group and its performance dynamics, so could be considered a group leader (De Souza & Klein, 1995; Hollander, 1961). The trumpet player was not the official leader of this group; however, his acknowledged ability to "read the audience" and understand its reactions to the group's performance placed him in a leadership position once the group's performance began. Consequently, other group members often deferred to him during performances regarding questions of tempo, music selection, and the timing of breaks. Clearly, he had a large amount of influence over the group and its performance dynamics, so could be considered a group leader (De Souza & Klein, 1995; Hollander, 1961).

Throughout the overall sample, incidents of the emergent leader interpreting an ambiguous situation were mentioned in 4 of the 10 jazz group interviews, and in 8 of the 10 rowing crew interviews (60% of the total sample). Interestingly, the times when emergent leaders of rowing crews interpreted ambiguous feedback occurred almost entirely within the context of practice sessions, suggesting that this rarely occurs when concrete feedback (i.e., winning or losing a race) is available. The lone time when an emergent leader of a rowing crew was able to provide a distinct interpretation of concrete performance feedback is illustrated next.

Group Norms

Emergent leaders take advantage of particular group norms as they establish and use their ability to manage group emotion. The most important of these are group norms regarding communication and the expression of emotion within the group setting. Emotional expression has been suggested as a key factor in overall group development (Bennis & Shepard, 1956), as impacting persuasion within a group (Mackie et al., 1992), and as a key indicator of psychological safety within a group (Edmondson, 1999). When a group has norms that allow for the expression and communication of emotion, then emotional contagion between group members may occur (Barsade, 2001; Hatfield, Cacioppo, & Rapson, 1994; Kelly & Barsade, 2001; Le Bon, 1896). If individual emotional reactions are not expressed and shared then there will be no way for the emergent leader to influence fellow group members via the display of emotion.

> Proposition 2: Emergent leaders will be more likely to engage in management of group emotion when the group has developed norms that allow and encourage the expression of emotion within the group context.

Another group leader helped her rowing crew through a potential crisis situation by redefining their goals and thus casting their performance into a new light. Jackie had been elected as the captain of her boat, a position that carried few responsibilities and no authority, but nevertheless was a mark of respect and leadership from her teammates. This collegiate women's rowing crew was fairly inexperienced; although they had practiced together for 3 months and engaged in informal races with other local crews, they had not yet competed in any official races. At their first official race, they were full of confidence and enthusiasm, talking optimistically about bringing home medals and victoriously tossing their coxswain into the river after the race. They raced well, considering their level of experience and practice; however, most of the other teams were more experienced, and Jackie's team placed sixth out of eight boats. As the boat crossed the finish line there was a disappointed silence within the boat, as the team had been expecting to finish much better than they had. Suddenly, Jackie began to cry out loudly and excitedly, exclaiming that they had beaten their local rivals, a team that they often engaged (and generally lost to) in scrimmage races. The women's spirits took an immediate upturn as they all began cheering because they had beaten their local rivals. Several of the members of this crew later described this experience as the best thing that occurred to them during their spring season, suggesting that it gave them confidence, resilience, and the realization that bringing home medals was not the only reason that they participated in the sport.

In this case, Jackie's ability to reshape the group's emotion helped the group as a whole in several ways. Rather than feeling completely defeated and losing confidence in themselves and their ability, they were able to take stock in their efforts, continue as a group, and find ways to improve their performance over the remainder of their racing season.

In an interview after this race, Jackie asserted that her actions were shaped by the group's norms. She realized retrospectively the impact her actions had on the group, and talked about the positive effects that had resulted from that change of heart that the group experienced at the finish line. However, she also said that the situation occurred because the group regularly expressed emotional reactions to events they experienced.

> "The boat I was on in high school, we were very uptight, very focused. We never would have let on that we were upset by coming in sixth, we would have decided individually that we had to work harder, or that we were worthless, or whatever. This group though, we always talk about how we feel about everything that happens to us as a group. So when I saw [the local rivals] behind us, and I got excited that we had beat them, I knew the others would want to know about that. I mean that was a really good thing, and I knew that they would be excited about it too! I never would have been able to cheer like that for sixth place in my old boat . . . they would have been all 'yeah, but we still blew it.' But with this boat, we all look for ways to keep each other up, so I knew they would want to know that this was good and this was exciting."

In this case, the group's history and well-established norm of allowing and encouraging emotional expression and communication allowed this individual to feel comfortable expressing her own emotional reactions, and thus bringing to light a new perspective on the group's performance. By showing her own emotional reaction to this new information, she encouraged the other group members to change their own perspectives to a more positive view of their performance. Consequently, group members felt encouraged by their performance, and left the competition feeling resolved to work harder over the next several weeks.

This relationship between openness of communication, especially emotional communication, and the ability of an emergent leader to manage group emotions was documented in the other groups as well. A scale designed to measure the prevalence of group norms of emotional expression was delivered to the groups before the observation and interview session took place. This six-item scale was adapted from the Open Group Process and Internal Fragmentation subscales of the Michigan Organizational Assessment Questionnaire on Work Group Functioning (Seashore, Lawler, Mirvis & Cammann, 1982). This scale was designed to measure two aspects of emotional expression within the group. First, it was designed to measure the individual's perception of his/her own ability to express emotions ("I say what is on my mind when I am with my teammates"). Second, this scale was designed to assess the individual's perception of other group members willingness to express their emotions within the group context ("my teammates are afraid to express their true feelings" [reverse coded]). The scale was aggregated to the group level, which may be justified empirically by the significant ICC F statistic ($M = 3.9$, $SD = 1.09$, alpha = .72, ICC F statistic = 3.60, $p < .01$) (Shrout & Fleiss, 1979). The ICC test has been discussed as difficult to pass because significance requires both high within-team agreement and low between-team agreement (see James, Demaree, & Wolf, 1984). A Pearson's R correlation was computed between the observation of emergent leaders managing group emotion and the group aggregate score for each of the 20 groups on the scale of norms regarding open emotional expression. This correlation was significant ($r = .53, p < .05$), further suggesting that emergent leaders take advantage of norms of emotional expression within the group in order to manage the group's emotional state.

Leader's Skills and Abilities

Charismatic and transformational theories of leadership emphasize emotions, values, and the importance of leader behavior in "making events meaningful for followers" (Boas, 1999). Indeed, some criticisms of charismatic leadership theories have been that they overemphasize the need for the leader to emotionally manipulate people in order to generate a groundswell of followers (Hogan, Raskin, & Fazzini, 1990; Sankowsky, 1995). Although these theories of leadership address directly the issues of leader and follower emotions, they typically do so from the perspective of a dyadic leader–follower relationship rather than looking at the effect of the leader on the group as a whole (Boas, 1999; Yukl, 1999).

Weber (1946) first introduced the concept of charismatic leadership. His discussion of charisma referred to it as being both a trait of the individual leader as well as an interactive process between actors (Mitzman, 1969). Wasielewski (1985) and Yukl (1999) further reinforce this interactive relationship aspect by suggesting that charismatic leadership is tied intimately to the leader's ability to model and redefine emotion and emotional responses. Wasielewski (1985) stated that the ability of charismatic leaders to identify, empathize with, and model emotions and emotional behavior is critical to their success, and that they gain legitimacy by modeling emotions for their followers.

Charismatic leaders gain legitimacy and power not only by identifying the emotions present in the situation, but also by modeling them in order to accentuate the meaning and intent of their communication, vision, and goals (Wasielewski, 1985).

Empathy is also an important factor in an emergent leader's ability to manage a group's emotional state, as it allows the leader to read, interpret, and understand the emotional reactions of individual group members (Eisenberg & Miller, 1987). Empathy has been proposed as an important prerequisite to effective leadership, particularly emergent leadership (Bell & Hall, 1954; Wolff et al., 2002). It is important to an emergent leader's ability to manage group emotion, not only because it allows a leader to read and understand group member emotional reactions, but also because it helps the leader craft an appropriate emotional response (Batson & Coke, 1981; Hoffman, 1984).

Proposition 3: Emergent leaders who exhibit both charisma and empathy will be more likely to engage in the management of group emotion.

Another case of an informal leader setting the emotional tenor for the group involved one of the rowing crews. This particular group was a highly competitive, collegiate men's team. This particular group was the "lightweight" team, meaning that they all weighed less than 155 pounds. Although this group was very successful against other lightweight teams, during everyday practice sessions they usually fell behind their "open weight" teammates, who were taller, stronger, and heavier young men. Sean, the informal leader of the lightweight rowers, led the group in thinking that their open-weight teammates should be regarded as competition. Consequently, for the lightweights, every practice session held the emotional intensity and importance of race day. It was not unusual to see this young man turn around in the middle of a practice and exhort his teammates to row faster, or encourage them by emphasizing how close they were to the open-weight crew. By the end of the spring racing season, the lightweight team had improved to the point where they would occasionally beat the open-weight team in practice sessions. After these victories the celebrations of the lightweight team, led by Sean, could easily be confused with the celebrations of their victories on the actual racecourse.

Other members of the lightweight team talked about Sean as one who helped to frame their emotional responses as a group. Several group members mentioned his almost relentless optimism as being a key to the group's success:

"We were down by a few seats and not gaining anymore, and I was ready to just quit because I was so tired and I didn't think we would be able to do it. Then I would hear Sean yell back 'That's it! We've almost got them!' Then I would realize that, yeah, we were a few seats down, but that meant that we were only a few seats away from being in front. He is always really good at keeping us up like that."

One of the reasons Sean was acknowledged as a leader of this group was because of the enthusiasm he showed and his personal commitment to the team and its goal. He personally held very high standards for the group's performance, as evidenced by the fact that he believed they should be able to beat a boat made up of significantly larger, stronger individuals. Other team members referred to his personal commitment to the team's success and his frequent assertions that they could perform at high levels as being key factors underpinning their own commitment to the group. Additionally, group members revealed that they looked to Sean for leadership because of his empathy, both in and out of their performance context: "No matter what we are going through, no matter how badly you feel during practice, you look at his face and you can tell that he is feeling it just as much as you are. He has been there before, and knows exactly what we are all feeling."

As the emergent leader for this team, one of Sean's primary roles was to help them reframe their performance situation so that group members would be encouraged rather than disheartened. He appeared to do this by focusing on key bits of information. For example, rather than focusing on the fact that the team was a few feet behind another boat, he would focus on the fact that they were closer than they had been a few moments ago. Sean was conscious of this role that he played on the team, saying:

> "You never, ever, say that you have lost ground. You tell them where you are in relation to the other boat, and if they can do the math at that point, well then that's their call. If you're behind, then you're gaining. If you're close, then you're right with them. If we're dead even, I say that we are up by just one seat, or up by just the bow ball. I always try to make them think that we are moving on the competition."

In the case of the lightweight team, Sean's ability to influence the emotions experienced in the group contributed to the group's success over the course of their racing season. His ability to get the other group members to think of the open-weight crew as competition undoubtedly made the crew work harder during its practice sessions than it otherwise might have. Additionally, his expressions of optimism and conviction that the crew could overtake its opponents kept the crew working hard during several situations when it would have been "easier" for the team to give up.

During group interviews, 5 of the jazz groups and 8 of the rowing crews made mention of an emergent leader exercising empathy with his or her fellow group members. Additionally, 6 of the 10 jazz groups and all 10 of the rowing crews made mention of an emergent leader enacting charisma, through exhortation and demonstrating a personal commitment to the goal. Of the 6 jazz groups that made mention of an emergent leader's charisma, 3 of them also specifically mentioned that individual's empathy. This suggests that emergent leaders can capitalize not only on their ability to express emotions and emotional messages (seen here as charisma), but also on their ability to perceive and understand the experience of other group members. Management of a group's emotional state, then, depends on an emergent leader's ability to convince others of the validity of a particular emotional response and also of that leader's demonstration that he or she has accurately understood their goals, their hopes, and their fears.

CONCLUSION

This chapter reports on a group leadership role that has been ignored previously, the role of manager of group emotions. I have described how emergent leaders within groups use their behavior to communicate messages to group members regarding group performance and contextual events, and do so in a way that sends a clear emotional message to the group members. As a result, group members take cues from the leader's behavior and craft emotional interpretations of the situation, which guide their own individual behavior. This suggests that one way in which emergent leaders influence group member behavior and group performance is through their management of group emotion.

Discussion and exploration of this role is particularly suited to emergent leaders. This is because emergent leaders rely on processes of influence in order to have an effect on the group of which they are a part. Because they are emergent rather than formal, they rely on this type of influence process rather than on formal processes of rewards and punishments (Druskat & Pescosolido, 2003). Additionally, emergent leaders are thought to be especially empathetic and responsive to follower needs (Wolff et al., 2002; Yammarino, 1996).

By putting forth initial observations and propositions regarding the management of group emotions, I hope to lay the groundwork for more formal studies of the emotional management process. These would take the form of more focused, hypothesis-testing studies and would involve clarity and ambiguity of performance, the measurement of group norms regarding emotional communication as well as actual communication, and personality characteristics of emergent leaders.

Additionally, the concept of the emergent leader as the manager of group emotions takes a step toward understanding how leaders influence interacting groups. Most leadership theories, particularly charismatic and transformational leadership theories, focus on leadership as a dyadic process (i.e., a leader interacting with one follower at a time) rather than as a process involving a whole, interacting group (Boas, 1999; Yukl, 1999). Boas (1999) suggested that it is important to understand how leaders influence group processes "because they are necessary to explain how a leader can influence the performance of an *interacting* group" (p. 295, emphasis added). By gaining a greater understanding of the characteristics and situations that influence management of group emotion, we will gain a greater understanding of the influence processes that are used by emergent leaders as they interact with whole groups, as well as with individual group members.

18

For Better or For Worse: Organizational Culture and Emotions

Michelle K. Pizer
Charmine E. J. Härtel

> ... *lest the land vomit you out, when you defile it, as it vomited out the nation that was before you. For whoever shall do any of these abominations, the persons that do them shall be cut off from among their people. (Leviticus 17:28–29, Revised Standard Version)*

An individual's failure to adapt to his or her cultural context, if not embrace it, can bring with it dire consequences, as illustrated in the preceding quote. Culture, or the shared assumptions, values, and beliefs of a social group, has a powerful influence over our lives. This is also true for the social groups within which we work. The culture of organizations and the ways in which it shapes people's thoughts, emotions, and behaviors, for better or for worse, are the subject of this chapter.

By combining an established although controversial construct, organizational culture, with a relatively new and topical area in contemporary organizational behavior, emotions in the workplace, we show that (a) culture is powerful; (b) its power is derived from the emotional needs of individuals; and (c) the way culture interacts with these emotional levers influences people for better or for worse.

Underpinning our approach is a positive perspective. Positive psychology (Seligman & Csikszentmihalyi, 2000) and its parallel in the organizational arena, positive organizational scholarship (Cameron, Dutton, & Quinn, 2001), are emerging areas representing a shift of focus—from what is wrong with people and organizations to identifying and nurturing our strongest qualities so that we flourish and thrive.

We suggest that management has a responsibility to strive for a positive, healthy organization where the organization and its members flourish and thrive. We argue that the key to creating such an organization in the contemporary business environment is through the strategic and intelligent design of organizational culture.

In the sections that follow, we draw from literature in management and psychology, social and developmental psychology, and the clinical literatures of psychotherapy and group dynamics, to identify the features of positive, healthy organizations; clarify what organizational culture is; explore how it operates as a form of social control at the emotional level; and demonstrate the range of outcomes it can have for individuals and organizations.

POSITIVE, HEALTHY ORGANIZATIONS

Miller (1995) discussed what makes for a healthy organization. He conceptualized an organization from a sociotechnical systems perspective and argued that it comprises three systems: a task system or system of work roles designed to achieve the tasks an organization is in business to perform; a sentient system, the system where employees' human needs for affiliation and identity are met; and an overarching management system that manages the relations between the two.

A healthy organization, one that jointly optimizes the outputs of each system, requires health in the task system, health in the sentient system, and health in the overarching management system (Miller, 1995). An organization is not healthy if, for example, it has a high output (illustrative of a healthy task system) combined with high turnover (illustrative of an unhealthy sentient system) or vice versa.

A healthy organization is a positive organization. Cameron et al. (2001) suggested that extraordinary, excellent, and virtuous organizational performance has largely been ignored, partly because of basic pressures to survive. Hence, organizational scholars have traditionally focused on repairing ineffective, inefficient, or error-prone performance or, at best, achieving effective, efficient, and reliable performance. In contrast, the focus of positive organizational scholars is on the organizational dynamics that lead to positive performance, and includes elements such as respectful encounters, compassion, forgiveness, dignity, integrity and wisdom, and optimism and positive affect (Cameron et al., 2001). Thus, one aspect of the organizational environment that plays a leading role in determining whether an organization is healthy or not are those phenomena that produce positive and negative emotions. It is little wonder then that "emotions in the workplace is shaping up as one of the principal areas of development in management thought and practice for the next decade" (Ashkanasy, Härtel, & Daus, 2003b, p. 307).

According to Ashkanasy et al. (2003b), one area receiving considerable support and identified as having significant implications for organizational research and organizational behavior is affective events theory (AET) (Weiss & Cropanzano, 1996). AET is a comprehensive model of emotions in the workplace (see Fig. 18.1). It is based on the notion that workplace conditions (work environment features) determine the occurrence of everyday hassles and uplifts (affective work events), which result in affective responses (moods and emotions) in workers. These feelings then lead to affect-driven behavior at that time, such as aggressive behavior, verbal abuse, or citizenship behavior. Over time this can accumulate to influence more stable work attitudes such as job satisfaction, which, in turn, influence cognitively driven behavior such as the intention to quit (Ashkanasy et al., 2003b).

An important aspect of AET is that emotions may be a crucial link between workplace contexts and employee behavior (Ashkanasy et al., 2003b). Ashkanasy et al. (2003b) pointed out that research to date has largely validated the basic premise that affect does mediate the effect of organizational variables on affective and behavioral outcomes. Nevertheless, the work environment features or organizational context component of AET is yet to be specifically researched.

Although there are two dominant and traditional approaches to assessing the organizational context: organizational culture and organizational climate (Denison, 1996); in this chapter we contribute to overcoming this gap in the research by illustrating the significance of organizational culture to emotions in the workplace, and, subsequently, the healthiness of the organization for its members. We adopt a cultural approach as our focus is on the relatively stable and more broadly based aspects of an organization, such as values, beliefs, assumptions, and associated artifacts, rather than the climate or more changeable shared perceptions of a particular workgroup (Ashkanasy & Nicholson, 2003).

Importantly, on the surface the differences between culture and climate are quite clear, yet in practice the distinction is blurred (Denison, 1996) and their differentiation controversial (Ashkanasy & Nicholson, 2003). As Denison (1996) concluded in his review of the differences between culture and climate,

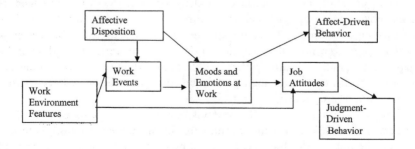

FIG. 18.1.　Affective events theory.

they represent different and overlapping interpretations of the same phenomenon. In this chapter we adopt Schein's (2000) resolution to the culture versus
climate dilemma by defining climate as a cultural artifact arising out of espoused values and shared underlying assumptions.

THE ORGANIZATIONAL CULTURE CONSTRUCT

Organizational culture is a central issue for organizational analysis and practice (Pettigrew, 2000) because it enables holistic thinking about organizations
(Ashkanasy, Wilderom, & Peterson, 2000) and provides a lens for studying organizations which brings to the fore the emotional side of organizational life
(Ancona, Kochan, Scully, Van Maanen, & Westney, 1999; Martin & Frost,
1996). It is, nevertheless, a controversial and contested field of intellectual en-
quiry (Pettigrew, 2000). It has been suggested that since the renaissance of interest in the construct in the late 1970s, there has been a struggle for intellectual dominance that has limited advances in knowledge in the field and
therefore threatened its potential (Martin & Frost, 1996; Pettigrew, 2000).
The struggle is, in effect, a paradigm war (Burrell & Morgan, 1979); according
to Pettigrew (2000), the construct has become "lost in its own definitional,
theoretical, and methodological disputes" (p. xiv).

The three cognitive interests identified by Habermas (1972) are one way to
distinguish between the many approaches to organizational culture (Alvesson,
2002; Knights & Willmott, 1987; Stablein & Nord, 1985). As identified by
Habermas (1972), approaches with a technical interest aim to enhance prediction and control within organizations by identifying and manipulating cultural
variables to achieve certain (managerial) outcomes. Approaches with a practical–hermeneutic interest aim to improve mutual understanding through the interpretation of symbolic communication to achieve common interpretations so
that coordinated action is possible. Approaches with an emancipatory interest
aim to liberate organizational participants from any repressive organizational
forces by exposing any domination or exploitation within the organization.

Alvesson (2002) noted that the relationship between the three approaches is
antagonistic, especially between the technical and emancipatory approaches,
as emancipatory approaches are concerned with ensuring that cultural projects are not subordinated to managerial interests. He argued for reducing the
gap, pointing out, for example, that "cultural interpretation as a knowledge resource for accomplishing managerial objectives is radically different from
questioning them" (Alvesson, 2002, p. 12).

Regardless of the approach taken toward organizational culture and the lack
of a fixed or broadly agreed-on meaning for the term, even in cultural anthropology, the field from which the organizational culture construct is borrowed
(Alvesson, 1993; Smircich & Calas, 1987), there are some areas of agreement

about its definition (Trice & Beyer, 1993). Recently Beyer, Hannah and Milton (2000) identified three such areas.

First and foremost is the general agreement that culture is about the sharing of meaning, although there is less agreement on where those shared cultural meanings reside (Beyer et al., 2000). One perspective is that cultural meanings are cognitive phenomena located in the mind, for example, basic assumptions, values or sets of understandings. For example, Schein (1990) argued that the cognitions a group comes to share, the learned common assumptions, are "the ultimate causal determinant of feelings, attitudes, espoused values and overt behavior" (p. 111). Others argue that cultural meanings are symbolic phenomena located in the context and manifest in behavior, language and artifacts. For these researchers, "cultural meanings reside in the concrete and observable things that provide the context for human behavior and thought" (Beyer et al., 2000, p. 324).

A second area where there is considerable agreement among scholars is in the reflexivity of cultural elements over time (Beyer at al., 2000). That is, cultural elements are viewed as mutually reinforcing and self-perpetuating. For example, De Dreu, West, Fischer, and MacCurtain (2001) argued that organizational culture shapes and is shaped by emotions.

Trice and Beyer (1993) referred to cultural forms (symbolic phenomena) as expressing, affirming, and communicating the substance or ideologies of a culture. Ideologies, as defined by Trice and Beyer (1993), are "shared, emotionally charged belief systems" (p. 2), which include the beliefs, values, and norms of an organization that inform its members as to "what is, how it got that way, and what ought to be" (Trice & Beyer, 1993, p. 2). Importantly, these cultural forms simultaneously contribute to the emergence and persistence of the organization's ideologies and vice versa.

Ancona et al. (1999) also illustrated the reflexivity of cultural elements and discussed how, through interpersonal relationships at work, an organization's culture both shapes and is shaped by its members. As they stated, organizational members "are actively engaged in organizational life, and through interaction with one another, they continually create, sustain, and modify organizational events, processes, and products" (Ancona et al., 1999, p. 64).

A third area where there has been a level of agreement amongst organizational researchers is the role of culture in the survival of the individual and/or organization (Beyer et al., 2000). In practice, however, culture is more commonly the context into which the individual is socialized and must adapt in order to survive as an organizational member. Rarely is culture constructed to help the organization survive and adapt to its members or its environment. The latter strategic use of culture is what authors such as Kets de Vries and Balazs (1997) argue is needed. They suggest that organizations would do well to continuously transform by aligning themselves with their environment and shaping a culture that encourages new challenges.

In a similar vein, Schneider (2000) suggested that the construct might benefit from being strategically focused, a culture *for* something. Pettigrew (2000) viewed this as a promising trend—using organizational culture as a stepping-stone to facilitate understanding related phenomena rather than studying it in its own right.

This trend is closest to a technical interest (Habermas, 1972), and not surprisingly, some noted authors in the field (Siehl & Martin, 1990, and Trice & Beyer, 1993) with a practical–hermeneutic interest suggest that a strategic focus for the culture construct debases it by focusing on outcome rather than process and meaning. However, following Alvesson's (2002) call to reduce the gap between the approaches, we advocate paradigm crossing (Schultz & Hatch, 1996), drawing on each approach while recognizing the similarities and differences between them. It is our contention that there is a need to understand and manage the process and meaning so as to achieve the desired outcome, which we argue should be for a positive, healthy organization.

In summary, we embrace in this chapter the assumption that organizational culture has the capacity to "*simultaneously* create order, meaning, cohesion and orientation, thus making collective action, indeed organizational life possible *and* to restrict autonomy, creativity and questioning, thereby preventing novel, potentially more ethically thought through ways of organizational social life being considered" (Alvesson, 2002, p. 13).

It is through shaping the meanings and actions of its members (Ashkanasy at al., 2000) that culture sets the stage for certain behaviors, thoughts, and feelings but not others, and provides a solution to the "age-old managerial dilemma: how to cause members to behave in ways compatible with organizational goals" (Kunda, 1992, p. 11). That is, culture enables control, and it does so through the promise of fulfilling our emotional needs, and at the same time, the threat of withdrawing this. Hence, culture's power is derived from the emotional needs of individuals and can be used to achieve a positive, healthy organization; however, as we show in the following sections, such an outcome is by no means guaranteed.

ORGANIZATIONAL CULTURE, A FORM
OF SOCIAL CONTROL

Various needs are met by employment, such as financial needs, a structured day, social contact, a sense of purpose, identity, and status, and enforced activity (Jahoda, 1981). In fact, the very needs met by employment are the leverage points an organization uses for control.

The dark side of organizational culture, referred to by some authors as the conscious use of culture by management as a form of social control, has largely been ignored (e.g., Karabanow, 2000; Van Maanan & Kunda, 1989). Van

Maanen and Kunda (1989) suggested that this is because culture is usually considered something people can do little about and, except in the case of conquest, seldom regarded as being deliberately imposed on people. However, we suggest that organizational culture is always used in organizations as a form of social control, whether consciously or unconsciously, and it is how it is used that determines whether it is healthy or not.

Social Control

Social control refers to "the regulation of individual behavior by means of group or institutional decisions' (Chaplin, 1979, p. 497). Its mere presence is neither good or bad; indeed, we show it is necessary. Without social control a system cannot be positive and healthy, yet its mere presence does not guarantee health.

Van Maanen and Kunda (1989) suggested that there are at least three generally recognized forms of social control used in organizations: market, technical, and bureaucratic. In addition, Van Maanen and Kunda (1989) suggested a fourth and less recognized form of social control, namely, organizational culture.

Market control refers to the control of labor based on the demands for products or services exchanged for a fee. Technical control refers to the control accorded to the production process itself whereby employees become as interchangeable as the products or services they produce. Bureaucratic control refers to the various administrative procedures such as career systems, selection and recruitment standards, and retirement plans, aimed to justify and direct individual contributions to the collective based on the self-interests they serve.

Culture control refers to emotion control. Van Maanen and Kunda (1989) argued that culture control is a particularly powerful form of social control because it seems to aim for a deeper level of employee compliance than other forms of control by operating on the emotional level. "Its aim is to influence and spark the felt involvement and attachment of organizational members" (Van Maanen & Kunda, 1989, p. 89). It is because culture operates on the emotional level that it can have a significant impact on an individual's experience of work, affecting personal development and even the degree of one's psychological health or disturbance.

The extent to which control in organizations results in positive or negative consequences for employees depends on the legitimate and transparent use of those leverage points for outcomes that include the well-being of the employee. If the use of those leverage points in situations of importance is perceived as fair, then organizational justice theory indicates that people will respond positively (Paterson & Härtel, 2002). Conversely, if their use is perceived as unfair, then the affective and behavioral response will be negative

(Paterson & Härtel, 2002). This, in turn, can result in positive or negative consequences for the organization.

The Increasing Importance of Organizational Culture as a Form of Social Control

Mastenbroek (2000a) traced the development of emotion control in organizations over time, starting with the meetings of rulers and authorities in the Middle Ages through to modern organizations. He noted the difficulties in doing business in the Middle Ages when control, including self-control, was less apparent. In those days, the emotions of the moment overruled plans and promises, and deception, assassination, and ambush were common. The organizations in those days, lacking any of the now generally recognizable forms of social control, would not be considered positive and healthy according to Miller's (1995) definition of organizational health described earlier in this chapter.

The generally accepted and unwritten code of conduct for what we now consider to be civilized and appropriate organizational behavior took over five centuries to evolve (Mastenbroek, 2000a). These unwritten rules for thinking, feeling, and behaving in organizations are found in organizational culture.

Furthermore, with the recent trend to fewer formal rules and procedures, these unwritten rules, and therefore organizational culture, are becoming more important in the management of organizations. Mastenbroek (2000a) referred to this trend of informalization as the controlled decontrolling of emotions (Mastenbroek, 2000a). Van Maanen and Kunda (1989) suggested that, in effect, culture replaces structure as a way of organizing, used to both explain and guide action. As Kunda (1992) illustrated: "His strategy is clear. 'Power plays don't work. You can't *make 'em* do *any*thing. They have to *want* to. So you have to work through the culture. The idea is to educate people without them knowing it. Have the religion and not know they ever got it!' " (p. 5).

Kunda (1992) referred to such strategies as normative control: "the attempt to elicit and direct the required efforts of members by controlling their underlying experiences, thoughts, and feelings that guide their actions" (p. 11). The issue we take up next is whether such control represents "an enhancement of freedom or a new and very manipulative form of tyranny" (Kunda, 1992, p. 22).

ORGANIZATIONAL CULTURE AND EMOTIONS: FOR BETTER OR FOR WORSE

In this section, we introduce five ways in which culture shapes emotions as identified by Beyer and Niño (2001) and use it as a framework for showing how culture operates on the emotional level in organizations, and how it influences people for better or for worse.

Managing Anxiety

Culture manages the anxieties resulting from uncertainties (Beyer & Niño, 2001). For example, Schein (1990) argued that organizational culture provides meaning, stability, and comfort for organizational members, thereby reducing the anxiety associated with the inability to understand or predict events in the environment. In this sense, aspects of culture are for the group as defense mechanisms are for the individual (Schein, 1990). This aspect of culture is particularly important for a positive, healthy organization in the uncertain contemporary business environment.

The capacity of organizations to be holding environments (Heifetz & Linsky, 2002; Kahn, 2001; Miller, 1995) refers to the extent to which employee anxiety can be contained or held so that the employee feels psychologically safe and therefore able to manage an anxiety-provoking situation that may otherwise be debilitating. The term *holding environment* is borrowed from Winnicott's (1965) notion of the holding environment that the mother provides for her child. In organizations, holding environments have been conceptualized as being based in interpersonal or group-based relationships (Kahn, 2001); in structural, procedural or virtual boundaries (Heifetz & Linsky, 2002); and, more broadly, in the organization itself (Miller, 1995).

Miller (1995) highlighted the need for organizations to be "good enough" holding environments and suggested that the increasing unpredictability both within and outside of organizations means it is increasingly difficult for them to provide containment, as evidenced by the widespread psychological withdrawal of employees (see also Kahn, 1992).

However, where an organization is able to provide psychological safety, employees are able to draw deeply on themselves in performing their work roles, for example, by expressing thoughts and feelings freely, questioning assumptions, and innovating. Kahn (1992) referred to this as psychological presence. *Psychological presence* is defined as comprising attentiveness, connection, integration and focus (Kahn, 1992). The indicators that someone is psychologically present include physical presence, eye contact, the fullness of speech and the choice of words, and the authenticity with which people respond to others at work. The result is, according to Kahn (1992), "personal accessibility to work (in terms of contributing ideas and effort), others (in terms of being open and empathetic), and one's self (in terms of growth and learning)" (p. 322).

Kahn (1992) suggested that an environment that facilitates psychological presence is indicative of a healthy organization. For instance, "the long-term implication of such presence is that people who are present and authentic in their roles help to create shared understandings of their systems that are equally authentic and responsive to change and growth" (Kahn, 1992, p. 331). Strazdins (2002) highlighted the need to be aware of the potential cost to the individual of an environment that facilitates psychological presence. As she said:

> It is *engagement* with other people's emotions that is the key pathway affecting health, not simply awareness of distress in the workplace. Employees may occupy work roles with extensive role demands, and they may be aware of these demands, but those who make the *effort* to engage with others and perform emotional work will be most at risk. (Strazdins, 2002, p. 237)

Emotional work involves those behaviors used to alter other people's feelings and includes companionship, help and regulation. Companionship involves mainly positive emotions, and feeling more positive than negative emotions increases feelings of well-being (Diener & Larson, 1993). Help and regulation both involve mainly negative emotions, and feeling more negative than positive emotions increases psychological distress (Fredrickson & Levenson, 1998). Strazdins (2002) pointed out that, through the process of emotional contagion (Hatfield, Cacioppo, & Rapson, 1994), emotional work poses a health risk by exposing employees to other people's negative feelings. Frost (2003) referred to such people as toxin handlers, those who deal with emotional pain (or toxicity) at work.

Hence, we advocate that organizations that facilitate employees engaging in emotion work also need to facilitate employees counteracting the associated health risks (Frost, 2003; Strazdins, 2002)—for example, by understanding the emotional impact of jobs and then ensuring they are designed to encourage appropriate emotional management (Ashkanasy & Daus, 2002), such as by encouraging employees to take time to manage their own anxiety so that they are able to restore their own emotions, calm down, soothe or return their emotions to equilibrium. For this to occur, the organization needs to value and recognize emotional work as part of, not in spite of, work (Strazdins, 2002).

Ways to Express Emotions

Culture provides ways to express emotions through cultural forms such as rites and rituals (Beyer & Niño, 2001). Any attempt to change such cultural practices is met with fierce opposition, even if they have outlasted their apparent relevance and usefulness. This is because they are an emotional matter imbued with meaning, not a matter for "rational" consideration.

Van Maanen and Kunda (1989) provided an example of employees participating in an organizational ritual. They described how all employees at an organizational retreat willingly and enthusiastically appear in foolish guise even though, they argue, their reasons for doing so may vary. They suggest that at the one extreme are the cynics expediently running "the three-legged race with furious effort" (Van Maanen & Kunda, 1989, p. 45) or applauding "a company slogan with wild abandon" (Van Maanen & Kunda, 1989, p. 45) in anticipation of future rewards. At the other extreme are the believers who not only have adapted to the organization's culture but have adopted it as their own. The believers' identities are inextricably linked to their identification with the firm.

We propose that positive, healthy organizations are mindful that on the one hand, participating in such rites and rituals may offer opportunities for self-expression, enjoyment, and social interaction (Strazdins, 2002), and that on the other, it may exact a health cost. For instance, when the culturally prescribed emotional expression is inconsistent with that which is felt, the emotional labor, or management of emotion in the self to express what is not felt or suppress what is, is necessarily high. The resultant emotional dissonance may lead to negative effects on employee well-being, such as emotional exhaustion (Morris & Feldman, 1996), and, in turn, may impair the health of the organization through, for example, increased absenteeism.

Although culture does provide ways to express emotions, Fineman (2001) suggested that it is a myth to think that the control of emotional expression comes about through managerial control. He asserted that its rhetoric "is just that—one of comforting hope and illusion" (Fineman, 2001, p. 222). It is our self-control, managing the tension between what we privately feel and publicly display, that enables control in organizations (Fineman, 2001).

We suggest that expressing emotions in the prescribed manner can become unhealthy when the culturally prescribed behavior is not felt, that is, the employee experiences emotional dissonance. Ashkanasy and Daus (2002) pointed out how emotional labor is, in fact, an important component of everyday work life, and we advocate their recommendation for training employees in emotional intelligence skills and healthy emotional expression to minimize the potentially negative effects of emotional labor.

Encouraging and Discouraging Emotions

Culture encourages and discourages emotional experience (Beyer & Niño, 2001). Geertz (1970) observed: "We are, in sum, incomplete or unfinished animals who complete ourselves through culture—and not through culture in general, but through highly particular forms of it" (p. 61). Here, Geertz (1970) referred to not only what we say but also how we say it; not only what we eat, but also how we prepare and consume it; and not only that we feel, but the distinctive emotions we feel. Hence, through culture we learn what specific emotions are appropriate to experience in different situations.

Tourish and Pinnington (2002) suggested that culture control can be an insidious form of social control. They argued that it is potentially sinister because of the subtle ways in which culture shapes the meanings and actions of its members: a "twinning of freedom and control" (Tourish & Pinnington, 2002, p. 163), and an example of Orwellian Doublethink. Tourish and Pinnington (2002) argued that, within organizations, people are habitually assured that they are empowered and free, and indeed are often encouraged to roam in any direction that they wish. The problem is that they roam at the end of a leash, constrained to move within an orbit sharply defined by the governing cultural assumptions of the organization. (p. 163)

These governing cultural assumptions can, however, result in an organization that is healthy and well functioning—that is, an organization in which "dissent is respected, people participate in decision making, and members at all times retain a foot in the real world" (Tourish & Wohlforth, 2000, p. 18). This is, we would suggest, an organization with an emancipatory interest, adopting the view that individuals are autonomous and self-managed and that both the individual and organization benefit from the relationship (Parker, 2000; Stablein & Nord, 1985).

Ashkanasy and Daus (2002) referred to the importance of modeling positive and friendly emotions given that "a negative emotional climate . . . can stymie organizational and individual growth" (p. 82). They highlighted the role of leaders in encouraging and discouraging emotions and the challenge they face in balancing healthy emotional expression with unbridled emotions running rampant. To this end, they recommended designing a rewards and compensation system that rewards desired behaviors and discourages unwanted behavior. However, as shown in subsequent sections, the intended outcomes of such systems may have unintended and unwanted consequences, and we advocate for the careful design, management, and monitoring of such systems.

Identification and Commitment

Culture engenders identification and commitment to the organization (Beyer & Niño, 2001). It is this aspect of culture, the ability to provide organizational members with a social identity and therefore an emotional bond or attachment to other members and the organization itself, that is fundamental to the power of organizational culture as a form of social control. It is therefore not surprising that "the strongest emotions that cultures engender seem to be those of belonging to social groups" (Beyer & Niño, 2001, p. 189).

Yet there is a natural tension between the need to belong and the need for an independent identity (Stokes, 1998). Although we have an innate need to feel we "belong somewhere instead of being transients or newcomers" (Hall & Lindzey, 1985, p. 204), the issue we all face, and not just when we first join an organization but also until we leave, is how much of ourselves to invest. As Goffman (1961) said, "Our sense of being a person can come from being drawn into a wider social unit; our sense of selfhood can arise through the little ways in which we resist the pull" (p. 320). There is a need to manage the boundaries between oneself and one's work role and the organization, as "too much separation is as discomforting as too much communion" (Van Maanen & Kunda, 1989, p. 85).

Nevertheless, our need to belong is fundamental (Baumeister & Leary, 1995; Maslow, 1970), and this is a basic need employment provides for us. Indeed, Maslow (1970) suggested that thwarting our basic need for belonging is at the core of most psychopathology, and subsequent research has repeatedly supported this proposition (Gardner, Pickett, & Brewer, 2000; for review, see Gardner, Gabriel, & Diekman, 2000). Thus, our need to belong is a very powerful leverage point, which can intentionally or unintentionally be exploited if it is not managed intelligently and ethically.

Attachment theory (Ainsworth, Blehar, Waters, & Wall, 1978; Bowlby, 1969) informs us that there is more than one way to attach or belong to others and organizations, and this, in turn, affects our emotions. Attachment theory describes and explains how infants become emotionally attached to their primary caregivers and emotionally distressed when separated from them. The theory's basic proposition is that attachment needs are primary, and that when an infant is confident that his or her primary caregiver will be available and responsive whenever desired, he or she will be more confident and interested in exploring and mastering the environment. This has been referred to as using the primary caregiver as a secure base (Ainsworth at al., 1978).

Ainsworth et al. (1978) identified three styles of attachment—secure, anxious/ambivalent, and avoidant—and observed that exploratory behavior differed accordingly. Mothers of secure infants were consistently sensitive and responsive, and their infants were confident and interested in exploring their environment; mothers of anxious/ambivalent infants were sometimes unavailable or unresponsive and at other times intrusive, and their infants explored less and became preoccupied with their mothers' availability; mothers of avoidant infants appeared to reject, rebuff, or deflect their infant's desire for proximity, so their infants avoided seeking contact and explored the neutral world of things but without the true interest of secure infants.

Hazan and Shaver (1990) applied attachment theory regarding the romantic love attachment of adults outside of work to their work relationships. Their basic premise is that adult attachment supports work activity just as infant attachment supports exploration. They hypothesized that securely attached adults, compared to their insecure counterparts, will have more job satisfaction, fewer worries about work and colleagues, and their work habits will not put health or relationships at risk. However, adults with anxious/ambivalent attachments will use work as a means of gaining approval, leading to a preference for working with others, a tendency to become overobligated combined with feeling underappreciated, a tendency to fantasize about success and praise, and a fear of failure and loss of self-esteem. The avoidant adult will use work as a means of avoiding unmet attachment needs and will tend to work long hours, take few holidays, be reluctant to finish projects, prefer working alone, and work at the expense of health and relationships. Research by Hazan and Shaver (1990) and subsequently Hardy and Barkham (1994) support these predictions.

If follows that adult attachment style influences the experience and expression of emotions (Magai, Hunziker, & Mesias, 2000). In terms of emotion regulation, Cassidy (1994) noted that secure adults have an open, flexible style in which a variety of emotions are experienced and expressed; anxious/ambivalent adults have a maximizing style; and avoidant adults have a minimizing style. De Dreu, West, Fischer, and MacCurtain (2001) suggested that, at the emotional level, a sense of belonging or secure attachment results in experiencing positive emotions such as happiness, elation, contentment, and calm. Conversely, feeling rejected is associated with negative emotions such as anxiety, depression, grief, jealousy, and loneliness. This is because object relations, or the internalized representations of self and other (Messer & Warren, 1995) are "at the *centre* of emotional life" (Klein, 1952/1975, p. 53).

Real, potential, or imagined belonging or exclusion affects our social relations at work and the extent to which we distance ourselves, attack, withdraw, or approach others (De Dreu et al., 2001). Given the interdependent nature of work, this will, in turn, influence our capacity to perform our tasks, and consequently will influence, to a greater or lesser degree, the success of the organization.

We therefore propose that a healthy organization will be one that understands and is accountable for employees' attachment needs. In such an organization, we anticipate a higher than average proportion of employees who feel securely attached; their needs for belonging will be met, and this will be evidenced, among other things, by a higher proportion of felt positive emotions and fewer felt negative emotions.

Ethnocentrism

Culture produces ethnocentrism (Beyer & Niño, 2001). It produces like-minded, like-feeling, like-behaving employees, and we argue that this aspect of culture needs to be managed against. It is a lack of diversity, and a lack of openness to diversity, that we argue results in an unhealthy organization (Härtel & Fujimoto, 2000).

The organizational culture literature has tended to emphasize the cohesive and integrative nature of culture (Van Maanan & Kunda, 1989), with monoculture the implied ideal state (Tourish & Pinnington, 2002). A key reason for this emphasis is that it has been considered as a way of securing a competitive advantage (Tourish & Pinnington, 2002).

Organizations commonly maintain their cultures through selection processes; and for a positive and healthy organization, Ashkanasy and Daus (2002) recommended including a positive emotional attitude as part of the selection criteria. However, we advocate being mindful of the risk in recruiting people similar in style, assumptions, values, and beliefs, as it weeds out those unlikely to fit with the culture, and is a common and often unconscious practice that facilitates control on the one hand and silences dissent on the other.

The Blue Eyes Brown Eyes exercise (Kral, 2000) illustrates this and is an example of the potential tyranny of power. Jane Elliott designed the exercise in the 1960s to show her fourth-grade students how harmful the White superiority myth is and what it means to be Black in America. To manipulate the culture, only those with blue or brown eyes were allowed to participate, and if any participant refused to abide by her rules, that person was immediately removed from the experiment.

Dissent, however, has been shown to have considerable benefits to organizations (Tourish & Pinnington, 2002). It improves the quality of decision making and performance (Janis, 1982) through encouraging multiple strategies to problem solution and challenging powerful majorities to consider other perspectives.

There is also a danger involved in not challenging powerful majorities through compliance (Milgram, 1963). Compliance (or obedience) is performing an act because someone asks you to even though you would rather not (Freedman, Sears, & Carlsmith, 1981). In Milgram's experiments, subjects administered what they thought were increasingly harmful electric shocks to others for answering questions incorrectly just because the experimenter asked them to. The majority of subjects continued to administer the increasingly harmful shocks because they saw themselves as merely following orders. Their view was that the experimenter was responsible for anything that happened in the experiment. Conversely, the minority who refused to continue to administer the shocks viewed themselves as responsible for their own actions.

Chattopadhyay (1995) offered hierarchy as an explanation for the dilution of personal responsibility, arguing that it allows for almost unlimited authority in the hands of a few senior managers and a simultaneous dilution of responsibility. Their authority derives from others giving it to them. When people join an organization "they delegate upwards their authority for time structuring, for dress, for placement, for promotions and demotions, for getting sacked and retirement" (Chattopadhyay, 1995, p. 17). Importantly, the process of upward delegation is forgotten largely because of the presence of hierarchy. As Chattopadhyay (1995) argued, the authority that comes with being more senior in the hierarchy is unquestionable to those who have roles below.

Milgram's experiments were criticized in that they could reduce participants to "the point of nervous collapse" (Schwartz, 1986, p. 118). Nonetheless, they stand as poignant reminders that social systems can be constructed that lead to potentially costly emotional consequences for the individuals involved (see also Menzies, 1970).

The Organizational Culture Paradox

To manage requires control over others and to be managed requires self-restraint. As Alvesson (2002) stated: "To some extent all forms of management mean domination and to some extent all social life presupposes constraint; the challenge is to identify and explore more problematic and arbitrary forms of power.... The line between legitimate and illegitimate exercise of power is thin and open to debate—it therefore should not be avoided but addressed" (pp. 12–13).

The paradox and difficult aspect of organizational culture is that many of the characteristics of cultures that have positive outcomes are similar to those that have negative outcomes. Hence, a healthy organizational culture has the potential to develop in "a dysfunctional and cultic direction" (Tourish & Wohlforth, 2000, p. 18). This is the potential dark side of organizational culture and one that is usually not considered or examined in the organizational literature. That is, having good intentions is not enough. Rather, organizations need to be aware of, assess, and manage their cultures, so that any destructive potential is not realized and healthy cultures are maintained.

Tourish and Pinnington (2002) illustrated how the defining traits of transformational leadership, the dominant model of leadership in the mainstream management literature in the last 20 years, are remarkably similar to those of cults. The defining traits of transformational leadership, similar to those of cults, are:

Charismatic leadership (which may be a socially engineered construct in the minds of the followers, rather than representing innate qualities on the part of the leader);

A compelling vision (one of a transcendent character, which imbues the individual's relationship to the organization with a new and higher purpose, beyond that of self interest);

Intellectual stimulation (generally, in the direction of transforming the follower's goals, so that they are subsumed into a new, collectivist objective on the part of the whole organization);

Individual consideration (or a feeling that the followers' interests are being attended to, and perhaps that they are in some way important to the charismatic leader);

Promotion of a common culture (a given way of thinking, doing and behaving, which is likely to minimize the overt expression of dissent, other than within carefully patrolled boundaries). (Tourish & Pinnington, 2002, p. 156)

Furthermore, other cultic elements are readily found in mainstream organizations. One such element is illusory causality, a potential outcome of self-categorization, which promotes in-group favoritism and out-group stigmatization. Illusory causality is the tendency to blame those on the receiving end of bias for its effects. The disadvantaged groups are considered naturally inferior rather than discriminated against. This is what Elliott found in the Blue Eyes Brown Eyes experiment: The brown-eyed participants came to believe those who were blue-eyed were inferior and treated them accordingly on the basis of their eye color.

Another cultic element is resisting exposing beliefs to empirical testing and therefore avoiding any possibility of their falsification. It has been shown that what is repeated is more likely to be believed as true (Tourish & Wohlforth, 2000). Hence, any suggestion of testing is met with increased rhetoric with the view to silencing any doubt or dissent. Elliott used this technique. She repeatedly told the brown-eyed participants they were superior and the blue-eyed participants they were inferior until there was no dissent. Further, she immediately removed any dissenting participants from the experiment.

Tourish and Wohlforth (2000) suggested that an organization cannot be simply defined as a cult or not; rather, there is a cult continuum along which organizations move depending on events. They also suggest that it is what organizations do rather than what they believe that determines whether an organization would be defined as a cult.

Hochman (1984) defined cults as:

> organizations which remold individuality to conform to the codes and needs of the cult, institute taboos which preclude doubt and criticism, and generate an elitist mentality whereby members see themselves as lone evangelists struggling to bring enlightenment to the hostile forces surrounding them. (cited in Tourish & Pinnington, 2002, p. 156)

Destructive Potential at the Individual Level

Not only are many of the characteristics of organizational cultures that have positive outcomes similar to those that have negative outcomes, so are the underlying individual dynamics. This indicates that, under certain circumstances, we all have destructive potential. As Tourish and Wohlforth (2000) pointed out:

> Many of the psychological dynamics that underlie prejudice formation (e.g., uncertainty reduction, stereotyping, expectancy effects) are not limited to members of hate groups. Rather, they are practiced to a greater or lesser extent by most of us ... it enables us to engage in stereotyping ourselves, while deploring its consequences in others—"we" belong to the civilised majority, while barbarian right wing fanatics stand as a solid phalanx on the other side of the barricades. (p. 37)

The experiments by Milgram (1963) on compliance, cited earlier, illustrate how easy it is to bring out an individuals' destructive potential. Similarly, the Blue Eyes Brown Eyes exercise demonstrates how easy it is to learn racism and to diminish self-worth, as well as how easy it is to set up the conditions for it to emerge and how quickly it occurs. Elliott stated, " 'It was just horrifying how quickly they became what I told them they were.' Within 30 minutes, a blue-eyed girl named Carol had regressed from a 'brilliant, self-confident carefree, excited little girl to a frightened, timid, uncertain little almost-person.' On the flip side, the brown-eyed children excelled under their newfound superiority" (cited in Kral, 2000). Elliott continued to find similar results when she conducted the experiment in organizations and with members of the general public from different countries. She argues that just as racism can be learned, it can be unlearned.

The Need for an Ethical Framework

Even with good intentions, it is not easy to achieve or maintain an ideal culture. As Schein (2000) stated, teamwork and cooperation cannot be created if "the underlying assumptions in the culture are individual and competitive, because those assumptions will have created a reward and control system that encourages individual competitiveness" (p. xxix). Similarly, participation and empowerment cannot be created in a culture where subordinates should do what they are told and expect their bosses to know what they are doing. Openness cannot be developed in an organization with a history of punishing the messenger for bad news.

Martin, Knopoff, and Beckman (1998) investigated bounded emotionality at The Body Shop. They point out that "the pressure to conform to the ideals of bounded emotionality paradoxically undermined some of its premises" (Martin et al., 1998, p. 460). This is not dissimilar to Kerr's (1995) notion of fouled-up reward systems. Kerr (1995) cited numerous examples of reward systems that reward the very behaviors they are trying to discourage. One example cited was how the government practice of determining next year's budget on the basis of this year's spending actually rewards spending and not the hoped-for economy and prudence.

Hence, with organizational culture as with rewards, it is not sufficient to have good intentions. There is a need to fully understand the dynamics involved, and to continuously assess and proactively manage the cultural strategy to ensure that what is intended is in fact achieved. Having good intentions is nevertheless necessary as a starting point for a healthy organization.

Nonetheless, we argue, it is essential to have an ethical or philosophical framework that underpins and guides the cultural strategy, and serves as a basis against which to evaluate it. Buller and McEvoy (1999) argued that an organization can develop a competitive advantage if it operates from an ethical framework. They identified the indicators of cultures driven by an ethical framework as what we have argued are positive and healthy: (a) leaders who manage with integrity and a strong sense of social responsibility, (b) the fostering of dialogue and dissent, and (c) the willingness to reflect on and learn from its actions (Gottlieb & Sanzgiri, 1996).

PRACTICAL IMPLICATIONS

In practice, a culture audit would be a useful first step in ensuring an organization's culture is positive and healthy. Based on our discussion, this would need to involve an assessment of the ways in which the culture impacts on organizational members' capacity to be psychologically present or withdrawn as well as securely or insecurely attached at work. This could be achieved by assessing the values statement of the organization against indicators of organizational health, such as the value placed and recognition of emotional work, and the extent to which employees are encouraged to bring their full selves to work (i.e., the extent to which employees are encouraged to express their thoughts and feelings freely without judgment and to question organizational assumptions).

Ashkanasy and Daus (2002) also suggested developing a values statement that emphasizes healthy emotional expression as a strategy for developing an emotionally healthy organization. They provided specific examples to illustrate their point, such as, "Our goal is to provide an emotionally healthy workplace atmosphere where the emotional challenges of the job are recognized, discussed, and managed in a way that simultaneously serves our customers well while also allowing employees a voice in the process" (Ashkanasy & Daus, 2002, p. 83).

Once the organization's value statement has been brought into line with the indicators of organizational health, it is necessary to ensure that organizational policies and practices are in alignment. Policies should not only align with the values statement, but also address all criteria associated with organizational health. For example, policies should be present that facilitate the hearing of grievances and openness to diversity and actively discourage harassment, favoritism, and bullying.

Once it is determined that the policies present in the organization address the activities associated with a healthy organization, then an assessment of practices should be undertaken. In particular, the placement and effectiveness of mechanisms for exposing domination and exploitation need to be examined. For example, do organizational members feel able to express their thoughts and feelings freely, question assumptions, and innovate, and when they do so, is their input responded to in a consistently sensitive and responsive manner?

Processes could also be evaluated, such as whether these outcomes are measured in performance management systems and whether training is provided to support their achievement. In particular, training is needed in ways to identify multiple strategies to encourage innovation, or in active listening skills so that employees are listened to well enough to know that their input was legitimately and fairly considered, even if their ideas were not adopted. These processes are also evidence of an ethical framework, and, by definition, encourage ethical practices such as the fostering of dialogue and dissent.

Ashkanasy and Daus (2002) also highlighted the importance of processes that promote emotionally healthy organizations. Given that negative emotions are especially contagious (Ashkanasy & Daus, 2002), one such process they discuss relates to the way particularly negative employees are managed, starting with targeted training, and moving through to punishment, reassignment, or firing as required.

Given that emotional experience and expression are an indicator of organizational health, the culture audit would also need to determine whether members experience and express a range of emotions, or whether they maximize or minimize them; whether there are more felt positive than negative emotions, or vice versa; the level of emotional dissonance and exhaustion experienced; the extent to which members engage in, or are the recipients of, emotional work; and whether time is allowed to restore emotional equilibrium.

Once the culture audit is complete, recommendations can be made regarding other changes at the values statement, policy, practice and process levels. Importantly, although these recommendations imply an organization-wide approach, in practice it may be appropriate for each division, department, or other relevant subgroup to develop its own set of recommendations for the achievement of a positive, healthy organization overall.

CONCLUSION

In this chapter, we sought to illustrate the significance of organizational culture to emotions in the workplace and its pivotal role in determining the healthiness of the organization for its members. Through discussion of organizational culture as a form of social control operating at the emotional level, we identified the features and processes that define a positive, healthy organizational culture for an organization's members and for itself.

Fundamental to a positive, healthy organizational culture is its capacity to provide a secure holding environment, underpinned by an ethical framework. A secure holding environment provides psychological safety, facilitating both psychological presence and secure attachments at work. An ethical framework helps ensure an organization will not develop in a dysfunctional and cultic direction, as it necessitates managing against repressive organizational forces such as ethnocentrism, and fosters healthy processes such as dialogue and dissent.

Although a culture audit is an important first step, we advocate for organizations to continuously assess and proactively manage their culture for a positive, healthy organization. To this end, we conclude that when an organization's culture provides a secure holding environment for its members and is underpinned by an ethical framework, it will be for better rather than for worse.

19

A Bounded Emotionality Perspective
on Organizational Change and Culture

Neal M. Ashkanasy
Charmine E. J. Härtel

Arguably, more than any other single factor, change lies at the core of organizational behavior. After all, why study organizational behavior if the aim is not to improve (change) behavior in organizations and, in effect, improve organizational effectiveness? Yet change, by its very nature, implies acceptance of a new status quo: a move away from the comfort and security of the familiar, toward an unfamiliar, possibly even threatening new environment. As such, change is, more often than not, likely to trigger the basic emotional instincts of survival.

In this instance, one of the first emotional reactions to change is likely to be fear. Indeed, as LeDoux (1996, 1998) argued, fear is one of the most primitive reactions to environmental stimuli. Consequently, distinct neurobiological mechanisms, centered on the amygdala, are dedicated to detecting environmental changes that may threaten survival and generate fear responses that ready the organism to meet the challenge. In this sense, Rachman (1974) posited that fear is a generalized emotional experience of the apprehension of uncertainty, and can be generated by changes in the working environment. Fear therefore generates defensive reactions (fight and/or flight) that can be difficult to manage.

Although not everyone is fearful of change—indeed, many who stand to benefit from the change will welcome it—the point still remains that many do experience fear as a powerful emotional reaction to change. In the sense of bounded emotionality, the consequence is that management of change re-

355

quires an understanding of the need to manage the strong emotions change elicits. These sentiments lie at the core of the three chapters in this section.

The corollary of this is that successful management of emotion during periods of organizational change represents a major challenge for managers. In this sense, managers are liable to demonstrate their best and worst traits. Managed inappropriately, fear and concomitant unmanageable emotion are a likely outcome. But change does not need to end up like this. Härtel and Zerbe (2002) stressed the more positive side of change management in a list of seven "myths of change management," which can be summarized as follows:

1. *Employees' negative emotional reactions reflect resistance to organizational change*. Not necessarily. Although poorly managed change can elicit unwanted negative emotions, many negative emotions experienced in the face of change represent genuine coping stress experienced by organizational members as they adapt to change.

2. *Emotions need to be managed away or overcome in order for change initiatives to succeed*. On the contrary, the point of the emotional revolution is that emotions need to be acknowledged as a natural part of human and organizational behavior, rather than something that needs to be eliminated.

3. *Emotions are the reason for employee withdrawal and destructive behavior during organizational change*. Although emotions can in part account for destructive behavior in change, other cognitive factors can contribute equally.

4. *People fear change in general and therefore oppose it*. Although this is often the case when change is not managed appropriately, it need not be so clear-cut. As the chapters in this section make clear, appropriate management strategies can assist employees to embrace change, and to work for positive change outcomes.

5. *Emotions represent chaotic or irrational responses*. In fact, emotions are a basic mechanism for survival. Thus, although emotion can appear irrational, emotions form a systematic pattern of responses designed to defend against threat.

6. *Negative emotions have negative consequences for the individual and the organization while positive emotions have positive consequences*. Although many negative responses do indeed lead to negative consequences, in many cases negative emotions are a prerequisite for appropriate coping behaviors.

7. *Emotions are solely the product of individuals*. In fact, the truth is quite the opposite. Emotions by and large are a product of the individual and the environment, and are reflected in collective, rather than individual, responses.

Importantly, the seven myths are most often a direct result of poor change management, and are self-reinforcing. Thus, a manager who believes that negative emotions are the inevitable outcome of all change efforts is at risk of engaging in the very practices that lead to the negative effects represented in the myths, including irrational behaviors, chaos, withdrawal, and, ultimately, destructive behavior that will defeat the change process. The three chapters in this section provide different perspectives on the management of changed, designed to avoid this trap.

Quy Huy, in chapter 16, describes how managers can "balance" their emotional and cognitive responses to avoid the management pitfalls (represented in the myths) in the instance of strategic change. Based on case-study data, he stresses that managers need to engage with emotion and employees' emotional reactions if change is to be managed positively. In this instance, managers need to shape their approaches to change management so as to match the emotional needs of the participants in the change process. Managers can achieve this through developing "emotional capabilities" that permit them to recognize, to understand, and to manage emotions at both the individual and collective levels. In many respects, Huy's model is parallel to Mayer and Salovey's (1997) model of emotional intelligence, but approached at the organizational management level, rather than at the individual level.

Anthony Pescosolido, in chapter 17, makes a point similar to that of Huy, but addressing change management at the group level of management, rather than the strategic level of analysis. Similar to Huy, Pescosolido argues that the key to effective change management in groups involves recognition and understanding of emotion, rather than a "rational" approach that assumes that emotions can somehow be dismissed as mere irrationality. Also consistent with Huy, Pescosolido stresses that emotions need to be managed as a group phenomenon, not at the individual level.

Michelle Pizer and Charmine Härtel take this point a step further in chapter 18. These authors present emotion as a core component of organizational culture—the set of values and ingrained practices that define the uniqueness of an organization. These authors argue that organizational change need not be cast as an inevitably negative process: that change can lead to a "healthy organizational culture," characterized by a focus on positive rather than negative emotion, consistent with the principles of positive psychology (Seligman & Csikszentmihalyi, 2000).

As in the two previous chapters in this section, Pizer and Härtel see appropriate management of emotion in cultural change as engaging the collective as well as the individual level. In this sense, the way in which culture interacts with individuals' emotional needs influences people, for better or for worse. The authors conclude that there is a need to focus on both the process and outcomes of culture so that it can be assessed and managed to achieve the outcome of organizational health.

In summary, the three chapters in this section stress that successful management of change is, to a large extent, dependent on managers' willingness to acknowledge and to deal actively with the emotions generated by change. The "natural" reaction to change is fear, and it is this uncontrolled reaction that represents the greatest challenge to managers of change. As represented in the seven myths, however, change management does not necessarily have to be associated with such negative emotions. Indeed, by appropriately managing organizational members' emotions, managers have the ideal opportunity to generate a new mindset among employees, leading to a genuinely healthy emotional working environment in their organizations.

20

What an Emotions Perspective of Organizational Behavior Offers

Charmine E. J. Härtel
Neal M. Ashkanasy
Wilfred J. Zerbe

By now, at this concluding chapter, we hope you have understood the important link between emotions and organizational behavior. Worklife is intertwined with emotion. We begin with the joy of successfully gaining employment and it ends with sometimes happiness, but more often sadness, at the loss of employment. But what about *during* employment? Where do emotions fit into the busy world of organizational behavior? We compiled this book from carefully selected papers, from scholars around the world, that identified the role that emotions play within organizations. The papers were presented at the Third Biannual Conference on Emotions, held on the Gold Coast in Australia. The strength of this compilation is that it views the emotion–organizational behavior link from a number of cultural viewpoints, and integrates different aspects of organizational life, such as the individual, interpersonal, and organizational processes that enhance the understanding and development of managing emotions in the workplace.

Our intent was to present a hands-on approach to understanding organizational behavior by using theories and models of emotions and current research examples. By taking an emotional approach to organizational behavior, we aim to increase understanding and awareness of the emotions existing within organizations. In this way, the book aims to advance individual diagnostic skills and knowledge and improve actual organizational behavior.

The soul of this book is to provide a different perspective of organizations and offer a fresh perspective in today's business world. In doing so, it opens our eyes to the role and importance of emotions and the methods by which we, as practitioners and scholars alike, can manage emotions at work. In turn, this creates a more efficient and effective workplace through carefully managed organizational behavior. We hope the book has provided you with a different perspective of organizational behavior.

EMOTIONS IN ORGANIZATIONAL BEHAVIOR

Emotions are an inevitable part of organizational life, yet if they are not responded to appropriately they may result in emotional pain, or toxicity. For the most part, discussion within organizational research has been based on Simon's (1976) notion of "bounded rationality," where talk of emotion in work situations was regarded as "weak" or "soft." As such, most organizations do not consider the effective management of emotions as necessary so that constant levels of high toxicity resound, which, in turn, become the focal point of employee attention and inevitably hinder performance levels. "People who are unhappy disconnect from work, turning their attention to their suffering and its causes rather than to doing excellent work" (Frost, 2003, p. 33). As Boyle discussed in chapter 3, the support of workmates, family, and the community at large is vitally important to dealing with emotions at work. Yet there is rarely recognition of the importance of this support from the organization. We hope that this volume will assist in the awareness of emotions in the workplace and the importance of recognizing those who support and handle the pain caused by organizational processes and practices.

This book examined organizational behavior within the realm of bounded emotionality, where the concept of emotionality is not intended to function as the exact opposite of rationality. Rather, it offers a "way of knowing that differs from but complements traditional rationality" (Mumby & Puttnam, 1993, p. 480). In this regard, the chapters in this volume offered research about how "nurturance, caring, community, supportiveness, and interrelatedness are fused with individual responsibility to shape organizational experiences" (Mumby & Puttnam, 1993, p. 474).

Dorothe Eide in part I examined the shift in viewing emotions as an "ugly duckling" to a valuable asset, which the organization can use to its advantage. She detailed the paradigm shift that has evolved and how emotions can now be viewed within an ontological framework aimed at enhancing organizational behavior through the careful management of emotions, knowledge, and learning.

Although emotions are gaining acceptance within the field of organizational behavior, we are only part of the way to gaining a full understanding of this fascinating new field. A happy worker may be a productive worker but what role do emotions really play in making this happen? Are they a bulldozer with brute force, or are they will-o'-the-wisps manipulating meaning? What is the difference between the impact of negative versus positive emotions? And does thinking play a role in the emotions we feel at work? This volume details the link in four areas.

First, research was presented that showed how individual behavior within organizations is affected by emotions. Part II focused on the individual within the organization and how individuals manage their emotions within the workplace. Together, the chapters in this section demonstrated the importance of emotions to individual behavior and work experiences, providing insight on the strategies that can enhance behavior and experience.

Maree Boyle's chapter dealt with the issue of thinking as a part of feeling. She discussed the link between coping with emotions, and the conflicting gender roles that societal rules impose upon us. The chapter by Yongmei Liu and Pamela Perrewe suggested that emotions play a powerful role in determining the productivity behaviors of employees. If managed inappropriately, emotions result in counterproductive work behavior, which can have a detrimental effect on both the employee and the organizational setting.

Yuka Fujimoto, Charmine Härtel, and Debra Panipucci followed Liu and Perrewé and detailed the destructive potential that negative emotions have through behavior such as prejudice overriding perception. They presented a model of how cognitive and affective reactions to dissimilar others impact on individual, group, and organizational outcomes such as hope, intergroup anxiety, trust, perceived fairness, deviant behavior, and task performance, and, importantly, how organizational human resource management practices can alter the cognitive and affective consequences of dissimilarity in the workforce.

Part III provided studies on interpersonal behavior and emotions, the second area. This section presented a combination of empirical and theoretical research on workgroup dynamics, communication and emotions. These chapters presented research on group interactions with a particular focus on problem solving and conflict/barriers to effective group interactions. The first chapter in this section presented a theorized model of group affect problem solving. The second chapter discussed communication and negotiation skills needed for effective cross-cultural interactions, and the final chapter illustrated the role that humor can play in effective communication.

Matthew Grawitch and David Munz led this section with a discussion of the cognition involved in feeling. They presented a theorized model of the relationship between affect and problem solving, showing that both individual and group affect are influenced by the problem-solving process, that as groups mature their level of affect becomes more influential over individual members' affect, that both positive and negative mood play an important role in effective problem solving, and that there is a reciprocal influence of individual affect on group-level affect in the group problem-solving process.

Following this, Stefan Meisiek and Xin Yao examined the role of positive emotions in coping with negative events. Specifically, their chapter suggested that humor could be used in the "storytelling" of emotional events to allow individuals to cope with the initial negative aspect of the event, in both a social and a psychological manner.

This section was concluded by Mona White, Charmine Härtel, and Debra Panipucci, in a review of the role emotions play in negotiation. In particular, they argued that negotiation breakdown occurs as a result of an accumulation of hassles or mishaps such as misunderstandings arising from the affective cultural background of the parties, emotional awareness and regulation, negative affect, and discrepancy in convergence–divergence on communicating style between the interactants.

Third, organizational processes, structure, and design are affected by emotions, as depicted in part IV. This section focused on organizational processes, structure, and design, and how the organization impacts individual and group emotions. Together, the chapters in this section introduced the reader to the demanding aspects of "emotional" jobs, that is, jobs that are designed to regulate emotional displays, the demands associated with emotional regulation itself, and behavioral responses to emotional regulation. If these emotional demands are different to the emotions the employee actually feels, then the employee will incur emotional dissonance or psychological discomfort. As a result, the employee will be internally motivated to try to reduce the discrepancy through pretending that he or she is experiencing the emotion or through regulating his or her own emotions so that they are consistent with that demanded. This motivated behavior is labeled *emotional labor*.

Certain individuals may never experience emotional dissonance as they experience the emotion demanded by their job. Thus, the chapter by Robert Rubin and colleagues proposed a moderated model whereby individual differences influence the amount of perceived dissonance felt and the resultant emotional labor and concomitant outcomes.

In the short term, organizations are expected to benefit from emotional labor, such as from customers expressing their satisfaction with the quality of the service interaction. However, in the long term, individual employees may become emotionally exhausted, leading to negative and potentially destructive outcomes such as violence, decreased job satisfaction, organizational commitment, negative job attitudes, turnover intention, stress, physical and psychological strain, burnout, emotional outbursts from suppression of actual felt emotion, withdrawal such as through taking long breaks, and reduction of work role inclusion.

Studies of emotional labor are inherently focused on negative emotions. There is a lack of research into the control of positive emotions. The section began with a detailed analysis of emotional labor by Robert Rubin, Vicki Staebler Tardino, Catherine Daus, and David Munz. This chapter illustrated the important part that thinking plays in the performance of emotional jobs, as it would be considered inappropriate to display certain feelings during task performance. It further illustrated the notion that emotions play a valuable part in manipulating meaning. That is, the purpose of regulating emotions is to manipulate how recipients of behavior feel and judge that behavior. It also presented a multifaceted model of emotional labor, separating behaviors, emotional states, and situational demands. In addition, it suggested that perceived emotional dissonance is an important mediator between situational demands and emotional labor behavior, which disentangles the emotional state from behavior.

Joyce Bono and Meredith Vey followed the introduction of the concept of emotional labor by Rubin et al. with a meta-analysis of emotional labor studies. They addressed the issue of whether emotions are holistic or multifaceted by drawing together the predictors of emotional labor, such as organizational display rules, job characteristics, social support, and individual difference, and the outcomes of emotional labor, such as emotional exhaustion, depersonalization, personal accomplishment, physical complaints, role internalization, self-esteem, and job satisfaction.

The issue of thinking as a part of feeling was also inherent in the concept of emotional intelligence. Chi-Sum Wong, Ping-Man Wong, and Kenneth Law examined this notion through their empirical analysis of emotional intelligence as an individual's ability to monitor his or her own and others' emotions and the regulation and use of these emotions in interactions. They further illustrated that emotions are multifaceted through segmenting the concept of emotional intelligence into self-appraisal of emotions, appraisal of others' emotions, the regulation of emotion, and use of one's emotions, classifying emotional labor as one part of emotional intelligence.

Certain jobs contain emotional demands. For instance, a doctor cannot listen to a patient's health problem and respond with tears, contempt, disregard, or an outburst such as "You're going to die!" In such a job, the employee is required to be calm, understanding, and empathetic. Therefore, organizations impact on the work experience of employees through placing emotional demands on their jobs. The chapter by Vanda Zammuner and Cristina Galli demonstrated that in a hospital setting, the emotional requirements of the job, the frequency and duration of an emotional task, and the seriousness of the patient problem impact on the degree to which employees depersonalize themselves from their job, leading to negative outcomes such as burnout. Regulation implies a certain amount of psychophysical effort and therefore implies a psychophysical cost (such as burnout, negative affect, dissatisfaction).

Finally, emotions play a large role in organizational change and changing organizations. It is vital for organizations to change, but it is equally vital that they recognize the impact of emotions in the workplace and also the support of others to those impacted by emotions.

Part IV concluded the book, and it is only fitting to finish the book with the concept of organizational change. Organizations must change because their environments change, and an organization's change process involves considerable emotional aspects. Organizations need to achieve an emotional balance between employee commitment to change (i.e., their enthusiasm for the change) and the need to manage the emotional disruption that comes with change (i.e., the need for incremental changes to allow acceptance and internalization of the changes). Emotions cannot be dissected from the change process, and to believe otherwise is to set yourself up for a big disappointment!

In chapter 16, Quy Huy illustrated the need for organizations to integrate their knowledge and awareness of emotions in order to develop emotional capabilities. A theoretical chapter on the notion of emotions and organizational change, it illustrated that in order to achieve effective continuous change, organizations must understand the emotional consequences of their change actions and use these emotions to advance the change. As such, the chapter also supported the notion that emotions are a powerful force that can push aside all else. Just as an individual can express an emotion, so too can an organization. During strategic change, the emotions of individuals can converge to the group level. Employees who share a common organizational culture are more likely to converge their emotions as they have similar beliefs. Group membership can also boost the individual's feelings of power as individuals may unconsciously respond to other people's emotional displays. An organization's emotional capability is greater than the sum of the emotional intelligence of its individual members.

Anthony Pescosolido illustrated the importance of emotions for leaders. He suggested that an individual is perceived as a leader by making an interpretation of the emotional response that would best serve the group's needs, and then modeling that response for the other group members. By modeling an emotional response to the situation, the leader resolves ambiguity and provides the group with the direction needed for action. At the same time, this leadership action can increase group solidarity by creating both shared emotion and shared action within the group.

The final research chapter within this text is by Michelle Pizer and Charmine Härtel. It encompassed all three of the issues discussed by Russell Cropanzano in the foreword. This chapter introduced the concept of a healthy organizational culture in terms of an organizational environment that induces positive emotions and reduces negative emotions. It also alluded to the power that emotions have. Culture's power is shown to derive from the emotional needs of individuals. The way in which culture interacts with individuals' emotional needs, these authors argued, influences people for better or for worse. The chapter also demonstrated the need to focus on a multifaceted view of emotions, examining both the process and outcomes of culture so that it can be assessed and managed to achieve the outcome of organizational health. Lastly, the chapter emphasized the need for organizations to think about their culture and emotions within their workplace in order to identify the key indicators associated with healthy and unhealthy, destructive, cultlike organizational cultures. Subsequently, organizations can create positive emotional experiences at work.

A MODEL OF EMOTIONS
IN ORGANIZATIONAL BEHAVIOR

There are many ways to approach the topic of organizational behavior. What we have done is to gather the latest research in emotions to demonstrate organizational behavior concepts. In essence, we have offered a view of organizational behavior through emotion-tinted glasses.

In drawing this book to a close we now present a model of organizational behavior developed by Charmine Härtel and Debra Panipucci. The model brings together the research assembled in this volume, summarizing it into a framework for looking at emotions within organizational behavior (Fig. 20.1).

The first level, the individual, depicts the everyday hassles and uplifts that may be experienced by an individual employee, within the organizational environment. This level includes the implications of emotion in employee counterproductive work behavior.

The second level, the interpersonal, addresses the influence of emotions between people, such as on group decision-making, intergroup dynamics and intragroup dynamics. (i.e., group affect problem solving, intergroup negotiation, and the social sharing of emotion [SSE] process, respectively).

The third level provides an analysis of the impact of the organization on the individual and group, in particular, the emotional requirements and affects of job design and organizational display rules and norms for emotion.

Finally, the fifth level depicts the ability of organizations to provide a healthy organizational culture, adaptable to the changing environment. It also addresses the important role that emotions play in socialization. This level reflects the power of the organization over emotions and the reciprocal power of emotions over the organization. Thus, in effect, this level reflects constraint. Organizational behavior can constrain emotions, while emotions can constrain organizational behavior. For instance, culture sets prescribed rules and norms for the emotions displayed, whereas emotions can hinder or help attempts at change (e.g., fear or happiness).

The field of organizational behavior itself models organizations based on a multilevel perspective (Weiss, 1996). We adapt this view in our model of emotions in organizational behavior. Emotions too are suggested to operate at the individual, group and organization levels (Ashkanasy, 2003b; Weiss, 2003). The model of organizational behavior we present incorporates how individual affect influences group-level affect, positive and negative mood, and problem solving, as well as emotional characteristics, emotional labor, and emotional intelligence. It examines the individual level and aggregates over people and

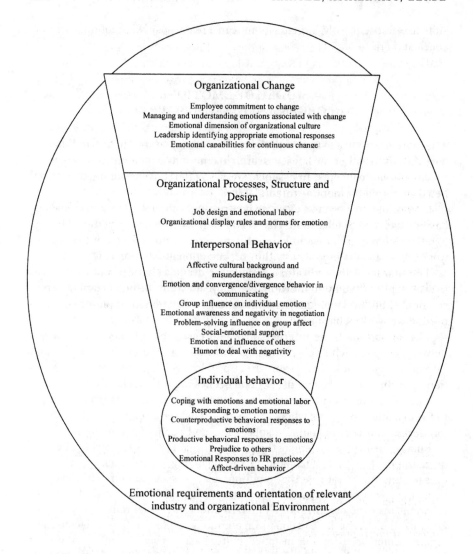

FIG. 20.1. A model of emotions in organizational behavior (Härtel & Panipucci).

time, as suggested by Weiss (2003), and it also considers the external environment within which the organization rests. Our model also shows how emotions translate across levels within organizational behavior. Thus we avoid crossing levels within one construct, without addressing the appropriateness for the construct at the level, as suggested by Weiss (2003). For instance, emotional intelligence at the individual level refers to how well the individual knows his or her emotions. At the interpersonal level, it refers to how well people assess and take actions on other people's emotions. At the organizational level, it refers to how well organizations design jobs for appropriate emotions. And at the culture and change level, it refers to how well organizations assess the emotional climate and address emotional issues during change.

We take both a bottom-up and a top-down approach to organizational behavior, whereby individual characteristics and emotions impact on the interpersonal, organizational, and change process levels, but so do the organization's change processes and culture impact on interpersonal and individual level emotions, such as through norms and rules prescribing appropriate emotional behavior and expression. Similarly, each level influences the other levels and constrains them at the same time (Weiss, 2003). Groups create powerful containers for social behavior, so are able to foster and discourage emotional experience and expression. Nonetheless, individuals can themselves exert powerful influences and change the emotional characteristics and norms of their groups.

Although the adoption of the study of emotions within organizational behavior has been slow, the studies accumulated in this volume indicate that research is addressing emotions at all levels in the organization. Emotions are not weak, or inferior to rationalizations. Rather, they are powerful influences on factors such as individual behavior, group problem solving, culture, and change processes.

FINAL WORDS

This volume of *Emotions in Organizational Behavior* presented state-of-the-art research from the world over, on emotions in organizational behavior. Yet it is not absolute. There is still much to know about the role emotions play in organizational behavior. This text simply provides a starting point for thinking about the notion ... the rest is up to you!

Nonetheless, we would like to remind you that this book is the third in a series of books on emotions. We encourage our readers to seek out the first book, *Emotions in the Workplace: Theory, Research, and Practice*, for constructive analysis of how people in organizational settings cope with and otherwise deal with emotions, and also the second book, *Managing Emotions in the Workplace*, which details the implications for managing emotions in the workplace. Further, we encourage scholars in the area to participate in the Biannual Conference on Emotions, with the 2004 conference to be held in London.

In conclusion, we hope that it has encouraged you to be more aware of, and sensitive to, the emotions within the workplace, not just during dramatic instances such as change where emotions are highly salient, but also during day-to-day tasks, as these are the emotions that frequently go undetected, influencing the behavior and performance of people at work. After all, that is what organizational behavior is all about!

References

Abraham, R. (1998). Emotional dissonance in organizations: Antecedents, consequences, and moderators. *Genetic, Social, and General Psychology Monographs, 124*(2), 229–246.

Abraham, R. (1999). Negative affectivity: Moderator or confound in emotional-dissonance relationships? *Journal of Psychology, 133*(1), 61–72.

Adelmann, P. A. (1995). Emotional labor as a potential source of job stress. In S. L. Sauter & L. R. Murphy (Eds.), *Organizational risk factors for job stress* (pp. 371–381). Washington, DC: American Psychological Association.

Adler, N. J., Brahm, R., & Graham, J. L. (1992). Strategy implementation: A comparison of face-to-face negotiations in the People's Republic of China and the United States. *Strategic Management Journal, 13*(6), 449–466.

Adler, R. B., & Rodman, G. (2000). *Understanding human communication.* Fort Worth, TX: Harcourt Brace.

Agar, M. H. (1996). *The professional stranger: An informal introduction to ethnography.* San Diego: Academic Press.

Ainsworth, M. D. S., Blehar, M. C., Waters, E., & Wall, S. (1978). *Patterns of attachment: A psychological study of the strange situation.* Hillsdale, NJ: Lawrence Erlbaum Associates.

Albert, S. (1984). A delete model for successful transitions. In J. Kimberly & R. Quinn (Eds.), *Managing organizational transitions* (pp. 149–191). Homewood, IL: Richard Irwin.

Allport, G. W. (1954). *The nature of prejudice.* Cambridge, MA: Addison-Wesley.

Altheide, D., Adler, P. A., Adler, P., & Altheide, D. A. (1978). The social meanings of employee theft. In J. M. Johnson & J. D. Douglas (Eds.), *Crime at the top: Deviance in business and the professions* (pp. 90–124). Philadelphia: J. B. Lippincott.

Alvesson, M. (1993). *Cultural perspectives on organizations.* Cambridge: Cambridge University Press.

Alvesson, M. (2002). *Understanding organizational culture.* London: Sage.

Alvesson, M., & Sköldberg, K. (1994). *Tolkning och reflektion: Vetenskapsfilosofi och kvalitative metod.* Lund: Studentlitteratur.

Amabile, T. M. (1988). A model of creativity and innovation in organizations. In L. L. Cummings & B. M. Staw (Eds.), *Research in organizational behavior* (Vol. 10, pp. 123–167). Greenwich, CT: JAI Press.

Ancona, D., Kochan, T. A., Scully, M., Van Maanen, J., & Westney, D. E. (1999). *Organizational behavior and processes.* Cincinnati, OH: South-Western College.

Andrews, F. M., & Robinson, J. P. (1991). Measures of subjective well-being. In J. P. Robinson, P. R. Shaver, & L. S. Wrightsman (Eds.), *Measures of personality and social psychological attitudes* (pp. 61–114). San Diego: Academic Press.

Antonacopoulou, E. P., & Gabriel, Y. (2001). Emotion, learning and organizational change: Towards an integration of psychoanalytic and other perspectives. *Journal of Organizational Change Management, 14*(5), 435–451.

Argyris, C. (1990). *Overcoming organizational defenses.* Boston: Allyn & Bacon.

Aristotle. (1998). *The Nicomachean ethics.* Oxford: Oxford World's Classics.

Ashforth, B. E., & Humphrey, R. H. (1993). Emotional labor in service roles: The influence of identity. *Academy of Management Review, 18*(1), 88–115.

Ashforth, B. E., & Humphrey, R. H. (1995). Emotion in the workplace: A reappraisal. *Human Relations, 48*(2), 97–125.

Ashforth, B. E., & Tomiuk, M. A. (2000). Emotional labour and authenticity: Views from service agents. In S. Fineman (Ed.), *Emotion in organizations* (2nd ed., pp. 184–203). Thousand Oaks, CA: Sage.

Ashkanasy, N. (1995). Organizational culture: Emotion or cognitions? *Managerial and Organizational Cognition Interest Group Newsletter (Mocig News), 5*(2), 1–2.

Ashkanasy, N. M. (2003a). Emotions in organizations: A multilevel perspective. In F. Dansereau & F. J. Yammarino (Eds.), *Research in multi-level issues, Vol. 2: Multi-level issues in organizational behavior and strategy* (pp. 9–54). Oxford, UK: Elsevier Science.

Ashkanasy, N. M. (2003b). Emotions at multiple levels: An integration. In F. Dansereau & F. J. Yammarino (Eds.), *Research in multi-level issues, Vol. 2: Multi-level issues in organizational behavior and strategy* (pp. 71–81). Oxford, UK: Elsevier Science.

Ashkanasy, N. M., & Daus, C. S. (2002). Emotion in the workplace: The new challenge for managers. *Academy of Management Executive, 16,* 76–86.

Ashkanasy, N. M., Härtel, C. E. J., & Daus, C. S. (2002a). Advances in organizational behavior: Diversity and emotions. *Journal of Management, 28,* 307–338.

Ashkanasy, N. M., Härtel, C. E. J., & Daus, C. S. (2002b). Diversity and emotion: The new frontiers in organizational behavior research. *Journal of Management, 28*(3), 307–338.

Ashkanasy, N. M., Härtel, C. E. J., & Zerbe, W. J. (Eds.). (2000). *Emotions in the workplace: Research, theory, and practice.* Westport, CT: Quorum Books.

Ashkanasy, N. M., & Nicholson, G. J. (2003). Climate of fear in organizational settings: Construct definition, measurement and test of theory. *Australian Journal of Psychology, 55,* 24–29.

Ashkanasy, N. M., & Tse, B. (2000). Transformational leadership as management of emotion: A conceptual review. In N. Ashkanasy, C. E. J. Härtel, & W. Zerbe (Eds.), *Emotions in the workplace: Research, theory, and practice* (pp. 221–235). Westport, CT: Quorum Books.

Ashkanasy, N. M., Wilderom, C., & Peterson, M. F. (Eds.). (2000). *Handbook of organizational culture and climate.* Thousand Oaks, CA: Sage.

Ashkanasy, N. M., Zerbe, W. J., & Härtel, C. E. J. (Eds.). (2000). *Managing emotions in the workplace.* Armonk, NY: M. E. Sharp.

Ashmore, R. D., & del Boca, F. K. (1981). Conceptual approaches to stereotypes and stereotyping. In D. Hamilton (Ed.), *Cognitive processes in stereotyping and intergroup behavior* (pp. 1–35). Hillsdale, NJ: Lawrence Erlbaum Associates.

Aspinwall, L. G., & Taylor, S. E. (1997). A stitch in time: Self-regulation and proactive coping. *Psychological Bulletin, 121*(3), 417–436.

Averill, J. R. (1973). Personal control over aversive stimuli and its relationship to stress. *Psychological Bulletin, 80*(4), 286–303.

Averill, J. R. (1980). A constructivist view of emotion. In R. Plutchik & H. Kellerman (Eds.), *Emotion: Theory, research, and experience* (pp. 305–339). New York: Academic Press.

Ayoko, O. B., & Härtel, C. E. J. (2000). *Culturally heterogeneous workgroups: The effects of leader behaviours and attitudes on conflict and its relationship to task and social outcomes.* Management Paper Series 87. Melbourne: Monash University, Faculty of Business and Economics.

Ayoko, O. B., & Härtel, C. E. J. (2002). The role of emotion and emotion management in destructive and productive conflict in culturally heterogeneous workgroups. In N. M. Ashkanasy, C. E. J. Härtel, & W. J. Zerbe (Eds.), *Managing emotions in the workplace* (pp. 77–97). Armonk, NY: M. E. Sharpe.

Ayoko, R., Härtel, C. E. J., Fisher, G., & Fujimoto, Y. (2003). Communication competence in cross-cultural business interactions. In D. Tourish & O. Hargie (Eds.), *Key issues in organizational communication* (pp. 157–171). New York: Routledge.

Babakus, E., Cravens, D. W., Johnston, M., & Moncrief, W. C. (1999). The role of emotional exhaustion in sales force attitude and behavior relationships. *Journal of the Academy of Marketing Science, 27*(1), 58–70.

Bales, R. F. (1950). *Interaction process analysis: A method for the study of small groups.* Cambridge, MA: Addison-Wesley.

Bales, R. F., & Slater, P. E. (1955). Role differentiation in small decision-making groups. In T. Parsons & P. E. Slater (Eds.), *The family, socialization and interaction processes* (pp. 259–306). Glencoe, IL: Free Press.

Balswick, J. O. (1988). *The inexpressive male.* Lexington, MA: Lexington Books.

Bandura, A. (1977). *Social learning theory analysis.* Englewood Cliffs, NJ: Prentice Hall.

Bandura, A. (1997). *Self-efficacy: The exercise of control.* New York: W. H. Freeman.

BarOn, R. (1997). *BarOn Emotional Quotient Inventory user's manual.* Odessa, FL: Psychological Assessment Resources, Inc.

Barrick, M. R., & Mount, M. K. (1991). The big five personality dimensions and job performance: A meta-analysis. *Personnel Psychology, 44*, 1–26.

Barsade, S. (2001). *The ripple effect: Emotional contagion in groups.* Working Paper. New Haven, CT: Yale University.

Barsade, S. G. (2002). The ripple effect: Emotional contagion and its influence on group behaviour. *Administrative Science Quarterly, 47*, 644–675.

Barsade, S., Brief, A. P., & Spataro, S. E. (2003). The affective revolution in organizational behavior: The emergence of a paradigm. In J. Greenberg (Ed.), *Organizational behavior: The state of the science* (pp. 3–52). Mahwah, NJ: Lawrence Erlbaum Associates.

Barsade, S., & Gibson, D. (1998). Group emotion: A view from top and bottom. In D. Gruenfeld, B. Mannix, & M. Neale (Eds.), *Research on managing groups and teams* (pp. 81–102). Stamford, CT: JAI Press.

Bartel, C. A., & Saavedra, R. (2000). The collective construction of work group moods. *Administrative Science Quarterly, 45*, 197–231.

Bartlett, F. C. (1932). *Remembering: A study in experimental and social psychology.* Cambridge: Cambridge University Press.

Bartlett, C., & Ghoshal, S. (1987, Fall). Managing across borders: New strategic requirements. *Sloan Management Review*, pp. 7–17.

Bass, B. M. (1990). *The Bass & Stogdill handbook of leadership* (3rd ed.). New York: Free Press.

Batson, C. D. (1998). Prosocial behavior and altruism. In D. T. Gilbert, S. T. Fiske, & G. Lindzey (Eds.), *Handbook of social psychology* (pp. 282–316). Boston: McGraw-Hill.

Batson, C. D., & Coke, J. S. (1981). Empathy: A source of altruistic motivation for helping? In J. P. Rushton & R. M. Sorrentino (Eds.), *Altruism and helping behavior: Social, personality, and developmental perspectives* (pp. 167–181). Hillsdale, NJ: Lawrence Erlbaum Associates.

Baumeister, R. F., & Leary, M. R. (1995). The need to belong: Desire for interpersonal attachments as a fundamental human motivation. *Psychological Bulletin, 117*, 497–529.

Beekun, R. I. (1989). Assessing the effectiveness of socio-technical interventions: Antidote or fad? *Human Relations, 47*, 877–897.

Bell, G. B., & Hall, H. E. (1954). The relationship between leadership and empathy. *Journal of Abnormal and Social Psychology, 49*, 156–157.

Bendelow, G., & Williams, S. J. (1998). *Emotions in social life*. London: Routledge.

Bennis, W., & Shepard, H. (1956). A theory of group development. *Human Relations, 9*, 415–437.

Berger, P. L., & Luckmann, T. (1966). *The social construction of reality*. New York: Doubleday.

Berkowitz, L., Jaffee, S., Jo, E., & Troccoli, B. T. (2000). On the correction of feeling-induced judgmental biases. In J. P. Forgas (Ed.), *Feeling and thinking: The role of affect in social cognition* (pp. 131–152). New York: Cambridge University Press.

Berry, D. S., & Pennebaker, J. W. (1998). Nonverbal and verbal emotional expression and health. In G. A. Fava & H. Freyberger (Eds.), *Handbook of psychosomatic medicine* (pp. 69–83). International Universities Press Stress and Health Series, Monograph 9. Madison, CT: International Universities Press.

Best, R. G., Downey, R. G., & Jones, R. G. (1997, April). *Job burnout: A dysfunctional consequence of contextual performance*. Paper presented at the Convention of the Society for Industrial and Organizational Life, San Diego, CA.

Beyer, J. M., Hannah, D. R., & Milton, L. P. (2000). Ties that bind. In N. M. Ashkanasy, C. Wilderom, & M. F. Peterson (Eds.), *Handbook of organizational culture & climate* (pp. 323–338). Thousand Oaks, CA: Sage.

Beyer, J. M., & Niño, D. (2001). Culture as a source, expression, and reinforcer of emotions in organizations. In R. Payne & C. L. Cooper (Eds.), *Emotions at work* (pp. 173–197). New York: Wiley.

Bhawuk, D. P., & Brislin, R. (1992). The measurement of intercultural sensitivity using the concepts of individualism and collectivism. *International Journal of Intercultural Relations, 16*, 413–436.

Biefhoff, H. W., & Müller, G. F. (1999). Positive feelings and cooperative support in project groups. *Swiss Journal of Psychology, 58*, 180–190.

Biggart, W. N. (1977). The creative destructive process of organizational change: The case of the post office. *Administrative Science Quarterly, 22*, 410–425.

Billikopf-Encina, G. (2000). Communicating across cultures. *International Journal of Conflict Management, 11*(4), 378–383.

Blackler, F., Reed, M., & Whitaker, A. (1993). Editorial introduction: Knowledge workers and contemporary organizations. *Journal of Management Studies, 30*(6), 851–862.

Boal, K. B., & Whitehead, C. J. (1992). A critique and extension of the stratified systems theory perspective. In R. L. Phillips & J. G. Hunt (Eds.), *Strategic leadership: A multiorganizational-level perspective* (pp. 237–255). Westport, CT: Quorum.

Boas, S. (1999). An evaluation of conceptual weaknesses in transformational and charismatic leadership theories. *Leadership Quarterly, 10*, 285–305.

Bochner, S., & Hesketh, B. (1994). Power distance, individualism/collectivism, and job-related attitudes in a culturally diverse work group. *Journal of Cross-Cultural Psychology, 25*, 233–257.

Boje, D. M. (1991). The storytelling organization: A study of story performance in an office-supply firm. *Administrative Science Quarterly, 36*, 106–126.

Bolina, M. C. (1999). Citizenship and impression management: Good soldiers or good actors. *Academy of Management Review, 24*, 82–98.

Bommer, W. H., & Rubin, R. S. (2001, August). *Antecedents and consequences of transformational leadership behaviors: The role of leader attitudes and social context upon leader behavior and performance outcomes*. Presented at the annual meeting of the Academy of Management, Washington, DC.

Bonino, S., Lo Coco, A., & Tani, F. (1998). *Empatia. I Processi di condivisione delle emozioni* [Empathy. Condivision processes of emotions]. Firenze, Italy: Giunti.

REFERENCES

Bono, J. E., & Judge, T. A. (2003). Self-concordance at work: Toward understanding the motivational effects of transformational leaders. *Academy of Management Journal, 29*(6), 831–857.

Borgen, F. H. (1986). New approaches to the assessment of interest. In W. B. Walsh & S. H. Osipow (Eds.), *Advances in vocational psychology. Vol. 1: The assessment of interests* (pp. 83–125). Hillsdale, NJ: Lawrence Erlbaum Associates.

Børli, H. (1972). *Samlede Dikt.* Oslo: Aschoug.

Bourdieu, P. (1990). *The logic of practice.* Stanford, CA: Stanford University Press.

Bower, J. L. (1986). *Managing the resource allocation process.* Homestead, IL: Irwin. (Original work published 1970)

Bowlby, J. (1969). *Attachment and loss: Vol. 1. Attachment.* New York: Basic Books.

Boye, M. W., & Jones, J. W. (1997). Organizational culture and employee counterproductivity. In R. A. Giacalone & J. Greenberg (Eds.), *Antisocial behavior in organization* (pp. 172–184). Newbury Park, CA: Sage.

Boyle, M. V. (2002). Sailing twixt Scylla and Charybdis: Managing multiple organizational masculinities. *Women in Management Review, 17*(3/4), 131–141.

Boyle, M. V., & Healy, J. (2003). Balancing Mysterium and Onus: Doing spiritual work within emotion-laden organizational contexts. *Organization, 10*(2), 351–373.

Breth, R., & Jin, K. (1991). *Business negotiations with the People's Republic of China.* Melbourne: Bowater Faculty of Business, Victoria College.

Brewer, M. B. (1979). Ingroup bias in the minimal intergroup situation: A cognitive-motivational analysis. *Psychological Bulletin, 86*, 307–324.

Brewer, M. B., & Gardner, W. (1996). Who is this "we"? Levels of collective identity and self-representations. *Journal of Personality and Social Psychology, 71*, 83–93.

Brickson, S. (2000). The impact of identity orientation on individual and organizational outcomes in demographically diverse settings. *Academy of Management Review, 25*, 82–101.

Bridges, W. (1980). *Making sense of life's transitions.* New York: Addison-Wesley.

Brief, A. P., & Weiss, H. M. (2002). Organizational behavior: Affect in the workplace. In S. T. Fiske, D. L. Schacter, & C. Zahn-Waxler (Eds.), *Annual Review of Psychology, 53*, 279–307. Palo Alto, CA: Annual Reviews, Inc.

Britt, T. W., Bonecki, K. A., Vescio, T. K., Biernat, M. R., & Brown, L. M. (1996). Intergroup anxiety as a form of social anxiety. *Personal and Social Psychology Bulletin, 22*, 1177–1188.

Brotheridge, C. M., & Grandey, A. A. (2002). Emotional labor and burnout: Comparing two perspectives of "people work." *Journal of Vocational Behavior, 60*, 17–39.

Brotheridge, C. M., & Lee, R. (1998). *On the dimensionality of emotional labor: Development and validation of an emotional labor scale.* Presented at the first conference on Emotions in Organizational Life, San Diego, CA.

Brotheridge, C. M., & Lee, R. (2002). Testing a conservation of resources model of the dynamics of emotional labor. *Journal of Occupational Health, 7*(1), 57–67.

Brown, D., & Brooks, L. (1990). *Career choice and development* (2nd ed.). San Francisco: Jossey-Bass.

Brown, P., & Levinson, S. (1987). *Politeness: Some universals in language usage.* Cambridge: Cambridge University Press.

Brown, S., & Eisenhardt, K. (1997). The art of continuous change: Linking complexity theory and time-paced evolution in relentlessly shifting organizations. *Administrative Science Quarterly, 42*, 1–34.

Brown, T. A., Chorpita, B. F., Korotitsch, W., & Barlow, D. H. (1997). Psychometric properties of the Depression Anxiety Stress Scales (DASS) in clinical samples. *Behaviour Research and Therapy, 35*, 79–89.

Bruner, J. (1990). *Acts of meaning.* Cambridge, MA: Harvard University Press.

Bryman, A. (1996). Leadership in organizations. In S. R. Clegg, C. Hardy, & W. R. Nord (Eds.), *Organizational studies* (pp. 276–292). London: Sage.

Buller, P. F., & McEvoy, G. M. (1999). Creating and sustaining ethical capability in the multinational corporation. *Journal of World Business, 34,* 326–343.

Burgelman, R. A. (1983). A process of model of internal corporate venturing in the diversified major firm. *Administrative Science Quarterly, 28,* 223–244.

Burgelman, R. A. (1994). Fading memoires: A process theory of strategic business exit in dynamic environments. *Administrative Science Quarterly, 39,* 24–56.

Burns, T., & Stalker, G. M. (1994). *The management of innovation* (2nd ed.). Oxford: Oxford University Press.

Buroway, M. (1979). *Manufacturing consent.* Chicago: Chicago University Press.

Burrell, G., & Morgan, G. (1979). *Sociological paradigms and organisational analysis.* Aldershot: Gower.

Byrne, B. M. (1993). The Maslach Burnout Inventory: Testing for factorial validity and invariance across elementary, intermediate and secondary teachers. *Journal of Occupational and Organizational Psychology, 66,* 197–212.

Byrne, D. (1971). *The attraction paradigm.* New York: Academic Press.

Calori, R. (1998). Essay: Philosophizing on strategic management models. *Organization Studies, 19*(2), 281–306.

Cameron, K., Dutton, J. E., & Quinn, R. (2001). *A new orientation to positive organizational scholarship.* http://www.bus.umich.edu/positiveorganizationalscholarship/neworientation.html (accessed 31 October 2002).

Campbell, A., Converse, P. E., & Rodgers, W. L. (1976). *The quality of American life: Perceptions, evaluation and satisfaction.* New York: Russell Sage.

Campion, M. A. (1988). Interdisciplinary approaches to job design: A constructive replication with extensions. *Journal of Applied Psychology, 73*(3), 467–481.

Campos, J., Campos, R., & Barrett, K. (1989). Emergent themes in the study of emotional development and emotion regulation. *Developmental Psychology, 25,* 394–402.

Carnall, C. (1995). *Managing change in organizations.* London: Prentice Hall.

Carrell, M. R., & Mann, E. E. (1993). Defining workforce diversity programs and practices in organizations. *Labor Law Journal, 44,* 755–764.

Carver, C. S. (2001). Affect and the functional bases of behavior: On the dimensional structure of affective experience. *Personality and Social Psychology Review, 5,* 345–356.

Carver, C. S., & Scheier, M. F. (1999). Stress, coping, and self-regulatory processes. In L. A. Pervin & O. P. John (Eds.), *Handbook of personality: Theory and research* (2nd ed., pp. 553–575). New York: Guilford Press.

Carver, C. S., & Scheier, M. F. (2002). Control processes and self-organization as complementary principles underlying behavior. *Personality and Social Psychology Review, 6,* 304–315.

Cascio, W. F. (1995). Whither industrial and organizational psychology in a changing world of work. *American Psychologist, 50*(11), 928–939.

Casio, W. (1995). *Managing human resources: Productivity, quality of work life, profits.* New York: McGraw-Hill.

Cassidy, J. (1994). Emotion regulation: Influences of attachment relationships. In N. Fox (Ed.), The development of emotion regulation: Biological and biobehavioral considerations. *Monographs of the Society of Research in Child Development* (Serial No. 240, Vol. 59, Nos. 2–3).

Chang, L. (2002). Cross-cultural differences in styles of negotiation between North Americans and Chinese. *Journal of American Academy of Business, 1*(2), 179–187.

Chaplin, J. P. (1979). *Dictionary of psychology* (Laurel ed.). New York: Dell.

Chapman, A. J., & Foot, H. C. (Eds.). (1976). *Humor and laughter: Theory, research, and applications.* London: Wiley.

Chattopadhyay, G. P. (1995). Hierarchy and modern organization: Strange bedfellows. In S. Long (Ed.), *International perspectives on organizations in times of turbulence* (pp. 13–22). Melbourne, Australia: Swinburne University of Technology.

Chen, C. C., & DiTomaso, N. (1996). Diversity: A strategic issue. In E. E. Kossek & S. A. Lobel (Eds.), *Managing diversity: Human resource strategies for transferring the workplace* (pp. 137–163). Massachusetts: Blackwell.

Chen, P. Y., & Spector, P. E. (1992). Relationship of work stressors with aggression, withdrawal, theft and substance use: An exploratory study. *Journal of Occupational and Organizational Psychology, 65*(3), 177–184.

Christophe, V., & Rimé, B. (1997). Exposure to the social sharing of emotion: Emotional impact, listener responses and secondary social sharing. *European Journal of Social Psychology, 27,* 37–54.

Ciarrochi, J. V., Chan, A. Y. C., & Caputi, P. (2000). A critical evaluation of the emotional intelligence construct. *Personality & Individual Differences, 28*(3), 539–561.

Cohen, S. G., Ledford, G. E., Jr., & Spreitzer, G. M. (1996). A predictive model of self-managing work team effectiveness. *Human Relations, 4,* 643–676.

Collins, J. M., & Griffin, R. W. (1998). The psychology of counterproductive job performance. In R. W. Griffin, A. O'Leary-Kelly, & J. M. Collins (Eds.), *Dysfunctional behavior in organizations: Nonviolent dysfunctional behavior* (pp. 219–242). Stamford, CT: JAI Press.

Collinson, D. L. (1988). "Engineering humor": Masculinity, joking and conflict in shop-floor relations. *Organization Studies, 9,* 181–199.

Collinson, D. L. (2002). Managing humour. *Journal of Management Studies, 39,* 269–288.

Connell, R. W. (1995). *Masculinities.* Sydney: Allen & Unwin.

Cooper, R. (2001). Un-timely mediations: Questing thought. *Ephemera, 1*(4), 321–347. (Electronic journal www.ephemerawb.org)

Cordes, C. L., & Dougherty, T. W. (1993). A review and an integration of research on job burnout. *Academy of Management Review, 18*(4), 621–656.

Coupland, N., Wiemann, J. M., & Giles, H. (1991). *Miscommunication and problematic talk.* Newbury Park, CA: Sage.

Cox, T. H., & Nkomo, S. M. (1993). Race and ethnicity. In R. Golembiewski (Ed.), *Handbook of organizational behavior* (pp. 205–229). New York: Marcel Decker.

Crandall, C. S., D'Anello, S., Nuray, S., Lazarus, E., Wieczorkowska, G., & Feather, N. T. (2001). An attribution-value model of prejudice: Anti-fat attitudes in six nations. *Journal of Personality and Social Psychology, 27*(1), 30–37.

Crawford, M., & Gressley, D. (1991). Creativity, caring, and context: Women's and men's accounts of humor preferences and practices. *Psychology of Women Quarterly, 15,* 217–231.

Cressey, A. (2001, May 14). Shut out of the car. *Evening Post Independent Newspapers,* p. 13.

Cropanzano, R., & Greenberg, J. (1997). Progress in organizational justice: Tunneling through the maze. In C. L. Cooper & I. T. Robertson (Eds.), *International review of industrial and organizational psychology* (pp. 317–372). New York: Wiley.

Cropanzano, R., Weiss, H. M., & Elias, S. M. (Eds.). (in press). *The impact of display rules and emotional labor on psychological well-being at work.* Greenwich, CT: JAI Press.

Cropanzano, R., Weiss, H. M., Hale, J. M. S., & Reb, J. (2003). The structure of affect: Reconsidering the relationship between negative and positive affectivity. *Journal of Management, 29*(6), 831–857.

Cropanzano, R., & Wright, T. A. (2001). When a "happy" worker is really a "productive" worker: A review and further refinements of the happy–productive worker thesis. *Consulting Psychology Journal, 53,* 182–199.

Cross, S. E., & Markus, H. R. (1991). *Cultural adaptation and the self: Self-construal, coping, stress.* Paper presented at the annual meeting of American Psychological Association, San Francisco.

Crystal, D. (2000). *English as a global language.* Cambridge: Cambridge University Press Canto.

Csikszentmihalyi, M. (1997a). *Creativity: Flow and the psychology of discovery and invention.* New York: Harper Perennial.

Csikszentmihalyi, M. (1997b). *Finding flow: The psychology of engagement with everyday life.* New York: Basic Books.

Csikszentmihalyi, M., & LeFevre, J. (1989). Optimal experience in work and leisure. *Journal of Personality and Social Psychology, 56,* 815–822.

Czarniawska, B. (1997). *Narrating the organization: Dramas of institutional identity.* Chicago: University of Chicago Press.

Damasio, A. R. (1994). *Descartes' error: Emotion, reason and the human brain.* New York: Grossett, Putnam & Sons.

Dandridge, T. C., Mitroff, I., & Joyce, W. F. (1980). Organizational symbolism: A topic to expand organizational analysis. *Academy of Management Review, 5,* 77–82.

Darwin, C. R. (1985). *The expression of emotion in man and animals.* Chicago: University of Chicago Press. (Original work published 1872)

Dass, P., & Parker, B. (1996). Diversity: A strategic issue. In E. E. Kossek & S. A. Lobel (Eds.), *Managing diversity: Human resource strategies for transferring the work place* (pp. 365–391). Malden, MA: Blackwell.

Daus, C. S. (2001). Rater mood and employee emotional expression in a customer service scenario: Interactions and implications for performance review outcomes. *Journal of Quality Management, 6,* 349–370.

Davies, M., Stankov, L., & Roberts, R. D. (1998). Emotional intelligence: In search of an elusive construct. *Journal of Personality and Social Psychology, 75*(4), 989–1015.

Davies, S. A., & Billings, R. S. (2002, April). *Emotional labor in academia: Developmental and initial validation of a new measure.* Paper presented in Emotional Labor: Emerging From Merky Waters With Multi-Method, Multimeasure Approaches, C. S. Daus & T. M. Glomb (Chairs), Symposium conducted at the 2002 meeting of the Society for Industrial Organizational Psychology, Toronto, Canada.

Davis, M. H. (1980). A multidimensional approach to individual differences in empathy. *JSAS Catalog of Selected Documents in Psychology, 10,* 85.

Davis, M. H. (1983). Measuring individual differences in empathy: Evidence for a multidimensional approach. *Journal of Personality and Social Psychology, 44*(1), 113–126.

Davis, T. R. V. (1984). The influence of the physical environment in offices. *Academy of Management Review, 9,* 271–283.

Dayringer, R. (1998). *The heart of pastoral counselling healing through relationship.* New York: Haworth Press.

Deci, E. L., Eghrari, H., Patrick, B. C., & Leone, D. R. (1994). Facilitating internalization: The self-determination theory perspective. *Journal of Personality, 62,* 119–142.

De Dreu, C., West, M., Fischer, A., & MacCurtain, S. (2001). Origins and consequences of emotions in organizational teams. In R. Payne & C. L. Cooper (Eds.), *Emotions at work* (pp. 199–213). New York: Wiley.

Denison, D. (1996). What is the difference between organizational culture and organizational climate? A native's point of view on a decade of paradigm wars. *Academy of Management Review, 21,* 619–654.

De Rivera, J. (1992). Emotional climate: Social structure and emotional dynamics. *International Review of Studies of Emotion, 2,* 197–218.

Deschamps, J. C., & Devos, T. (1998). Regarding the relationship between social identity and personal identity. In S. J. Worchel, J. F. Morales, D. Páez, & J. C. Deschamps (Eds.), *Social identity* (pp. 1–12). Thousand Oaks, CA: Sage.

De Souza, G., & Klein, H. J. (1995). Emergent leadership in the group goal-setting process. *Small Group Research, 26,* 475–496.

Deutsch, M., Katz, I., & Jensen, A. R. (Eds.). (1968). *Social class, race, and psychological development.* New York: Holt, Rinehart & Winston.

Devine, P. G. (1989). Stereotypes and prejudice: Their automatic and controlled components. *Journal of Personality and Social Psychology, 56*(1), 5–18.

Dibben, K. (2001, July 8). Big pay out for age bias. *The Sunday Tasmanian.*

Dieffendorff, J. M., & Richard, E. M. (in press). Antecedents and consequences of emotional display rule perceptions. *Journal of Applied Psychology.*

Diehl, M., & Stroebe, W. (1991). Productivity loss in idea-generating groups: Tracking down the blocking effect. *Journal of Personality and Social Psychology, 61,* 392–403.

Diener, E. (1984). Subjective well-being. *Psychological Bulletin, 95*(3), 542–575.

Diener, E., Emmons, R. A., Larsen, R. J., & Griffin, S. (1985). The satisfaction with life scale. *Journal of Personality Assessment, 49*(1), 71–75.

Diener, E., & Larsen, R. J. (1993). The experience of emotional wellbeing. In M. L. Haviland & J. M. Haviland (Eds.), *Handbook of emotions* (pp. 405–415). New York: Guilford.

Dodier, N., & Camus, A. (1998). Openness and specialization: Dealing with patients in a hospital emergency service. *Sociology of Health and Illness, 20*(4), 413–444.

Doherty, R. W. (1998). Emotional contagion and social judgment. *Motivation and Emotion, 22,* 187–209.

Domagalski, T. A. (1999). Emotion in organizations: Main currents. *Human Relations, 52*(6), 833–852.

Doucet, L. (1998, August). *Responsiveness: Emotion and information dynamics in service interactions.* Paper presented at the First Conference of Emotions in Organizational Life, San Diego, CA.

Dougherty, D., & Bowman, E. (1995). The effects of organizational downsizing on product innovation. *California Management Review, 37,* 28–44.

Dovidio, J. F., Gaertner, S. L., Validzic, A., Matoka, K., Johnson, B., & Frazier, S. (1997). Extending the benefits of recategorization: Evaluations, self-disclosure, and helping. *Journal of Experimental Social Psychology, 33,* 401–420.

Dreyfus, H. L. (1991). *Being-in-the-world: A commentary on Heidegger's being and time.* London: MIT Press.

Drucker, P. F. (1993). *Post-capitalist society.* New York: Butterworth Heineman.

Drucker, P. F. (2001, November 3). The next society. *The Economist,* pp. 3–22.

Druskat, V. U., & Kayes, D. C. (1999). The antecedents of team competence: Toward a fine-grained model of self-managing team effectiveness. In M. A. Neale & E. A. Mannix (Series Eds.) & R. Wageman (Vol. Ed.), *Research on managing groups and teams* (Vol. 2, pp. 201–231). Context. Stamford, CT: JAI Press.

Druskat, V. U., & Pescosolido, A. T. (2003). *Leading self-managing teams from the inside: Informal leader behavior and team effectiveness.* Manuscript under review.

Dunbar, E., Saiz, J. L., Stela, K., & Saez, R. (2000). Personality and social group value determinants of out-group bias: A cross-national comparison of Gough's Pr/To scale. *Journal of Cross-Cultural Psychology, 31*(2), 267–275.

Duncan, W. J. (1982). Humor in management: Prospects for administrative practice and research. *Academy of Management Review, 7,* 136–142.

Duncan, W. J., & Feisal, J. P. (1989). No laughing matter: Patterns of humor in the workplace. *Organizational Dynamics, 17,* 18–30.

Duncan, W. J., Smeltzer, L. R., & Leap, T. L. (1990). Humor and work: Applications of joking behavior to management. *Journal of Management, 16,* 255–278.

Duncombe, J., & Marsden, D. (1993). Love and intimacy: The gender division of emotion and emotion work. *Sociology, 27,* 221–241.

Duncombe, J., & Marsden, D. (1995). " 'Workaholics' and 'Whingeing' women": Theorising intimacy and emotion work—The last frontier of gender inequality? *Sociological Review, 43,* 150–169.

Dutton, J. E., & Dukerich, J. M. (1991). Keeping an eye on the mirror: Image and identity in organizational adaptation. *Academy of Management Journal, 34,* 517–554.

Dutton, J. E., Dukerich, J. M., & Harquail, C. V. (1994). Organizational images and member identification. *Administrative Science Quarterly, 39,* 239–263.

Eagly, A. H., & Wood, W. (1999). The origins of sex differences in human behaviour: Evolved dispositions versus social roles. *American Psychologist, 54*, 408–423.

Earley, P. C., & Northcraft, G. B. (1989). Goal setting, resource interdependence, and conflict. In M. A. Rahim (Ed.), *Managing conflict: An interdisciplinary approach* (pp. 161–170). New York: Praeger.

Edmondson, A. (1999). Psychological safety and learning behavior in work teams. *Administrative Science Quarterly, 44,* 350–383.

Eide, D. (2000, July). *Learning across interactions: Which voices matters where?* Paper presented at the 16th EGOS Colloquia, Track 2: Action, Learning and Collective Practices. Helsinki, Finland.

Eide, D. (in press). *A situated-relational approach to knowing and learning: Integrating emotions and social relational sides.* PhD dissertation, Tromsø University, Tromsø.

Eide, D., Jensen, Ø., & Lilleby, E. (1996, November 1). Arbeidsmiljø snudd på hodet. *Næringslivets Ukeavis*, p. 7.

Eide, D., & Lindberg, F. (1997, August). *Exploring external interactions and consequences for knowing: A critical analysis of service firms.* Paper presented at the 14th Nordic Conference on Business Studies, Bodø.

Eisenberg, N., & Miller, P. A. (1987). The relation of empathy to prosocial and related behaviors. *Psychological Bulletin, 101*, 91–119.

Eiteman, D. K. (1990, Winter). American executives' perceptions of negotiating joint ventures with the People's Republic of China: Lessons learned. *Columbia Journal of World Business*, pp. 59–67.

Ekman, P. (1972). Universal and cultural differences in facial expressions of emotion. In J. K. Cole (Ed.), *Nebraska Symposium on Motivation* (pp. 207–283). Lincoln: University of Nebraska Press.

Ekman, P. (1973a). Cross culture studies of facial expression. In P. Ekman (Ed.), *Darwin and facial expression: A century of research in review* (pp. 169–222). New York: Academic Press.

Ekman, P. (1973b). *Darwin and facial expression: A century of research in review.* New York: Academic Press.

Ekman, P. (1984). Expression and the nature of emotion. In K. R. Scherer & P. Ekman (Eds.), *Approaches to emotion* (pp. 197–219). Hillsdale, NJ: Lawrence Erlbaum Associates.

Ekman, P. (1994). Strong evidence for universals in facial expressions: A reply to Russell's mistaken critique. *Psychological Bulletin, 115*(2), 268–287.

Ekman, P., & Friesen, W. V. (1969). The repertoire of nonverbal behavior—Categories, origins, usage, and coding. *Semiotica, 1*, 49–98.

Ekman, P., Friesen, W. V., & Ancoli, S. (1980). Facial signs of emotional experience. *Journal of Personality and Social Psychology, 39*, 1125–1134.

Engholm, C. (1989). *The China venture: America's corporate encounter with the People's Republic of China.* Glenview, IL: Scott, Foresman.

Erez, A., & Isen, A. M. (2002). The influence of positive affect on the components of expectancy motivation. *Journal of Applied Psychology, 87*, 1055–1067.

Erickson, R. J., & Ritter, C. (2001). Emotional labor, burnout, and inauthenticity: Does gender matter? *Social Psychology Quarterly, 64*, 146–163.

Espinoza, J. A., & Garza, R. T. (1985). Social group salience and interethnic cooperation. *Journal of Experimental Social Psychology, 21*, 697–715.

Evans, B. K., & Fischer, D. G. (1993). The nature of burnout: A study of the three-factor model of burnout in human service and non-human service samples. *Journal of Occupational and Organizational Psychology, 66*, 29–38.

Eysenck, H. J. (1942). The appreciation of humour: An experimental and theoretical study. *British Journal of Psychology, 32*, 295–309.

Eysenck, H. J. (1943). An experimental analysis of fine tests of "appreciation of humour." *Educational and Psychological Measurement, 32*, 191–214.

Eysenck, H. J. (1972). Foreword. In J. H. Goldstein & P. E. McGhee (Eds.), *The psychology of humor* (pp. xiii–xvii). New York: Academic.

Faulkner, B., & Patiar, A. (1997). Workplace induced stress among operational staff in the hotel industry. *International Journal of Hospitality Management, 16*(1), 99–117.

Feldenkirchen, W. (1996). Werner von Siemens. *Erfinder und internationaler Unternehmer.* Berlin: Pieper.

Fenigstein, A., Scheier, M. F., & Buss, A. H. (1975). Public and private self-consciousness: Assessment and theory. *Journal of Consulting and Clinical Psychology, 43*(4), 522–527.

Ferraro, G. P. (2002). *The cultural dimension of international business.* Upper Saddle River, NJ: Prentice Hall.

Feshback, S. (1986). Reconceptualizations of anger: Some research perspectives. *Journal of Social and Clinical Psychology, 4*(2), 123–132.

Festinger, L. (1957). *A theory of cognitive dissonance.* Stanford, CA: Stanford University Press.

Fiedler, F. E. (1967). *A theory of leadership effectiveness.* New York: McGraw-Hill.

Fiedler, F. E., Chemers, M. M., & Mahar, L. (1977). *Improving leadership effectiveness: The leader match concept.* New York: Wiley.

Finch, J. (1983). *Married to the job: Wives' incorporation in men's work.* Boston: Allen & Unwin.

Fineman, S. (1993a). *Emotion in organizations.* London: Sage.

Fineman, S. (1993b). Organizations as emotional arenas. In S. Fineman (Ed.), *Emotion and organization* (pp. 3–11). London: Sage.

Fineman, S. (1997). Emotion and management learning. *Management Learning, 28*(1), 13–25.

Fineman, S. (2000). *Emotion in organizations* (2nd ed.). Thousand Oaks, CA: Sage.

Fineman, S. (2001). Emotions and organizational control. In R. Payne & C. L. Cooper (Eds.), *Emotions at work* (pp. 214–239). New York: Wiley.

Finkenauer, C., & Rimé, B. (1998). Socially shared emotional experiences vs. emotional experiences kept secret: Differential characteristics and consequences. *Journal of Social and Clinical Psychology, 3*, 47–58.

Fischer, A. H. (Ed.). (2000). *Gender and emotion.* Cambridge: Cambridge University Press.

Fisher, C. D. (2000). Mood and emotions while working: Missing pieces of job satisfaction? *Journal of Organizational Behavior, 21*(2), 185–202.

Fisher, C. D., & Ashkanasy, N. M. (2000a). The emerging role of emotions in work life: An introduction. *Journal of Organizational Behavior, 21*(3), 123–129.

Fisher, C. D., & Ashkanasy, N. M. (Eds.). (2000b). Special edition on emotions in work life. *Journal of Organizational Behavior, 21*(2), 123–129.

Flanagan, J. C. (1954). The critical incident technique. *Psychological Bulletin, 51*, 327–358.

Fløistad, G. (1993). *Heidegger—En innføring I hans filosofi.* Oslo: Pax Forslag A/S.

Floyd, S. W., & Lane, P. J. (2000). Strategizing throughout the organization: Managing role conflict in strategic renewal. *Academy of Management Review, 25*, 154–177.

Floyd, S. W., & Woolridge, B. (1996). *The strategic middle manager.* San Francisco: Jossey-Bass.

Folger, R., & Skarlicki, D. P. (1998). A popcorn metaphor for employee aggression. In R. W. Griffin, A. O'Leary-Kelly, & J. M. Collins (Eds.), *Dysfunctional behavior in organizations: Nonviolent dysfunctional behavior* (pp. 43–82). Stamford, CT: JAI Press.

Forgas, J. P. (2000). Introduction. In J. P. Forgas (Ed.), *Thinking and feeling: The role of affect in social cognition* (pp. 1–30). Cambridge: Cambridge University Press.

Forgas, J. P. (2002). Feeling and doing: Affective influences on interpersonal behavior. *Psychological Inquiry, 13*, 1–28.

Forgas, J. P., & George, J. M. (2001). Affective influences on judgments and behavior in organizations: An information processing perspective. *Organizational Behavior and Human Decision Processes, 86*, 3–34.

Forgas, J. P., & Vargas, P. T. (2000). The effects of mood on social judgment and reasoning. In M. Lewis & J. M. Haviland-Jones (Eds.), *Handbook of emotions* (2nd ed., pp. 350–367). New York: Guilford Press.

Forseth, U. (2001). *Boundless work: Emotional labor and emotional exhaustion in interactive service work*. Published PhD dissertation. Trondheim: Department of Sociology and Political Science, Norwegian University of Technology and Natural Science.

Forzi, M., Arcuri, L., & Kodilja, R. (1987). Aspetti differenziali nella percezione del sè e processi attribuzionali [Differential aspects in self perception and attributional processes]. *Reports from the Institute of Psychology*. University of Trieste, Trieste, Italy.

Fox, S. (Ed.). (2000). Special issue on emotions in the workplace. *Human Resource Management, 12*(2).

Fox, S., & Spector, P. E. (1999). A model of work frustration-aggression. *Journal of Organizational Behavior, 20*(6), 915–931.

Fox, S., & Spector, P. E. (2000). Relationship of emotional intelligence, practical intelligence, general intelligence, and trait affectivity with interview outcomes: It's not all just "g." *Journal of Organizational Behavior, 21*, 203–220.

Fox, S., Spector, P. E., & Miles, D. (2001). Counterproductive work behavior (CWB) in response to job stressors and organizational justice: Some mediator and moderator tests for autonomy and emotions. *Journal of Vocational Behavior, 59*(3), 291–309.

Francis, L. E. (1994). Laughter, the best medicine: Humor as emotion management in interaction. *Symbolic Interaction, 17*(2), 147–163.

Fredrickson, B. L. (1998). What good are positive emotions? *Review of General Psychology, 2*(3), 300–319.

Fredrickson, B. L. (2001). The role of positive emotions in positive psychology: The broaden-and-build theory of positive emotions. *American Psychologist, 56*, 218–226.

Fredrickson, B. L., & Levenson, R. W. (1998). Positive emotions speed recovery from the cardiovascular sequelae of negative emotions. *Cognition and Emotion, 12*, 191–220.

Freedman, J. L., Sears, D. O., & Carlsmith, J. M. (1981). *Social psychology* (4th ed.). Englewood Cliffs, NJ: Prentice-Hall.

French, W. L., & Bell, C. H., Jr. (1990). *Organization development: Behavioral science interventions for organization improvement* (4th ed.). Englewood Cliffs, NJ: Prentice Hall.

Freud, S. (1922). *Group psychology and the analysis of the ego*. New York: W. W. Norton.

Freud, S. (1928). Humour. *International Journal of Psychoanalysis, 9*, 1–6.

Fried, Y., & Ferris, G. R. (1987). The validity of the job characteristics model: A review and meta-analysis. *Personnel Psychology, 40*, 287–322.

Friedman, R. S., & Förster, J. (2001). The effects of promotion and prevention cues on creativity. *Journal of Personality and Social Psychology, 81*, 1001–1013.

Friesen, C. M. (1972). *The political economy of East–West trade*. New York: Praeger.

Frijda, N. H. (1986). *The emotions*. Cambridge: Cambridge University Press.

Frijda, N. H. (1993). Moods, emotion episodes and emotions. In M. Lewis & J. M. Haviland (Eds.), *Handbook of emotions* (pp. 381–403). New York: Guilford Press.

Frijda, N. H. (1999). Emotions and hedonic experience. In D. Kahneman, E. Diener, & N. Schwarz (Eds.), *Well-being: The foundations of hedonic psychology* (pp. 190–210). New York: Sage.

Frost, P. (2003). *Toxic emotions at work*. Boston: Harvard Business School Press.

Fry, W. (1963). *Sweet madness: A study of humor*. Palo Alto, CA: Pacific Books.

Fujimoto, Y., & Härtel, C. E. J. (2002). *Emotional experience of individualist-collectivist workgroups: Findings from a study of 14 multinationals located in Australia*. 3rd International Conference on Emotions and Organisational Life, best papers.

Fujimoto, Y., Härtel, C. E. J., Härtel, G. F., & Baker, N. J. (2000). Openness to dissimilarity moderates the consequences of diversity in well-established groups. *Asia Pacific Journal of Human Resources, 38*(3), 46–61.

Fullerton, H. N. (1987). Labor force projections: 1986–2000. *Monthly Labor Review, 110*(9), 19–29.

Gabrenya, W. K., & Barba, L. (1987, March). *Cultural differences in social interaction during group problem solving.* Paper presented at the Southeastern Psychological Association, Atlanta, GA.

Gabriel, Y. (1998). An introduction to the social psychology of insults in organizations. *Human Relations, 51*(11), 1329–1254.

Gardner, H. (1993). *Multiple intelligences: The theory in practice.* New York: Basic Books.

Gardner, W. L., Gabriel, S., & Diekman, A. (2000). The psychophysiology of interpersonal processes. In J. T. Cacioppo, L. G. Tassinary, & G. G. Bertson (Eds.), *The handbook of psychophysiology* (2nd ed., pp. 613–644). Cambridge, MA: Cambridge University Press.

Gardner, W. L., Pickett, C. L., & Brewer, M. B. (2000). Social exclusion and selective memory: How the need to belong influences memory for social events. *Personality and Social Psychology Bulletin, 26*, 486–496.

Gasper, K., & Clore, G. L. (2002). Attending to the big picture: Mood and global versus local processing of visual information. *Psychological Science, 13*, 34–40.

Geertz, C. (1970). The impact of the concept of culture on the concept of man. In E. A. Hammal & W. S. Simmons (Eds.), *Man makes sense* (pp. 47–65). Boston: Little, Brown.

Gendolla, G. H. E. (2001). On the impact of mood on behavior: An integrative theory and a review. *Review of Psychology, 4*, 378–408.

George, J. M. (1990). Personality, affect, and behavior in groups. *Journal of Applied Psychology, 75*, 107–116.

George, J. M. (1992). The role of personality in organizational life: Issues and evidence. *Journal of Management, 18*, 185–210.

George, J. M. (1995). Leader positive mood and group performance: The case of customer service. *Journal of Applied Social Psychology, 25*, 778–794.

George, J. M. (1996). Trait and state affect. In K. M. Murphy (Ed.), *Individual differences in behavior in organizations* (pp. 145–171). San Francisco, CA: Jossey-Bass.

George, J. M. (2000). Emotions and leadership: The role of emotional intelligence. *Human Relations, 53*, 1027–1055.

George, J. M., Jones, G., & Gonzalez, J. A. (1998). The role of affect in cross-cultural negotiations. *Journal of International Business Studies, 29*(4), 749–772.

George, J. M., & Zhou, J. (2002). Understanding when bad moods foster creativity and good ones don't: The role of context and clarity of feelings. *Journal of Applied Psychology, 87*, 687–697.

Gerard, H. B., & Hoyt, M. F. (1974). Distinctiveness of social categorization and attitude toward ingroup members. *Journal of Personality and Social Psychology, 29*, 836–842.

Gergen, K. (1994). *Realities and relationships.* Cambridge, MA: Harvard University Press.

Gerth, H., & Mills, C. W. (1953). *Character and social structure: The psychology of social institutions.* New York: Harcourt, Brace and World.

Gherardi, S. (1999). Learning as problem-driven or learning in the face of mystery? *Organization Studies, 20*(1), 101–124.

Giacalone, R. A., & Knouse, S. B. (1990). Justifying wrongful employee behavior: The role of personality in organizational sabotage. *Journal of Business Ethics, 9*(1), 55–61.

Giddens, A. (1991). *Modernity and self-identity.* Cambridge: Polity Press.

Gilbert, J. A., & Ivancevich, J. M. (2000). Valuing diversity: A tale of two organizations. *Academy of Management Executives, 24*(1), 93–105.

Giles, H. (1973). Communication effectiveness as a function of accented speech. *Speech Monographs, 40*, 330–331.

Ginsberg, A. (1988). Measuring and modelling changes in strategy: Theoretical foundations and empirical directions. *Strategic Management Journal, 9*, 559–575.

Glomb, T. M., Miner, A. G., & Tews, M. J. (2002, April). *An experience sampling analysis of emotional dissonance at work.* Paper presented in Emotional Labor: Emerging From Merky Waters With Multi-Method, Multimeasure Approaches, C. S. Daus & T. M. Glomb (Chairs), Symposium conducted at the 2002 meeting of the Society for Industrial Organizational Psychology, Toronto, Canada.

Glomb, T. M., & Tews, M. J. (2004). Emotional labor: A conceptualization and scale development. *Journal of Vocational Behavior, 64*, 1–23.

Goffman, E. (1959). *The presentation of the self in everyday life [Vårt rollespill til daglig]*. New York: Doubleday Anchor.

Goffman, E. (1961). *Encounters*. Indianapolis, IN: Bobbs-Merrill.

Goleman, D. (1995). *Emotional intelligence: Why it can matter more than IQ*. New York: Bantam Books.

Goleman, D. (1998). *Working with emotional intelligence*. London: Bloomsbury.

Gollwitzer, P. M. (1990). Action phases and mind-sets. In E. T. Higgins & R. M. Sorrentino (Eds.), *Handbook of motivation and cognition: Foundations of social behavior* (pp. 53–92). New York: Guilford Press.

Gordon, S. (1981). The sociology of sentiments and emotion. In M. Rosenberg & R. Turner (Eds.), *Social psychology: Sociological perspectives* (pp. 562–592). New York: Basic Books.

Gordon, S. (1989). Institutional and impulsive orientations in selectively appropriating emotions to self. In D. D. Franks & E. Doyle McCarthy (Eds.), *The sociology of emotions: Original essays and research paper* (pp. 115–136). Greenwich, CT: JAI Press.

Gordon, S. (1990). Social structural perspectives on emotions. In T. D. Kemper (Ed.), *Research agendas in the sociology of emotions* (pp. 145–179). Albany: State University of New York Press.

Gottleib, J. Z., & Sanzgiri, J. (1996). Towards an ethical dimension of decision making in organizations. *Journal of Business Ethics, 15*, 1275–1285.

Graham, E. E. (1995). The involvement of sense of humor in the development in social relationships. *Communication Reports, 8*(2), 158–169.

Grandey, A. (1998, August). *Emotional labor: A concept and its correlates*. Paper presented at the First Conference on Emotions in Organizational Life, San Diego, CA.

Grandey, A. A. (1999). *The effects of emotional labor: Employee attitudes, stress and performance (customer service)*. Unpublished doctoral dissertation, Colorado State University, Denver.

Grandey, A. A. (2000, April). Emotion regulation in the workplace: A new way to conceptualize emotional labor. *Journal of Occupational Health Psychology, 5*(1), 95–110.

Grandey, A. A. (2001). *A dramaturgical perspective of emotional labor: Surface acting and deep acting as predictors of friendly service and burnout*. Unpublished manuscript, Pennsylvania State University, State College.

Grandey, A. A. (2002, April). *Emotional labor as emotional regulation: Test of a framework*. Paper presented in Emotional Labor: Emerging From Merky Waters With Multi-Method, Multi-measure Approaches, C. S. Daus & T. M. Glomb (Chairs), Symposium conducted at the 2002 meeting of the Society for Industrial Organizational Psychology, Toronto, Canada.

Grandey, A. A. (2003). When the "show must go on": Surface acting and deep acting as determinants of emotional exhaustion and peer-rated service delivery. *Academy of Management Journal, 46*(1), 86–96.

Graves, L. M., & Powell, G. N. (1995). The effect of sex similarity on recruiters' evaluations of actual applicants: A test of the similarity-attraction paradigm. *Personnel Psychology, 48*, 85–97.

Grawitch, M. J., Munz, D. C., Elliott, E. K., & Mathis, A. (2001). *Observing the group process of creative performance in temporary workgroups*. Unpublished manuscript, Saint Louis University, St. Louis, MO.

Grawitch, M. J., Munz, D. C., Elliott, E. K., & Mathis, A. (in press). Temporary workgroups and creativity: The effects of member mood and autonomy on group process and performance. *Group Dynamics: Theory, Research & Practice*.

Grawitch, M. J., Munz, D. C., & Kramer, T. J. (2003). Effects of member mood states on creative performance in temporary workgroups. *Group Dynamics: Theory, Research, and Practice, 7*, 41–54.

Greenberg, J. (1990). Employee theft as a reaction to underpayment inequity: The hidden cost of pay cuts. *Journal of Applied Psychology, 75*(5), 561–568.

Greenberg, J. (1993). Stealing in the name of justice: Informational and interpersonal moderators of theft reactions to underpayment inequity. *Organizational Behavior and Human Decision Processes, 54*(1), 81–103.

Greenberg, L., & Barling, J. (1999). Predicting employee aggression against coworkers, subordinates and supervisors: The roles of person behaviors and perceived workplace factors. *Journal of Organizational Behavior, 20*(6), 897–913.

Greenglass, E. R. (1995). Gender, work stress, and coping: Theoretical implications. *Journal of Social Behavior and Personality, 10*(2), 121–134.

Greenhaus, J. H., Prasuraman, S., & Wormley, W. M. (1990). Effects of race on organizational experiences, job performance evaluations, and career outcomes. *Academy of Management Journal, 33*, 64–86.

Griffeth, R. W., Hom, P. W., & Gaertner, S. (2000). A meta-analysis of antecedents and correlates of employee turnover: Update, moderator tests, and research implications for the next millennium. *Journal of Management, 26*(3), 463–488.

Grimen, H. (1995). Starka värderingar och holistisk liberalism. Inledning till Charles Taylors filosofi. In H. Grimen (Ed.), *Identitet, frihet och gemenskap* (pp. 1–93). Göteborg: Daidalos.

Grimsmo, A. (1996a, November 1). Arbeidsmiljøet verst i hotell og restaurant. *Næringslivets Ukeavis*. Oslo.

Grimsmo, A. (1996b). Norsk arbeidsmiljø i en endringstid: En rapport fra statistisk sentralbyrås Arbeidslivsundersøkelser 1989 og 1993. *AFIs Rapportserie* no. 4. Oslo: AFI.

Gross, J. J. (1998a). The emerging field of emotion regulation: An integrated review. *Review of General Psychology, 2*(3), 271–299.

Gross, J. J. (1998b). Antecedent- and response-focused emotion regulation: Divergent consequences for experience, expression, and physiology. *Journal of Personality and Social Psychology, 74*(1), 224–237.

Gross, J. J. (1999). Emotion regulation: Past, present, future. *Cognition and Emotion, 13*(5), 551–573.

Gross, J. J., Feldman-Barrett, L., & Richards, J. M. (1991). *Emotion regulation in everyday life.* Manuscript in preparation.

Gross, J. J., & Levenson, R. W. (1993). Emotional suppression: Physiology, self-report and expressive behavior. *Journal of Personality and Social Psychology, 64*, 970–986.

Gross, J. J., & Levenson, R. (1997). Hiding feelings: The acute effects of inhibiting negative and positive emotions. *Journal of Abnormal Psychology, 106*(1), 95–103.

Gudykunst, W. B., Yoon, Y., & Nishida, T. (1987). The influence of individualism–collectivism on perceptions of communication in in-group and out-group relationships. *Communication Monographs, 54*, 295–306.

Guerrier, Y. (1999). *Organizational behaviour in hotels and restaurants: An international perspective.* Chichester: Wiley.

Gump, B. B., & Kulick, J. A. (1997). Stress, affiliation, and emotional contagion. *Journal of Personality and Social Psychology, 72*, 305–319.

Guneriussen, W. (1996). *Aktør, handling, struktur: Grunnlagsproblemer I samfunnsvitenskapene.* Aurskog: Tano.

Guth, W. D., & MacMillan, I. C. (1986). Strategy implementation versus middle management self-interest. *Strategic Management Journal, 7*, 313–327.

Habermas, J. (1972). *Knowledge and human interests.* London: Heinemann.

Hackman, J. R., & Oldham, G. R. (1975). Development of the job diagnostic survey. *Journal of Applied Psychology, 60*(2), 159–170.

Hall, E. T. (1976). *Beyond culture.* Garden City, NY: Anchor Press.

Hall, C. S., & Lindzey, G. (1985). *Introduction to theories of personality.* New York: Wiley.

Hardy, G. E., & Barkham, M. (1994). The relationship between interpersonal attachment styles and work difficulties. *Human Relations, 47*, 263–282.

Hardy, C., Lawrence, T. B., & Phillips, N. (1998). Talk and action: Conversations and narrative in interorganizational collaboration. In C. Grand, T. B. Keenoy, & N. Orswick (Eds.), *Discourse and organizations* (pp. 65–83). London: Sage.

Harlos, K. P., & Pinder, C. C. (2000). Emotion and injustice in the workplace. In S. Fineman (Ed.), *Emotion in Organizations* (pp. 255–276). London: Sage.

Harquail, C. V. (1998). Organizational identification and the "whole person": Integrating affect, behavior and cognition. In D. A. Whetten & P. C. Godfrey (Eds.), *Identity in organizations: Developing theory through conversations* (pp. 223–231). Thousand Oaks, CA: Sage.

Harrison, D. A., Price, K. H., & Bell, M. P. (1998). Beyond relational demography: Time and the effects of surface- and deep level diversity on work group cohesion. *Academy of Management Journal, 41*, 96–107.

Härtel, C. E. J., & Fujimoto, Y. (1999). Explaining why diversity sometimes has positive effects in organizations and sometimes has negative effects in organizations: The perceived dissimilarity openness moderator model. *Academy of Management Best Papers Proceedings* (CD-ROM).

Härtel, C. E. J., & Fujimoto, Y. (2000). Diversity is not the problem: Openness to perceived dissimilarity is. *Journal of the Australian and New Zealand Academy of Management, 5*, 14–27.

Hartel, C. E. J., Hsu, A. C. F., & Boyle, M. V. (2002). A conceptual examination of the causal sequences of emotional labor, emotional dissonance, and emotional exhaustion: The argument for the role of contextual and provider characteristics. In N. M. Ashkanasy, C. E. J. Härtel, & W. J. Zerbe (Eds.), *Managing emotions in a changing workplace* (pp. 25–44). Armonk, NY: M. E. Sharpe.

Härtel, C. E. J., Kibby, L., & Pizer, M. (2003). Intelligent emotions management. In D. Tourish & O. Hargie (Eds.), *Key issues on organizational communication* (pp. 130–143). London: Routledge.

Härtel, C. E. J., & Zerbe, W. J. (2000). Commentary: Emotions as an organizing principle. In N. M. Ashkanasy, C. E. J. Härtel, & W. J. Zerbe (Eds.), *Emotions in the workplace: Research, theory, and practice* (pp. 97–100). Westport, CT: Quorum Books.

Härtel, C. E. J., & Zerbe, W. J. (2002). Myths about emotions during change. In N. M. Ashkanasy, C. E. J. Härtel, & W. J. Zerbe (Eds.), *Managing emotions in the workplace* (pp. 70–74). Armonk: M. E. Sharpe.

Hatch, M. J. (1997). Irony and the social construction of contradiction in the humor of a management team. *Organization Science, 8*, 275–288.

Hatch, M. J., & Ehrlich, S. B. (1993). Spontaneous humor as an indicator of paradox and ambiguity in organizations. *Organization Studies, 14*, 505–526.

Hatfield, E., Cacioppo, J. T., & Rapson, R. L. (1992). Primitive emotional contagion. In M. S. Clark (Ed.), *Review of personality and social psychology: Emotion and social behavior* (pp. 25–59). Newbury Park, CA: Sage.

Hatfield, E., Cacioppo, J., & Rapson, R. (1994). *Emotional contagion.* New York: Cambridge Press.

Hays, R. B. (1984). The development and maintenance of friendship. *Journal of Social and Personal Relationships, 1*, 75–98.

Hazan, C., & Shaver, P. (1990). Love and work: An attachment-theoretical perspective. *Journal of Personality and Social Psychology, 59*, 270–280.

Heidegger, M. (1996). *Being and time.* Albany: State University of New York Press. (Original work published 1927)

Heifetz, R. A., & Linsky, M. (2002). *Leadership on the line.* Boston: Harvard Business School Press.

Hewstone, M., & Ward, C. (1985). Ethnocentrism and causal attribution in Southeast Asia. *Journal of Personality and Social Psychology, 48*(3), 614–623.

Higgins, C. A., Judge, T. A., & Ferris, G. R. (2003). Influence tactics and work outcomes: A meta-analysis. *Journal of Organizational Behavior, 24*(1), 89–106.

Higgins, E. T. (1998). Promotion and prevention: Regulatory focus as a motivational principle. *Advances in Experimental Social Psychology, 30*, 1–46.

Hobbes, T. (1994). *The element of law, natural, and politic (Part I)*. New York: Oxford University Press. (Original work published 1650)

Hochschild, A. R. (1979). Emotion work, feeling rules and social structure. *American Journal of Sociology, 85*(3), 551–575.

Hochschild, A. R. (1983). *The managed heart: Commercialization of human feeling.* Berkeley: University of California Press.

Hochschild, A. R. (1993). Preface. In S. Fineman (Ed.), *Emotion in organizations* (pp. ix–xiii). London: Sage.

Hoffman, M. L. (1984). Interaction of affect and cognition in empathy. In C. E. Izard, J. Kagan, & R. B. Zajonc (Eds.), *Emotions, cognition, and behavior* (pp. 103–131). Cambridge, England: Cambridge University Press.

Hofstede, G. (1980). *Culture's consequences: International differences in work-related values.* Beverly Hills, CA: Sage.

Hofstede, G. (1986). Cultural differences in teaching and learning. *International Journal of Intercultural Relations, 10*, 301–320.

Hofstede, G. (2001). *Culture's consequences* (2nd ed.). Thousand Oaks, CA: Sage.

Hogan, R. (1969). Development of an empathy scale. *Journal of Consulting and Clinical Psychology, 33*, 307–316.

Hogan, R., Raskin, R., & Fazzini, D. (1990). The dark side of charisma. In K. E. Clark & M. B. Clark (Eds.), *Measures of leadership* (pp. 343–354). West Orange, NJ: Leadership Library of America.

Hogg, M. A., & Vaughan, G. M. (1998). *Social psychology* (2nd ed.). Hemel Hempstead, UK: Prentice Hall Europe.

Holland, J. L. (1959). A theory of vocational choice. *Journal of Counseling Psychology, 6*, 35–45.

Holland, J. L. (1985). *Making vocational choices: A theory of vocational personalities and work environments* (2nd ed.). Englewood Cliffs, NJ: Prentice Hall.

Hollander, E. P. (1961). Emergent leadership and social influence. In L. Petrullo & B. Bass (Eds.), *Leadership and interpersonal behavior* (pp. 30–47). New York: Holt, Rinehart & Winston.

Hollander, E. P. (1964). *Leaders, groups, and influence.* New York: Oxford University Press.

Hollander, E. P. (1985). Leadership and power. In G. Lindzey & E. Aronson (Eds.), *Handbook of social psychology* (3rd ed., pp. 485–537). New York: Random House.

Hollander, E. P., & Offerman, L. R. (1990). Power and leadership in organizations: Relationships in transition. *American Psychologist, 45*, 179–189.

Hollinger, R. C. (1986). Acts against the workplace: Social bonding and employee deviance. *Deviant Behavior, 7*(1), 53–75.

Holman, D., Chissick, C., & Totterdell, P. (2002). The effects of performance monitoring on emotional labor and well-being in call centers. *Motivation and Emotion, 16*(1), 57–81.

Höpfl, H., & Linstead, S. (1997). Introduction. Learning to feel and feeling to learn: Emotion and learning in organizations. *Management Learning, 28*(1), 5–12.

Hornsey, M., & Gallois, C. (1998). The impact of interpersonal and intergroup communication accommodation on perceptions of Chinese students in Australia. *Journal of Language & Social Psychology, 17*(3), 323–348.

Hosking, D., & Fineman, S. (1990). Organizing processes. *Journal of Management Studies, 27*(6), 583–604.

Hubbard, G., Backett-Milburn, K., & Kemmer, D. (2001). Working with emotion: Issues for the researcher in fieldwork and teamwork. *International Journal of Social Research Methodology, 4*(2), 119–137.

Hulin, C. L. (1990). Adaptation, persistence, and commitment in organizations. In M. D. Dunnette & L. M. Hough (Eds.), *Handbook of industrial organizational psychology* (2nd ed., pp. 445–505). Palo Alto, CA: Consulting Psychologists Press.

Hulin, C. L., Roznowski, M., & Hachiya, D. (1985). Alternative opportunities and withdrawal decisions: Empirical and theoretical discrepancies and an integration. *Psychological Bulletin, 97*, 233–250.

Humphrey, R. H. (2000). The importance of job characteristics to emotional displays. In N. M. Ashkanasy, C. E. J. Härtel, & W. J. Zerbe (Eds.), *Emotions in the workplace: Research, theory, and practice* (pp. 236–249). Westport, CT: Quorum Books.

Humphrey, R. H. (2002). Special issue on emotions in leadership. *Leadership Quarterly, 13*(5), 493–504.

Hunter, J. E., & Schmidt, F. L. (1990). *Methods of meta-analysis: Correcting errors and biases in research findings*. Newbury Park, CA: Sage.

Huy, Q. (1999). Emotional capability, emotional intelligence, and radical change. *Academy of Management Review, 24*(2), 325–345.

Huy, Q. (2001). In praise of middle managers. *Harvard Business Review, 79*(8), 72–79.

Huy, Q. (2002). Emotional balancing: The role of middle managers in radical change. *Administrative Science Quarterly, 47*, 31–69.

Ibarra, H. (1999). Provisional selves: Experimenting with image and identity in professional adaptation. *Administrative Science Quarterly, 44*, 764–791.

Ilgen, D. R., Major, D. A., & Tower, S. L. (1994). The cognitive revolution in organizational behavior. In J. Greenberg (Ed.), *Organizational behavior: The state of the science* (pp. 1–22). Hillsdale, NJ: Lawrence Erlbaum Associates.

Isen, A. M. (1985). The asymmetry of happiness and sadness in effects on memory in normal college students. *Journal of Experimental Psychology, 114*, 388–391.

Isen, A. M. (2000). Positive affect and decision making. In M. Lewis & J. M. Haviland-Jones (Eds.), *Handbook of emotions* (2nd ed., pp. 417–435). New York: Guilford Press.

Isen, A. M., & Baron, R. A. (1991). Positive affect as a factor in organizational behavior. In B. M. Staw & L. L. Cummings (Eds.), *Research in organizational behavior* (Vol. 13, pp. 1–54). Greenwich, CT: JAI Press.

Isen, A. M., & Means, B. (1983). The influence of positive affect on decision-making strategy. *Social Cognition, 2*(1), 18–31.

Izard, C. E., & Ackerman, B. P. (2000). Motivational, organizational and regulatory functions of discrete emotions. In M. Lewis & J. M. Haviland-Jones (Eds.), *Handbook of emotions* (2nd ed., pp. 253–264). New York: Guilford Press.

Jackson, S. E., Schwab, R. L., & Schuler, R. S. (1986). Toward an understanding of the burnout phenomenon. *Journal of Applied Psychology, 71*, 630–640.

Jackson, S. E., Stone, V. K., & Alvarez, E. B. (1993). Socialization amidst diversity: Impact of demographics on work team oldtimers and newcomers. In L. L. Cumming & B. M. Staw (Eds.), *Research in organizational behavior* (pp. 45–109). Greenwich, CT: JAI Press.

Jahoda, M. (1981). Work, employment, and unemployment: Values, theories, and approaches to social research. *American Psychologist, 36*, 184–191.

James, L. R., Demaree, R. G., & Wolf, G. (1984). Estimating within-group interrater reliability with and without response bias. *Journal of Applied Psychology, 69*, 85–98.

James, N. (1989). Emotional labour: Skill and work in the social regulation of feelings. *Sociological Review, 37*(1), 15–28.

James, N. (1993). Divisions of emotional labour: Disclosure and cancer. In S. Fineman (Ed.), *Emotion in organizations* (pp. 94–117). London: Sage.

James, W. (1884). What is an emotion? *Mind, 9*(34), 188–205.

Janis, I. L. (1972). *Victims of groupthink*. Boston: Houghton Mifflin.

Janis, I. L. (1982). *Victims of groupthink: A psychological study of foreign policy decisions and fiasco* (2nd ed.). Boston: Houghton Mifflin.

Jehn, K. (1997). A qualitative analysis of conflict types and dimensions in organizational groups. *Administrative Science Quarterly, 42*, 530–557.

Jessor, R., & Jessor, S. (1977). *Problem behaviour and psychosocial development*. New York: Academic Press.

Jones, E., Gallios, C. E., Callan, V., & Barker, M. (1995). Language and power in an academic context: The effects of status, ethnicity, and sex. *Journal of Language and Social Psychology, 14*(4), 434–461.

Jones, E., Gallios, C. E., Callan, V., & Barker, M. (1999). Strategies of accommodation: Development of a coding system for conversational interaction. *Journal of Language and Social Psychology, 18*(2), 123–153.

Jones, H. B. (2001). Magic, meaning and leadership: Weber's model and the empirical literature. *Human Relations, 54*, 753–771.

Jordan, P. J., Ashkanasy, N. M., & Härtel, C. E. J. (2000). Job insecurity and innovation. A bounded emotionality analysis. In L. N. Dosier & J. B. Keys (Eds.), *Academy of Management Best Paper Proceedings* (CD-ROM). Pleasantville, NY: Academy of Management.

Jordan, P. J., Ashkanasy, N. M., Härtel, C. E. J., & Hooper, G. S. (2002). Work group emotional intelligence: Scale development and relationship to team process effectiveness and goal focus [Special Issue]. *Human Resource Management Review, 12*(2), 195–214.

Jöreskog, K. G., & Sörbom, D. (1993). *LISREL 8: Structural equation modeling with the SIMPLIS command language*. Chicago: Scientific Software International, Inc.

Josselson, R. (1992). *The space between us*. San Francisco: Jossey-Bass.

Judge, T. A., & Larsen, R. J. (2001). Dispositional affect and job satisfaction: A review and theoretical extension. *Organizational Behavior and Human Decision Processes, 86*, 67–98.

Kahn, R., & Katz, D. (1960). Leadership practices in relation to productivity and morale. In D. Cartwright & A. Zander (Eds.), *Group dynamics: Research and theory* (pp. 612–628). Elmsford, NY: Row, Paterson.

Kahn, R. L., Wolfe, D. M., Quinn, R. P., Snoek, J. D., & Rosenthal, R. A. (1964). *Organizational stress: Studies in role ambiguity and conflict*. New York: Wiley.

Kahn, W. A. (1992). To be fully there: Psychological presence at work. *Human Relations, 45*, 321–350.

Kahn, W. A. (2001). Holding environments at work. *Journal of Applied Behavioral Science, 37*, 260–279.

Kant, I. (1914). *Critique of judgment*. London: Macmillan. (Original work published 1790)

Kanter, R. A. (1977). *Men and women of the corporation*. New York: Harper.

Kanter, R. M. (1983). *The change masters*. New York: Simon & Schuster.

Karabanow, J. (2000). The organizational culture of a street kid agency: Understanding employee reactions to pressures to feel. In N. M. Ashkanasy, C. E. J. Härtel, & W. J. Zerbe (Eds.), *Emotions in the workplace: Research, theory, and practice* (pp. 165–176). Westport, CT: Quorum Books.

Katzenbach, J. R., & Smith, D. K. (1994). *The wisdom of teams: Creating the high-performance organization*. New York: HarperBusiness.

Kelly, J., & Barsade, S. (2001). Moods and emotions in small groups and work teams. *Organizational Behavior and Human Decision Processes, 86*, 99–130.

Keltner, D., & Anderson, C. (2000). Saving face for Darwin: The functions and uses of embarrassment. *Current Directions in Psychological Science, 9*, 187–191.

Keltner, D., & Buswell, B. (1997). Embarrassment: Its distinct form and appeasement functions. *Psychological Bulletin, 122*, 250–270.

Keltner, D., & Gross, J. J. (1999). Functional accounts of emotions. *Cognition and Emotion, 13*(5), 467–480.

Kemper, T. (1978). *A social interactional theory of emotions*. New York: Wiley.

Kemper, T. D. (1984). Power, status, and emotions: A sociological contribution to a psychophysiological domain. In K. Scherer & P. Ekman (Eds.), *Approaches to emotion* (pp. 369–384). Hillsdale, NJ: Lawrence Erlbaum Associates.

Kerr, S. (1995). On the folly of rewarding A, while hoping for B. *Academy of Management Executive, 9*(1), 7–14.

Kets de Vries, M. F. R., & Balazs, K. (1997). The downside of downsizing. *Human Relations, 50*(1), 11–50.

Kidd, J. M. (1998). Emotion: An absent presence in career theory. *Journal of Vocational Behavior, 52*, 275–288.

Kim, U., Triandis, H. C., Kagitcibasi, C., Choi, S., & Yoon, G. (1994). Introduction. In U. Kim, H. C. Triandis, C. Kagitcibasi, S. Choi, & G. Yoon (Eds.), *Individualism collectivism: Theory, method and applications* (pp. 1–16). Newbury Park, CA: Sage.

Kirkeby, O. F. (2001). *Organisationsfilosofi—En studie i liminalitet.* København: Samfundslitteratur.

Klein, M. (1975). *The origins of transference, envy and gratitude and other works.* London: Hogarth Press. (Original work published 1952)

Knights, D., & Willmott, H. C. (1987). Organizational culture as management strategy: A critique and illustration from the financial service industries. *International Studies of Management & Organization, 17*, 40–63.

Kossek, E. E., & Lobel, S. A. (1996). *Managing diversity: Human resource strategies for transferring the work place.* Malden, MA: Blackwell.

Kotter, J. P. (1995). Leading change: Why transformation efforts fail. *Harvard Business Review, 73*(1), 59–67.

Kral, B. (2000). *The eyes of Jane Elliott.* http://www.horizonmag.com/4/jane-elliott.asp (retrieved 7 March 2002).

Kramer, T. J., Fleming, G. P., & Mannis, S. M. (2001). Improving face-to-face brainstorming through modeling and facilitation. *Small Group Research, 32*, 558–575.

Kruml, S., & Geddes, D. (1998a, August). *Exploring the dimensions of emotional labor: The heart of Hochschild's work.* Paper presented at the First Conference of Emotions in Organizational Life, San Diego, CA.

Kruml, S., & Geddes, D. (1998b, August). *Catching fire without burning out: Is there an ideal way to perform emotion labor.* Paper presented at the First Conference of Emotions in Organizational Life, San Diego, CA.

Kruml, S. M., & Geddes, D. (2000). Catching fire without burning out: Is there an ideal way to perform emotional labor? In N. M. Ashkanasy, C. E. J. Härtel, & W. J. Zerbe (Eds.), *Emotions in the workplace: Research, theory, and practice* (pp. 177–188). Westport, CT: Quorum Books.

Kuhl, J., & Beckmann, J. (1985). *Action control: From cognition to behavior.* New York: Springer-Verlag.

Kunda, G. (1992). *Engineering culture.* Philadelphia: Temple University Press.

Kunda, G., & Van Maanen, J. (1999, January). Changing scripts at work: Managers and professionals. *Annals of American Political and Social Science, 561*, 64–80.

Laird, J. D., Alibozak, T., Davainis, D., Deignan, K., Fontanella, K., Hong, J., Levy, B., & Pacheco, C. (1994). Individual differences in the effects of spontaneous mimicry on emotional contagion. *Motivation and Emotion, 18*, 231–247.

Langer, E. J. (1975). The illusion of control. *Journal of Personality and Social Psychology, 32*(2), 311–328.

Larsen, R. J. (2000). Toward a science of mood regulation. *Psychological Inquiry, 11*, 129–141.

Larsen, R. J., & Diener, E. E. (1992). Promises and problems with the circumplex model of emotion. In M. S. Clark (Ed.), *Review of personality and social psychology: Emotion and social behavior* (pp. 25–59). Newbury Park, CA: Sage.

Larsson, H. (1920). *Intuition.* Stockholm: Albert Bonniers Förlag. (Original work published 1892)

Lave, J., & Wenger, E. (1991). *Situated learning: Legitimate peripheral participation.* New York: Cambridge University Press.

Law, K. S., Wong, C. S., & Mobley, W. H. (1998). Toward a taxonomy of multidimensional constructs. *Academy of Management Review, 23*(4), 741–755.

Law, K. S., Song, L. J., & Wong, C. S. (2002, August). *Emotional intelligence as an intelligence facet: Construct validation and its predictive power of job outcomes.* Paper presented at the Academy of Management Meeting, Denver, CO.

Lawler, E. E., III. (1998). *Strategies for high performance organizations.* San Francisco: Jossey-Bass.

Lazarus, R. S. (1984). On the primacy of cognition. *American Psychologist, 39*(2), 124–129.

Lazarus, R. S. (1991). *Emotion and adaptation.* New York: Oxford University Press.

Le Bon, G. (1896). *The crowd: A study of the popular mind.* Marietta, GA: Cherokee Publishing.

LeDoux, J. (1996). *The emotional brain.* New York: Simon & Schuster.

LeDoux, J. (1998). Fear and the brain: Where have we been, and where are we going. *Biological Psychiatry, 44,* 1229–1238.

Lee, R. T., & Ashforth, B. E. (1996). A meta-analytic examination of the correlates of the three dimensions of job burnout. *Journal of Applied Psychology, 81*(2), 123–133.

Lefcourt, H. M. (2001). The humor solution. In C. R. Snyder (Ed.), *Coping with stress: Effective people and processes* (pp. 28–92). New York: Oxford University Press.

Lefcourt, H. M. & Martin, R. A. (1986). *Humor and life stress.* New York: Springer-Verlag.

Leidner, R. (1993). *Fast food, fast talk: Service work and the routinization of everyday life.* Berkeley: University of California Press.

Levenson, R. W., & Ruef, A. M. (1992). Empathy: A physiological substrate. *Journal of Personality and Social Psychology, 63,* 234–246.

Levine, J. (1977). Humour as a form of therapy: Introduction to symposium. In A. J. Chapmena & H. Foot (Eds.), *It's a funny thing, humour* (pp. 127–137). Oxford: Pergamon.

Levine, J. B. (1976). The feminine routine. *Journal of Communication, 26,* 173–175.

Levine, J. M., Higgins, E. T., & Choi, H. S. (2000). Development of strategic norms in groups. *Organizational Behavior and Human Decision Processes, 82,* 88–101.

Lindberg, F. (2001). *Ontological consumer research: Outline of the conceptual argument. Illustrated through tourist experiences.* Published doctoral dissertation, PhD series no. 16, Center of Market Economics. Copenhagen: Copenhagen Business School.

Linge, D. E. (1976). *Philosophical hermeneutics.* Berkeley: University of California Press.

Linnehan, F., & Konrad, A. M. (1999). Diluting diversity: Implications for intergroup inequality in organisations. *Journal of Management Inquiry, 8,* 399–414.

Linstead, S. (1985). Jokers wild: The importance of humour in the maintenance of organizational culture. *Sociological Review, 33,* 741–767.

Loher, B. T., Noe, R. A., Moeller, N. L., & Fitzgerald, M. P. (1985). A meta-analysis of the relation of job characteristics to job satisfaction. *Journal of Applied Psychology, 70,* 280–289.

Lois, J. (2001). Managing emotions, intimacy, and relationships in a volunteer search and rescue group. *Journal of Contemporary Ethnography, 30*(2), 131–179.

Lord, R. G., Klimoski, R. J., & Kanfer, R. (Eds.). (2002). *Emotions in the workplace: Understanding the structure and role of emotions in organizational behavior.* San Francisco: Jossey-Bass.

Lovibond, S. H., & Lovibond, P. F. (1995). *Manual for the depression anxiety stress scales* (2nd ed.). Sydney, Australia: Psychology Foundation of Australia.

Lucas, R. E., Diener, E., & Suh, E. (1996). Discriminant validity of well-being measures. *Journal of Personality and Social Psychology, 71*(3), 616–628.

Luijpen, W. A. (1962). *Existential phenomenology.* Pittsburgh: Duquesne University Press.

Luminet, O., Bouts, P., Delie, F., Manstead, A. S. R., & Rimé, B. (2000). Social sharing of emotion following exposure to a negatively valenced situation. *Cognition and Emotion, 14,* 661–688.

Lundberg, C. C. (1969). Person-focused joking: Patterns and function. *Human Organization, 28,* 22–28.

Mackie, D., Asuncion, A., & Rosselli, F. (1992). The impact of affective states on persuasion processes. In M. S. Clark (Ed.), *Review of personality and social psychology* (Vol. 14, pp. 247–270). Thousand Oaks, CA: Sage.

Magai, C., Hunziker, J., & Mesias, W. (2000). Adult attachment styles and emotional biases. *International Journal of Behavioral Development, 24,* 301–309.

Mainemelis, C. (2001). When the muse takes it all: A model for the experience of timelessness in organizations. *Academy of Management Review, 26*(4), 548–565.

Malone, P. B. (1980). Humor: A double-edged tool for today's managers? *Academy of Management Review, 5*, 357–360.

Manganelli Rattazzi, A. M., Canova, L., & Macorin, R. (1999). *La desiderabilità sociale. Un' analisi di forme brevi della scala di Marlow e Crowne* [Social desirability. Analysis of a short version of Marlow & Crowne's scale]. Manuscript, University of Padova, Padua, Italy.

Mann, S. (1999). Emotion at work: To what extent are we expressing, suppressing, or faking it? *European Journal of Work and Organizational Psychology, 8*(3), 347–369.

Manning, P. (1992). *Erving Goffman and modern sociology.* Cambridge, England: Polity Press.

Marks, M. A., Mathieu, J. E., & Zaccaro, S. J. (2001). A temporally based framework and taxonomy of team processes. *Academy of Management Review, 26,* 356–376.

Markus, H. R., & Kitayama, S. (1991). Culture and the self: Implications for cognition, emotion, and motivation. *Psychological Review, 98*(2), 224–253.

Marlow, D., & Crowne, D. P. (1961). Social desirability and response to perceived situational demands. *Journal of Consulting Psychology, 25,* 109–115.

Marsella, A. J., Devos, G., & Hsu, F. L. K. (1985). *Culture and the self.* London: Tavistock.

Martin, J. (1992). *Cultures in organizations: Three perspectives.* New York: Oxford University Press.

Martin, R. A. (2000). Humor and laughter. In A. E. Kazdin (Ed.), *Encyclopedia of psychology* (Vol. 4, pp. 202–204). Washington, DC: American Psychological Association.

Martin, J., & Frost, P. (1996). The organizational culture war games: A struggle for intellectual dominance. In S. R. Clegg, C. Hardy, & W. R. Nord (Eds.), *Handbook of organization studies* (pp. 599–621). London: Sage.

Martin, J., Knopoff, K., & Beckman, C. (1998). An alternative to bureaucratic impersonality and emotional labor: Bounded emotionality at The Body Shop. *Administrative Science Quarterly, 43,* 429–470.

Martin, L. L., Ward, D. W., Achee, J. W., & Wyer, R. S. (1993). Mood as input: People have to interpret the motivational implications of their moods. *Journal of Personality and Social Psychology, 64,* 317–326.

Martinez-Pons, M. (1997). The relation of emotional intelligence with selected areas of personal functioning. *Imagination, Cognition and Personality, 17*(1), 3–13.

Martinko, M. J., Gundlach, M. J., & Douglas, S. C. (2001, March). *Toward an integrative theory of counterproductive workplace behavior: A causal reasoning perspective.* Paper presented at the meeting of Southern Management Association, New Orleans, LA.

Martinko, M. J., & Zellars, K. L. (1998). Toward a theory of workplace violence and aggression: A cognitive appraisal perspective. In R. W. Griffin, A. O'Leary-Kelly, & J. M. Collins (Eds.), *Dysfunctional behavior in organizations: Nonviolent dysfunctional behavior* (pp. 1–42). Stamford, CT: JAI Press.

Martinsen, K. (1989). *Omsorg, sykepleie og medisin: Historisk-filosofiske essays.* Otta: Tano.

Mascolo, W. F., & Griffin, S. (1998). Alternative trajectories in the development of anger-related appraisals. In M. F. Mascolo & S. Griffin (Eds.), *What develops in emotional development?* (pp. 219–249). New York: Plenum Press.

Mascolo, W. F., & Harkins, D. (1998). Toward a component systems model of emotional development. In M. F. Mascolo & S. Griffin (Eds.), *What develops in emotional development?* (pp. 189–217). New York: Plenum Press.

Maslach, C. (1982). *Burnout: The cost of caring.* Englewood Cliffs, NJ: Prentice Hall.

Maslach, C., & Jackson, S. E. (1981a). *The Maslach Burnout Inventory.* Palo Alto, CA: Consulting Psychologist Press.

Maslach, C., & Jackson, S. E. (1981b). The measurement of experienced burnout. *Journal of Occupational Behavior, 2,* 99–113.

Maslach, C., & Jackson, S. E. (1984). Patterns of burnout among a national sample of public contact workers. *Journal of Health and Human Resources Administration, 7,* 189–212.

Maslow, A. H. (1970). *Motivation and personality* (2nd ed.). New York: Harper.

Mastenbroek, W. (2000). Organizational behavior as emotion management. In N. M. Ashkanasy, C. E. J. Härtel, & W. J. Zerbe (Eds.), *Emotions in the workplace: Research, theory, and practice* (pp. 19–35). Westport, CT: Quorum Books.

Matsumoto, D. (1993). Ethnic differences in affect intensity. *Motivation and Emotion, 17*(2), 107–123.

Matteson, M. T., & Ivancevich, J. M. (1987). *Controlling work stress: Effective human resource and management strategies.* San Francisco, CA: Jossey-Bass.

May, R. (1983). *The discovery of being.* New York: W. W. Norton.

Mayer, J. D. (2000). Understanding personality organization helps clarify mood regulation. *Psychological Inquiry, 11,* 196–199.

Mayer, J. D. (2001). A field guide to emotional intelligence. In J. Ciarrochi, J. P. Forgas, & J. D. Mayer (Eds.), *Emotional intelligence in everyday life* (pp. 3–24). Philadelphia, PA: Psychology Press.

Mayer, J. D., Caruso, D. R., & Salovey, P. (2000). Emotional intelligence meets traditional standards for an intelligence. *Intelligence, 27*(4), 267–298.

Mayer, J. D., DiPaolo, M., & Salovey, P. (1990). Perceiving affective content in ambiguous visual stimuli: A component of emotional intelligence. *Journal of Personality Assessment, 54*(3/4), 772–781.

Mayer, J. D., & Salovey, P. (1997). What is emotional intelligence? In P. Salovey & D. J. Sluyter (Eds.), *Emotional development and emotional intelligence: Educational implications* (pp. 3–34). New York: Basic Books.

McLead, P. L., & Lobel, S. A. (1992). The effects of ethnic diversity on idea generation in small groups. *Academy of Management Best Paper Proceeding,* pp. 227–231.

McLean Parks, J., & Kidder, D. L. (1994). Till death us do part . . . : Changing work relationships in the 1990s. In C. L. Cooper & D. M. Rousseau (Eds.), *Trends in organizational behavior* (pp. 112–133). New York: Wiley.

McLean Parks, J., & Schmedemann, D. A. (1994). When promises become contracts: Implied contract and handbook provisions on job security. *Human Resource Management, 33*(3), 403–423.

Menzies, I. E. P. (1970). *The functioning of social systems as a defense against anxiety: A report on a study of the nursing service at a general hospital.* London: Tavistock Institute of Human Relations.

Meisiek, S. (2002). *Social sharing of emotion in strategic adaptation: Evidence from a small business venture.* Unpublished manuscript, Stockholm School of Economics, Stockholm.

Messer, S. B., & Warren, C. S. (1995). *Models of brief psychodynamic therapy: A comparative approach.* New York: Guilford Press.

Mesquita, B., & Frijda, N. H. (1992). Cultural variations in emotions: A review. *Psychological Bulletin, 112*(2), 179–204.

Meyer, J. P., & Allen, N. J. (1991). A three-component conceptualization of organizational commitment. *Human Resource Management Review, 1,* 61–98.

Meyer, J. P., Allen, N. J., & Smith, C. A. (1993). Commitment to organizations and occupations: Extensions and test of a three-component conceptualization. *Journal of Applied Psychology, 78*(4), 538–555.

Middleton, D. (1989). Emotional style: The culture ordering of emotions. *Ethos, 17,* 187–207.

Milgram, S. (1963). Behavioral study of obedience. *Journal of Abnormal and Social Psychology, 67,* 371–378.

Milkie, M. A., & Peltola, P. (1999). Playing all the roles: Gender and the work–family balancing act. *Journal of Marriage and the Family, 61*(2), 476–490.

Miller, D. (1990). Organizational configurations: Cohesion, change, prediction. *Human Relations, 43,* 771–789.

Miller, E. (1995). The healthy organization for the 1990s. In S. Long (Ed.), *International perspectives on organizations in times of turbulence* (pp. 1–12). Melbourne, Australia: Swinburne University of Technology.

Miller, F. A. (1998). Strategic culture change: The door to achieving high performance and inclusion. *Public Personnel Management, 27*(2), 151–160.

Mintzberg, H. (1990, March–April). The manager's job: Folklore and fact. *Harvard Business Review*, pp. 163–177.

Mischel, W., Cantor, N., & Feldman, S. (1996). Principles of self-regulation: The nature of willpower and self-control. In E. T. Higgins & A. W. Kruglanski (Eds.), *Social psychology: Handbook of basic principles* (pp. 329–360). London: Guilford Press.

Mishkinsky, M. (1977). Humour as a "courage mechanism." *Israel Annals of Psychiatry and Related Disciplines, 15*, 352–363.

Mitchell, J. T. (1984, January). The 600-run limit. *Journal of Emergency Medical Services*, pp. 52–54.

Mitzman, A. (1969). *The iron cage: An historical interpretation of Max Weber.* New York: Enkopf.

Moliner, C., Martínez-Tur, V., Peiró, J. M., Ramos, J., & Cropanzano, R. (2003). *Linking justice to extra-role customer service: Does well-being at work mediate?* Unpublished manuscript.

Moody, R. (1978). *Laugh after laugh: The healing power of humor.* Jacksonville, FL: Headwaters Press.

Mor Barak, M. E. (2000). Beyond affirmative action: Toward an inclusive model of diversity and organizational inclusion. *Administration in Social Work, 23*(3/4), 47–68.

Moreland, R. L. (1985). Social categorization and the assimilation of "new" group members. *Journal of Personality and Social Psychology, 48*(5), 1173–1190.

Morgan, G. (1986). *Images of organizations.* Newbury Park, CA: Sage.

Morris, J. A., & Feldman, D. C. (1996). The dimensions, antecedents, and consequences of emotional labor. *Academy of Management Review, 21*(4), 986–1010.

Morris, J. A., & Feldman, D. C. (1997). Managing emotions in the workplace. *Journal of Managerial Issues, 9*(3), 257–274.

Morris, M. W., Williams, K. Y., Leung, K., Larrick, R., Mendoza, M. T., Bhatnagar, D., Li, J., Kondo, M., Luo, J., & Hu, J. (1998). Conflict management style: Accounting for cross-national differences. *Journal of International Business Studies, 29*(4), 729–748.

Morrison, E., & Robinson, S. L. (1997). When employees feel betrayed: A model of how psychological contract violation develops. *Academy of Management Review, 22*(1), 226–256.

Moscovici, S., & Paicheler, G. (1978). Social comparison and social recognition: Two complementary processes of identification. In H. Tajfel (Ed.), *Differentiation between social groups* (pp. 251–266). London: Academic Press.

Moses, J. L. (1987, March). A psychologist assesses today's AT&T managers. *Teleconnect*, pp. 32–36.

Motowidlo, S. J. (1986). Information processing in personnel decisions. In *Research in personnel and human resources management* (pp. 1–44). Greenwich, CT: JAI Press.

Motowidlo, S. J., Carter, G. W., Dunnette, M. D., Tippins, N., Werner, S., Burnett, J. R., & Vaughan, M. J. (1992). Studies of the structured behavioral interview. *Journal of Applied Psychology, 77*, 571–587.

Mumby, D. K., & Putnam, L. A. (1992). The politics of emotion: A feminist reading of bounded rationality. *Academy of Management Review, 17*(3), 465–486.

Mundy, L. (1998). The crying game. *Working Woman, 23*(6), 27–28.

Munz, D. C., Benaka, A., & Walters, J. (2000). *Thinking versus talking: Differential effects on mood and anticipated task performance.* Unpublished manuscript, Saint Louis University, St. Louis, MO.

Munz, D. C., Huelsman, T. J., Konold, T. R., & McKinney, J. J. (1996). Are there methodological and substantive roles for affectivity in job diagnostic survey relationships? *Journal of Applied Psychology, 81*(6), 795–805.

Muraven, M., Tice, D. M., & Baumeister, R. F. (1998). Self-control as a limited resource: Regulatory depletion patters. *Journal of Personality and Social Psychology, 74*, 774–789.

Myers, D. G., & Diener, E. (1995). Who is happy? *Psychological Science, 6*, 10–19.

Myhr, K. I. (2001, May 14). Syk av å smile på job. *Dagbladet*, p. 18.

Næss, A. (1998). *Livsfilosofi. Et personlig bidrag om følelser og fornuft*. Oslo: Universitetsforlaget.

Nelson, R. R., & Winter, S. G. (1982). *An evolutionary theory of economic change*. Cambridge, MA: Harvard University Press.

Nemanick, R. C., Jr., & Munz, D. C. (1997). Extraversion and neuroticism, trait mood, and state affect: A hierarchical relationship? *Journal of Social Behavior and Personality, 12*, 1079–1092.

Nerhardt, G. (1976). Incongruity and funniness: Towards a new descriptive model. In A. J. Chapman & H. C. Foot (Eds.), *Humor and laughter: Theory, research, and applications* (pp. 55–62). London: Wiley.

Neubert, M. J. (1999). Too much of a good thing or the more the merrier? Exploring the dispersion and gender composition of informal leadership in manufacturing teams. *Small Group Research, 30*, 635–646.

Neumann, R., & Strack, F. (2000). "Mood contagion": The automatic transfer of mood between persons. *Journal of Personality and Social Psychology, 79*, 211–223.

Noble, B. P. (1994, November 6). Still in the dark on diversity. *New York Times*, p. F27.

Noer, D. M. (1993). *Healing the wounds*. San Francisco: Jossey-Bass.

Nonaka, I. (1988, Spring). Toward middle-up-down management: Accelerating information creation. *Sloan Management Review*, pp. 9–18.

Nonaka, I. (1994). Dynamic theory of organizational knowledge creation. *Organization Science, 1*(3), 267–292.

Nonaka, I., & Takeuchi, N. (1995). *The knowledge-creating company*. New York: Oxford University Press.

Nord, W., & Fox, S. (1995). The individual in organizational studies: The great disappearing act? In *Handbook of organizational studies* (pp. 148–175).

Nussbaum, M. C. (1995). *Känslans skärpa tankens inlevelse: Essäer om etik och politik*. Stockholm: Brutus Östlings Bokförlag.

Nyeng, F. (2000). *Det autentiske menneske—Med Charles Taylors blikk på menneskevitenskap og moral*. Oslo: Fagbokforlaget.

Nygren, R., & Levine, E. L. (1996). Leadership of work teams: Factors influencing team outcomes. In M. M. Beyerlein, D. A. Johnson, & S. T. Beyerlein (Eds.), *Advances in interdisciplinary studies of work teams* (pp. 67–105). Greenwich, CT: JAI Press.

O'Connell, W. E. (1960). The adaptive function of wit and humor. *Journal of Abnormal and Social Psychology, 61*, 263–270.

Offner, A. K., Kramer, T. J., & Winter, J. P. (1996). The effects of facilitation, recording, and pauses on group brainstorming. *Small Group Research, 27*, 283–298.

O'Leary-Kelly, A. M., Griffin, R. W., & Glew, D. J. (1996). Organization-motivated aggression: A research framework. *Academy of Management Review, 21*(1), 225–253.

O'Neill, H. M., & Lenn, J. (1995). Voices of survivors: Words that downsizing CEOs should hear. *Academy of Management Executive, 9*(4), 23–34.

Organ, D. W., & Ryan, K. (1995). A meta-analytic review of attitudinal and dispositional predictors of organizational citizenship behavior. *Personnel Psychology, 48*(4), 775–802.

Orlitzky, M., & Hirokawa, R. Y. (2001). To err is human, to correct for it is divine: A meta-analysis of research testing the functional theory of group decision-making effectiveness. *Small Group Research, 32*, 313–341.

Palmer, C. E. (1983). "Trauma junkies" and street work: Occupational behaviour of paramedics and emergency medical technicians. *Urban Life, 12*(2), 162–183.

Parker, M. (2000). *Organizational culture and identity: Unity and division at work*. London: Sage.

Parkinson, B. (1996). Emotions are social. *British Journal of Psychology, 87*(4), 663–683.

Parkinson, B., & Totterdell, P. (1999). Classifying affect-regulation strategies. *Cognition and Emotion, 13,* 277–303.

Parkinson, B., Totterdell, P., Briner, R. B., & Reynolds, S. (1996). *Changing moods: The psychology of mood and mood regulation.* New York: Longman.

Paterson, J. M., & Härtel, C. E. J. (2002). An integrated affective and cognitive model to explain employees' responses to downsizing. In N. M. Ashkanasy, C. E. J. Härtel, & W. J. Zerbe (Eds.), *Managing emotions in a changing workplace* (pp. 25–44). Armonk, NY: M. E. Sharpe.

Paulus, P. B. (2000). Groups, teams, and creativity: The creative potential for idea-generating groups. *Applied Psychology: An International Review, 49,* 237–262.

Pavot, W., & Diener, E. (1993). Review of the Satisfaction With Life Scale. *Psychological Assessment, 5,* 164–172.

Payne, R., & Cooper, C. L. (Eds.). (2001). *Emotions at work: Theory, research and applications for management.* New York: Wiley.

Pearce, J. L., Sommer, S. M., Morris, A., & Frideger, M. (1992). *A configurational approach to interpersonal relations: Profiles of workplace social relations and task interdependence.* Working paper no. OB92015. Graduate School of Management, University of California, Irvine.

Pedrabissi, L., & Santinello, M. (1988). Professione infermieristica e sindrome del burnout: Un contributo alla taratura del Maslach Inventory Burnout [Nurses and burnout: A contribution in standardization of Maslach Inventory Burnout]. *Bollettino di Psicologia Applicata, 187–188,* 41–46.

Pekrun, R., & Frese, M. (1992). Emotions in work and achievement. *International Review of Industrial and Organizational Psychology, 7,* 153–200.

Pelled, L. H. (1996). Demographic diversity, conflict, and workgroup outcomes: An intervening process study. *Organizational Science, 7,* 615–631.

Pennebaker, R. W., & Hoover, C. W. (1986). Inhibition and cognition: Toward an understanding of trauma and disease. In R. J. Davidson, G. E. Schwartz, & D. Shapiro (Eds.), *Consciousness and self-regulation* (Vol. 4, pp. 107–136). New York: Wiley.

Perdue, C. W., Dovidio, J. F., Gurtman, M. B., & Tyler, R. B. (1990). Us and them: Social categorization and the process of intergroup bias. *Journal of Personality and Social Psychology, 59,* 475–486.

Perlow, L. A. (1999). The time famine: Toward a sociology of work time. *Administrative Science Quarterly, 44,* 57–81.

Perrewé, P. L., & Ganster, D. C. (1989). The impact of job demands and behavioral control on experienced job stress. *Journal of Organizational Behavior, 10,* 213–229.

Pescosolido, A. T. (2000). *Emotional intensity in groups.* Unpublished doctoral dissertation, Department of Organizational Behavior, Case Western Reserve University, Cleveland, OH.

Pescosolido, A. T. (2001). Informal leaders and the development of group efficacy. *Small Group Research, 32,* 74–93.

Petronio, S., Ellemers, N., Giles, H., & Gallois, C. (1998). (Mis)communicating across boundaries: Interpersonal and intergroup considerations. *Communication Research, 25*(6), 571–596.

Pettigrew, A. M. (2000). Foreword. In N. M. Ashkanasy, C. Wilderom, & M. F. Peterson (Eds.), *Handbook of organizational culture & climate* (pp. xiii–xv). Thousand Oaks, CA: Sage.

Phatak, A. V., & Habib, M. H. (1996). The dynamics of international business negotiations. *Business Horizons, 39*(3), 30–38.

Pierce, J. (1999). Emotional labor among paralegals. *Annals of the American Academy of Political and Social Science, 561,* 127–142.

Pierce, J. L., Gardner, D. G., Cumming, L. L., & Dunham, R. B. (1989). *Academy of Management, 32*(3), 622–648.

Pierro, A., & Fabbri, S. (1995). Modelli di analisi fattoriale confirmatoria: Il caso del MBI [Models of confirmatory factor analysis: The MBI]. *Bollettino di Psicologia Applicata, 213,* 51–57.

Pine, B. J., & Gilmore, J. H. (1998). *The experience economy: Work is theatre & every business a stage.* Boston: Harvard Business School Press.

Pirola-Merlo, A., Härtel, C. E. J., Mann, L., & Hirst, G. (2002). How leaders influence the impact of affective events on team climate and performance in R&D teams. *Leadership Quarterly*, *13*(5), 561–581.

Plutchik, R. (1980). A general psychoevolutionary theory of emotion. In R. Plutchik & H. Kellerman (Eds.), *Emotion: Theory, research, and experience* (pp. 3–33). New York: Academic Press.

Plutchik, R. (1989). Measuring emotions and their derivatives. In R. Plutchik & H. Kellerman (Eds.), *Emotion: Theory, research and experience* (pp. 1–35). New York: Academic Press.

Plutchik, R. (2001). The nature of emotions. *American Scientist, 89*(4), 344–344.

Podsakoff, P. M., MacKenzie, S. B., Paine, J. B., & Bachrach, D. G. (2000). Organizational citizenship behaviors: A critical review of the theoretical and empirical literature and suggestions for future research. *Journal of Management, 26*(3), 513–563.

Polanyi, M. (1958). *Personal knowledge*. Chicago: University of Chicago Press.

Polanyi, M. (1969). *Knowing and being*. Chicago: University of Chicago Press.

Polanyi, M. (1983). *The tacit dimension*. Gloucester, MA: Peter Smith. (Original work published 1966)

Polanyi, M., & Prosch, H. (1975). *Meaning*. Chicago: Phoenix.

Polkinghorne, D. E. (1988). *Narrative knowing and the human sciences*. Albany: State University of New York Press.

Pondy, L. R. (1967). Organizational conflict: Concepts and models. *Administrative Science Quarterly, 2*, 296–320.

Porter, R. E., & Samovar, L. A. (1998). Cultural influences on emotional expression: Implications for intercultural communication. In P. A. Andersen & L. K. Guerrero (Eds.), *Handbook of communication and emotion: Research, theory, applications, and contexts* (pp. 351–472). San Diego, CA: Academic Press.

Probst, T. M., Carnevale, P. J., & Triandis, H. C. (1999). Cultural values in intergroup and single-group social dilemmas. *Organizational Behavior and Human Decision Processes, 77*(3), 171–191.

Pugh, D. S. (1998, August). *Why do happy employees have happy customers? Emotional contagion as an explanatory concept in research on customer service*. Paper presented at the First Conference of Emotions in Organizational Life, San Diego, CA.

Pugh, S. D. (2001). Service with a smile: Emotional contagion in the service encounter. *Academy of Management Journal, 44*(5), 1018–1027.

Pugliesi, K. (1999). The consequences of emotional labor: Effects on work stress, job satisfaction, and well-being. *Motivation and Emotion, 23*(2), 135–154.

Pye, L. W. (1982). *Chinese commercial negotiating style*. Cambridge, MA: Oelgeschlager, Gunn & Hain.

Pye, L. W. (1990, July–August). The China trade: Making the deal. *Harvard Business Review*, pp. 74–84.

Quick, J. C. (1992). Crafting an organizational culture: Herb's hand at Southwest Airlines. *Organizational Dynamics, 21*, 45–56.

Quinn, J. B. (1992). *Intelligent enterprise*. New York: Free Press.

Rachman, S. (1974). *The meanings of fear*. Harmondsworth, UK: Penguin.

Rafaeli, A. (1989). When clerks meet customers: A test of variables related to emotion. *Journal of Applied Psychology, 74*(3), 385–394.

Rafaeli, A., & Sutton, R. I. (1987). Expression of emotion as part of the work role. *Academy of Management Review, 12*, 23–37.

Rafaeli, A., & Sutton, R. I. (1989). The expression of emotion in organizational life. In L. L. Cummings & B. M. Staw (Eds.), *Research in organizational behavior* (pp. 11–42). Greenwich, CT: JAI Press.

Rafaeli, A., & Sutton, R. I. (1990). Busy stores and demanding customers: How do they affect the display of positive emotion? *Academy of Management Journal, 33*(3), 623–637.

Ramamoorthy, N., & Carroll, J. (1998). Individualism/collectivism orientations and reactions toward alternative human resource management practices. *Human Relations, 51*(5), 571–588.

Ramina, S., & Huy, Q. (2002). *Streamline: The ABC of a merger. Case (A), (B) & (C).* INSEAD, Fontainebleau, France.

Redlich, F. C., Levine, J., & Sohler, T. P. (1951). A mirth response test: Preliminary report on a psychodiagnostic technique utilizing dynamics of humor. *American Journal of Orthopsychiatry, 21*, 717–734.

Redmond, M. V. (1989). The functions of empathy (decentering) in human relations. *Human Relations, 42*(7), 593–605.

Reger, R. K., Gustafson, L. T., Demarie, S. M., & Mullane, J. V. (1994). Reframing the organization: Why implementing total quality is easier said than done. *Academy of Management Review, 19*, 565–584.

Reichers, A. E., & Schneider B. (1990). Climate and culture: An evolution of constructs. In B. Schneider (Ed.), *Organizational climate and culture* (pp. 5–39). San Francisco: Jossey-Bass.

Reichers, A. E., Wanous, J. P., & Austin, J. T. (1997). Understanding and managing cynicism about organizational change. *Academy of Management Executive, 11*, 48–59.

Reisenzein, R., & Schoenpflug, W. (1992). Stumpf's cognitive-evaluation theory of emotion. *American Psychologist, 47*, 34–45.

Richards, J. M., & Gross, J. J. (1999). Composure at any cost? The cognitive consequences of emotional suppression. *Personality and Social Psychology Bulletin, 25*, 1033–1044.

Richards, J. M., & Gross, J. J. (2000). Emotion regulation and memory: The cognitive costs of keeping one's cool. *Journal of Personality and Social Psychology, 79*(3), 410–424.

Rimé, B. (1995). The social sharing of emotional experience as a source for the social knowledge of emotion. In J. A. Russell, J. M. Fernandez-Dols, A. S. R. Manstead, & J. C. Wellenkamp (Eds.), *Everyday conceptions of emotions. An introduction to the psychology, anthropology, and linguistics of emotion* (pp. 475–489). Dordrecht, the Netherlands: Kluwer.

Rimé, B., Finkenauer, C., Luminet, O., Zech, E., & Philippot, P. (1998). Social sharing of emotion: New evidence and new questions. *European Review of Social Psychology, 9*, 145–189.

Rimé, B., Mesquita, B., Philippot, P., & Boca, S. (1991). Beyond the emotional event: Six studies on the social sharing of emotion. *Cognition and Emotion, 5*, 435–465.

Rimé, B., Philippot, P., Boca, S., & Mesquita, B. (1992). Long-lasting cognitive and social consequences of emotion: Social sharing and rumination. In W. Stroebe & M. Hewstone (Eds.), *European review of social psychology* (Vol. 3, pp. 225–258). Chichester: Wiley.

Rimé, B., Philippot, P., & Cisamolo, D. (1990). Social schemata of peripheral changes in emotion. *Journal of Personality and Social Psychology, 59*, 38–49.

Robbins, S. P. (2003). *Organizational behavior.* Upper Saddle River, NJ: Prentice Hall.

Robinson, S. L., Kraatz, M. S., & Rousseau, D. M. (1994). Changing obligations and the psychological contract: A longitudinal study. *Academy of Management Journal, 37*(1), 137–152.

Robinson, S. L., & O'Leary-Kelly, A. M. (1998). Monkey see, monkey do: The influence of work groups on the antisocial behavior of employees. *Academy of Management Journal, 41*(6), 658–672.

Roeckelein, J. E. (2002). *The psychology of humor: A reference guide and annotated bibliography.* Westport, CT: Greenwood Press.

Rogers, E. M. (1995). *Diffusion of innovations* (4th ed.). London: Free Press.

Rokeach, K. (1960). *The open and closed mind.* New York: Basic Books.

Rokeach, M., & Mezei, L. (1966). Race and shared belief as actors in social choice. *Science, 151*, 167–172.

Romanelli, E., & Tushman, M. L. (1994). Organizational transformation as punctuated equilibrium: An empirical test. *Academy of Management Journal, 37*(5), 1141–1166.

Ronan, W. W., & Latham, G. P. (1974). The reliability and validity of the critical incident technique: A closer look. *Studies in Personnel Psychology, 6*, 53–64.

Roosevelt, T. R., Jr. (1996). *Redefining diversity.* New York: American Management Association.

Ross, L., & Nisbett, R. E. (1991). *The person and the situation: Perspectives of social psychology.* Philadelphia: Temple University Press.

Rousseau, D. M. (1989). Psychological and implied contracts in organizations. *Employee Responsibilities and Rights Journal, 2,* 322–337.

Roy, D. F. (1960). Banana time: Job satisfaction and informal interaction. *Human Organization, 18,* 158–168.

Rubin, J. Z., Pruitt, D. G., & Kim, S. H. (1994). *Social conflict: Escalation, stalemate, and settlement* (2nd ed.). New York: McGraw-Hill.

Russell, J. A. (1980). A circumplex model of affect. *Journal of Personality and Social Psychology, 39,* 1161–1178.

Russell, J. A (1991). Culture and the categorization of emotions. *Psychological Bulletin, 110*(3), 426–450.

Russell, J. A., Lewicka, M., & Niit, T. (1989). A cross-cultural study of a circumplex model of affect. *Journal of Personality and Social Psychology, 57,* 848–856.

Ryan, R. M., & Deci, E. L. (2000). Self-determination theory and the facilitation of intrinsic motivation, social development, and well-being. *American Psychologist, 55,* 68–78.

Saarni, C. (1993). Socialization of emotion. In M. Lewis & J. M. Haviland (Eds.), *Handbook of emotion* (pp. 435–446). New York: Guilford Press.

Saavedra, R., & Kwun, S. K. (2000). Affective states in job characteristics theory. *Journal of Organizational Behavior, 21,* 131–142.

Salovey, P., Bedell, B. T., Detweiler, J. B., & Mayer, J. D. (2000). Current directions in emotional intelligence research. In M. Lewis & J. M. Haviland-Jones (Eds.), *Handbook of emotions* (2nd ed., pp. 504–520). New York: Guilford Press.

Salovey, P., Hsee, C. K., & Mayer, J. D. (1993). Emotional intelligence and the self-regulation of affect. In D. M. Wegner & J. W. Pennebaker (Eds.), *Handbook of mental control* (pp. 258–277). Englewood Cliffs, NJ: Prentice Hall.

Salovey, P., & Mayer, J. D. (1990). Emotional intelligence. *Imagination, Cognition, and Personality, 9*(3), 185–211.

Salovey, P., Mayer, J. D., Goldman, S. L., Turvey, C., & Palfai, T. P. (1995). Emotional attention, clarity, and repair: Exploring emotional intelligence using the trait meta-mood scale. In J. W. Pennebacker (Ed.), *Emotion disclosure and health* (pp. 125–154). Washington, DC: American Psychological Association.

Sandelands, L. E., & Boudens, C. J. (2000). Feeling at work. In S. Fineman (Ed.), *Emotion in organizations* (2nd ed., pp. 46–63). London: Sage.

Sankowsky, D. (1995). The charismatic leader as narcissist: Understanding the abuse of power. *Organizational Dynamics, 23,* 57–75.

Schaubroeck, J., & Jones, J. R. (2000). Antecedents of workplace emotional labor dimensions and moderators of their effects on physical symptoms. *Journal of Organizational Behavior, 21*(2), 163–183.

Schein, E. H. (1990). Organizational culture. *American Psychologist, 45*(2), 109–119.

Schein, E. H. (1992). *Organizational culture and leadership* (2nd ed.). San Francisco: Jossey-Bass.

Schein, E. H. (1996). Kurt Lewin's change theory in the field and in the classroom: Notes toward a model of managed learning. *Systems Practice, 9,* 27–47.

Schein, E. H. (2000). Sense and nonsense about culture and climate. In N. M. Ashkanasy, C. Wilderom, & M. F. Peterson (Eds.), *Handbook of organizational culture and climate* (pp. xxiii–xxx). Thousand Oaks, CA: Sage.

Scherer, K. R. (1984). Emotions as a multicomponent process. A model and some cross-cultural data. In P. Shaver (Eds.), *Review of personality and social psychology: Vol. 5. Emotions, relationships, and health* (pp. 37–63). London: Sage.

Scherer, K. R. (1986). Vocal affect expression: A review and a model for future research. *Psychological Bulletin, 99*(2), 143–165.

Schneider, B. (1987). The people make the place. *Personnel Psychology, 40,* 437–453.

Schneider, B. (2000). The psychological life of organizations. In N. M. Ashkanasy, C. Wilderom, & M. F. Peterson (Eds.), *Handbook of organizational culture and climate* (pp. xvii–xxi). Thousand Oaks, CA: Sage.

Schneider, B., & Bowen, D. E. (1999). Understanding customer delight and outrage. *Sloan Management Review, 41*(1), 35–45.

Schön, D. (1983). *The reflective practitioner: How professionals think in action.* New York: Basic Books.

Schultz, M., & Hatch, M. J. (1996). Living with multiple paradigms—The case of paradigm interplay in organizational culture studies. *Academy of Management Review, 21*, 529–557.

Schwartz, S. (1986). *Classic studies in psychology.* Palo Alto, CA: Mayfield.

Scodel, A., & Mussen, P. (1953). Social perceptions of authoritarian and nonauthoritarian. *Journal of Abnormal and Social Psychology, 48*, 181–184.

Seashore, S. E., Lawler, E. E., Mirvis, P., & Cammann, C. (Eds.). (1982). *Observing and measuring organizational change: A guide to field practice.* New York: Wiley.

Seligman, M. E. P., & Csikszentmihalyi, M. (2000). Positive psychology. *American Psychologist, 55*, 5–14.

Shaver, P., Schwartz, J., Kirson, D., & O'Connor, L. (1987). Emotion knowledge: Further exploration of a prototype approach. *Journal of Personality and Social Psychology, 52*, 1061–1086.

Sheldon, K. M., & Elliott, A. J. (1999). Goal striving, need satisfaction and longitudinal well-being: The self-concordance model. *Journal of Personality and Social Psychology, 76*, 482–497.

Shell, G. R. (2001). Bargaining styles and negotiation: The Thomas-Kilmann Conflict Mode Instrument in negotiation training. *Negotiation Journal, 17*(2), 155–174.

Shenkar, O., & Simcha, R. (1987). The cultural context of negotiations: The implications of Chinese interpersonal norms. *Journal of Applied Behavioral Science, 23*(2), 263–275.

Sherif, M. (1966). *Common predicament: Social psychology of intergroup conflict and cooperation.* Boston: Houghton Mifflin.

Shott, S. (1979). Emotion and social life: A symbolic interactionist analysis. *American Journal of Sociology, 84*(6), 1317–1334.

Shrivastava, P. (1986). Is strategic management ideological? *Journal of Management, 12*(3), 363–377.

Shrout, J. L., & Fleiss, P. E. (1979). Intraclass correlations: Uses in assessing rater reliability. *Psychological Bulletin, 86*(2), 420–428.

Siehl, C., & Martin, J. (1990). Organizational culture: A key to financial performance? In B. Schneider (Ed.), *Organizational climate and culture* (pp. 241–281). San Francisco: Jossey-Bass.

Simon, B., Pantaleo, G., & Mummendey, A. (1995). Unique individual or interchangeable group member? The accentuation of intragroup differences versus similarities as an indicator of the individual self versus the collective self. *Journal of Personality and Social Psychology, 69*(1), 106–119.

Simon, H. (1997). *Administrative behavior.* New York: Free Press.

Simon, H. A. (1976). *Administrative behavior: A study of decision-making processes in administrative organization* (3rd ed.). New York: Free Press.

Sinclair, M., & Ashkanasy, N. (2001, July). *Intuition: Myth or a decision-making tool?* Paper presented at the 17th Colloquium of EGOS, Lyon.

Singelis, T. M. (1994). The measurement of independent and interdependent self-construals. *Personality and Social Psychology Bulletin, 20*(5), 580–591.

Sirigatti, S., & Stefanile, C. (1992). Aspetti e problemi dell'adattamento italiano del MBI [Aspects and problems of Italian adaptation of MBI]. *Bollettino di Psicologia Applicata, 202–203*, 3–12.

Sirigatti, S., Stefanile, C., & Menoni, E. (1988). Per un adattamento italiano del Maslach Burnout Inventory (MBI) [Italian adaptation of Maslach Burnout Inventory]. *Bollettino di Psicologia Applicata, 187–188*, 33–39.

Sjöstrand, S.-E. (1997). *The two faces of management: The Janus factor.* London: International Thomson Business Press.

Skårderud, F. (2002). Kunsten å forholde seg. In J. Skavlan (Ed.), *Frisk nok for livet* (pp. 227–241). Oslo: Pantagruel Forlag.

Smircich, L., & Calas, M. B. (1987). Organizational culture: A critical assessment. In F. M. Jablin, L. L. Putnam, K. H. Roberts, & L. W. Porter (Eds.), *Handbook of organizational communication: An interdisciplinary perspective* (pp. 228–263). Newbury Park, CA: Sage.

Smith, A. C., & Kleinman, S. (1989). Managing emotions in medical school: Students' contacts with the living and the dead. *Social Psychology Quarterly, 52*(1), 56–69.

Smith, J. A., & Foti, R. J. (1998). A pattern approach to the study of leader emergence. *Leadership Quarterly, 9,* 147–160.

Snyder, C. R., Harris, C., Anderson, J. R., Holleran, S. A., Irving, L. M., Sigmon, S. T., Yoshinobu, L., Gibb, J., Langelle, C., & Harney, P. (1991). The will and the ways: Development and validation of an individual-differences measure of hope. *Journal of Personality and Social Psychology, 60,* 570–585.

Snyder, M. (1974). Self-monitoring of expressive behavior. *Journal of Personality and Social Psychology, 30,* 526–537.

Snyder, M., & Miene, P. K. (1994). Stereotyping of the elderly: A functional approach. *British Journal of Social Psychology, 33*(1), 63–82.

Solomon, R. C. (2000). The philosophy of emotions. In M. Lewis & J. M. Haviland (Eds.), *Handbook of emotions* (pp. 3–15). New York: Guilford Press.

Spector, P. E. (1978). Organizational frustration: A model and review of the literature. *Personnel Psychology, 31*(4), 815–829.

Spector, P. E. (1996). *Industrial and organizational psychology: Research and practice.* New York: Wiley.

Spector, P. E. (1997). The role of frustration in antisocial behavior at work. In R. A. Giacalone & J. Greenberg (Eds.), *Antisocial behavior in organization* (pp. 1–17). Newbury Park, CA: Sage.

Spector, P. E., & Fox, S. (2002). An emotion-centered model of voluntary work behavior: Some parallels between counterproductive work behavior (CWB) and organizational citizenship behavior (OCB) [Special issue]. *Human Resource Management Review, 12*(2), 269–292.

Spencer-Oatey, H. (1997). Unequal relationships in high and low power distance societies: A comparative study of tutor-student role relations in Britain and China. *Journal of Cross-Cultural Psychology, 28,* 284–302.

Spitzer, W. J., & Neely, K. (1992). Critical incident stress: The role of hospital-based social work in developing a statewide intervention system for first responders delivering emergency services. *Social Work in Health Care, 18*(1), 39–58.

Stablein, R., & Nord, W. R. (1985). Practical and emancipatory interests in organizational symbolism: A review and evaluation. *Journal of Management, 11,* 13–28.

Staw, B. M., & Barsade, S. G. (1993). Affect and managerial performance: A test of the sadder-but-wiser vs. happier-and-smarter hypotheses. *Administrative Science Quarterly, 38*(2), 304–331.

Staw, B., Sandelands, L., & Dutton, J. (1981). Threat-rigidity effects in organizational behavior: A multi-level analysis. *Administrative Science Quarterly, 26*(4), 501–524.

Staw, B. M., Sutton, R. R., & Pelled, L. H. (1994). Employee positive emotion and favorable outcomes at the workplace. *Organization Science, 5*(1), 51–71.

Steiner, I. D. (1972). *Group process and productivity.* New York: Academic Press.

Stephan, W. G. (1999). *Reducing prejudice and stereotyping in schools.* New York: Teachers College Press.

Stephan, W. G., & Stephan, C. W. (1993). Cognition and affect in stereotyping: Parallel interactive networks. In D. Makie & D. Hamilton (Eds.), *Affect, cognition and stereotyping: Interactive processes in group perception* (pp. 111–136). Orlando, FL: Academic Press.

Stephan, W. G., Ybarra, O., Martínez, C. M., Schwarzwald, J., & Tur-Kaspa, M. (1998). Prejudice toward immigrants to Spain and Israel: An integrated threat theory analysis. *Journal of Cross-Cultural Psychology, 29*(4), 559–576.

Stipek, D. (1998). Differences between Americans and Chinese in the circumstances evoking pride, shame, and guilt. *Journal of Cross-Cultural Psychology, 29*(5), 616–629.

Stokes, J. (1998). The unconscious at work in groups and teams: Contributions from the work of Wilfred Bion. In A. Obholzer & V. Z. Roberts (Eds.), *The unconscious at work* (pp. 19–27). London: Routledge.

Stone, R. J. (2002). *Human resource management.* Milton, Queensland: John Wiley & Sons Australia.

Storms, P. L., & Spector, P. E. (1987). Relationships of organizational frustration with reported behavioral reactions: The moderating effect of perceived control. *Journal of Occupational Psychology, 60*(3), 227–234.

Strati, A. (1998). Organizational symbolism as a social construction: A perspective from the sociology of knowledge. *Human Relations, 51*(11), 1379–1402.

Strati, A. (2000, July). *Aesthetics, tacit knowledge and organizational learning.* Paper presented at 16th EGOS Colloquium, Helsinki, 2nd theme group on Action, Learning and Collective Practice.

Strati, A. (2001, July). *Aesthetics, tacit knowledge and symbolic understanding: Going beyond the pillars of cognitivism in organization studies.* Paper presented at 17th EGOS Colloquium, Lyon, Group: Knowing as Desire.

Strauss, A. L., & Corbin, J. (1994). Grounded theory methodology: An overview. In Y. Lincoln & N. Denzin (Eds.), *Handbook of qualitative research* (pp. 273–285). Thousand Oaks, CA: Sage.

Strazdins, L. (2002). Emotional work and emotional contagion. In N. M. Ashkanasy, W. J. Zerbe, & C. E. J. Härtel (Eds.), *Managing emotions in the workplace* (pp. 232–250). Armonk, NY: M. E. Sharpe.

Stroebe, W., & Stroebe, M. (1996). The social psychology of social support. In E. T. Higgins & A. W. Kruglanski (Eds.), *Social psychology: Handbook of basic principles* (pp. 597–621). New York: Guilford Press.

Sturdy, A., & Fleming, P. (2001, July). *Talk as technique—A critique of the words and deeds distinction in the diffusion of customer service cultures.* Paper presented at 17th EGOS Colloquium, Lyon Conference.

Styre, A., Ingelgard, A., Beausang, P., Castenfors, M., Mulee, K., & Roth, J. (2002). Emotion management and stress: Managing ambiguities. *Organization Studies, 23*(1), 83–103.

Suh, E., Diener, E., Oishi, S., & Triandis, H. C. (1998). The shifting basis of life satisfaction judgements across cultures: Emotions versus norms. *Journal of Personality and Social Psychology, 74*, 482–493.

Suls, J. M. (1972). A two-stage model for the appreciation of jokes and cartoons: An information processing analysis. In J. H. Goldstein & P. E. McGhee (Eds.), *The psychology of humor* (pp. 81–100). New York: Academic Press.

Sundstrom, E., DeMeuse, K. P., & Futrell, D. (1990). Work teams: Applications and effectiveness. *American Psychologist, 45*, 120–133.

Sutton, R. I. (1991). Maintaining norms about expressed emotions: The case of bill collectors. *Administrative Science Quarterly, 36*(2), 245–268.

Sutton, R. I., & Rafaeli, A. (1988). Untangling the relationship between displayed emotions and organizational sales: The case of convenience stores. *Academy of Management Journal, 31*(3), 461–487.

Swierczek, F. W. (1990). Culture and negotiation in the Asian context: Key issues in the marketing of technology. *Journal of Managerial Psychology, 5*(5), 17–24.

Swinkels, A., & Giuliano, T. A. (1995). The measurement and conceptualization of mood awareness: Monitoring and labeling one's mood states. *Personality and Social Psychology Bulletin, 21*, 934–949.

Sykes, A. J. M. (1966). Joking relationships in an industrial setting. *American Anthropologist, 68*, 188–193.

Taggar, S., Hackett, R., & Saha, S. (1999). Leadership emergence in autonomous work teams: Antecedents and outcomes. *Personnel Psychology, 52*, 899–926.

Tajfel, H. (1981). *Human groups and social categories: Studies in social psychology.* Cambridge: Cambridge University Press.

Tangney, J. P. (1995). Shame and guilt in interpersonal relationships. In J. P. Tangney & K. W. Fischer (Eds.), *Self-conscious emotions: Shame, guilt, and embarrassment, and pride* (pp. 114–139). New York: Wiley.

Tangney, J. P., & Fischer, K. W. (Eds.). (1995). *Self-conscious emotions: Shame, guilt, and embarrassment, and pride.* New York: Wiley.

Taylor, C. (1985). Human agency and language. *Philosophical Papers, Vol. 1.* Cambridge: Cambridge University Press.

Taylor, C. (1995). *Identitet, frihet och gemenskap.* Göteborg: Daidalos.

Taylor, D. M., & Jaggi, V. (1974). Ethnocentrism and causal attribution in a south Indian context. *Journal of Cross-Cultural Psychology, 5*(2), 162–171.

Tews, M. J., & Glomb, T. M. (2000, August). *The feelings at work scale: Theoretical basis, development of the instrument, and preliminary validity testing.* Paper presented at the Second Conference on Emotions and Organizational Life, Toronto, Ontario.

Tews, M. J., & Glomb, T. M. (2004). Emotional labor: A conceptualization and scale development. *Journal of Vocational Behavior, 64*(1), 1–23.

Thakerar, J. N., Giles, H., & Cheshire, J. (1982). Psychological and linguistic parameters of speech accommodation theory. In C. Fraser & K. R. Scherer (Eds.), *Advances in the social psychology of language* (pp. 205–255). Cambridge: Cambridge University Press.

Thayer, R. E. (1967). Measurement of activation through self-report. *Psychological Reports, 20*, 663–678.

Thayer, R. E. (1978). Factor analytic and reliability studies on the Activation-Deactivation Adjective Check List. *Psychological Reports, 42*, 747–756.

Thayer, R. E., Newman, J. R., & McClain, T. M. (1994). Self-regulation of mood: Strategies for changing a bad mood, raising energy, and reducing tension. *Journal of Personality and Social Psychology, 67*, 910–925.

Thoits, P. (1984). Coping, social support and psychological outcomes: The central role of emotion. In P. Shaver (Ed.), *Review of personality and social psychology* (pp. 219–238). Beverly Hills, CA: Sage.

Thoits, P. (1985). Self-labelling processes in mental illness: The role of emotional deviance. *American Journal of Sociology, 91*, 221–249.

Thoits, P. A. (1989). The sociology of emotions. *Annual Review of Sociology, 15*, 317–342.

Thoits, P. A. (1991). Patterns in coping with controllable and uncontrollable events. In E. M. Cummings, A. L. Greene, & K. H. Karraker (Eds.), *Life-span developmental psychology: Perspectives on stress and coping* (pp. 235–258). Hillsdale, NJ: Lawrence Erlbaum Associates.

Thompson, J. D. (1967). *Organizations in action: Social science bases of administrative theory.* New York: McGraw-Hill.

Thompson, S. C. (1981). Will it hurt less if I can control it? A complex answer to a simple question. *Psychological Bulletin, 90*(1), 89–101.

Thompson, S. C., Armstrong, W., & Thomas, C. (1998). Illusions of control, underestimations, and accuracy: A control heuristic explanation. *Psychological Bulletin, 123*(2), 143–161.

Thorndike, E. L. (1920). Intelligence and its uses. *Harper's Magazine, 140*, 227–235.

Ting-Toomey, S., & Oetzel, J. G. (2001). *Managing intercultural conflict effectively.* Thousand Oaks, CA: Sage.

Tomkins, S. S. (1984). Affect theory. In P. Ekman (Ed.), *Emotion in the human face* (2nd ed., pp. 353–395). New York: Cambridge University Press.

Tourish, D., & Pinnington, A. (2002). Transformational leadership, corporate cultism and the spirituality paradigm: An unholy trinity in the workplace? *Human Relations*, *55*, 147–172.

Tourish, D., & Wohlforth, T. (2000). Prophets of the Apocalypse: White supremacy and the theology of Christian identity. *Cultic Studies Journal*, *17*, 15–41.

Triandis, H. C. (1972). *The analysis of subjective culture*. New York: Wiley.

Triandis, H. C. (1980). *Values, attitudes and interpersonal behavior*. Lincoln: University of Nebraska Press.

Triandis, H. C. (1986). The measurement of the etic aspects of individualism and collectivism across cultures. *Australian Journal of Psychology*, *38*(3), 257–265.

Triandis, H. C. (1989). The self and social behavior in differing cultural contexts. *Psychological Review*, *96*, 506–520.

Triandis, H. C. (1990). Cross-cultural studies of individualism and collectivism. In J. Berman (Ed.), *Cross-cultural perspective. Current theory and research in motivation* (pp. 41–133). Nebraska Symposium on Motivation. Lincoln: University of Nebraska Press.

Triandis, H. C. (1998). Vertical and horizontal individualism and collectivism: Theory and research application for international comparative management. In J. Cheng & R. Peterson (Eds.), *Advances in international comparative management* (pp. 7–35). Stamford, CT: JAI Press.

Triandis, H. C., Dunnette, M. D., & Hough, L. M. (1994). *Handbook of industrial and organizational psychology* (Vol. 4, 2nd ed.). Palo Alto, CA: Consulting Psychologists Press.

Trice, H. M., & Beyer, J. M. (1993). *The cultures of work organizations*. Englewood Cliffs, NJ: Prentice Hall.

Trompenaars, F. (1993). *Riding the waves of culture: Understanding cultural diversity in business*. London: Nicholas Brearey.

Tse, D. K., Francis, F., & Walls, J. (1994). Cultural differences in conducting intra- and intercultural negotiations: A Sino-Canadian comparison. *Journal of International Business Studies*, *25*(3), 537–555.

Tsui, A. S., Egan, T. D., & O'Reilly, C. A. (1992). Being different: Relational demography and organizational attachment. *Administrative Science Quarterly*, *37*, 549–579.

Tsui, A. S., Egan, T. D., & Porter, L. W. (1994, August). *Performance implications of relational demography in vertical dyads*. Paper presented at the 54th annual meeting of the Academy of Management, Dallas.

Tsui, A. S., & O'Reilly, C. A. (1989). Beyond simple demographic effects: The importance of relational demography in superior-subordinate dyads. *Academy of Management Journal*, *32*(2), 402–423.

Tuckman, B. W. (1965). Developmental sequence in small groups. *Psychological Bulletin*, *63*, 384–399.

Tung, R. L. (1991). Handshakes across the sea: Cross-cultural negotiating for business success. *Organizational Dynamics*, *19*(3), 30–40.

Tunstall, W. B. (1985). *Disconnecting parties*. New York: McGraw-Hill.

Turner, J. C., & Oakes, P. J. (1989). Self-categorization theory and social influence. In P. B. Paulus (Ed.), *Psychology of group influence* (pp. 233–275). Hillsdale, NJ: Lawrence Erlbaum Associates.

Tushman, M. L., & Romanelli, E. (1985). Organizational evolution: A metamorphosis model of convergence and reorientation. In L. L. Cummings & B. Staw (Eds.), *Research in organizational behavior* (pp. 171–222). Greenwich, CT: JAI Press.

Uhl-Bien, M., & Graen, G. B. (1998). Individual self-management: Analysis of professionals' self-managing activities in functional and cross-functional work teams. *Academy of Management Journal*, *41*, 340–350.

Unsworth, K. (2001). Unpacking creativity. *Academy of Management Review*, *26*, 289–297.

Uyterhoeven, H. (1989). General managers in the middle. *Harvard Business Review*, *5*, 136–145.

Van Maanen, J. (1988). *Tales of the field: On writing ethnography*. Chicago: University of Chicago Press.

Van Maanen, J. (1991). The smile factory: Work in Disneyland. In P. Frost, L. F. Moore, M. Reis Louis, C. C. Lundberg, & J. Martin (Eds.), *Reframing organizational culture* (pp. 58–76). Greenwich, CT: JAI Press.

Van Maanen, J., & Kunda, G. (1989). "Real feelings": Emotional expression and organizational culture. In L. L. Cummings & B. M. Staw (Eds.), *Research in organizational behavior* (Vol. 11, pp. 43–103). Greenwich, CT: JAI Press.

Vince, R., & Broussine, M. (1996). Paradox, defense and attachment: Accessing and working with emotions and relations underlying organizational change. *Organization Studies, 17*(1), 1–21.

Vinton, K. L. (1989). Humor in the workplace: It is more than telling jokes. *Small Group Behavior, 20*, 151–166.

Wagner, F. R., & Morse, J. J. (1975). A measure of individual sense of competence. *Psychological Reports, 36*, 451–459.

Wagner, J. A., & Moch, M. K. (1986). Individualism–collectivism: Concept and measure. *Group and Organization Studies, 11*(3), 280–304.

Wakefield, J. C. (1989). Levels of explanation in personality theory. In D. M. Buss & N. Cantor (Eds.), *Personality psychology: Recent trends and emerging directions* (pp. 333–346). New York: Springer-Verlag.

Wasielewski, P. L. (1985). The emotional basis of charisma. *Symbolic Interaction, 8*, 207–222.

Watson, D. (2000). *Mood and temperament*. New York: Guilford Press.

Watson, D., & Clark, L. A. (1997). Measurement and mismeasurement of mood: Recurrent and emergent issues. *Journal of Personality Assessment, 68*, 267–296.

Watson, D., Clark, L. A., & Tellegen, A. (1988). Development and validation of brief measures of positive and negative affect: The PANAS scales. *Journal of Personality and Social Psychology, 54*, 1063–1070.

Watson, D., Wiese, D., & Vaidya, J. (1999). The two general activation systems of affect: Structural findings, evolutionary considerations, and psychobiological evidence. *Journal of Personality and Social Psychology, 76*(5), 820–838.

Wayne, S. J., & Ferris, G. R. (1990). Influence tactics, affect and exchange quality in supervisor–subordinate interactions: A laboratory experiment and field study. *Journal of Applied Psychology, 75*, 487–499.

Weber, M. (1946). The sociology of charismatic authority. In H. H. Gerth & C. W. Mills (Eds.), *Max Weber: Essays in sociology* (pp. 245–250). New York: Oxford University Press.

Weber, M. (1947). *The theory of social and economic organization*. London: Free Press.

Weick, K. (1979). *The social psychology of organizing*. New York: McGraw-Hill.

Weick, K. E. (1995). *Sensemaking in organization*. Thousand Oaks, CA: Sage.

Weiss, H. M. (Ed.). (2001). Special issue—Affect at work: Collaborations of basic and organizational research. *Organizational Behavior and Human Decision Processes, 86*(1).

Weiss, H. M. (Ed.). (2002). Special issue on emotional experiences at work. *Motivation and Emotions, 26*(1).

Weiss, H. M. (2003). Connecting levels in the study of emotions in organizations. In F. Dansereau & F. J. Yammarino (Eds.), *Research in multi-level issues, Vol. 2: Multi-level issues in organizational behavior and strategy* (pp. 9–54). Oxford, UK: Elsevier Science.

Weiss, H. M., & Brief, A. P. (2001). Affect at work: An historical perspective. In R. L. Payne & C. L. Cooper (Eds.), *Emotions at work: Theory, research, and application in management* (pp. 133–177). Chichester, UK: Wiley.

Weiss, H. M., & Cropanzano, R. (1996). Affective events theory: A theoretical discussion of the structure, causes and consequences of affective experiences at work. In B. M. Staw & L. L. Cummings (Eds.), *Research in organizational behavior* (pp. 1–74). Greenwich, CT: JAI Press.

Weiss, H. M., Nicolas, J. P., & Daus, C. S. (1999). An examination of the joint effects of affective experience and job beliefs on job satisfaction and variations in affective experience over time. *Organizational Behavior and Human Decision Processes, 78,* 1–24.

Weiss, J. W. (1996). *Organizational behavior and change: Managing diversity, cross-cultural dynamics and ethics.* St. Paul, MN: West.

Westley, F. (1990). Middle managers and strategy: Microdynamics of inclusion. *Strategic Management Journal, 11,* 337–351.

Wharton, A. S. (1993). The affective consequences of service work: Managing emotions on the job. *Work & Occupations, 20*(2), 205–232.

Wharton, A. S., & Erickson, R. J. (1993). Managing emotions on the job and at home: The consequences of multiple emotional roles. *Academy of Management Review, 18*(3), 457–486.

Wharton, A. S., & Erickson, R. J. (1995). The consequences of caring: Exploring the links between women's job and family emotion work. *Sociological Quarterly, 36*(2), 273–296.

Wheelan, S. A., & Johnston, F. (1996). The role of informal member leaders in a system containing formal leaders. *Small Group Research, 27,* 33–55.

Whitener, E. M. (1990). Confusion of confidence intervals and credibility intervals in meta-analysis. *Journal of Applied Psychology, 75*(3), 315–321.

Williams, L. J., Gavin, M. B., & Williams, M. L. (1996). Measurement and nonmeasurement processes with negative affectivity and employee attitudes. *Journal of Applied Psychology, 81,* 88–101.

Williams, K. J., Suls, J., Alliger, G. M., Learner, S. M., & Wan, C. K. (1991). Multiple role juggling and daily mood states in working mothers: An experience sampling study. *Journal of Applied Psychology, 76,* 664–674.

Willemyns, M., Gallois, C., Callan, V. J., & Pittam, J. (1997). Accent accommodation in the job interview: Impact of interviewer accent and gender. *Journal of Language and Social Psychology, 16*(1), 3–22.

Winnicott, D. W. (1965). *The maturational process and the facilitating environment.* New York: International University Press.

Wittgenstein, L. (1992). *Filosofiske undersökningar.* Stockholm: Basil Blackwell. (Original work published 1953)

Wolff, S. B., Pescosolido, A. T., & Druskat, V. U. (2002). Emotional intelligence as the basis of leadership emergence in self managing work teams. *Leadership Quarterly, 13,* 505–522.

Wong, C. S. (1997, May). The effects of organizational commitment and job satisfaction on turnover: The case of Hong Kong. *Proceedings of the Eighth International Conference on Comparative Management,* pp. 134–140. National Sun Yat-Sen University, Kaohsiung, Taiwan.

Wong, C. S., & Campion, M. A. (1991). Development and test of a task level model of motivational job design. *Journal of Applied Psychology, 76*(6), 825–837.

Wong, C. S., & Law, K. S. (2002). The effect of leaders' and followers' emotional intelligence on performance and attitudes: An exploratory study. *Leadership Quarterly, 13,* 243–274.

Wright, T. A., & Bonnett, D. G. (1997). The contribution of burnout to work performance: Results of a longitudinal field study. *Journal of Occupational and Organizational Psychology, 66,* 277–284.

Wright, T. A., & Cropanzano, R. (1998). Emotional exhaustion as a predictor of job performance and voluntary turnover. *Journal of Applied Psychology, 83*(3), 486–493.

Wright, T. A., & Staw, B. M. (1999). Affect and favorable work outcomes: Two longitudinal tests of the happy-productive worker thesis. *Journal of Organizational Behavior, 20,* 1–13.

Wysocki, B. J., Jr. (1995, July 5). Some companies cut costs too far, suffer corporate anorexia. *Wall Street Journal,* p. A1.

Yamada, A. M., & Singelis, T. M. (1999). Biculturalism and self-construal. *International Journal of Intercultural Relation, 23*(5), 697–709.

Yammarino, F. J. (1996). Group leadership: A levels of analysis perspective. In M. A. West (Ed.), *Handbook of work group psychology* (pp. 189–224). New York: Wiley.

Yik, M. S. M., Russell, J. A., & Feldman Barrett, L. (1999). Structure of self-reported current affect: Integration and beyond. *Journal of Personality and Social Psychology, 77*, 600–619.

Yukl, G. (1999). An evaluative essay on current conceptions of effective leadership. *European Journal of Work and Organizational Psychology, 8*, 33–48.

Zajonc, R. B. (1984). On the primacy of affect. *American Psychologist, 39*(2), 117–123.

Zammuner, V. L. (1995). Naive theories of emotional experience: Jealousy. In J. A. Russell, J. M. Fernandez Dols, A. S. R. Manstead, & J. C. Wellenkamp (Eds.), *Everyday conceptions of emotion* (pp. 435–456). Dordrecht: Kluwer.

Zammuner, V. L. (1996). Felt emotions, and verbally communicated emotions: The case of pride. *European Journal of Social Psychology, 26*, 233–245.

Zammuner, V. L. (2000a). Men's and women's lay theories of emotion. In A. H. Fischer (Ed.), *Gender and emotion* (pp. 48–60). Cambridge: Cambridge University Press.

Zammuner, V. L. (2000b). *The regulation of emotions, life satisfaction, and burnout in post office service-job employees*. Paper presented at the XI Meeting of the International Society for Research on Emotion (ISRE), Quebec City, Canada.

Zammuner, V. L., & Canato, M. (2000). Emotion regulation and its correlates in bank service jobs. In E. Holtz (Ed.), *Fairness & cooperation* (pp. 525–530). IAREP-SABE2000. Conference Proceedings, Vienna, Austria.

Zammuner, V. L., & Galli, C. (2002). *Emotion regulation and its correlates in job-services*. Paper presented at the XII Meeting of the International Society for Research on Emotion (ISRE) [Symposium: Taking Sides: The Politics of Emotion in Everyday Life], Cuenca, Spain.

Zammuner, V. L., Lotto, L., & Galli, C. (2002). Regulation of emotions in the helping professions: Nature, antecedents and consequences. In L. Morrow, I. Verins, & E. Willis (Eds.), *Mental health and work: Issues and perspectives* (pp. 217–231). Flinders University South Australia: Auseinet. Republished in Australian e-Journal for the Advancement of Mental Health (AeJAMH), March 2(1), 2003 (www.auseinet.com/journal).

Zapf, D., Vogt, C., Seifert, C., Mertini, H., & Isic, A. (1999). Emotion work as a source of stress. *European Journal of Work and Organizational Psychology, 8*(3), 371–400.

Zeithaml, V. Parasuraman, A., & Berry, L. L. (1990). *Delivering quality service: Balancing customer perceptions and expectations*. New York: Free Press.

Zenger, T. R., & Lawrence, B. S. (1989). Organizational demography: The differential effects of age and tenure distribution on technical communication. *Academy of Management Journal, 32*, 353–376.

Zerbe, W. J. (2000). Emotional dissonance and employee well-being. In N. M. Ashkanasy, C. E. J. Härtel, & W. J. Zerbe (Eds.), *Emotions in the workplace: Research, theory, and practice* (pp. 189–214). Westport, CT: Quorum Books.

Zhang, Y., & Neelankavil, J. P. (1997). The influence of culture on advertising effectiveness in China and the USA. *European Journal of Marketing, 31*(1/2), 134–150.

Zhao, J. J. (2000). The Chinese approach to international business negotiation. *Journal of Business Communication, 37*(3), 209–237.

Ziller, R. C. (1965). Toward a theory of open and closed groups. *Psychological Bulletin, 64*, 164–182.

Zillmann, D., & Stocking, S. H. (1976). Putdown humor. *Journal of Communication, 26*, 154–163.

Zurcher, L. A. (1982). The staging of emotion: A dramaturgical analysis. *Symbolic Interaction, 5*(1), 1–22.

Author Index

417

Snyder, M., 88, 109, 257
Sohler, T. P., 160
Solomon, R. C., 74
Song, L. J., 242
Spataro, S. E., 3
Spector, P. E., 67, 68, 69, 76, 78, 79, 80, 81, 82, 83, 84, 85, 203
Spencer-Oatey, H., 155, 156
Spitzer, W. J., 58
Spreitzer, G. M., 319
Staebler Tardino, V. M., xxiii, 189
Stablein, R., 338, 346
Stalker, G. M., 315
Staw, B. M., 2, 74, 78, 85
Stefanile, C., 268
Steiner, I. D., 323
Stela, K., 92
Stephan, C. W., 90
Stephan, W. G., 90, 92
Stipek, D., 92
Stocking, S. H., 146, 160
Stokes, J., 346
Stone, R. J., 172
Stone, V. K., 92
Storms, P. L., 78
Strack, F., 127
Strati, A., 15, 32
Strazdins, L., 343, 344, 345
Stroebe, M., 136, 311
Stroebe, W., 311
Styhre, A., 2
Suh, E., 258, 269
Suls, J., xi, 146
Sundstrom, E., 131, 132, 138, 141
Sutton, R. I., xi, 74, 190, 197, 199, 208, 215, 231, 239, 253
Swierczek, F. W., 181
Swinkels, A., 126
Sykes, A. J. M., 156

T

Taggar, S., 318, 319, 320
Tajfel, H., 92
Takeuchi, N., 11
Tangney, J. P., xiii
Tani, F., 269
Taylor, C., 17, 28, 29, 30, 31, 32
Taylor, D. M., 92
Taylor, S. E., 301
Tellegen, A., 121, 122, 268

Tews, M. J., 189, 195, 215, 216, 227, 228
Thayer, R. E., 121, 122, 125
Thoits, P. A., 46, 48, 49, 64, 71, 72, 75
Thomas, C., 81
Thompson, S. C., 81, 83
Tice, D. M., 206
Ting-Toomey, S., 181
Tippins, N., 325, 326
Tomiuk, M. A., 189, 201
Tomkins, S. S., 227
Totterdell, P., 120, 121, 125, 215
Tourish, D., 345, 346, 348, 349, 350, 351
Tower, S. L., 3
Triandis, H. C., 90, 92, 94, 95, 96, 97, 269
Trice, H. M., 339, 340
Troccoli, B. T., 203
Trompenaars, F., 170, 179
Tse, B., 181, 308, 319, 320
Tsui, A. S., 93
Tuckman, B. W., 136
Tung, R. L., 172
Tunstall, W. B., 304
Tur-Kaspa, M., 92
Turner, J. C., 91
Tushman, M. L., 310
Tyler, R. B., 96

U

Uhl-Bien, M., 119, 129, 139, 140
Unsworth, K., 131

V

Vaidya, J., 300
Validzic, A., 109
Van Maanen, J., 3, 13, 17, 48, 50, 215, 338, 339, 340, 341, 342, 344, 346, 348
Vargas, P. T., 121
Vaughan, G. M., 90
Vaughan, M. J., 325, 326
Vey, M. A., xxiii, 213
Vince, R., 84
Vinton, K. L., 148, 156
Vogt, C., 216

W

Wagner, F. R., 91, 104, 108

Subject Index

A

Absenteeism, 89, 93, 208, 345
Activation, 121, 122, 259, 299, 300, 301, 314, 401
Affect
  contagion, 127
  management norms, 127, 128, 139
Affective events, viii, 4, 6, 90, 97, 110, 111, 113, 167, 169, 172, 178, 182, 184, 192, 337
  theory (AET), viii, 4, 6, 113, 167, 169, 172, 178, 184, 192, 337
Affective neutrality, 53, 54, 56, 252
Age, 53, 60, 88, 150, 241, 243, 245, 246, 247, 261, 262, 264, 270, 275, 315, 340
Aggression, 80, 81, 83
  hostility, 146
  violation, 67
  violence, 67, 78
Alienation, 63, 96, 101, 105, 107, 109
Ambiguity, 7, 37, 79, 154, 158, 162, 223, 224, 225, 317, 321, 333, 364
Ambivalence, 53, 56, 300
Anger, 15, 29, 37, 48, 61, 68, 71, 76, 80, 81, 82, 85, 114, 154, 163, 171, 174, 179,
194, 202, 215, 238, 251, 254, 258, 260, 261, 268, 297, 301, 302, 305, 312, 314
  consequences, 29
  and fear, 297, 302, 314
  relational aspects, 68
Anxiety, 19, 30, 38, 51, 54, 56, 81, 88, 92, 96, 104, 107, 110, 123, 251, 295, 297, 300, 312, 343, 344, 348, 361
Approach system, 122, 123, 124, 126
Arousal, 121, 146, 157, 255, 297, 300, 307, 308, 113
Attitudes, xxiv, 4, 5, 33, 89, 90, 91, 92, 93, 98, 100, 101, 110, 111, 115, 127, 171, 172, 173, 182, 192, 204, 205, 206, 224, 225, 226, 231, 240, 243, 257, 263, 274, 337, 339, 362
Attraction, 92, 93, 96
Attribution theory, 68
Attachment, 54, 55, 309, 312, 315, 341, 346, 347, 348
Australia, xx, xxi, xxiii, 4, 5, 101, 102, 167, 168, 174, 359
Authenticity, 17, 24, 201, 236, 306, 307, 312, 343
Autonomy, 6, 21, 24, 197, 221, 222, 230, 231, 288, 290, 308, 325, 340
Avoidance, 56, 68, 76, 77, 121, 122, 123, 124, 125, 126, 127, 128, 133, 137, 297, 301

Tasl